HISTORY

OF

LATIN CHRISTIANITY.

HISTORY

OF

LATIN CHRISTIANITY;

INCLUDING THAT OF

THE POPES

TO

THE PONTIFICATE OF NICOLAS V.

BY HENRY HART MILMAN, D.D.,

DEAN OF ST. PAUL'S.

IN EIGHT VOLUMES.

VOLUME II.

NEW YORK:
SHELDON AND COMPANY.
BOSTON: GOULD AND LINCOLN.
M DCCC LXI.

RIVERSIDE, CAMBRIDGE:
STEREOTYPED AND PRINTED BY
H. O. HOUGHTON.

CONTENTS

OF

THE SECOND VOLUME.

BOOK III. (*continued.*)

CHAPTER VI.

Western Monasticism.

CHAPTER VII.

Gregory the Great.

BOOK IV.

CHAPTER I.

MOHAMMED.

CHAPTER II.

SUCCESSORS OF MOHAMMED.

CHAPTER III.

CONVERSION OF ENGLAND.

CHAPTER IV.

Wilrid — Bede.

CHAPTER V.

Conversion of the Teutonic Races beyond the Roman Empire.

CHAPTER VI.

The Papacy from the time of Gregory the Great to Gregory II.

CHAPTER VII.

ICONOCLASM.

CHAPTER VIII.

SECOND COUNCIL OF NICEA — CLOSE OF ICONOCLASM.

CHAPTER IX.

Severance of Greek and Latin Christianity.

CHAPTER X.

Hierarchy of France.

CHAPTER XI.

Pepin King of France.

CHAPTER XII.

Charlemagne on the Throne.

BOOK V.

CHAPTER I.

Charlemagne.

CHAPTER II.

Louis the Pious.

HISTORY

OF

LATIN CHRISTIANITY.

BOOK III. (Continued.)

CHAPTER VI.

WESTERN MONASTICISM.

Monasticism ascended the papal throne in the person of Gregory the Great. As our history approaches this marked period in the annals of Latin Christianity, it is necessary to describe the rise and progress of those institutions, which at once tended so powerfully to propagate, to maintain, and to give its peculiar character to the Christianity of Western Christendom.

Western monasticism

Western monasticism was very different from that of the East. It was practical more than speculative; it looked more to the performance of rigid duty, the observance of an austere ritual, the alternation of severe toil with the recitation of certain stated offices or the reading appointed portions of sacred books, than to dreamy indolence and meditative silence, only broken by the discussion of controverted points of theology. Labor was part of the rule of all the eastern monks; it was urged by the wiser advocates of the monastic state, Athanasius, Basil, Chrys-

contrasted with Eastern.

ostom, even Jerome: it was enforced in the law of the monastic life brought by Cassianus from the East;[1] and it is singular that it was first repudiated by Martin of Tours and his disciples;[2] yet the eastern element predominated over the rule almost throughout Greek Christianity. The Greek monks have done little or nothing to advance the cultivation of barren lands, for the arts, for knowledge, or for civilization. But the hermits in the West were in general content with the wild recesses of nature, and with a rigid but secret discipline. They had neither the ingenious nor the ostentatious self-tortures which were common in the East. They had hardly one Stylites, men who stood for decades of years[3] on a lofty pillar, a pillar elevated in height as the saint drew nearer to heaven and to perfection[4]—as yet no rambling and vagabond monks, astonishing mankind by the public display of their miserable self-inflicted sufferings. Nor did Cœnobites disburb the peace of the western cities by crowding with arms in their hands, ready with unscrupulous and sanguinary fanaticism for slaughter, or worse than slaughter, in the maintenance of some favorite doctrine, or some favorite prelate. Under their founder

1 "A laboring monk is troubled by one devil, an idle one by a host of devils."—Cassian. x. 23. Augustine wrote a book, de Opere Monachorum. M. Villemain has this striking observation: "De cette rude école du désert il sortait des grands hommes et des fous."—Mélanges, Eloquence Chrétienne, p. 356. The East had few great men, many madmen; the West, madmen enough, but still very many great men.

2 Paulin. de vit. Martini, l. ii. Sulpic. Severus, c. 7.

3 Fifty-six, according to Evagrius, t. iii. i. 13; Theodoret. Hist. Relig., p. 882. For Wulfilas the one Stylites of the West at Treves, see Fleury, xxiv. 22.

4 "The Gallic bishops ordered a pillar to be destroyed on which an ambitious Western aspired to rival the East."—Greg. Tur. i. 17. Compare Schroeck, viii. p. 231.

in Northern France, Martin of Tours, they might lend their tumultuous aid in the demolition of some heathen shrine or temple; but their habits were usually those of profound peace; they aspired not yet to rule the world which they had forsworn: it was not till much later that their abbots, now endowed with enormous wealth, poured upon them by blind admiration of their holiness, assumed political existence. The western monks partook of that comparative disinclination to the more subtle religious controversy which distinguished Roman from Greek and Oriental Christendom. Excepting the school of semi-Pelagianism, propagated by the Oriental Cassianus among the monasteries in the neighborhood of Marseilles (still to a certain extent a Greek city, and with the Greek language spoken around it), the monasteries were the seats of submissive, uninquiring orthodoxy. They were not as yet the asyla of letters. Both the ancient Latin prose and ancient Latin poetry were too repulsively and dangerously heathen to be admitted into the narrow cell or the mountain cloister. This perilous tendency to intellectual indulgence which followed Jerome into his cave in Palestine, and could only be allayed by the scourge and unintermitting fast, as yet did not penetrate into the solitudes of the western recluses. But if the reason was suppressed with such unmitigated proscription, the imagination, while it shrunk from those metaphysic abstractions, which are so congenial to eastern mysticism, had full scope in the ordinary occurrences of life, which it transmuted into perpetual miracle. The mind was centered on itself; its sole occupation was the watching the emotions, the pulsations of the religious life; it impersonated its impulses, it attributed to external or to foreign but indwelling powers the whole strife within. Everything fostered, even the daily labor, which might have checked, carried on in solitude and in silence, encouraged the vague and desultory dreaminess of the fancy. Men plunged into the desert alone, or united themselves with others (for there is no contagion so irresistible as that of religious emotion) under a deep conviction that there was a fierce contest taking place for the soul of each individual, not between moral influences and unseen and spiritual agencies, but between beings palpable, material, or at least having at their command material agents, and constantly controlling the course of nature. All the monks' scanty reading was of the miracles of our Lord or his Apostles, or still more the legends of saints. Their singing was of the same subjects. Their fasts were to expel demoniacal possessions, their festivals to celebrate the actual presence of the tutelar saint. And directly the soul escaped, as it could not but escape, from the narrow internal world, it carried into the world without, not merely that awful reverence which sees God in everything, but a wonderful ignorance of nature and of man, which made miracle the ordinary rather than the exceptional state of things. The scenes among which they settled were usually such as would promote this tendency—strange, desolate, gloomy, fearful, the interminable sea or desert, the mountain immeasurable by the eye, the unfathomed glen ; in Italy volcanic regions, either cleft or distorted by ancient eruptions, and still liable to earthquake and disorder. Their solitudes ceased to be solitary ; they were peopled with sounds, with apparitions unaccountable and therefore supernatural. Wherever a few met together, they met upon the principle of encouraging each other, of vying with each other, of measuring the depth of their faith by their unhesitating belief. The state of mind was contagious; those around them were mostly peasants, serfs, who admired their austerities, reverenced their holiness; and whom even if their credulity outran their own, they would not disabuse, lest they should disturb instead of deepen their religious impressions. When they went still further forth into the world, the fame of their recluse sanctity, of their miracle-working holiness preceded them. Men were prepared for wonders, and he who is prepared for wonders will usually see them. Emulation, zeal for the glory of their founder, the awe, often the salutary awe, which controlled multitudes, the mind unbalanced by brooding upon itself, and the frame distempered by the wildest ascetic usages, the self-walled, self-barred, the sunless dreary dungeons, which they made themselves in the midst of populous cities, wrought the same effects on the monks in Rome, or Milan, or Tours. Thus religion, chiefly through monasticism, conspired with barbarism to throw back mankind into a new childhood, a second imaginative youth. The mythic period of Christianity had begun and continued for centuries: full of the materials of poetry, producing a vast mass of what was truly poetic, but wanting form and order, destined to await the creation of new languages before it should culminate in great Christian poems, commencing with the Divine Comedy and closing with the Paradise Lost.

Early monasticism in the West.

Monasticism, as we have seen, was introduced into the West by the authority and by the writings of the great Athanasius. In the time of Jerome it had found its proselytes among the patricians and highborn matrons and virgins of Rome. Many monasteries in that city excited the admiration of Augustine;[1] and that of Nola, celebrated by St. Paullinus, did not stand alone in Southern Italy.[2] Milan[3] vied with Rome in the antiquity, in the severe sanctity of her monastery, which rose in one of the suburbs under the fostering care of St. Ambrose; and Ambrose acknowledged that he had but followed the holy example of Eusebius of Vercelli. Monasticism had now spread throughout the West. In the recesses of the Apennines; in the secluded islands along the coast of Italy; in Gaul, where it had been disseminated by the zeal of Martin of Tours; in Ireland; in the parts of Britain yet unwasted by the heathen Saxons; in Spain; in Africa, these young republics rose in all quarters, and secluded themselves from the ordinary duties, occupations, pursuits, and as they fondly thought, the passions and the sins of men. In Gaul the earliest monasteries were those of Ligugé, near Toulouse, and of Tours, both founded by St. Martin, of the Isle Barbe, in the Saone above Lyons, Toulouse, in the Islands of the Hieres and of Lerins. Cæsarius, the Bishop of Arles, whom his age considered to unite in an unparalleled degree the virtues of the ecclesiastic and the monk, and Cassianus, who, originally an Oriental, settled at Marseilles, and endeavored to realize in his monastery of St. Victor in that city the severity of his institutes,

[1] De Morib. Eccl. c. 33.

[2] Ambros. Epist. lxiii. St. August. Confess. iv. 6.

[3] Constructâ statuit requiescere cellâ
Heic ubi gaudentem nemoris vel palmitis umbris
Italiam pingit pulcherrima Mediolanum."

Paul. in vit. St. Mart.

The Western monks already loved the beauties of nature.

maintained and extended the dominion of monasticism in that province. The settlements of Columban will appear as the great initiatory measure which prepared and accomplished the conversion of Germany.

But even now no kingdom of the West is inaccessible to the rapid migrations, or sudden apparitions of these religious colonies.

The origin of Spanish monasticism is obscure. It is recognized by the decrees of various councils, those of Tarragona, of Lerida, of Barcelona, of Saragossa. It received a strong impulse from Donatus, an African, who landed with seventy monks from that country.

In Spain.

In Africa, monasticism, under St. Augustine, assumed a peculiar form, intermediate between the ordinary sacerdotal institutions and the monastery. The clergy were to live in common under a rule, in some respects rigidly monastic, yet to discharge all the ordinary duties of the priesthood. They were the first regular canons; but the Augustinian Order formed, as it was designed, on this ancient and venerable model, is of much later date, the twelfth century.[1]

In Africa.

In Britain, monasticism had arrived before the Saxon invasion. It fled with Christianity to the fastnesses of Wales; the monks of Banchor, long established on the border, encountered the Saxon monks, who accompanied Augustine into the Island. Ireland and the Western Isles were already studded with these religious retreats; Iona had its convent, and these institutions, which were hereafter to send forth St. Columban to convert and monasticize the German

In Britain.

[1] Compare Thomassin, La Discipline de l'Eglise, i. 31.

forests, were already at least in their early and initiatory state.

St. Benedict of Nursia.

But the extension and organization of monasticism in the West owes its principal strength and uniformity to Benedict of Nursia.[1] The life of Benedict, from infancy to death, is the most perfect illustration of the motives which then worked upon the mind of man. In him meet together and combine all those influences which almost divided mankind into recluses or cœnobites, and those who pursued an active life; as well as all the effects, in his case the best effects, produced by this phasis of human thought and feeling. Benedict, it was said, was born at that time, like a sun to dispel the Cimmerian darkness which brooded over Christendom, and to revive the expiring spirit of monasticism. The whole world was desolated by the inroads of the northern conquerors; the thrones of the new western kingdoms were filled by barbarian heretics; the East was distracted with controversy. War had not respected the monastic institutions; and those were fortunate who were shrouded in the mountain glens of the Apennines, or lay hid in some remote and sea-girt island. His age acknowledged Benedict as the perfect type of the highest religion, and Benedict impersonated his age.

In the time of Benedict no man could have made a profound impression or exercised an enduring influence upon the mind of man, without that enthusiasm in himself which would environ him with wonder, or without exciting that enthusiasm in others which would eagerly accept, propagate, and multiply the miracles which avouched his sanctity.

[1] Baronius sub ann., but chiefly Mabillon, Hist. Ordin. Benedict.

How perfectly the whole atmosphere was impregnated with this inexhaustible yearning for the supernatural, appears from the ardor with which the monastic passions were indulged at the earliest age. Children were nursed and trained to expect at every instant more than human interferences; their young energies had ever before them examples of asceticism, to which it was the glory, the true felicity of life, to aspire. The thoughtful child had all his mind thus preoccupied; he was early, it might almost seem intuitively, trained to this course of life; wherever there was gentleness, modesty, the timidity of young passion, repugnance to vice, an imaginative temperament, a consciousness of unfitness to wrestle with the rough realities of life, the way lay invitingly open — the difficult, it is true, and painful, but direct and unerring way — to heaven. It lay through perils, but was made attractive by perpetual wonders; it was awful, but in its awfulness lay its power over the young mind. It learnèd to trample down that last bond which united the child to common humanity, filial reverence; the fond and mysterious attachment of the child and the mother, the inborn reverence of the son to the father. It is the highest praise of St. Fulgentius that he overcame his mother's tenderness by religious cruelty.[1]

History, to be true, must condescend to speak the language of legend; the belief of the times is part of the record of the times; and, though there may occur what may baffle its more calm and searching philoso-

[1] The approving bishop said, "Facile potest juvenis tolerare quemcunque imposuerit laborem qui poterit maternum jam despicere dolorem.' —Fulgent. Vit. apud Mabillon.

phy, it must not disdain that which was the primal, almost universal, motive of human life.

Benedict was born at Nursia, in the province of Spoleto, of respectable parents. He was sent to Rome, according to still-prevailing custom, to be instructed in the liberal arts. But his pure spirit shrunk instinctively from the vices of the capital. He gave up the perilous study of letters, and preferred a holy ignorance.[1] He fled secretly from the society of his dangerous associates, from the house of his parents, who, it seems, had accompanied him, as of old the father of Horace his son to Rome.[2] His faithful nurse alone discovered his design and accompanied his flight. This incident seems to imply that his flight took place at a very tender age; a circumstance, told at a later period, intimates that it was not before the first impulses of youthful passion. He took refuge in a small village called Effide, about two miles from Subiaco. The rustic inhabitants, pleased with his modesty and sweetness of disposition, allowed him to inhabit a cell near their church. Here took place his first miracle. The faithful nurse, Cyrilla, had borrowed a stone sieve, commonly used in that part of the country to make bread. It fell from her hands, and broke in two. Benedict, moved by her distress, united the two pieces, prayed over them, and the vessel became whole. The wondering rustics are said to have hung the miraculously restored sieve over their church door. But the sensitive youth shrunk from fame, as

A.D. 480.

Youth of Benedict.

1 "Scienter nesciens, et sapienter indoctus." Such are the words of Gregory the Great. — Dial. l. 2.

2 Compare (how strange the comparison!) the life of Horace and the life of St. Benedict.

be had from vice: he sought a deeper solitude. In the neighborhood of Subiaco, by the advice and assistance of a monk, named Romanus, he found a wild and inaccessible cavern, into which he crept, and for three years the softly and delicately educated boy lay hid in this cold and dismal dwelling from the sight of men. His scanty food was supplied by Romanus, who took it by stealth from his own small pittance in his monastery. The cave was at the foot of the hill on which the monastery stood, but there was no path down the precipitous rock. The food, therefore, was let down by a rope, and a small bell tied to the rope gave notice of its coming. Once the devil broke the rope; but he could not baffle the inventive charity of Romanus. To an imagination so prepared, what scene could be more suited to nurture the disposition to wonders and visions than the wild and romantic region about Subiaco? The cave of Benedict is still shown as a hallowed place, high on the crest of a toppling rock, with the Anio roaring beneath in a deep ravine, clothed with the densest forest, and looking on another wild, precipitous crag. Half-way up the zigzag and laborious path stands the convent of Benedict's sister, St. Scolastica.[1] So entirely was Benedict cut off from the world that he ceased to mark not merely the progress of ordinary time, but even the fasts and festivals of the Church. A certain priest had prepared for himself

[1] According to the annalist of the order, Subiaco, properly Sub-lacu, was a town at the foot of a lake made by the waters of the Anio, which had been dammed up by the Emperor Claudius. On the 20th February, 1325, the lake burst its dam, swept away the road and bridge to San Lorenzo, and left only its dry bed, through which the torrent of the Anio still pours. —Annal. Ordin. Benedict. i. c. viii. The old monastery must have been on a peak higher than Benedict's cave.

some food of unusual delicacy for the festival of Easter. A mysterious admonition within his heart reproved him for this luxurious indulgence, while the servant of God was pining with hunger. Who he was, this holy and heaven-designated servant, or where he dwelt, the priest knew not, but he was led through the tangled thickets and over the rugged rocks to the cave of Benedict. Benedict was ignorant that it was Easter, and not till he was assured that it was that festal day, would he share in the heaven-sent banquet.

The secret of his hiding-place was thus betrayed, and some of the rude shepherds of the country, seeing the hermit in his coarse attire, which was no more than a sheepskin thrown round him, mistook him at first for a wild beast: but when they approached him, they were so melted by his gentle eloquence, that their hearts yielded at once, and they were subdued to courtesy of manners and Christian belief. But the young hermit had not escaped the notice or the jealousy of the enemy of mankind. One day (we must not omit puerilities so characteristic, and this is gravely related by a late serious and learned writer) he appeared in the shape of a blackbird, and flapped him over the eyes with his wings, so as almost to blind him. The evil one took a more dangerous form, the unforgotten image of a beautiful woman whom young Benedict had known at Rome (he could not, then, have left it so very young). This was a perilous probation, and it was only by rushing forth and rolling his naked body upon the brambles and sharp points of the rocks that Benedict obtained the hard-wrung victory. Never after this, as he said to his familiar friends, was he exposed to these fleshly trials. Yet his warfare was not over. He had triumphed over sensual lust, he was to be tempted by religious ambition. A convent of monks in the neighborhood, excited by the fame of his sanctity, determined to choose Benedict for their head. He fairly warned them of the rigorous and uncompromising discipline which he should think it his duty to enforce. Either fondly believing their own sincerity, or presuming on the latent gentleness of Benedict, they could not be dissuaded from the design. But in a short time the firm severity of the young abbot roused their fierce resentment; hatred succeeded to reverence and love. They attempted to poison him; but the cup with the guilty potion burst asunder in the hands of Benedict, who calmly reproved them for their crime, prayed for the divine forgiveness, reminded them of his own warnings before he undertook their government, and withdrew into his happier solitude.

Fame of Benedict.

It was no longer a solitude. The sanctity of Benedict, and the fame of his miracles, drew together daily fresh aspirants to the holiness or the quietness of his recluse life. In a short time arose in the poetic district, on the peaks and rent clefts, under the oaks and chestnuts round Subiaco, twelve monasteries, each containing twelve votaries (Benedict considered that less or more than this number led to negligence or to discord). The names of many of these cloisters designate their romantic sites; the Monastery of the Cavern, St. Angelo and St. Clement by the Lake, St. John by the Stream, St. Victor at the foot of the Mountain; Eternal Life, or the Holy Valley; and one now called Santa Scolastica, rising amid embowering woods on a far-seen ridge of the Apennines. The fame of these institutions soon spread to Rome. Some of the nobles joined the young fraternities, others sent their sons for the benefit of a severe and religious education; and already considerable endowments in farms and other possessions were bestowed by the piety and gratitude of parents or admirers. Maurus (afterwards St. Maur) was one of these young nobles, who became before long the friend, assistant, and successor of Benedict. To Maurus was soon attributed a share in the miraculous powers, as in the holiness of Benedict. Though wells of waters had broken out at the prayer of Benedict, on the thirsty summits of the rocks, where the hermitages hung aloft, they were not always at hand or always full. A noble youth of fifteen, Placidus, in drawing water from the lake, fell in, and was carried by the waves far from the shore. Benedict cried to Maurus to assist. Maurus rushed in, and, walking on the water, drew out the fainting youth by the hair. A contest of humility began: Maurus attributed the wonder to the holiness of his master, Benedict to the devotion of Maurus. It was decided by the youth, who declared that he had seen the sheepskin cloak of Benedict hovering over him. It would not be difficult to admit all the facts of this miracle, which might be easily accounted for by the excitement of all parties.

The Priest Florentius.

It is strange to see the blackest crimes constantly, as it were, in collision with this high-wrought holiness. Florentius, a neighboring priest, was envious of the holy Benedict. He attempted to poison him in some bread which he sent as a present.[1]

[1] Compare the attempt of the ambitious archdeacon to poison the aged Bishop of Canosa. The bishop drank the cup, having made the sign of the cross, and the *archdeacon fell dead*, as if the poison had found its way to his stomach. — Greg. Dial. iii. 5.

Benedict had a prescient consciousness of the treason; and a raven at his command flew away with the infected food. Florentius, baffled in his design upon the life of the master, plotted against the souls of the disciples. He turned seven naked girls into the garden of one of the monasteries. Benedict determined to withdraw from the dangerous neighborhood. He had set forth on his journey when Maurus hastily overtook him, and, not without some signs of joy, communicated the tidings of the death of Florentius. The wicked priest had been buried in the ruins of his chamber, which had fallen in, while the rest of the house remained standing. Benedict wept over the fate of his enemy, and imposed penance on his disciple for his unseemly and unchristian rejoicing in the calamity even of the wicked.

Benedict pursued his way (as the more poetic legend added, under the guidance of two visible angels) to Monte Casino, about fifty miles from Subiaco. On Monte Casino still arose a temple of Apollo amid its sacred grove; and in the midst, as it were, of Christianity, the pagan peasants brought their offerings to their ancient god. But there was no human resistance when the zealous recluse destroyed the profane and stately edifice, broke the idol, overturned the altar, and cut down the grove. Unreluctant the people received the religion of Christ from the eloquent lips of Benedict. The enemy of mankind attempted some obstruction to the building of the church devoted to St. Martin. The obstinate stones would not move but at the prayers of Benedict. They fell and crushed the builders, who were healed by his intercession. The last stronghold of paganism was replaced by a Benedictine monastery; and here arose that great model republic, which gave its laws to almost the whole of Western Monasticism. If we might imagine the pagan deity to have any real and conscious being, and to represent the Sun, he might behold the monastic form of Christianity, which rose on the ruins of his ancient worship, almost as univerally spread throughout the world, as of old the adoration of his visible majesty.

Rule of St. Benedict.

Three virtues constituted the sum of the Benedictine discipline. Silence with solitude and seclusion, humility, obedience, which, in the strong language of its laws, extended to impossibilities. All is thus concentrated on self. It was the man isolated from his kind who was to rise to a lonely perfection. All the social, all patriotic virtues were excluded: the mere mechanic observance of the rules of the brotherhood, or even the corporate spirit, are hardly worthy of notice, though they are the only substitutes for the rejected and proscribed pursuits of active life.

The three occupations of life were the worship of God, reading, and manual labor. The adventitious advantages, and great they were, of these industrious agricultural settlements, were not contemplated by the founder: the object of the monks was not to make the wilderness blossom with fertility, to extend the arts and husbandry of civilized life into barbarous regions, it was solely to employ in engrossing occupation that portion of time which could not be devoted to worship and to study.[1]

For the divine service the monks awoke at midnight; they retired again, and rose after a brief repose for matins. After matins they did not return to their

[1] "Cuivis piæ mentis agitationi," says Mabillon, p. 52.

beds, but spent the time in reading, meditation, or the singing of psalms. From prime to noon, and all after the brief meal, and another period of reading or meditation, was devoted to labor. At particular periods, as at harvest, the laboring brothers did not return home to their religious service; they knelt and performed it in the fields. The mass was not celebrated on ordinary days, only on Sundays and holidays.

Abstinence from flesh, at least that of four-footed animals, was perpetual and universal; from that of fowls was prescribed with less rigor. The usual food was vegetable broth, bread, and a small measure of wine. From Easter to Pentecost there was no fast. From Pentecost to the ides of September, fasts on two days in the week; the rest of the year to Easter perpetual fast, with one evening meal of eggs or fish. Lent was still more rigorously enforced by abstinence not from food only, but from sleep and from speech. The punishment of delinquents was sequestration from the oratory, the table, and the common meetings; the contumacious and incorrigible were expelled from the community. The monastery contained within its walls the mill, the bakehouse, and everything necessary for life. It was strictly forbidden to partake of food without the walls; all wandering to any distance was prohibited; and if the monk was obliged to be absent during the whole day, he was enjoined to fast rather than partake of food abroad.

So were self-doomed to live the monks of St. Benedict; so all monks, whose number is incalculable, for the long centuries during which Latin Christianity ruled the western world. The two sexes were not merely to be strangers, but natural, irreconcilable enemies. This strong repulsion was carried not only into their judgments upon themselves, but into their judgments of those who were yet in the world without. All monks inevitably embraced, with the most extreme severity, the dominant notion of the absolute sinfulness of all sexual intercourse; at least, its utter incompatibility with religious service. A noble lady is possessed with a legion of devils, for compliance with her husband, before a procession in honor of the bones of St. Sebastian. The less questionable natural affections were proscribed with equal severity. Attachment to the order was to be the one absorbing affection. A boy monk, who loved his parents too fondly and stole forth to visit them, was not merely suddenly struck with death, but the holy earth refused to retain his body, and cast it forth with indignation. It was only by the influence of Benedict, who commanded the Holy Eucharist to be placed upon the body, that it was permitted to repose in the grave.[1]

But the later days of Benedict, at Monte Casino, though adorned with perpetual miracle, did not seclude him or his peaceful votaries from the disastrous times which overwhelmed Italy during the fall of the Gothic monarchy and the reconquest by the Eastern Emperor. War respected not these holy sanctuaries; and in prophetic vision Benedict saw his

Ravages in Italy.

[1] Gregor. Dial. i. 10. There is another strange story of the power of Benedict: he had excommunicated certain nuns for the unbridled use of their tongues. They were buried, however, in the church. But when the sacrament was next administered, at the voice of the deacon, commanding all who did not communicate to depart, the bodies rose from their graves and walked out of the church. This was seen by their nurse, who communicated the fact to Benedict. The pitying saint commanded an oblation to be made for them, and ever after they rested quietly in their graves. — Greg Dial. ii. 23.

establishment laid waste, and all its lofty buildings in ruins before the ravages of the spoiler. He was consoled, however, it is added, by visions of the extension of his rule throughout Europe, and the rise of flourishing Benedictine monasteries in every part of the West. Nor were the virtues of Benedict without influence in assuaging the horrors of the war. Totila himself, the last and not least noble Gothic sovereign, came to consult the prophetic saint of Monte Casino as an oracle. He attempted to practise a deception upon him, by dressing one of his chieftains in the royal attire. Benedict at once detected the fraud, and Riggo, the chieftain, returned to his master, deeply impressed with awe at the supernatural knowledge of the saint. Totila.

Totila himself, it is said, fell prostrate at the feet of Benedict, who raised him up, solemnly rebuked his cruelties, foretold his conquest of Rome, his passage of the sea, his reign of nine years, his death during the tenth. The greater humanity with which Totila from this time conducted the war, his severity against his soldiers for the violation of female chastity, the virtues, in short, of this gallant warrior, are attributed to this interview with Benedict. Considering the uncertainty of the date assigned to this event, it is impossible to estimate how far the fierce warrior was already under the control of those Christian feelings which led him to seek the solitude of the saint, or was really awe-struck into more thoughtful religiousness by these prophetic admonitions.[1]

[1] There are several other anecdotes of Totila in the Dialogues of Gregory. He went to consult the Bishop of Canosa, as a prophet, and tried to deceive him. See likewise the odd story of Cassius, Bishop of Narni, whom Totila, from his red nose, unjustly suspected of drunkenness. In several other instances Totila was compelled to reverence the sanctity of bishops, whom he had begun to persecute. — c. x. and xi.

Benedict did not live to witness the ruin of Monte St. Scolastica. Casino; his sister, St. Scolastica, preceded him in her death but a few days. There is something striking in the attachment of the brother and sister, the human affection struggling with the hard spirit of monasticism. St. Scolastica was a female Benedict. Equally devout, equally powerful in attracting and ruling the minds of recluses of her own sex, the remote foundress of convents almost as numerous as those of her brother's rule. With the most perfect harmony of disposition, one in holiness, one in devotion, they were of different sexes, and met but once a year. The feminine weakness of the dying Scolastica for once extorted an unwilling breach of his rule from her severer brother.[1] He had come to visit her, probably for the last time; she entreated him to rest for the night in her convent; but Benedict had never, so spake his own laws, passed a night out of his own monastery. But Heaven was more indulgent than the monk. Scolastica reclined her head in profound prayer. Suddenly the serene sky was overcast, lightnings and thunders flashed and roared around, the rain fell in torrents. "The Lord have mercy upon you, my sister!" said Benedict; "what have you done?" "You," she replied, "have rejected my prayers; but the Lord hath not. Go now, if you can." They passed the night in devout spiritual exercises. Three days after Benedict saw the soul of his sister soaring to heaven in the shape of a dove. Only a short time elapsed, and Benedict was seized with a mortal sickness. Six days before his death he ordered his grave to be opened, and at the end breathed his last in prayer. His death was not without its

[1] Greg. Dial. 2, xxxiii.

prophetic announcements. It was revealed to a monk in his cell at Monte Casino, and to his chosen disciple, St. Maurus, who had already left Italy to establish the rule of his master in the monasteries of Gaul. In a convent near Auxerre, Maurus was wrapt in spirit, and beheld a way strewn with garments and lighted with lamps, which led direct from the cell of Benedict to heaven. "May God enable us to follow our master along this heavenward way." Benedict was buried in the oratory of John the Baptist, which stood upon the site of the sanctuary of Apollo.

The vision of St. Benedict of the universal diffusion of his order was accomplished with a rapidity wonderful even in those times. In Italy, from Calabria to the Alps, Benedictine monasteries began to rise on the brows of beetling mountains, sometimes in quiet valleys. Their buildings gradually grew in spaciousness and splendor;[1] nor did they absolutely abandon the cities, as dangerous to themselves or beyond the sphere of their exemplary rigor. Few, if any of the great towns are without their Benedictine convent. Every monastery sent forth its colonies. The monks seemed to multiply with greater fecundity than the population of the most flourishing cities, and were obliged to throw off their redundant brethren to some new settlement. They swarmed, according to their language, like bees.[2] Wherever was the abode of

[1] It did not often happen that a monastery, ashamed of its magnificence, like one built by the desire, but not according to the modest notions, of St. Waltruda, fell of its own accord, and gave place to a humbler edifice. — Mabillon, Ann. i. p. 405.

[2] "Tanquam apes ex cœnobiali alveario de more egressi, nova monasteria, sive dicas cellas, construere amabant." — Note of Angelo della Noce, Abbot of Monte Casino, on the Chron. Casinen.

men was the abode of these recluses, who had put off the ordinary habits, attire, occupations of men ; wherever they settled in the waste wilderness men gathered around them, as if to partake of their sanctity and security.[1] Maurus, the faithful friend and associate of Benedict, had crossed the Alps even before his death. Bishop Innocent, of Le Mans, who had invited him to Gaul, had died before his arrival; but he was hospitably received in Orleans. The first Benedictine monastery in France rose at Glanfeuille, on the Loire, not far from Angers; it was but the first of many rich and noble foundations — foundations which, as they grew in wealth and splendor, and, in consequence, in luxury and ease, were either themselves brought back by some stern reformer, who wrought them up to their old austere discipline, or rivalled and supplanted by new monasteries, which equalled or surpassed the rigor of Benedict himself.[2] The name of St. Maur is dear to letters. Should his disciples have in some degree departed from the iron rule of their founder, the world, even the enlightened Christian world, will pardon them if their profound and useful studies have withdrawn them from mechanical and

[1] The Benedictine rule was universally received even in the older monasteries of Gaul, Britain, Spain, and throughout the West; not as that of a rival order (all rivalry was of later date), but as a more full and perfect rule of the monastic life; as simply completing the less consummate work of Cassian, Martin of Tours, or Columban. It gave, therefore, not only a new impulse to monasticism, as founding new monasteries, but as quickening the older ones into new life and energy.

[2] Noirmoutier, founded by St. Meudon, accepted the rule of St. Benedict, and became the head of the Benedictine order in France; other great monasteries were St. Benignus at Dijon; St. Denys; the Chaise Dieu, near Puy de Velay; Fleury, near the Loire. In England, Canterbury, Westminster, Glastonbury, St. Albans. In the north, Wearmouth, Yarrow, Lindisfarn. — Helyot.

automatic acts of devotion. In Spain the monasteries mostly fell in the general wreck of Christianity on the Mahommedan conquest; few scanty and doubtful records survived, to be gleaned by the industry of their successors, as Christianity slowly won back the land.[1]

With St. Augustine the rule of St. Benedict passed to England; but there it might seem as if the realm, instead of banishing them, or permitting their self-banishment, to the wild heath or the mountain crest, had chosen for them, or allowed them to choose, the fairest spots in the land for their settlements. In every rich valley, by the side of every clear and deep stream, arose a Benedictine abbey. The labors of the monks in planting, in cultivation, in laying out the sunny garden, or hanging the hill with trees, may have added much to the picturesque grace of these scenes; but, in general, if a district in England be surveyed, the most convenient, most fertile, most peaceful spot, will be found to have been the site of a Benedictine abbey.

Their numbers at any one time it may be difficult to estimate.[2] Abbeys rose and fell, like other human institutions; the more favored, however, handed down the sacred tradition of their foundation, of their endowments, of their saints, of their miracles, of their good deeds to civilization, till the final wreck of monastic

1 Flores, España Sagrada, passim. This valuable work gives the religious history of Spain, according to its provinces, so that the annals of each church or abbey must be followed out.

2 Mabillon, Ann. Ordin. Benedict. passim. The number of great monasteries founded in Italy, Rhenane Germany, and France, between 520 and 700, is astonishing. There are some after the conversion of Recared, Toledo, Merida, &c., in Spain.

institutions during the last century; and even from that wreck a few have survived, or lifted up again their venerable heads.[1]

[1] Sarpi (p. 78, delle Mater Benefic.) quotes the Abbot Trithemius as asserting that in his day there were 15,000 Benedictine convents.

CHAPTER VII.

GREGORY THE GREAT.

THE sixth century of Christianity was drawing towards its close. Anarchy threatened the whole West of Europe; it had already almost enveloped Italy in ruin and desolation. Italy had been a Gothic kingdom, it was now a province of the Eastern Empire. Rome had been a provincial city of Theodoric's kingdom, it was now a provincial, at least only the second, city in the monarchy of Justinian. But the Byzantine government, though it had overthrown the Gothic kingdom, had exhausted itself in the strife. The eunuch Narses had drained by his avarice that wealth which had begun to recover under the vigor of his peaceful administration. But Narses, according to the popular belief, had revenged himself upon the groaning province, which had appealed to Constantinople against his oppressive rule, and upon the jealous Emperor who had feared his greatness. He had summoned the Lombards to cross the Alps. The death of Narses had left his successor, the Exarch of Ravenna, only the dignity of a sovereignty which he was too weak to exercise for any useful purpose of government. Already the Lombards occupied great part of the north of Italy, and were extending their desolating inroads towards the south. The ter-

Close of sixth century.

Lombard invasion.

rors of the defenceless province cowered before, no doubt exaggerated, the barbarity of these new invaders. The Catholics and the Romans had leagued with the East to throw off the Gothic yoke; they were not even to rest under the more oppressive rule of their new masters; they were to be the prey, the victims, the slaves of a new race of barbarians. The Goths had been to a great degree civilized and Romanized before their conquest of Italy; their enlightened rulers had endeavored to subdue them to the arts of peace, at least to a less destructive system of warfare. The Lombards were still obstinate barbarians; the Christianity which they had partially embraced was Arianism; and it had in no degree, if justly described, mitigated the ferocity of their manners. They had no awe of religious men, no reverence for religious places; they burned churches, laid waste monasteries, slew ecclesiastics, and violated consecrated virgins with no more dread or remorse than ordinary buildings or profane enemies.[1] So profound was the terror of the Lombard invasion, that the despairing Italians, even the highest ecclesiastics, beheld it as an undoubted sign of the coming day of judgment. The great writer of the times describes the depopulated cities, the ruined castles, the churches burned, the monasteries of males and females destroyed, the farms wasted and left without cultivation, the whole land a solitude, and wild beasts wandering over fields once occupied by multitudes of human beings. He draws the inevitable conclusion: "what is happening in other parts of the world we know not, but in this the end of all things not merely announces itself as approaching, but shows

[1] On the ravages in Italy by these conflicts, Greg. Epist. v. 21, xiii. 38.

itself as actually begun."[1] This terror of the Lombards seemed to survive and to settle down into an unmitigated detestation. Throughout the legends of the piety and the miracles wrought by bishops and monks in every part of Italy, the most cruel and remorseless persecutor is always a Lombard.[2] And this hatred was not in the least softened when the popes, rising to greater power, became to a certain extent the defenders of Italy: it led them joyfully to hail the appearance of the more warlike and orthodox Franks, whom first the Emperor Maurice, and afterwards the popes, summoned finally to crush the sinking kingdom of the Lombards. The internecine and inextinguishable hatred of the Church, and probably of the Roman provincials, to the Lombards, had many powerful workings on the fortunes of Italy and of the popedom.

The Byzantine conquest had not only crushed the independence of reviving Italy, prevented the quiet infusion of Gothic blood and of Gothic institutions into the frame of society; it had almost succeeded in trampling down the ecclesiastical dignity of Rome. There are few popes whose reigns have been so inglorious as those of the immediate successors of that unhappy Vigilius, who closed his disastrous and dishonorable life at a distance from his see, Pelagius I., Benedict I., Pelagius II. They rose at the command, must obsequiously obey the mandates, not of the Emperor, but of the Emperor's representative, the Exarch of Ra-

1 "Finem suum mundus jam non nunciat, sed ostendit." — Greg. Mag. Dial. iii. sub fine: compare ii. 29, vii. ii. 192. Gregory was fully persuaded of the approaching Day of Judgment. The world gave manifest signs of its old age. — Hom. v. on Matt. c. 10.

2 See the Dialogues of Gregory, passim, and frequent notices in the Epistles.

venna. They must endure, even if under solemn but
A.D. 553. to 560. unregarded protests, the pretensions of the bishop of the Emperor's capital, to equality, perhaps to superiority. Western bishops seem to take advantage of their weakness, and supported, as they expect to be, by Imperial Constantinople, defy their patriarch.

Times of emergency call forth great men — men at least, if not great in relation to the true intellectual, moral, and spiritual dignity of man, great in relation to the state and to the necessities of their age; engrossed by the powerful and dominant principles of their time, and bringing to the advancement of those principles surpassing energies of character, inflexible resolution, the full conviction of the wisdom, justice, and holiness of their cause, in religious affairs of the direct and undeniable sanction of God. Such was Gregory I., to whom his own age and posterity have assigned the appellation of the Great.

Now was the crisis in which the Papacy must reawaken its obscured and suspended life. It was the only power which lay not entirely and absolutely prostrate before the disasters of the times — a power which had an inherent strength, and might resume its majesty. It was this power which was most imperatively required to preserve all which was to survive out of the crumbling wreck of Roman civilization. To Western Christianity was absolutely necessary a centre, standing alone, strong in traditionary reverence, and in acknowledged claims to supremacy. Even the perfect organization of the Christian hierarchy might in all human probability have fallen to pieces in perpetual conflict: it might have degenerated into a half secular feudal caste with hereditary benefices, more and more entirely subservient to the civil authority, a priesthood of each nation or each tribe, gradually sinking to the intellectual or religious level of the nation or tribe. On the rise of a power both controlling and conservative, hung, humanly speaking, the life and death of Christianity — of Christianity as a permanent, aggressive, expansive, and, to a certain extent, uniform system. There must be a counterbalance to barbaric force, to the unavoidable anarchy of Teutonism, with its tribal, or at the utmost national independence, forming a host of small, conflicting, antagonistic kingdoms. All Europe would have been what England was under the Octarchy, what Germany was when her emperors were weak; and even her emperors she owed to Rome, to the Church, to Christianity. Providence might have otherwise ordained, but it is impossible for man to imagine by what other organizing or consolidating force the commonwealth of the Western nations could have grown up to a discordant, indeed, and conflicting league, but still to a league, with that unity and conformity of manners, usages, laws, religion, which have made their rivalries, oppugnancies, and even their long ceaseless wars, on the whole to issue in the noblest, highest, most intellectual form of civilization known to man. It is inconceivable that Teutonic Europe, or Europe so deeply interpenetrated with Teutonism, could have been condensed or compelled into a vast Asiatic despotism, or succession of despotisms. Immense and interminable as have been the evils and miseries of the conflict between the southern and northern, the Teutonic and Roman, the hierarchical and civil elements of our social system; yet out of these conflicts has at length arisen the balance and harmony of the great states which constitute European Christendom, and are now peopling other continents with kindred and derivative institutions. It is impossible to conceive what had been the confusion, the lawlessness, the chaotic state of the middle ages, without the mediæval Papacy; and of the mediæval Papacy the real father is Gregory the Great. In all his predecessors there was much of the uncertainty and indefiniteness of a new dominion. Christianity had converted the Western world — it had by this time transmuted it: in all except the Roman law, it was one with it. Even Leo the Great had something of the Roman dictator. Gregory is the Roman altogether merged in the Christian bishop. It is a Christian dominion, of which he lays the foundations in the Eternal City, not the old Rome associating Christian influence to her ancient title of sovereignty.

Birth and descent of Gregory.

Gregory united in himself every qualification and endowment which could command the veneration and attachment of Rome and of his age.[1] In his descent he blended civil and ecclesiastical nobility. He was of a senatorial family; his father bore the imperial name of Gordian, his mother that of Sylvia. A pope (Felix II.) was his ancestor in the fourth degree — the pope who had built the church of Sts. Cosmos and Damianus, close to the temple of Romulus. Two sainted virgins, Thirsilla and Sylvia, were his aunts. To his noble descent was added considerable wealth; and all that wealth, directly he be-

[1] Homil. 38, in Evang. Dialog. Epist. iv. 16; Joh. Diac. in Vit. The date of his birth is uncertain; it was about the year 540 — Lau, Gregor. I. der Grosse, page 10.

come master of it by the death of his father, was at once devoted to religious uses. He founded and endowed, perhaps from Sicilian estates, six monasteries in that island; a seventh, in Rome, he chose for his own retreat; and having lavished on the poor all his costly robes, his silk, his gold, his jewels, his furniture, he violently wrenched himself from the secular life (in which he had already attained to the dignity of prætor of the city[1]), and not even assuming the abbacy of his convent, but beginning with the lowest monastic duties, he devoted himself altogether to God.[2] His whole time was passed in prayer, reading, writing, and dictation.[3] The fame of his unprecedented abstinence and boundless charity spread abroad, and, as usual, took the form of miracle. He had so destroyed his health by fasting, vigil, and study, that his brethren were obliged to feed him by compulsion. His life hung on a thread, and he feared that he should not have strength to observe the indispensable fast even on Good Friday. By the prayers of the holy Eleutherius his stomach was endowed with supernatural strength, and never after (he had manifestly, however, undermined his constitution) refused the sacred duty of abstinence.[4] His charity was tried by an angel in the garb of a shipwrecked sailor, whose successive visits exhausted all he

1 He describes his secular state, Præfat. ad Job. "Diu longeque conversionis gratiam distuli, et postquam cœlesti sum desiderio affectus, seculari habitu contegi melius putavi . . . . Cumque adhuc me cogeret animus præsenti mundo quasi specie tenus deservire, cœperunt multa contra me ex ejusdem mundi curâ succrescere, ut in eo jam non specie, sed quod est gravius, mente retinerer."

2 The date of Gregory's monkhood is again uncertain — probably not earlier than 573, nor later than 577. — Lau, p. 21.

3 Greg. Tur. x. 1. According to Jaffè, the Register of Gregory's Letters not only marks the year (the indiction), but the month of their date.

4 Dial. iii. 13; Joh. Diac. i. p. 9.

had, except a silver vessel set apart for the use of his mother. This too he gave, and the satisfied angel at length revealed himself.[1] The monastery of St. Andrew was a perpetual scene of preternatural wonder. Fugitive monks were seized upon by devils, who confessed their power to Gregory; others were favored with visits of angels summoning them to peace; and one brother, whose whole life, excepting the intervals of food and sleep, was spent in psalmody, was not merely crowned by invisible hands with white flowers, but fourteen years after, a fragrance, as of the concentrated sweetness of all flowers, breathed from his tomb. Such was the poetry of those days.

Gregory Abbot.

Gregory became abbot;[2] and that severe discipline which he had imposed upon himself, he enforced with relentlessness, which hardened into cruelty, upon others. Many were tempted to embrace the monastic life who had not resolution to adhere to it, who found no consolation in its peace, and grew weary of its monotonous devotion. Fugitive monks were constantly revolting back to the world which they had forsaken: on these Gregory had no mercy. On the more faithful he exercised a tyranny of discipline which crushed out of the heart not only every lingering attachment to the world, but every sense and pulsation of humanity. The most singular history of this discipline, combining ingratitude and cruelty under the guise of duty, with a strange confidence in his own powers of appeasing the divine wrath, and in the influ-

1 See Præf. ad Dial., a pleasing passage, in which, oppressed by the cares and troubles of the papacy, he looks back on the quiet of his monastery.

2 Lau insists, I think on unsatisfactory grounds, that he was abbot only after his return from Constantinople. — p. 37.

ence of the eucharistic sacrifice, is the death of Justus, related by Gregory himself. Before he became a monk, Justus had practised physic. During the long illness of Gregory, Justus, now a monk, had attended him day and night with affectionate care and skill. On his own death-bed Justus betrayed to his brother that he possessed three pieces of gold. This was in direct violation of that law as to community of property established in the monastery. After long search the guilty money was found concealed in some medicine. Gregory determined to strike the offender with a due sense of his crime, and to awe the brotherhood by the terror of his example. He prohibited every one from approaching the bed of the dying man, the new Simon Magus. No word of consolation or of hope was to soothe his departure. His brother alone might approach to tell him that he died detested by all the community. Nor did the inhuman disciplinarian rest here. The body was cast out upon the dunghill, with the three pieces of gold, the whole convent shouting aloud, "Thy money perish with thee!" After thirty days of fiery burnings, the inevitable fate of an unabsolved outlaw, the heart of Gregory began to relent. He permitted the mass to be celebrated for the afflicted soul. The sacrifice was offered for thirty days more, at the end of which the spirit of Justus appeared to his brother, and assured him of his release from penal torture.[1]

But a mind of such force and ability as Gregory's could not be permitted to slumber in the holy quiet of

[1] "Mira sunt quæ narras et non mediocriter læta." Such, at the close of this story, is the quaint language of Gregory's obsequious hearer. Greg. Mag. Dial. iv. 55.

a monastery. He himself began to comprehend that there were higher religious avocations and nobler services to God. He was still a monk of St. Andrew when that incident took place which, by the divine blessing, led to the conversion of our Saxon ancestors. The tale, though often repeated, is too pleasing not to find a place here. In the market-place of Rome Gregory saw some beautiful and fair-haired boys exposed for sale. He inquired from whence they came. "From Britain." "Are they Christians?" "They are still pagans." "Alas! that the Prince of Darkness should possess forms of such loveliness! That such beauty of countenance should want that better beauty of the soul!" He asked of what nation they were. "Angles" was the reply. "Truly," he said "they are angels! From what province?" "That of Deira." "Truly they must be rescued *de irâ* (from the wrath of God). What is the name of their king?" "Ælla." "Yea," said Gregory, "Alleluia must be sung in the dominions of that king." To be the first missionary to this beautiful people, and win this remote and barbarous island, like a Christian Cæsar, to the realm of Christ, became the holy ambition of Gregory. His long-suppressed humanity burst forth in this new channel. He extorted the unwilling consent of the Pope: he had actually set forth, and travelled three days' journey, when he was overtaken by messengers sent to recall him. All Rome had risen in pious mutiny, and compelled the Pope to revoke his permission.

Gregory aspires to convert Britain.

But Gregory was not to retire again to his monastery. He was forced to embark in public affairs. He was ordained deacon (he was one

Gregory in Constantinople.

of the seven deacons of the Church of Rome, the Regionarii), and sent by Pope Benedict on an important embassy to Constantinople. But his occupations were not confined to his negotiations with the court. He was the Pope's apocrisiarius or secretary. These negotiations were but partially successful. He reconciled, indeed, the two successive emperors, Tiberius and Maurice, with the person of the Pope, Pelagius; but the aid against the Lombards was sent reluctantly, tardily, inefficiently. The schism between the East and West was still unallayed. He entered into a characteristic controversy with Eutychius, Bishop of Constantinople, on the nature of the body after the resurrection.[1] The metaphysical Greek imagined an impalpable body, finer and more subtile than the air. The Western theologian, unembarrassed by the materialism from which the Greek endeavored to escape, strenuously asserted the unrefined identity of the renovated body with that of the living man.

In Constantinople[2] Gregory commenced, if he did not complete, his great work, the 'Magna Moralia, or Exposition of the Book of Job,' at which the West stood astonished, and which may even now excite our wonder at the vast superstructure raised on such narrow foundations. The book of Job, according to Gregory, comprehended in itself all natural, all Christian, theology, and all morals. It was at once a true and

[1] The controversy must have been somewhat perplexing, as Gregory was ignorant of Greek, and good translators were not to be found. "Quia hodie in Constantinopolitanâ civitate, qui de Latino in Græcum dictata *bene* transferant non sunt. Dum enim verba custodiunt et sensus minimè attendunt, nec verba intelligi faciunt, et sensus frangunt." — Greg. Mag. Epist. vi. 27.

[2] Gregory resided three years in Constantinople: 584–587.

wonderful history, an allegory containing, in its secret sense, the whole theory of the Christian Church and Christian sacraments, and a moral philosophy applicable to all mankind. As an interpreter of the history, Gregory was entirely ignorant of all the Oriental languages, even of Greek.[1] He read the book partly according to the older, partly according to the later Latin version. Of ancient or of Oriental manners he knew nothing. Of the book of Job as a poem (the most sublime of all antiquity) he had no conception: to him it is all pure, unimaginative, unembellished history. As an allegory, it is surprising with what copious ingenuity Gregory discovers latent adumbrations of all the great Christian doctrines, and still more the unrelenting condemnation of heresies and of heretics. The moral interpretation may be read at the present time, if with no great admiration at the depth of the philosophy, with respect for its loftiness and purity. It is ascetic, but generally, except when heretics are concerned, devout, humane and generous.[2]

Magna Moralia.

[1] "Nam nos nec Græcè novimus, nec aliquod opus Græcè aliquando conscripsimus." — Greg. Mag. Epist. ix. 69.

[2] It may be safely said that, according to Gregory's license of interpretation, there is nothing which might not be found in any book ever written; there is no single word which may not be pregnant with unutterable mysteries, no syllable which may not mean everything, no number which may not have relation to the same number, wherever it may occur, to every multiple or divisible part of such number. "The seven sons of Job mean the twelve apostles, and therefore the clergy, because seven is the perfect number, and multiplied within itself, four by three or three by four, produces twelve. The three daughters mean the faithful laity, because they are to worship the Trinity." "In septem ergo filiis ordo predicantium, in tribus vero filiabus multitudo auditorum signatur." The three daughters may likewise mean the three classes of the faithful, the pastores, continentes, and conjugati. The curious reader may see the mystery which is found in the sheep and the camels, the oxen and the asses, — Lib. i. c. vi., and Lib. ii. c. xiv. — where the friends of Job are shown, from the latent meaning of their names, to signify the heretics.

So congenial, however, was this great work to the Christian mind, that many bishops began to read it publicly in the churches; and it was perhaps prevented from coming into general use only by the modest remonstrance of Gregory himself; and thus Gregory, if his theology and morals had been sanctioned by the authority of the Church, would have become the founder of a new religion. It never appears to have occurred to the piety of that or indeed of other ages, that this discovery of latent meanings in the books of inspiration, and the authoritative enforcement of those interpretations as within the scope of the Holy Spirit, is no less than to make a new revelation to mankind. It might happen that the doctrines thus discovered were only those already recognized as Christianity, and the utmost error then would be the illustration of such doctrines by forced and inapplicable texts. But it cannot be denied that by this system of exposition the sacred writings were continually made to speak the sense of the interpreter; and if once we depart from the plain and obvious meaning of the Legislator, all beyond is the enactment of a new, a supplementary, an unwarranted law. Compare the Great Morals of Gregory, not with the book of Job, but with the New Testament; and can we deny that there would have been a new authoritative proclamation of the Divine will?

Gregory in Rome.

So far Gregory had kept his lofty way in every situation, not only fulfilling, but surpassing, the highest demands of his age. In his personal character austerely blameless; as an abbot (he resumed on his return to Rome the abbacy in his monastery of St. Andrew), mercilessly severe, the model of a strict disciplinarian; as an ambassador, displaying consummate ability; as a controversialist, defeating in the opinion of the West the subtleties of the rival Bishop of Constantinople; as a theologian, already taking that place which was assigned him by the homage of posterity, that of the fourth great father of the Latin Church.[1] Soon after his return to Rome the city became a scene of misery and desolation, so that all eyes could not but be turned on a man so highly favored of God. The Lombard invasions continued to waste Italy; the feeble Exarch acknowledged that he had no power to protect Rome; the supplications for effectual aid from Constantinople had been unavailing. More dire and pressing calamities darkened around. The Tiber overflowed its banks, and swept away the granaries of corn. A dreadful pestilence ensued, of which the Pope Pelagius was among the first victims.[2] With one voice the clergy, the senate, and the people summoned Gregory to the pontifical throne.[3] His modest remonstrances were in vain. His letter entreating the Emperor Maurice to relieve him from the perilous burden, by refusing the imperial consent to his elevation, was intercepted by the loving vigilance of his admirers. Among these was the prefect of the city, who substituted for Gregory's letter the general petition for his advancement. But, until the answer of the Emperor could arrive, Gregory assumed the religious

A.D. 587.

State of the City.

Gregory Pope.

[1] Pelag. Epist. ad Greg. apud J. Diaconum in Vit.

[2] The pestilence was attributed to a vast number of serpents and a great dragon, like a beam of timber, carried down the Tiber to the sea, and cast back upon the shore, where they putrefied, and caused the plague. — Greg. Turon.

[3] 589–590, Jaffè.

direction of the people. He addressed them with deep solemnity on the plague, and persuaded them to acts of humiliation.[1] On an appointed day the whole city joined in the religious ceremony. Seven litanies, or processions with prayers and hymns, and the greatest pomp, traversed the streets. That of the clergy set out from the Church of St. John the Baptist; that of the men from St. Marcellus; the monks from that of the martyrs John and Paul; the holy virgins from Sts. Cosmos and Damianus; the married women from St. Stephen; the widows from St. Vitalis; that of the poor and the children from St. Cæcilia. But the plague was not stayed; eighty victims fell dead during the procession;[2] but Gregory still urged the people to persist in their pious supplications.

To the end Gregory endeavored to elude the compulsory honor of the Papacy. It was said that, knowing the gates to be jealously watched, he persuaded some merchants to convey him to a solitary forest in disguise; but a light, like a pillar of fire, hovered over his head, and betrayed his flight. He was seized, hurried to the Church of St. Peter, and forcibly consecrated as Supreme Pontiff.[3]

1 The speech in Greg. Tur. x. i.; Paul. Diac. Ep. ii.; Joh. Diac. i. 41.

2 The picturesque legend, from which the monument of Hadrian took the name of the Castle of St. Angelo, cannot be reconciled with the Letters of Gregory. It ran, that as the last procession reached this building, an angel was seen sheathing his sword, as though the work of divine vengeance was over. The statue of the angel in this attitude commemorated the wonder.

3 The biographer of Gregory (John the Deacon) thinks it necessary to adduce evidence of the sincerity of this reluctance, which had been questioned by "certain perfidious Lombards." He cites a curious letter to Theoctista, the emperor's sister, among the strange expressions in which is this: "Ecce serenissimus Dominus Imperator fieri Simiam Leonem jussit et quidem pro jussione illius vocari Leo potest; fieri autem Leo

Monkhood of Gregory.

Monasticism ascended the Papal throne in the person of Gregory. In austerity, in devotion, in imaginative superstition, Gregory was a monk to the end of his days.[1] From this turmoil of affairs, civil and spiritual; the religious ambition of maintaining and extending the authority of his see; the affairs of pure Christian humanity in which he was involved, as almost the only guardian of the Roman population against the barbarian invasions; oppressed with business, with cares, with responsibilities, he perpetually reverts to the peace of his monastery, where he could estrange himself entirely from sublunary things, yield himself up to the exclusive contemplation of heaven, and look forward to death as the entrance into life.[2]

Consecrated Sept. 3. Jaffè.

But he threw off at once and altogether the dreaming indolence of the contemplative life, and plunged into affairs with the hurried restlessness of the most ambitious statesman. His letters offer a singular picture of the incessant activity of his mind,

non potest." Compare letter to John of Constantinople, i. 24, and the following epistles; also Epist. vii. 4, and Regula Past. in init.

1 "Cum quibus (amicis) Gregorius diu nocteque versatus nihil monasticæ perfectionis in palatio, nihil pontificalis institutionis in ecclesiâ dereliquit. Videbantur passim cum eruditissimis clericis adhærere Pontifici religiosissimi monachi, et in diversissimis professionibus habebatur vita communis; ita ut talis esset tunc sub Gregorio penes urbem Romam ecclesia, qualem *hanc fuisse sub apostolis Lucas* et sub *Marco* Evangelistâ penes Alexandriam Philo commemorat." Was Joh. Diaconus as ignorant of St. Luke's writings as of Philo's? — Joh. Diac. ii. 12.

2 "Infelix quippe animus meus, occupationis suæ pulsatus vulnere, meminit qualis aliquando in monasterio fuit, quomodo ei labentia cuncta subter erant; quantum rebus omnibus, quæ volvuntur, eminebat; quod nulla nisi cœlestia cogitare consueverat; quod etiam retentus corpore, ipsa jam carnis claustra contemplatione transibat: quod mortem quoque quæ pæne cunctis pœna est, videlicet ut ingressum vitæ, et laboris sui præmium amabat." — Præfat. in Dial. Oper. iii. p. 233: compare Epist. i. 4 to 7.

the variety and multiplicity of his occupations. Nothing seems too great, nothing too insignificant for his earnest personal solicitude; from the most minute point in the ritual, or regulations about the papal farms in Sicily, he passes to the conversion of Britain, the extirpation of simony among the clergy of Gaul, negotiations with the armed conquerors of Italy, the revolutions of the Eastern empire, the title of Universal Bishop usurped by John of Constantinople.

Threefold character of Gregory.

The character of Gregory, as the representative of his times, may be considered I. as a Christian bishop organizing and completing the ritual and offices of the Church; as administrator of the patrimony of the Roman See, and its distribution to its various pious uses. II. As the patriarch of the West, exercising authority over the clergy and the churches in Italy, in Gaul, and other parts of Europe; as the converter of the Lombards from Arianism, and the Saxons of Britain from heathenism; and in his conduct to pagans, Jews, and heretics, as maintaining the independence of the Western ecclesiastical power against the East. III. As virtual sovereign of Rome, an authority which he was almost compelled to assume; as guardian of the city, and the protector of the Roman population in Italy against the Lombards; and in his conduct to the Emperor Maurice, and to the usurper Phocas.

Services of the Church.

I. Under Gregory the ritual of the Church assumed more perfect form and magnificence. The Roman ordinal, though it may have received additions from later pontiffs, in its groundwork and distribution belongs to Gregory. The organization of the Roman clergy had probably been long complete; it comprehended the whole city and suburbs. The fourteen regions were divided into seven ecclesiastical districts. Thirty *titles* (corresponding with parishes) were superintended by sixty-six priests; the chief in each title was the cardinal priest. Each ecclesiastical district had its hospital or office for alms, over which a deacon presided; one of the seven was the archdeacon. Besides these, each hospital had an administrator, often a layman, to keep the accounts. The clergy of the seven regions officiated on ordinary occasions, each on one day of the week. Gregory appointed the *stations*, the churches in which were to be celebrated the more solemn services during Lent and at the four great festivals. On these high days the Pope proceeded in state, usually on horseback, escorted by the deacons and other officers, from his palace in the Lateran to St. Peter's, St. Maria Maggiore, or some other of the great churches. He was received with obsequious ceremony, robed by the archdeacons, conducted to the choir with the incense and the seven candlesticks borne before him. Psalms were sung as he proceeded to his throne behind the altar. The more solemn portions of the service were of course reserved for the Supreme Pontiff.[1] But Gregory did not stand aloof in his haughty sanctity, or decline to exercise more immediate influence over the minds of the people. He constantly ascended the pulpit himself, and in those days of fear and disaster was ever preaching in language no doubt admirably adapted to their state of mind,

Gregory as preacher.

1 The reader who may not be inclined to consult Gregory's own Sacramentarium and Antiphonarium, or the learned labors of Mabillon on the Ordo Romanus, will find a good popular view of the Roman service in Fleury, H. E. xxxvi. 16 *et seq.*

tracing to their sins the visible judgments of God, exhorting them to profound humiliation, and impressing them with what appears to have been his own conviction — that these multiplying calamities were the harbingers of the Last day.

Music.

The music, the animating soul of the whole ritual, was under the especial care of Gregory. He introduced a new mode of chanting, which still bears his name, somewhat richer than that of Ambrose at Milan, but still not departing from solemn simplicity. He formed schools of singers, which he condescended himself to instruct; and from Rome the science was propagated throughout the West: it was employed even to soothe and awe the barbarians of Britain. Augustine, the missionary, was accompanied by a school of choristers, educated in their art at Rome.[1]

Gregory as administrator of the See.

As administrator of the Papal patrimony Gregory was active and vigilant, unimpeachably just and humane. The Churches, especially that of Rome, now possessed very large estates, chiefly in Calabria, in Sicily;[2] in the neighborhood of Rome, Apulia, Campania, Liguria; in Sardinia and Corsica; in the Cozian Alps; in Dalmatia and Illyricum; in Gaul; and even in Africa, and the East.[3] There are letters addressed to the administrators of the Papal

[1] The original copy of Gregory's Antiphonary, the couch on which he reclined while he instructed the singers, and the rod with which he threatened the boys, were preserved, according to John the Deacon, down to his time. — Vit. Greg. M. ii. 6.

[2] These estates were called the patrimony of the patron saints of the city, in Rome of St. Peter, in Milan of St. Ambrose, in Ravenna of St. Apollinaris. Ravenna and Milan had patrimonies in Sicily.

[3] Pope Celestine, writing, in the year 432, to the Emperor of the East, mentions "possessiones in Asiâ constitutas quas illustris et sanctæ recordationis Proba longâ a majoribus vetustate reliquerat Romanæ ecclesiæ." He prays the emperor that they may not be disturbed.

estates in all these territories; and in some cities, as Otranto, Gallipoli, perhaps Norcia, Nepi, Cuma, Capua, Corsealano; even in Naples, Palermo, Syracuse. Gregory prescribes minute regulations for these lands, throughout which prevails a solicitude lest the peasants should be exposed to the oppressions of the farmer or of the Papal officer. He enters into all the small vexatious exactions to which they were liable, fixes the precise amount of their payments, orders all unfair weights and measures to be broken and new ones provided; he directs that his regulations be read to the peasants themselves; and, lest the old abuses should be revived after his death, they were to be furnished with legal forms of security against such suppressed grievances.[1] Gregory lowered the seignorial fees on the marriages of peasants not free. Nor, in the protection of the poor peasant, did he neglect the rights and interests of the farmer; he secured to their relatives the succession to their contracts, and guarded the interests of their families by several just regulations. His maxim was, that the revenue of the Church must not be defiled by sordid gains.[2]

The revenue thus obtained with the least possible intentional oppression of the peasant and the farmer was distributed with the utmost publicity, and with

[1] Securitatis libellos. The whole of this letter (i. 42) should be read to estimate the character of Gregory as a landlord. The peasants were greatly embarrassed by the payment of the first term of their rent, which being due before they could sell their crops, forced them to borrow at very high interest. Gregory directed that they should receive an advance from the church treasury, and be allowed to pay by instalments.

[2] In more than one instance Gregory represses the covetousness of the clergy, who were not scrupulous in obtaining property for the church by unjust means. — Epist. vii. 2, 23, ii. 43. Bequests to monasteries continually occur.

rigid regard for the interests of the diocese.[1] Rome, which had long ceased to receive the tributary harvests of Africa and of Egypt, depended greatly on the bounty of the Pope. Sicily alone had escaped the ravages of war, and from her cornfields, chiefly from the Papal estates, came the regular supplies which fed the diminishing, yet still vast, poor population.[2] In a synod at Rome it was enacted that the Pope should only be attended by ecclesiastics, who ought to enjoy the advantage of the example of his life, to the privacy of which the profane laity should not be admitted.[3]

The shares of the clergy and of the papal officers, the churches and monasteries, the hospitals, deaconries or ecclesiastical boards for the poor, were calculated in money, and distributed at four seasons of the year, at Easter, on St. Peter's day, St. Andrew's day, and that of the consecration of Gregory. The first day in every month he distributed to the poor in kind, corn, wine, cheese, vegetables, bacon, meat, fish, and oil.[4] The sick and infirm were superintended by persons appointed to inspect every street. Before the Pope sat down to his own meal a portion was separated and sent out to the hungry at his door. A great volume,

1 The quadripartite division, to the bishop, the clergy, the fabric and services of the church, and the poor, generally prevailed in the West. — Epist. iii. 11.

2 Sicily, since its conquest, had paid as tribute a tenth of its corn to the metropolis; the papal patrimony was liable to this burden. But in case of shipwreck the farmers or peasants were obliged to make good the loss. Gregory relieves his tenants from this iniquitous burden.

3 Epist. iv. 44.

4 Among the instances of munificent grants by Gregory, see that of Aquæ Salviæ, with its farms and vineyards, two gardens on the banks of the Tiber, and other lands, part of the patrimony of St. Peter, to the church of St. Paul, to maintain the lights. — xiv. 14.

containing the names, the ages, and the dwellings of the objects of papal bounty, was long preserved in the Lateran with reverential gratitude. What noble names may have lurked in that obscure list! The descendants of Consuls and Dictators, the Flamens and the Augurs of elder Rome, may have received the alms of the Christian prelate, and partaken in the dole which their ancestors distributed to their thousand clients. So severe was the charity of Gregory that one day, on account of the death of an unrelieved beggar, he condemned himself to a hard penance for the guilt of neglect as steward of the Divine bounty.[1]

[1] It would be curious to obtain even an approximation to the value of the patrimony of St. Peter at these times. These facts may be collected from the letters. 1. The patrimony in Gaul was comparatively small: it is repeatedly called (Epist. iv. 14, vi. 6) patrimoniolum. At one time the Pope received 400 solidi in money, it does not appear clearly whether the residue of the annual rent. But the patrimony in Gaul seems to have been chiefly transmitted, or expended (there were no bills of exchange) in coarse cloths of Gallic manufacture for the poor. Besides this, Gregory ordered the purchase of English youths, of 17 or 18, to be bred in monasteries for missionary purposes. — vi. 33. These 400 solidi (putting the ordinary current solidus at from 11*s.* to 12*s.* — the Gallic solidus was one third less, say 7*s.* 6*d.*) would not be above 160*l.* In one case the Gallic bishops seem to have withheld part of the patrimony — in Gregory's eyes a great offence. "Valde est execrabile, ut quod a regibus gentium servatum est, ab episcopis dicatur ablatum." — vi. 53, 4. But in Sicily Gregory orders Peter the subdeacon, his faithful administrator, to invest 280 pounds of gold in his hands in corn. Taking the pound of gold at 40*l.* (see Gibbon on Greaves, ch. xvii.; Epist. vi. 35, note), this would amount to 2000*l.*; if the value of money was one and a half more than now, 5000*l.* But the produce of Sicily cannot be estimated at the money-rent. It had great quantities of cattle, especially horses (to the improvement of which Gregory paid great attention) in the plains about Palermo and Syracuse. One mass or farm had been compelled by a dishonest factor to pay double rent to the amount of 507 aurei, nearly 280*l.* Gregory ordered it to be restored out of the property of the factor. The number of farms cannot be known, but suppose 100, and this an average rent. Rather more than a century later, the Emperor Leo the Isaurian confiscated to the public treasury the rights of the Roman See in Sicily, valued at three talents and a half. — Theophanes, Chron. p. 631, edit. Bonn. This passage, which at first sight promises the

Nor was Gregory's active beneficence confined to the city of Rome. His letters are full of paternal interpositions in favor of injured widows and orphans. It was even superior to some of the strongest prejudices of the time. Gregory sanctioned that great triumph of the spirit over the form of religion, by authorizing not merely the alienation of the wealth of the clergy, but even the sale of the consecrated vessels from the altar for the redemption of captives — those captives not always ecclesiastics, but laymen.[1]

most full and accurate information, unfortunately offers almost insuperable difficulties. In the first place, the reading is not quite certain; nor is it absolutely clear whether it means some charge on the revenue of the island, or the full rents and profits of the patrimony of St. Peter. But the chief perplexity arises from our utter ignorance of what is meant by a talent. The loss inflicted on the hostile see of Rome must no doubt have been considerable; otherwise the emperor would not have inflicted it on him whom he considered a refractory subject; nor would it have commanded the notice of the historian. But any known talent, above all the small gold talent of Sicily, would give but an insignificant sum, under 900*l.* It had occurred to me, and has been suggested by a high authority, that it may mean 3½ talents in weight, paid in gold money. Fines in the Theodosian code are fixed at so many pounds of gold. 1½ cwt. of gold (if Gibbon be about right, according to Greaves, in taking the pound of gold at 40*l.*) would give a large, perhaps not an improbable, sum: * and, if the relative value of money be taken into account, must have been a most serious blow to the papal revenue.

[1] Gregory's humility is amusingly illustrated by his complaint, that of all his valuable stud in Sicily, his subdeacon had only sent him a sorry nag, and five fine asses. The horse he could not mount because it was so wretched a one, the asses because they were asses. "Præterea unum nobis caballum miserum, et quinque bonos asinos transmisisti; caballum istum sedere non possum quia miser est, illos autem bonos sedere non possum quia asini sunt." — ii. 32.

* Compare, however, Paolo Sarpi, who, probably taking the ordinary talent, makes a much lower estimate (delle Mat. Benefic. c. ix.); but where did he find three talents of silver, half a one of gold, directly contrary to the text in Theophanes, and to the translation of Anastasius? Much of this has been worked out, but far too positively, by the writer of a modern book for popular use, and therefore with no citation of authorities. — Bianchi-Giovini, Storia dei Pape. Capolago, 1851, t. iii. pp. 159-160.

Gregory Patriarch of the West.

II. Gregory did not forget the Patriarch of the West in the Bishop of Rome. Many churches in Italy were without pastors: their priests had been sold into slavery.[1] He refused to intermeddle in the election of bishops,[2] but his severe discipline did not scruple to degrade unworthy dignitaries and even prelates. Laurence, the first of the seven deacons, was deposed for his pride and other unnamed vices;[3] the Bishop of Naples for crimes capital both by the laws of God and man.[4] The Bishop of Salona is reproved for neglect of his solemn duties, and indulgence in convivial pleasures; for his contumacy in refusing to reinstate his archdeacon, he is deprived of his pallium; if he continues contumacious, he is to be excluded from communion. The Pope reproves the Bishop of Sipontum, in more than one angry letter, for his criminal and irreligious remissness in allowing the daughter of a man of rank to throw off her religious habit and return to a secular life.[5] He commands the bishop to arrest the woman who has thus defiled herself, and imprison her in a monastery till further instructions.[6] He commands Andrew Bishop of Tarentum, if guilty of concubinage, to abdicate his see; if of cruelty to a female, to be suspended from his functions for two months.[7] To Januarius, the Bishop of Cagliari, he

[1] Epist. i. 8, 15. There is an instance of a clericus sold for 12 solidi, at which price he might be redeemed. Gregory directs the Bishop of Sipontum to take that sum, if it cannot be obtained elsewhere, from the captives' church. — iii. 17.

[2] Epist. ii. 29.

[3] Epist. ii. in Præf.

[4] Epist. ii.; the ordo and plebs were to elect his successor.

[5] Epist. ii. 18.

[6] Epist. iii. 43.

[7] Epist. iii. 45.

speaks in still more menacing terms for a far more heinous offence — ploughing up the harvest of a proprietor on a Sunday before mass, and removing the landmark after mass. Nothing but the extreme age of Januarius saved him from the utmost ecclesiastical punishment.[1] He gave a commission to four bishops to degrade the Bishop of Melita for some serious crime: certain presbyters, his accomplices, were, it seems, to be imprisoned in monasteries.[2] We find the Bishop of Rome exercising authority in Greece over the Bishops of Thebes[3] and Larissa and Corinth.[4] The Bishops of Istria were less submissive. His attempts, at the commencement of his pontificate, to force them to condemn the three Chapters, were repressed by the direct interference of the Emperor.

In Gaul, simony and the promotion of young or unworthy persons to ecclesiastical dignities constantly demanded the interference of the Pontiff. The greater the wealth and honors attached to the sacred office, and the greater their influence over the barbarian mind, the more they were coveted for themselves, and sought by all the unscrupulous means of worldly ambition.[5] The epistles of Gregory to the bishops, to Queen Brunehild, to Thierry and Theodobert, and to Chlotaire kings in Gaul, are full of remonstrances against these irregularities.[6]

1 This seems to be the sense of the passage vii. ii. 1, which is obscure, probably corrupt. Januarius seems to have given Gregory much trouble. Another epistle censures him for exacting exorbitant burial fees. — vii. ii. 56. Oblations for lights might be received for those buried in the church.

2 vii. ii. 63.

3 Epist. iii. 6, 7

4 iv. 51.

5 iv. 54.

6 ix. 50 to 57. The privilegium said to have been granted by Gregory

Of all the great events of his pontificate, Gregory looked on none with more satisfaction than the conversion of the Arian-Gothic kingdom of Spain to Catholicism. He compares, in his humility, the few who in the last day will bear witness to his own zeal and influence, to the countless multitudes who would owe their salvation to the orthodox example of King Recared.[1]

The Council of Toledo, at which Spain publicly proclaimed its Catholicity, closes the history of the old Teutonic Arianism. The Lombards, indeed, remained to be subdued by the mild and Christian wisdom of Gregory; but in Burgundy and in Visigothic Gaul, the zeal and organization of the Catholic clergy, and the terror, the power, the intrigues of the orthodox Franks, had driven it from the minds of the kings, and from the hearts of the people. Twice Arianism had assailed the independence of Burgundy; twice it fell before the victorious arms of the Franks, the prayers, and no doubt more powerful aid than prayers, of the Catholic hierarchy. The Council of Epaona (though Arianism rallied for the last desperate conflict under the younger Godemar after that Council) witnessed what might be considered the act of submission to Latin Christianity.

May 8, 589.

Fall of Arianism in Gaul. A.D. 517.

The history of Visigothic Arianism in Spain is a more dire and awful tragedy. During the early reigns, both of the Suevian and Visigothic kings,

In Spain.

to the monastery of St. Medardus, anathematizing kings and all secular persons who should infringe the decrees of his apostolic authority, and ranking them with Judas, is proved to be spurious by Launoi, and by Dupin. — Dissert. 7, de Antiq. Eccl. Discip.

1 Epist. ad Rechared. Reg. vii. 128.

the Catholic bishops had held their councils undisturbed; Arianism had maintained its lofty or prudent or indifferent toleration. Leovigild ascended the throne, the ablest, most ambitious monarch 572 to 586. who had set on an Arian-Gothic throne, except Theodoric the Ostrogoth. Leovigild aspired to subdue the lawless Gothic lords who dwelt apart in their embattled mountain fastnesses, to compel the whole land (where each race, each rank, each creed asserted its wild freedom) to order and to law. He would be a king. He carried out his schemes with rigor and success. But he would compel religious differences also to unity. Himself a stern Arian, he even condescended to approximate, and with consummate art, to Catholicism; he sought by confounding to harmonize the contending parties; but he could not deceive the quick sight of the more vigilant, more intellectual Catholic hierarchy.

His young son, Hermenegild, became a Catholic — the Catholic a rebel. Seville and the southern cities rose against the King; Hermenegild was besieged in Seville; the Guadalquivir was blocked up; the city suffered the extremity of famine. Hermenegild fled to Cordova: he was sold by the Greeks, who possessed some of the havens under allegiance to the Byzantine Emperor. He was imprisoned first, less rigorously, in pleasant Valencia; afterwards more harshly in Tarragona. He was shut up in a noisome dungeon, with manacles on his hands. The young martyr (he was but twenty-one years old) increased his own sufferings by the sackcloth which chafed his soft and delicate limbs. He resisted all the persuasions, all the arts of his father. A fierce Goth, Sisebert, was sent into his cell, and clove his skull with an axe. The rebellious but orthodox Hermenegild, about ten centuries after, was canonized by Pope Sixtus V., through the influence of Philip II., the father of the murdered Don Carlos.[1]

Leovigild, before his death, was compelled at least to adopt milder measures towards his Catholic subjects. He is even said to have renounced his Arianism.

The first act of his son Recared was to avenge his brother's death on the murderer Sisebert. He hardly condescended to disguise, even for a year, his Catholicism; yet Recared was obliged to proceed with caution and reserve. It was not till the year before Gregory ascended the pontifical throne that Spain declared her return to Roman unity.[2]

Africa.

In Africa Gregory endeavored to suppress the undying remains of the Donatist factions, which even now aspired to the primacy of the Numidian Churches; but Donatism expired only with the Christianity of Northern Africa.

Britain.

By Gregory Britain was again brought within the pale of Christian Europe. The visions of his own early spiritual ambition were fulfilled by his missionary, the monk Augustine. In a letter to the Bishop of Alexandria he relates with triumph the tidings of this conquest, as communicated by Augustine,

[1] The religion was not an affair of race: Massona, the Catholic bishop of Merida, was a Goth. Leovigild set up Sanna as a rival bishop of Merida. Leovigild threatened the holy Massona with exile. "If you know where God is not, command your servants to conduct me thither." A thunderclap pealed in the heavens. "That is the King of whom we and you should stand in awe. He is not a king like you." — Florez, España Sagrada.

[2] Gregory of Tours and John of Bisclar are the great authorities for this period of Spanish history.

who boasts already of ten thousand baptized converts.[1] But in the conversion of the heathen Gregory was neither a fierce nor intolerant iconoclast. He deprecated the destruction of the pagan temples; he enjoined their sanctification by Christian rites;[2] the idols only were to be destroyed without remorse. Even the sacrifices of oxen[3] were to continue, but to be celebrated on the saints' days, in order gently to transfer the adoration of the people from their old to their new objects of worship. In his letters to the King and Queen, Ethelred and Bertha, he is gentle, persuasive, but he intimates the rapidly approaching end of the world in those awful terms which might appall the mind of a barbarian.[4] Even Ireland was not beyond the sphere of Gregory's patriarchal vigilance. He was consulted by certain bishops of that island on the question of rebaptizing heretics. He thought it necessary to inform those remote prelates, who perhaps were utterly ignorant of the controversy, as to his views on the three Chapters. The Irish bishops contrast their own state of peace with the calamities of Italy, and seem disposed to draw the inference that God approved their views on the contested points rather than those of the Italian prelates. Gregory replies that the miseries of Italy were rather signs of God's chastening love. The

[1] Epist. vii. 31.

[2] We find a singular illustration of the commercial intercourse kept up by means of religion: timber was to be brought from Britain to build the churches of St. Peter and St. Paul in Rome; and in several letters to the Bishop of Alexandria, Gregory informs him that he has sent him timber, an acceptable present in Egypt.

[3] It is curious to find the theory of the Egyptian origin of many of the Hebrew rites, received with so much apprehension in the writings of Spencer and Warburton, unsuspectingly promulgated by Gregory.—Epist. ix. 71.

[4] ix. 60.

unconvinced Irish, however, adhered to their own opinions.[1]

But if to these remote and yet unsubdued regions Gregory showed this wise forbearance, his solicitude to extirpate the last vestiges of heathenism which still lingered in Sardinia,[2] and a few other barbarous parts, was more uncompromising and severe. Towards those obstinate heathens he forgot on one occasion his milder language. He instructs the Bishop of Cagliari to preach to them. If his preaching is without effect, to compel them to repentance by imprisonment and other rigorous measures.[3]

Everywhere throughout the spiritual dominions of Gregory — in Gaul, in Italy, in Sicily, in Spain — the Jews dwelt mingled with his Christian subjects. To them Gregory was on the whole just and humane.[4] He censured the Bishop of Terracina for unjustly expelling the Jews from some place where they had been accustomed to celebrate their festivals. He condemned the forcible baptism of Jews in Gaul, which had been complained of by certain itinerant Jewish merchants.[5] Conviction by preaching was the only legitimate means of conversion. He did not scruple, however, to try the milder method of

Gregory and the Jews.

1 Letter of Columbanus published by Usher. — Biblioth. Vet. Patr. Lugd.

2 Epist. iii. 23, 26; vii. 1, 2: compare 20.

3 "Siquidem servi sunt, verberibus, cruciatibusque, quibus ad emendationem pervenire valeant, castigare. Si vero sunt liberi, inclusione dignâ distinctâque sunt in pœnitentiam dirigendi; ut qui salubria et a mortis periculo revocantia audire contemnunt, cruciat*us* (*ibus*, *qu.?*) saltem eos corporis ad desiderandam mentis valeas reducere sanitatem." — vii. ii. 67.

4 "Eos enim qui a religione Christianâ discordant, mansuetudine, benignitate, admonendo, suadendo, ad unitatem fidei necesse est congregare." — Epist. i. 33.

5 Epistle to the bishops of Arles and Marseilles, i. 45.

bribery. Certain Jewish tenants of Church property are told that if they embrace Christianity their rents will be lowered.[1] Even if their conversion be not sincere, that of their children may be so.[2] He denied them, however, the possession of Christian slaves, though where the slaves belonged as coloni to their estates (the Jews appear here, as in Sicily, in the unusual condition of landowners and cultivators of the soil), they were to maintain their uninvaded rights.[3] Slaves of Jewish masters, who, whether pagans or Jews, had taken refuge in a church from the desire of embracing Christianity, were to be purchased from their owners.[4] Gregory endeavored to check the European slave-trade, which was chiefly in the hands of the Jews, but his efforts were by no means successful.[5] Gregory reproved the Bishop of Cagliari, who had permitted a Jewish convert named Peter to seize the synagogue, and to set up within it a cross and an image of the Virgin. The Jews had been forbidden to build new synagogues, but were not to be deprived of those which they possessed. In one the images were to be removed with due respect, and the building restored to

1 iv. 6. This is remarkable as showing the Jews in the rare situation not only as cultivators of the soil, but as cultivators of church lands. In another passage he is extremely indignant at the sale of church vessels to a Jew, who was to be compelled to restore them. — i. 51.

2 ii. 37. See the curious story of a Jew who had deceived the Christians by setting up an altar to St. Elias, at which they were tempted to worship. (He must have been a singularly heretical Jew.) He was to be punished for the offence.

3 Epistle to the Bishop of Luna. To Queen Brunehild Gregory expresses his wonder that in her dominions Jews were permitted to possess Christian slaves. — vii. ii. 115, 116.

4 v. 31. In the next epistle Gregory expresses his indignation that certain Samaritans in Catana had presumed to circumcise their slaves. Compare vii. 1, 2, and xi. 15.

5 vii. ii. 30: compare Hist. of Jews, iii.

its rightful owners.[1] Directions in a similar spirit were given to the Bishop of Palermo.

Gregory and the heretics.

Gregory's humanity was hardly tried by the temptation of persecuting heretics. He was happily wanting both in power and in opportunity. The heresies of the East, excepting as to the three Chapters, had almost died away in the West. The Pelagian controversy had almost argued itself to rest; and even Manicheism, which was later to spring up in new forms, lurked only in obscure places, undetected by the searching jealousy of orthodoxy. Arianism in Spain had recanted its errors; among the Lombards it was an armed antagonist which could only be assailed, as it was victoriously assailed, by the gentle means of persuasion and love.

Bishop of Constantinople Universal Bishop.

While Gregory was thus, by his Christian virtues, establishing a substantial claim to Christian supremacy, and by superstitions congenial to the age still further unconsciously confirming his authority over the mind of man, he heard with astonishment and indignation that John the Patriarch of Constantinople had publicly, openly, assumed the title of Universal Bishop, a title which implied his absolute supremacy over the Christian world. This claim rested on the civil supremacy of Constantinople. The Western empire had perished, Italy had sunk into a province, Rome into a provincial city. Constantinople was the seat of empire, the capital of the world; the bishop of the capital was of right the chief pontiff of Christendom. The pretensions of the successors of St. Peter were thus contemptuously set aside; the religious supremacy became a kind of appanage to the

[1] vii. ii. 59: compare xi. 15.

civil sovereignty; it lost at once its permanence, its stability, its independence; it might fluctuate with all the vicissitudes of political dominion, or the caprice of human despotism.[1]

The letter of Gregory to the Emperor Maurice pours forth his indignation with the utmost vehemence, yet not without skill. All the calamities of the empire are traced to the pride and ambition of the clergy, yet there is a prudent reservation for the awfulness of their power, if applied, as it ought to be, as mediators between earth and heaven. "What fleshly arm would presume to lift itself against the imperial majesty, if the clergy were unanimous in insuring, by their prayers and by their merits, the protection of the Redeemer? Were the clergy what they should be, the fiercest barbarians would cease to rage against the lives of the innocent." "And is this a time, chosen by an arbitrary prelate, to invade the undoubted rights of St. Peter by a haughty and pompous title? Every part of Europe is abandoned to the dominion of the barbarians; cities are destroyed, fortresses overthrown, provinces depopulated, lands without inhabitants, the worshippers of idols are daily revelling in the massacre of the faithful, and the priests, who ought to A.D. 595.
be wailing in dust and ashes, are inventing new and profane appellations to gratify their pride. Am I defending my own cause? Is this any special injury to

[1] From the jealous and even angry tone in which Gregory writes to John Archbishop of Ravenna, who had dared to wear the pallium out of the church, and had ventured on other irregularities, at the same time that he protests that he always renders due honor to the church of Ravenna, it may be suspected that, as the residence of the Exarch, the emperor's representative, Ravenna was beginning to aspire towards some peculiar ecclesiastical superiority, at least to independence. — Epist. iv. ii. 15.

the Bishop of Rome? It is the cause of God, the cause of the whole Church. And who is he that usurps this uncanonical dignity? — the prelate of a see repeatedly ruled by heretics, by Nestorians, by Macedonians. Let all Christian hearts reject the *blasphemous* name. It was once applied, by the Council of Chalcedon, in honor of St. Peter, to the Bishop of Rome; but the more humble pontiffs of Rome would not assume a title injurious to the rest of the priesthood. I am but the servant of those priests who live as becomes their order. But 'pride goes before a fall;' and 'God resisteth the proud, but giveth grace to the humble.'" [1]

To the Empress (for on all religious questions the Empress is usually addressed as well as the Emperor), Gregory brands the presumption of John as a sign of the coming of Antichrist; and compares it to that of Satan, who aspired to be higher than all the angels.[2]

Among the exhortations to humility addressed to John himself, he urges this awful example: — "No one in the Church has yet sacrilegiously dared to usurp the name of Universal Bishop. Whoever calls himself Universal Bishop is Antichrist." [3] Gregory appeals also to the Bishops of Antioch and Alexandria to unite with him in asserting the superior dignity of St. Peter, in which they have a common interest; and it is remarkable with what address he endeavors to enlist those prelates in his cause, without distinctly admitting their equal claim to the inheritance of St. Peter, to which Antioch at least might adduce a plausible title.[4]

1 Epist. Maurit. Augusto. Epist. iv. 32.

2 Ad Constant. Imperatric., Epist. iv. 33.

3 Joanni Constant. Epist. iv. 38.

4 "Itaque cum multi sunt apostoli, pro ipso tamen principatu sola apostolorum principis sedes in auctoritate convaluit quæ in tribus locis unius est.

Gregory as temporal sovereign.

III. In the person of Gregory the Bishop of Rome first became, in act and in influence, if not in avowed authority, a temporal sovereign. Nor were his acts the ambitious encroachments of ecclesiastical usurpation on the civil power. They were forced upon him by the purest motives, if not by absolute necessity. The virtual sovereignty fell to him as abdicated by the neglect or powerlessness of its rightful owners: he must assume it, or leave the city and the people to anarchy. He alone could protect Rome and the remnant of her citizens from barbaric servitude; his authority rested on the universal feeling of its beneficence; his title was the security afforded by his government.

Nothing could appear more forlorn and hopeless than the state of Rome on the accession of Gregory to the pontificate — continual wars, repeated sieges, the capture and recapture of the city by barbarian Goths and Vandals, and no less barbarous Greeks.[1] Fires, tempests, inundations had raged with indiscriminating fury. If the heathen buildings of the city had suffered most, it was because, from their magnitude and splendor, they were more exposed to plunder and devastation. The Christian city was indebted for its comparative security, if partially to its sanctity, in a great degree to its humility. Epidemic plagues, the offspring of these calamities, had been constantly completing the work of barbarian enemies and of the destructive elements.

. . . Cum ergo unius atque una sit sedes, cui ex auctoritate divinâ his nunc episcopi præsident, quicquid ego de vobis boni audio, hoc mihi imputo, quod de me boni creditis hoc vestris meritis imputate." — Epist. vi. 37.

[1] Denina thinks that greater misery was inflicted upon Italy by the Grecian reconquest than by any other invasion. — Revoluz. d' Italia, t. i. l. v. p. 247.

After the pestilence which raged at the accession of Gregory had been arrested (an event attributed no doubt to the solemn religious ceremonies of the Bishop), his first care was that of a prefect of the city — to supply food for the famishing people. This, as has been shown, was chiefly furnished from Sicily and from the estates of the Church. During this whole period the city was saved from the horrors of famine only by the wise and provident regulations of the Pope.[1]

The Lombards.

But it was the Lombard invasion which compelled the Pope to take a more active part in the affairs of Italy. For seven and twenty years, says Gregory, we have lived in this city in terror of the sword of the Lombards. If during the few later years of Gregory's pontificate of thirteen years Rome enjoyed a precarious peace, that peace it owed to the intervention of her Bishop.

In their first invasion of Italy, under Alboin,[2] the Lombards extended their conquests as far as Tuscany and Umbria. Rome, Ravenna, and a few cities on the sea-coast, alone escaped their devastations, and remained under the jurisdiction of the Exarch of Ravenna, the representative of the Byzantine empire. The tragedy of Alboin's death, and that of his adulterous Queen, Rosmunda; the cup made out of her father's skull, with which Alboin pledged her in a public banquet, her revenge, her own murder by her guilty paramour, though in the latter event the Exarch

[1] Gregory, in a letter to one of his agents in Sicily, writes thus: — "Quia si quid minus huc transmittetur, non unus quilibet homo, sed cunctus simul populus trucidatur." — Epist. i. 2.

[2] A.D. 567, twenty-three years before the popedom of Gregory, A.D. 590.

of Ravenna had taken part, belong, nevertheless, to the unmitigated ferocity of the barbarian. The Lombard host comprehended wild hordes of Teutonic or Sclavonian tribes.[1] They occupied all the cities of northern Italy, to which they gave the name of Lombardy; civilization retreated as they advanced; the bishop, at their approach, fled from Milan. Nothing withheld them from the immediate and total subjugation of Italy but their wars with the Franks — wars excited by the intrigues of the Byzantine court, who by these means alone averted for a time the loss of their Italian territories.

After the short reign of Cleph, the elected successor of Alboin, the kingdom was divided into A.D. 573. dukedoms, and these martial independent princes continued to extend their ravages over the still retiring limits of the Roman dominion. They compelled the cultivators of the soil to pay a third part of their produce; they plundered churches and monasteries without scruple; massacred the clergy, destroyed the cities, and mowed down the people like corn.[2]

The perpetual wars with the Franks, who still poured over the Alps, demanded from the Lombards A.D. 584. a firmer government. Autharis was raised by acclamation to the Lombard throne. Within his own dominions the reign of Autharis was that of prosperity and peace. So only can any truth be assigned to the poetic description of his rule by the Latin historian the Deacon Paul, in whose glowing words the savage and desolating Lombards almost suddenly became an order-

[1] "Unde usque hodie eorum in quibus habitant vicos, Gepidos, Bulgares, Sarmatas, Pannonios, Suavos, Noricos, sive aliis hujuscemodi nominibus appellamus." — Paul. Dial. de Gestis Longobard., ii. 26.

[2] De Gestis Longobard., ii. 32.

ly, peaceful, Christian people. "Wonderful was the state of the Lombard kingdom: violence and treachery were alike unknown; no one oppressed, no one plundered another; thefts and robberies were unheard of; the traveller went wherever he would in perfect security."[1] How strange a contrast with the bitter and unceasing complaints in the works of Gregory of the savage manners, remorseless cruelties, and sacrilegious impieties, of these most wicked Lombards,[2] these heathen or Arian enemies of Rome and of true religion! During a period of cessation in his wars with the Franks, King Autharis swept unresisted over the whole of Southern Italy. At Reggio, the extreme point, the conqueror rode his horse into the sea, and with his spear struck a column, which had been erected there, exclaiming, "This is the boundary of the Lombard kingdom." During this or former expeditions Lombard dukedoms had been founded in the south, of which the most formidable were those of Spoleto and Benevento. These half-independent chieftains waged war upon the Romans; the latter especially carried his ravages to the gates of Rome.

The Italians sent earnest supplications, and the Pope pressing message after message for succor, to the successive Emperors, Tiberius and Maurice. The Byzantine government was too feeble, or too much occupied by nearer enemies, to render effectual aid to this remote province: their allies, the Franks, were the only safeguards of Italy.

It was towards the close of the reign of Autharis that Gregory became bishop of the plague-stricken

1 Paul. Diac. iii. 16.

2 "Nefandissimos Lombardos" is Gregory's standing epithet.

city. In the second year of his pontificate, Agilulf became the husband of Theodelinda, the widow of Autharis, and king of the Lombards.[1] The Exarch, who had not the power to avert, had the folly to provoke the Lombards to new invasions. He surprised Perugia and some other cities, and, to protect them, withdrew great part of the insufficient garrison of Rome. Agilulf poured his unresisted swarms into Southern Italy.[2]

Gregory compelled to act in temporal affairs.

Already had Gregory made peace with one formidable enemy, Ariulf, the Duke of Spoleto.[3] The predatory bands of the Lombard had threatened the city, where the walls were scarcely manned by a diminished and unpaid garrison. Agilulf, with his army, appeared at the gates of Rome.[4] Gregory suddenly brought to an end his exposition of the Temple of Ezekiel, on which he was preaching to the people. His work closes with these words:—"If I must now break off my discourse, ye are my witnesses for what reason, ye who share in my tribulations. On all sides we are girt with war; everywhere is the imminent

[1] Gregory ascribes the death of "Nefandissimus" Autharis to a direct judgment of God, for his prohibiting the baptism of Lombard children in the Catholic faith, "pro quâ culpâ eum divina majestas extinxit." Autharis was reported to have died by poison (Epist. i. 16, Nov.–Dec. 590)—probably an idle tale.—Paul. Diac. iii. 36.

[2] "Non Romanorum," wrote Gregory, "sed Longobardorum episcopus factus sum."

[3] Gregory's letter to the Archbishop of Ravenna shows how these affairs were thrown upon him. "Movere vos non debet Romani patricii animositas. Age cum eo ut pacem cum Ariulpho faciamus, quia miles de Româ ablatus est. Theodosiani vero, qui remanserunt, rogam non accipientes vix ad murorum custodiam se accommodant, et destituta ab omnibus civitas, si pacem non habet, quomodo subsistat?"—Epist. ii. 32.

[4] Chronologists differ as to the date of this siege. Sigonius gives 594, Baronius 595. I should agree with Muratori for 592, or at latest 593. Jaffè dates it 592, July.—Epist. ii. 46.

peril of death. Some return to us with their hands chopped off, some are reported as captives, others as slain. I am constrained to cease from my exposition, for I am weary of life. Who can expect me now to devote myself to sacred eloquence, now that my harp is turned to mourning, and my speech to the voice of them that weep?"[1]

Gregory defends Rome.

At least, by encouraging the commanders of the garrison, who seem to have done their duty, Gregory contributed to avert the impending capture of the city. While all the Romans, even those of the highest rank and family, without the city, were dragged like dogs into captivity,[2] at least those within were in safety, and owed their safety to the Pope; and the pacific influence which Gregory obtained in this momentous crisis led, after some years, to a definitive treaty of peace.[3]

Yet while Gregory was thus exercising the real power, and performing the protecting part of a sovereign, the Exarch, the feeble and insolent Romanus, affected to despise the weakness of Gregory, in supposing the barbarous Lombards disposed to peace.[4] The Emperor Maurice, safe in his palace at Constantinople, looked with jealousy on the proceedings of Gregory,

1 Job. xxx. 31, Exposit. in Ezekiel. sub fin.

2 It is not quite clear at what period the noble Romans, whom Gregory was anxious to ransom from the nefandissimi Lombardi, were carried into captivity upon the taking of Crotona. — Epist. vi. 23.

3 Sigonius places the final peace in 599; so also Jaffè, March. — Epist. ix. 42.

4 According to Gregory, the oppressions of the Exarchs were even worse than the hostilities of the Lombards. "Quia ejus in nos malitia gladios Longobardorum vicit: ita ut benigniores videantur hostes, qui nos interimunt quam reipublicæ judices, qui nos malitiâ suâ, rapinis atque fallaciis in cogitatione consumunt." — Epist. ad Sebast. Episc. vi. 42.

who thus presumed to save the narrow remnant of his dominions without his sanction, and disowned the peace, made, it should seem, by Gregory on his own authority.[1] Gregory, indeed, according to his own statement, possessed greater powers than he displayed. The fate of the whole Lombard race depended on his will. On the occasion of a charge made against him, as having been accessory to the death of a bishop, he is not content with repelling the accusation as false and alien to his humane disposition, but he desires the Emperor to be reminded, that if he had been disposed to mingle himself up with the death of the Lombards, the nation would have been without king, duke, or count, and would have fallen into utter confusion. But the fear of God had forbidden him to be concerned in the death of any human being.[2] It is difficult to reject this as an idle boast; more difficult to fix any period or to point to any juncture in which the Pope's humanity was exposed to this temptation.

Conversion of Lombards. March, 599.

But it is most singular that the influence of Gregory was obtained by means not only more mild and legitimate, but purely religious. In their very hour of conquest he was subduing the conqueror. While the Lombard king was at the gates of Rome, at the head of a hostile and ferocious army, Gregory was pursuing the triumphs of the Catholic faith, entertaining a friendly correspondence with the orthodox

[1] Epist. v. 40: compare v. 42.

[2] "Quod breviter suggeras domino nostro, quia si ego servus eorum in morte Longobardorum miscere me voluissem, hodie Longobardorum gens nec Regem, nec Duces nec Comites haberet, atque in summâ confusione esset divisa." —Epist. vii. 1, ad Sabin., quoted also in Paul. Diacon. This seems to point at some conspiracy devised to massacre the Lombard chiefs. It cannot mean any fanatic confidence in his own prayers, as of power to pluck down divine vengeance upon them.

Queen Theodelinda, and beginning, at least, to wean the sovereign and his subjects from what he thought, doubtless, the worst part of their character, their Arianism. Theodelinda was a Bavarian princess, bred up in Trinitarian belief, and to her Gregory appeals to show her genuine Christianity by her love of peace. Great would be her reward if she should check the prodigal effusion of blood. To Theodelinda Gregory addressed his memorable Dialogues; and perhaps the best excuse which can be made for the wild and extravagant legends thus stamped with his authority, and related apparently with such undoubting faith, may be found in the person to whom he dedicated this work. They might be, if not highly colored, selected with less scruple in order to impress the Lombard queen with the wonder-working power of the Roman clergy, of the orthodox monks and bishops of Italy. Profound as was the superstition of Gregory, many of these stories need some such palliation.[1]

Gregory employed the influence which he had obtained over Queen Theodelinda not merely to secure for Rome the blessings of peace; through him likewise, according to the annalist of the Lombards, from heathens, or, at most Arians, who paid no regard to the sacred possessions, the edifices, or the ministers of the Church, the whole nation, with Agilulf, their king, became orthodox Christians. Agilulf restored the wealth which he had plundered from the churches, reinstated the ejected bishops, and raised those who

[1] Some writers have endeavored to relieve the memory of Gregory the Great from the authorship of the Dialogues. But there can be no reasonable doubt of their authenticity; they are entirely in his style and manner, and alluded to more than once in his unquestioned writings.

had remained in their sees from abject poverty and degradation to dignity and power.[1] At what period this conversion took place it is difficult to decide; throughout Gregory's writings the Lombards are mentioned with unmitigated abhorrence; it could only, therefore, be towards the close of his life that this important event can be thought possible.

Still, however, Gregory acknowledged himself a subject of the Emperor. Though constrained to negotiate a separate peace, this measure was submissively excused as compelled by hard necessity. Even in his strongest act of opposition to the Byzantine court, in which the civil power of the Emperor and the monastic spirit of the Pope seemed to meet in irreconcilable hostility, his resistance to the law which prohibited soldiers actually enrolled or enlisted by a mark on the hand from deserting their duty to their country and taking refuge in monasteries, Gregory did not dare to resist the publication of the edict.[2] His language is that of supplication rather than remonstrance; the humble expostulation of a subject, not the bold assertion of spiritual power. "I confess, my Sovereigns, that I am struck with terror at this edict, by which heaven is closed against so many; and that which before was lawful to all, is prohibited to some. Many, indeed, may lead a religious life in a secular habit, but the most of men cannot be saved before God but by leaving all they have. What am I, who thus address my Sovereigns? Dust, and a worm! But I cannot be silent before my Sovereigns, because this edict is directed against God, the author

Imperial law about monastics.

1 Paull. Diac. iv. 6.

2 This edict dates 593. Gregory's letter, Aug. 593. — Jaffè.

of all things. Power was given to my Sovereigns over all men, to assist the good, to open wide the way to heaven; and that the kingdom of earth might be subservient to the kingdom of heaven. And now, behold, it is proclaimed that no one who is marked as an earthly soldier, unless he has completed his service, or is discharged from infirmity, shall be allowed to be a soldier of Jesus Christ. To this Christ answers, by me, the lowliest of his servants and yours: 'From a notary I made you captain of the guards; from captain of the guards, Cæsar; from Cæsar, emperor; and, more than that, the father of emperors. I commended my priests to your care, and you withdraw your soldiers from my service.' Tell your servant what answer you will make to the Lord when he comes to judgment. It is supposed, perhaps, that such conversions are not sincere; but I, your unworthy servant, know many converted soldiers who in our own days have worked miracles and done many signs and wonders. And will you prohibit the conversion of such men by law? Inquire what emperor it was that first issued such a statute.[1] Consider seriously, is this the time to prohibit men from leaving the world, when the end of the world is at hand? But a short time, and the earth and the heavens will burn, and among the blazing elements, amid angels and archangels, and thrones and dominions, and principalities and powers, the terrible Judge will appear. And what, if all your sins be remitted and this law

1 The allusion is to Julian the Apostate. — See Epist. 65. In the same letter Gregory asserts the temporal dominion of the sovereign in still stronger terms. "Qui dominari eum non solum militibus, sed etiam sacerdotibus concessit."

rise up against you, will be your excuse? By that terrible Judge I beseech you, let not so many tears, so many prayers, and alms, and fastings be obscured before the sight of God. Either mitigate or alter this law. The armies of my Sovereigns will be strengthened against their enemies in proportion as the armies of God, whose warfare is by prayer, are increased. I, who am subject to your authority, have commanded the law to be transmitted throughout the empire, but I have also avowed to my Sovereigns that I esteem it displeasing to God. I have done my duty in both cases; I have obeyed the Emperor, and not compromised my reverence for God."[1]

Usurpation of Phocas.

The darkest stain on the name of Gregory is his cruel and unchristian triumph in the fall of the Emperor Maurice — his base and adulatory praise of Phocas, the most odious and sanguinary tyrant who had ever seized the throne of Constantinople. It is the worst homage to religion to vindicate or even to excuse the crimes of religious men; and the apologetic palliation, or even the extenuation of their misdeeds rarely succeeds in removing, often strengthens, the unfavorable impression.

The conduct of the Emperor Maurice to Gregory had nothing of that vigor or generosity which had commended him to his Eastern subjects, while the avarice which had estranged their affections contributed manifestly towards the abandonment of Italy to the Lombard invader. Gregory owed not his elevation to Maurice. The cold consent of the Byzantine Emperor had ratified his election, and from that time the Emperor had treated him with neglect and contempt.

1 Ad Maurit. Imperat. — Epist. ii. 62.

On one occasion Maurice had called him in plain terms a fool for allowing himself to be imposed upon by the craft of the Lombard Ariulf. "A fool indeed I am," replied Gregory, "to suffer, as I do, among the swords of the Lombards."[1] Throughout his reign Maurice had impotently resented the enforced interference of Gregory in temporal affairs. He had thwarted and repudiated his negotiations, by which Rome was saved. The only act of vigor by which the Emperor had attempted to recruit his Italian armies had been that which Gregory in his monastic severity had denounced as a flagrant impiety. Maurice had, at least, connived at the arrogant usurpation of the title of Universal Bishop by the patriarch of Constantinople, even if he had not deliberately sanctioned it.[2]

Could it be expected that Gregory should rise superior to all these causes of animosity; that he should altogether suppress or disguise what might appear his patriotic and religious hopes from a change of dynasty? Such revolutions were of so frequent occurrence on the throne of Byzantium as to awaken little surprise and less sympathy, in the remote provinces; and the allegiance of Italy was but of recent date — an allegiance which subjected the land to all the tyranny and oppression, and afforded none of the protection and security, of a regular government.

[1] Epist. iv. 31. The craft which has been imputed to Gregory may perhaps be traced in this remarkable letter. He acknowledges himself and the priesthood in general subject to the censure of the emperor. "Sed excellenti consideratione propter eum cujus servi sunt, eis *ita dominetur*, ut etiam *debitam reverentiam* impendat. Nam in divinis eloquiis sacerdotes aliquando dii, aliquando angeli vocantur."

[2] Maurice, according to the biographer of Gregory, had meditated more violent hostility against the Pope, but had been deterred by the alarming prophecy of a monk. — Vit. Greg.

At the time of his insurrection Phocas was an undistinguished soldier, raised by the acclamations of the army to the post of peril and honor;[1] his mean and cruel character, even his repulsive and hideous person, might be unknown in Rome; and Gregory might suppose that in such an exigency the choice of the army would not fall upon a man without courage, energy, or ability. It was no uncommon event in the annals of the empire to transfer the diadem to some bold military adventurer; Rome and Constantinople owed some of their best rulers to such revolutions.

But the common usage of such revolutions could not vindicate to a Christian prelate the barbarities with which Maurice and his infant family were put to death; and the high-wrought resignation of Maurice, it might have been supposed, would awaken ardent admiration in a mind like Gregory's. "If he is a coward, he will be a murderer!" such was the prophetic language of Maurice concerning the successful usurper. Maurice had taken refuge in a sanctuary; but when Phocas appeared as Emperor at the gates, when, in discharge of the first imperial duty at Constantinople, he interfered between the blue and the green factions in the Circus, which still excited fiercer animosities than those of the state, the Blues, against whom the usurper took part, broke out into menacing and significant shouts, "Maurice is not dead!" Phocas imme-

1 Theophylact, viii. 1, vol. i. p. 706, edit. Bonn. His person and character are thus described by the hatred of later writers. He was short, deformed, with a fierce look, and red hair, with his brows meeting and his chin shaved. He had a scar on his cheek, which looked black when he was angry. He was a drunkard, lewd, sanguinary, stern and savage in speech, pitiless, brutal, and a heretic! His wife Leonto was as bad.— Cedren. Lib. i. p. 708.

diately ordered the fallen emperor to be dragged from his sanctuary. His five sons were butchered before his face. The unmoved and tearless father, as each received the fatal blow, exclaimed, "Just art thou, O Lord, and righteous are thy judgments!" With a sterner feeling of self-sacrifice, if it were not, indeed, despair which took the form of frenzy, he betrayed the pious fraud of a nurse, who had substituted her own child for the youngest of the Emperor. Maurice was beheaded the last;[1] the heads were cast before the throne of Phocas, who would not allow them, till compelled by their offensiveness, to be buried.

The intelligence of these events, with most, at least, of their revolting circumstances, must have arrived at Rome at the same time with that of the fall of Maurice and the elevation of Phocas. It is astonishing that even common prudence did not temper the language of the triumphant Pontiff, who launches out into a panegyric on the mercy and benignity of the usurper, calls on earth and heaven to rejoice at his accession, augurs peace and prosperity to the empire from his pious acts, and even seems to anticipate the return of the old republican freedom under the rule of the devout and gentle Phocas.[2]

[1] According to the biographer, Maurice owed profound obligations to Gregory, which might overbalance such merciless rejoicings at his worldly fate. He owed his eternal salvation to the prayer of Gregory. "Et quia oratio Gregorii, quâ illum petierat in terribili Dei judicio liberum ab omnibus delictis inveniri, *vacua esse non potuit:* idem Mauricius id recepit quod meruit et in cunctis suis incommodis Deum benedicens, a sempiterno supplicio meruit liberari." — Joann. Diac. iii. 19.

[2] "Lætentur cœli et exultet terra; et de benignis vestris actibus universæ reipublicæ populus, nunc usque vehementer afflictus, hilarescat. . . . Hoc namque inter reges gentium et reipublicæ Imperatores distat, quod reges gentium domini servorum sunt; Imperatores vero reipublicæ domini liberorum." — Epist. xi. 38.

The sad truth is, that Gregory was blinded by the one great absorbing object, the interest of the Church, which to him involved the interest of religion, of mankind, and of God. Loyalty, justice, candor, even humanity, yielded to the dominant feeling. Maurice was not above suspicion of heresy; the unscrupulous hostility, no doubt, of political enemies taunted him as a Marcionist. At all events, he had countenanced th usurpation of the Bishop of Constantinople. John of Constantinople, with his sanction, called himself Universal Bishop. The new emperor, out of enmity to the old, would probably espouse the opposite side. Already Phocas seems to have invited in some way the adulation of Gregory; and reverence for the see of Rome, obedience to legitimate ecclesiastical authority, were in themselves, or gave the promise of, such transcendant virtues, that rebellion, murder, brutal barbarity, were overlooked, as the accidental result of circumstances, the inevitable evils of a beneficial revolution. So completely, by this time, had the sacerdotal obtained the superiority over the moral influence of Christianity, that even a man of Gregory's unquestioned Christian gentleness and natural humanity could not escape the predominant passion.

June, 603.

Phocas Emperor. A.D. 602-610.

Gregory was spared the pain and shame of witnessing the utter falsehood of his pious vaticinations as to the glorious and holy reign of Phocas. In the second year of the tyrant's reign he closed the thirteen important years of his pontificate. The ungrateful Romans paid but tardy honors to his memory. His death was followed by a famine, which the starving multitude attributed to his wasteful dilapi-

Death of Gregory, March 10, 604.

dation of the patrimony of the Church — that patrimony which had been so carefully administered, and so religiously devoted to their use. Nothing can give a baser notion of their degradation than their actions. They proceeded to wreak their vengeance on the library of Gregory, and were only deterred from their barbarous ravages by the interposition of Peter, the faithful archdeacon. Peter had been interlocutor of Gregory in the wild legends contained in the Dialogues. The archdeacon now assured the populace of Rome that he had often seen the Holy Ghost, in the visible shape of a dove, hovering over the head of Gregory as he wrote. Gregory's successor therefore hesitated, and demanded that Peter should confirm his pious fiction or fancy by an oath. He ascended the pulpit, but before he had concluded his solemn oath he fell dead. That which to an hostile audience might have been a manifest judgment against perjury, was received as a divine testimony to his truth.[1] The Roman Church has constantly permitted Gregory to be represented with the Holy Ghost, as a dove, floating over his head.[2]

1 Joann. Diacon. Vit. iv. 69.

2 I am disposed to insert the epitaph on Gregory as an example of the poetry and of the religious sentiment of the times: —

Suscipe, terra, tuo corpus de corpore sumptum,
Reddere quod valeas, vivificante Deo.
Spiritus alta petit, leti nil jura nocebunt,
Cui vitæ alterius mors magis illa via est.
Pontificis summi hoc clauduntur membra sepulcro,
Qui innumeris semper vivit ubique bonis.
Esuriem dapibus superavit, frigora veste,
Atque animas monitis texit ab hoste suis.
Implebatque actu quicquid sermone docebat,
Esset ut exemplum mystica verba loquens.
Anglos ad Christum vertit, pietate ministrâ,
Acquirens fideique agmina gente nova.

The historian of Christianity is arrested by certain characters and certain epochs, which stand as landmarks between the close of one age of religion and the commencement of another. Such a character is Gregory the Great; such an epoch his pontificate, the termination of the sixth century.

Gregory, not from his station alone, but by the acknowledgment of the admiring world, was intellectually, as well as spiritually, the great model of his age. He was proficient in all the arts and sciences cultivated at that time; the vast volumes of his writings show his indefatigable powers; their popularity and their authority his ability to clothe those thoughts and those reasonings in language which would awaken and command the general mind.

His epoch was that of the final Christianization of the world, not in outward worship alone, not in its establishment as the imperial religion, the rise of the church upon the ruin of the temple, and the recognition of the hierarchy as an indispensable rank in the social system, but in its full possession of the whole mind of man, in letters, arts as far as arts were cultivated, habits, usages, modes of thought, and in popular superstition.

Not only was heathenism, but, excepting in the laws and municipal institutions, Romanity itself absolutely extinct. The reign of Theodoric had been an attempt to fuse together Roman, Teutonic, and Christian usages. Cassiodorus, though half a monk, aspired

Hic labor, hoc studium, hæc tibi cura, hoc, pastor, agebas,
Ut Domini offerres plurima lucra greges.
Hisque Dei consul factus lætare triumphis,
Nam mercedem operum jam sine fine tenes.

Remark the old Roman image in the last line but one.

to be a Roman statesman, Boethius to be a heathen philosopher. The influence of the Roman schools of rhetoric is betrayed even in the writers of Gaul, such as Sidonius Apollinaris; there is an attempt to preserve some lingering cadence of Roman poetry in the Christian versifiers of that age. At the close of the sixth century all this has expired; ecclesiastical Latin is the only language of letters, or rather, letters themselves are become purely ecclesiastical. The fable of Gregory's destruction of the Palatine Library is now rejected, as injurious to his fame; but probably the Palatine Library, if it existed, would have been so utterly neglected that Gregory would hardly have condescended to fear its influence. His aversion to such studies is not that of dread or hatred, but of religious contempt; profane letters are a disgrace to a Christian bishop; the truly religious spirit would loathe them of itself.[1]

What, then, was this Christianity by which Gregory ruled the world? Not merely the speculative and dogmatic theology, but the popular, vital, active Christianity, which was working in the heart of man; the dominant motive of his actions, as far as they were affected by religion; the principal element of his hopes and fears as regards the invisible world and that future life which had now become part of his conscious belief.

Christian mythology.

The history of Christianity cannot be understood without pausing at stated periods to survey the progress and development of this Christian mythology, which, gradually growing up and

[1] See the pious wonder with which he reproves a bishop of Gaul. "Post hæc pervenit ad nos quod *sine verecundiâ* memorare non possumus, fraternitatem tuam grammaticam quibusdam exponere. . . . Quam grave nefandumque sit episcopos canere, quod nec laico religioso conveniat, ipse considera." — Epist. ix. 48.

springing as it did from natural and universal instincts, took a more perfect and systematic form, and at length, at the height of the Middle Ages, was as much a part of Latin Christianity as the primal truths of the Gospel. This growth, which had long before begun, had reached a kind of adolescence in the age of Gregory, to expand into full maturity during succeeding ages. Already the creeds of the Church formed but a small portion of Christian belief. The highest and most speculative questions of theology, especially in Alexandria and Constantinople, had become watchwords of strife and faction, had stirred the passions of the lowest orders; the two Natures, or the single or double Will in Christ, had agitated the workshop of the artisan and the seats in the Circus. But when these great questions had sunk into quiescence, or, as in Latin Christianity, had never so fully occupied the general mind; when either the triumph of one party, or the general weariness, had worn out their absorbing interest, the religious mind subsided into its more ordinary occupations, and these bore but remote relation to the sublime truths of the Divine Unity and the revelation of God in Christ. As God the Father had receded, as it were, from the sight of man into a vague and unapproachable sanctity; as the human soul had been entirely centred on the more immediate divine presence in the Saviour; so the Saviour himself might seem to withdraw from the actual, at least the exclusive, devotion of the human heart, which was busied with intermediate objects of worship. Christ assumed gradually more and more of the awfulness, the immateriality, the incomprehensibleness, of the Deity, and men sought out beings more akin to themselves, more open, it might seem, to human sympathies. The Eucharist, in which the Redeemer's spiritual presence, yet undefined and untransubstantiated, was directly and immediately in communion with the soul, had become more and more wrapt in mystery; though the great crowning act of faith, the interdiction of which was almost tantamount to a sentence of spiritual death, it was more rarely approached, except by the clergy. Believers delighted in those ceremonials to which they might have recourse with less timidity; the shrines and the relics of martyrs might deign to receive the homage of those who were too profane to tread the holier ground. Already the worship of these lower objects of homage begins to intercept that to the higher; the popular mind is filling with images either not suggested at all, or suggested but very dimly, by the sacred writings; legends of saints are supplanting, or rivalling at least, in their general respect and attention, the narratives of the Bible.

Of all these forms of worship, the most captivating, and captivating to the most amiable weaknesses of the human mind, was the devotion to the Virgin Mary. The worship of the Virgin had first arisen in the East;[1] and this worship, already more than initiate, contributed, no doubt, to the passionate violence with which the Nestorian controversy was agitated, while that controversy, with its favorable issue to those who might seem most zealous for the Virgin's glory, gave a strong impulse to the worship. The denial of the title "The Mother of God," by Nestorius, was that which sounded most offensive to the general ear; it was the intelligible odious point in his heresy. The worship of

[1] Evagr. ii. E. v. 19.

the Virgin now appears in the East as an integral part of Christianity. Among Justinian's splendid edifices arose many churches dedicated to the Mother of God.[1] The feast of the Annunciation is already celebrated under Justin and Justinian.[2] Heraclius has images of the Virgin on his masts when he sails to Constantinople to overthrow Phocas.[3] Before the end of the century the Virgin is become the tutelar deity of Constantinople, which is saved by her intercession from the Saracens.[4]

Worship of the Virgin.

In the time of Gregory the worship of the Virgin had not assumed that rank in Latin Christianity to which it rose in later centuries, though that second great impulse towards this worship, the unbounded admiration of virginity, had full possession of his monastic mind. With Gregory celibacy was the perfection of human nature; he looked with abhorrence on the contamination of the holy sacerdotal character, even in its lowest degree, by any sexual connection.[5] No subdeacon, after a certain period, was to be admitted without a vow of chastity; no married subdeacon to be promoted to a higher rank. In one of his expositions[6] he sadly relates the *fall* of one of his aunts, a consecrated virgin; she had been guilty

1 Procop. de Edif. c. 6.

2 Niceph. H. E. xvii. 28.

3 Theophanes, p. 429, edit. Bonn.

4 Theophan. p. 609 *et passim.*

5 "Nullus debet ad ministerium altaris accedere, nisi cujus castitas ante susceptum ministerium sit approbata." — Epist. i. 42. He protests against the election of a bishop who had a young daughter; this bishop, however, was also simplex, and charged with usury. — viii. 40. No bigamist, or one who had married a wife not a virgin, to be received into orders. Marriages, however, Gregory declares, cannot be dissolved on account of religion; *both* parties must consent to live continently in marriage. — ix. 39.

6 That on the text, "many are called, but few chosen."

of the sin of marriage. Of all his grievances against the Exarch of Ravenna none seems more worthy of complaint than that he had encouraged certain nuns to throw off their religious habits, and to marry.[1] Gregory does not seem to have waged this war against nature, however his sentiments were congenial with those of his age, with his wonted success.[2] His letters are full of appeals to sovereigns and to bishops to repress the incontinence of the clergy; even monasteries were not absolutely safe.[3]

It was not around the monastery alone, the centre of this preternatural agency, that the ordinary providence of God gave place to a perpetual interposition of miraculous power. Every Christian was environed with a world of invisible beings, who were constantly putting off their spiritual nature, and assuming forms, uttering tones, distilling odors, apprehensible by the soul of man, or taking absolute and conscious possession of his inward being. A distinction was drawn between the pure, spiritual, illimitable, incomprehensible nature of the Godhead, and the thin and subtile, but bodily forms of angels and archangels. These were perceptible to the human senses, wore the human form, spoke with human language: their substance was the thin air, the impalpable fire; it resem-

Angels.

1 Epist. iv. 18.

2 The absurd story about Gregory's fish-ponds paved with the sculls of the drowned infants of the Roman clergy, is only memorable as an instance of what writers of history will believe, and persuade themselves they believe, when it suits party interest. But by whom, or when, was it invented? It is much older than the Reformation.

3 Epist. viii. 21. The regulations of Gregory about the monastic life are in a wiser spirit. None were to be received as monks under 18 (Epist. i. 41); none without two years' probation (iv. 44, viii. 23); but monks who left their monasteries were to be confined for life (i. 33, 40, xii. 28). He mentions also the wandering Africans, who were often secret Manicheans.

bled the souls of men, but yet, whenever they pleased, it was visible, performed the functions of life, communicated not with the mind and soul only, but with the eye and ear of man.[1]

The hearing and the sight of religious terror were far more quick and sensitive. The angelic visitations were but rare and occasional; the more active Demons were ever on the watch, seizing and making every opportunity of beguiling their easy victims.[2] They were everywhere present, and everywhere betraying their presence. They ventured into the holiest places; they were hardly awed by the most devout saints; but, at the same time, there was no being too humble, to whose seduction they would not condescend — nothing in ordinary life so trivial and insignificant but that they would stoop to employ it for their evil purposes. They were without the man, terrifying him with mysterious sounds and unaccountable sights. They were within him, compelling all his faculties to do their bidding, another indwelling will besides his own, compelling his reluctant soul to perform their

Devils.

1 The following definition is of a later period, but represents the established notion: — *Περὶ τῶν ἀγγέλων καὶ ἀρχαγγέλων, καὶ τῶν ὑπὲρ τούτους ἁγίων δυνάμεων, προσθήσω δὲ καὶ τὰς ἡμετέρας ψυχὰς τῶν ἀνθρώπων, νοερούς μὲν αὐτοὺς ἡ καθολικὴ ἐκκλησία γινώσκει, οὐ μὴν ἀσωμάτους πάντη καὶ ἀοράτους, ὡς ὑμεῖς οἱ Ἑλλῆνες φατέ· λεπτοσωμάτους δὲ καὶ ἀερώδεις ἢ πυρώδεις κατὰ τὸ γεγραμμένον, ὁ ποιῶν τοὺς ἀγγελόυς αὐτοὺς πνεύματα καὶ τοὺς λειτουργοὺς αὐτοῦ πῦρ φλέγον.* — Joann. Episcop. Thessalon. apud Concil. Nic. ii., Labbe, p. 354.

2 Read Cassian, who writes indeed of monks, but the belief was universal. "Nosse debemus non omnes universas dæmones passiones ingerere, sed unicuique vitio certos spiritus incubare: et alios quidem immunditiis ac libidinum sordibus delectari; alios blasphemiis, alios iræ furoriquæ proclivius imminere, alios cenodoxiâ superbiâque mulceri; et unumquemque illud vitium humanis cordibus, quo ipse gaudet, inserere: sed non cunctos pariter suas ingerere pravitates, sed vicissim prout temporis vel loci vel suscipientis opportunitas provocaverit." — Cass. Coll. 7, c. 17.

service. Every passion, every vice, had its especial demon; lust, impiety, blasphemy, vainglory, pride, were not the man himself, but a foreign power working within him. The slightest act, sometimes no act at all, surrendered the soul to the irresistible indwelling agent. In Gregory's Dialogues a woman eats a lettuce without making the sign of the cross; she is possessed by a devil, who had been swallowed in the unexorcised lettuce. Another woman is possessed for admitting her husband's embraces the night before the dedication of an oratory.

Martyrs.

Happily there existed, and existed almost at the command of the clergy, a counterworking power to this fatal diabolic influence, in the perpetual presence of the saints, more especially in hallowed places, and about their own relics.[1] These relics were the treasure with which the clergy, above all the bishops of Rome, who possessed those of St. Peter and St. Paul, with countless others, ruled the mind; for by these they controlled and kept in awe, they repaired the evils wrought by this whole world of evil spirits. Happy were the churches, the monasteries, whose foundations were hallowed and secured by these sacred talismans. To doubt their presence in these dedicated shrines, in the scenes of their martyrdom, obstinately to require the satisfaction of the senses as to their presence, was an impious want of faith; belief, in propor-

1 Gregory thus lays down the doctrine of his age: "Ubi in suis corporibus sancti martyres jacent, dubium, Petre, non est, quod multa valeant signa demonstrare, sicut et fecerunt, et purâ mente quærentibus innumera miracula ostendunt. Sed quia ab infirmis mentibus potest dubitari, utrumne ad exaudiendum ibi præsentes sunt, ubi constat, quia in suis corporibus non sunt, ita necesse est eos majora signa ostendere, ubi de eorum præsentiâ potest mens infirma dubitare. Quorum vero mens in Deo fixa est, tanto magis habet fidei meritum, quando eos novit, et non jacere corpore, et tamen non deesse ad exaudiendum."

tion to the doubtfulness of the miracle, was the more meritorious. Kings and queens bowed in awe before the possessors and dispensers of these wonder-working treasures,[1] which were not only preservative against worldly calamities, but absolved from sin.[2]

Relics had now attained a self-defensive power; profane hands which touched them withered; Relics. and men who endeavored to remove them were struck dead.[3] Such was the declaration of Gregory himself, to one who had petitioned for the head or some part of the body of St. Paul. It was an awful thing even to approach to worship them. Men who had merely touched the bones of St. Peter, St. Paul, and St. Lawrence, though with the pious design of changing their position or placing the scattered bones together, had fallen dead, in one case to the number of ten. The utmost that the Church of Rome could bestow would be a cloth which had been permitted to touch them; and even such cloths had been known to bleed. If, indeed, the chains of St. Paul would yield any of their precious iron to the file, which they often refused to do, this, he writes, he would transmit to the Empress; and he consoles her for the smallness of the gift by the miraculous power which it will inherently possess.[4]

1 See letters to the Bishop of Xaintonge and Brunechild Queen of France.

2 "Ut quod illius collum ligat ad martyrium, vestrum ab omnibus peccatis solvat." — Dialog. vi. 25.

3 On relics, especially those of St. Peter, compare Epist. i. 29, 30, ii. ii. 32, iii. 30, v. 50, 51, vi. 23, 25, vii. 2, 112, vii. ii. 88, xii. 17. They were formerly defended by law, their removal and sale prohibited. "Nemo martyrem distrahat, nemo mercetur." — C. Theod. ix. 17. Compare C. Justin. i. t. 2. Augustine speaks of vagabond monks, who traded in false relics. "Membra martyrum, si tamen martyrum venditant." — De Oper. Monach. c. 28.

4 All this is verbatim from the curious letter to the Empress Constantia.

Gregory doled out such gifts with pious parsimony. A nail which contained the minutest filings from the chains of St. Peter[1] was an inestimable present to a patrician, or an ex-consul, or a barbaric king. Sometimes they were inserted in a small cross; in one instance with fragments of the gridiron on which St. Lawrence was roasted.[2] One of the *golden* nails of the chains of St. Peter had tempted the avarice of a profane, no doubt a heathen or Arian, Lombard; he took out his knife to sever it off; the awe-struck knife sprung up and cut his sacrilegious throat. The Lombard king, Autharis, and his attendants, were witnesses of the miracle, and stood in terror, not daring to lift the fearful nail from the ground. A Catholic was fortunately found, by whom the nail permitted itself to be touched, and this peerless gift, so avouched, Gregory sends to a distinguished civil officer.[3]

Sanctity of the clergy.

That sanctity, which thus dwelt in the relics of the saints, was naturally gathered, as far as possible, around their own persons by the clergy, hallowed as they were, and set apart by their ordination from the common race of man; and if the hierarchy had only wielded this power for self-protection; if they had but arrayed themselves in this defensive awe against the insults and cruelties of barbarians, such as the Lombards are described, it would be stern censure which would condemn even manifest imposture. We might excuse the embellishment, even the inven-

— iii. 30. Gregory had forgotten that he had been allowed to transport from Constantinople to Rome an arm of St. Andrew and the head of St. Luke, and owed a more liberal return.

1 Epist. i. 29, 30. King Childebert, vi. vi. "Quæ collo vestro suspensæ a malis vos omnibus tueantur."

2 Epist. ii. ii. 32.

3 Dial. vi. 23; see also 25.

tion of the noble story of the Bishop Sanctulus, who offered his life for that of a captive deacon, before whom the Lombard executioner, when he lifted up his sword to behead him, felt his arm stiffen, and could not move it till he had solemnly sworn never to raise that sword against the life of a Christian.[1] But this conservative respect for the sanctity of their order darkens too frequently into pride and inhumanity; the awful inviolability of their persons becomes a jealous resentment against even unintentional irreverence. A demoniac accused the holy Bishop Fortunatus of refusing him the rights of hospitality; a poor peasant receives the possessed into his house, and is punished for this inferential disrespect to the Bishop by seeing his child cast into the fire and burnt before his eyes. A poor fellow with a monkey and cymbals is struck dead for unintentionally interrupting a Bishop Boniface in prayer.[2]

The sacred edifices, the churches, especially, approachable to all, were yet approachable not without profound awe; in them met everything which could deepen that awe; within were the relics of the tutelar saint, the mysteries, and the presence of the Redeemer, of God himself, beneath were the remains of the faithful dead.[3]

Burial in churches had now begun; it was a special privilege. Gregory dwells on the advantage of being thus constantly suggested to the prayers of friends and relatives for the repose of the soul. But that which was a blessing to the holy was but more perilous to

1 Dial. iii. 37.

2 Dial. i. 10, i. 9.

3 Gregory forbade the *worship* of images, though he encouraged them as suggestive memorials.—vii. ii. 54; compare vii. 33, iii. "Pro lectione pictura est."—ix. 9.

the unabsolved and the wicked. The sacred soil refused to receive them; the martyrs appeared and commanded the fetid corpses to be cast out of their precincts. They were seized by devils, who did not fear to carry off their own even from those holy places.[1] But oblations were still effective after death. The consecrated host has begun to possess in itself wonder-working powers. A child is cast forth from his grave, and is only persuaded to rest in quiet by a piece of the consecrated bread being placed upon his breast. Two noble women, who had been excommunicated for talking scandal, were nevertheless buried in the church; but every time the mass was offered, their spirits were seen to rise from their tombs, and glide out of the church. It was only after an oblation had been "immolated" for them that they slept in peace.[2]

State after death.

The mystery of the state after death began to cease to be a mystery. The subtile and invisible soul gradually materialized itself to the keen sight of the devout. A hermit declared that he had seen Theodoric, the Ostrogothic king, at the instant of death, with loose garments and sandals, led between Symmachus the patrician and John the Pope, and plunged into the burning crater of Lipari.[3] Benedict, while waking, beheld a bright and dazzling light, in which he distinctly saw the soul of Germanus, Bishop of Capua, ascend to heaven in an orb of fire, borne by angels.[4]

1 Dial. iv. 50, &c.

2 Dial. ii. 22, 23. Compare the last two chapters of Book iv.

3 "Discinctus et discalceatus" — such was the confusion of the attributes of soul and body. — Dial. iv. 30.

4 Dial. iv. 30.

Hell was by no means the inexorable dwelling which restored not its inhabitants. Men were transported thither for a short time, and returned to reveal its secrets to the shuddering world. Gregory's fourth book is entirely filled with legends of departing and of departed spirits, several of which revisit the light of day. On the locality of hell Gregory is modest, and declines to make any peremptory decision. On purgatory too he is dubious, though his final conclusion appears to be that there is a purgatorial fire which may purify the soul from very slight sins.[1] Some centuries must elapse before those awful realms have formed themselves into that dreary and regular topography which Dante partly created out of his own sublime imagination, partly combined from all the accumulated legends which had become the universal belief of Christendom.

Hell.

The most singular of these earlier journeys into the future world are the adventures of a certain Stephen, the first part of which Gregory declares he had heard more than once from his own mouth,[2] and which he relates, apparently intending to be implicitly believed. Stephen had to all appearance died in Constantinople, but, as the embalmer could not be found, he was left unburied the whole night. During that time he went down into hell, where he saw many things which he had not before believed. But when he came before the Judge, the Judge said, I did not send for this man, but for Stephen the smith. Gregory's friend Stephen was too happy to get back, and on his return found

1 "Sed tamen de quibusdam levibus culpis esse ante judicium purgatorius ignis credendus est." — Dial. iv. 39.

2 "De semet ipso mihi narrare *consueverat*."

his neighbor Stephen the smith dead. But Stephen learned not wisdom from his escape. He died of the plague in Rome, and with him appeared to die a soldier, who returned to reveal more of these fearful secrets of the other world, and the fate of Stephen. The soldier passed a bridge, beneath it flowed a river, from which rose vapors, dark, dismal, and noisome. Beyond the bridge (the imagination could but go back to the old Elysian fields) spread beautiful, flowery, and fragrant meadows, peopled by spirits clothed in white. In these were many mansions, vast and full of light. Above all rose a palace of golden bricks, to whom it belonged he could not read. On the bridge he recognized Stephen, whose foot slipped as he endeavored to pass. His lower limbs were immediately seized by frightful forms, who strove to drag him to the fetid dwellings below. But white and beautiful beings caught his arms, and there was a long struggle between the conflicting powers. The soldier did not see the issue of the conflict.

Such were among the stories avouched by the highest ecclesiastical authority, and commended it might seem by the uninquiring faith of the ruling intellect of his age — such among the first elements of that universal popular religion which was the Christianity of ages. This religion gradually moulded together all which arose out of the natural instincts of man, the undying reminiscences of all the older religions, the Jewish, the Pagan, and the Teutonic, with the few and indistinct glimpses of the invisible world and the future state of being in the New Testament, into a vast system, more sublime perhaps for its indefiniteness, which, being necessary in that condition of mankind, could not but grow up out of the kindled imagination and religious faith of Christendom; and such religion the historian who should presume to condemn as a vast plan of fraud, or a philosopher who should venture to disdain as a fabric of folly, only deserving to be forgotten, would be equally unjust, equally blind to its real uses, assuredly ignorant of its importance and its significance in the history of man. For on this, the popular Christianity, popular as comprehending the highest as well as the lowest in rank, and even in intellectual estimation, turns the whole history of man for many centuries. It is at once the cause and the consequence of the sacerdotal dominion over mankind; the groundwork of authority at which the world trembled; which founded and overthrew kingdoms, bound together or set in antagonistic array nations, classes, ranks, orders of society. Of this, the parent, when the time arrived, of poetry, of art, the Christian historian must watch the growth and mark the gradations by which it gathered into itself the whole activity of the human mind, and quickened that activity till at length the mind outgrew that which had been so long almost its sole occupation. It endured till faith, with the Schoolmen, led into the fathomless depths of metaphysics, began to aspire after higher truths; with the Reformers, attempting to refine religion to its primary spiritual simplicity, gradually dropped, or left but to the humblest and most ignorant, at least to the more imaginative and less practical part, of mankind, this even yet prolific legendary Christianity, which had been the accessory and supplementary Bible, the authoritative and accepted, though often unwritten, Gospel of centuries.

BOOK IV.

CONTEMPORARY CHRONOLOGY.

POPES. A.D. — A.D.	PATRIARCHS OF CONSTANTINOPLE. A.D. — A.D.	EMPERORS OF THE EAST. A.D. — A.D.	EXARCHS OF RAVENNA. A.D. — A.D.
	Cyriacus 610		Callinicus 602
Gregory I. died 604		602 Phocas 610	
			608 Smaragdus (restored) 610
604 Sabinianus 606			
606 Boniface III. 607			
608 Boniface IV. 615			
	610 Sergius 638	610 Heraclius 641	610 John Remigius 615
615 Deusdedit 618			615 Eleutherius 619
619 Boniface V. 625			619 Isaac 643
625 Honorius I. 638			
638 Severinus 640			
	639 Pyrrhus, deposed 641		
640 John IV. 642			
	641 Paul II. 654	641 Constantine III., Heracleonas	
642 Theodorus I. 649		642 Constans II. 668	
649 Martin I. 655			643 Calliopas 650
654 Eugenius I. 657	654 Pyrrhus, reinstated 655		650 Olympius 652
			652 Calliopas again 687
	655 Peter 666		
657 Vitalian 672			
	666 Thomas II. 669		
		668 Constantine Pogonatus 685	
	669 John V. 675		
672 Adeodatus 676			
	675 Constantine, deposed 677		
676 Donus 678			
	677 Theodorus, deposed 678		
678 Agatho 681	678 George I. 683		
682 Leo II. 683			
683 (?) Benedict II. 685	683 Theodorus, reinstated 686		
685 Conon 687	686 Paul III. 693	685 Justinian II. 694	687 John Platon 702
687 Paschal (antipope) 692			
687 Theodorus			
687 Sergius I. 701	693 Callinicus, deposed 705		
		694 Leontius I. 697	
		697 Tiberius 704	
701 John VI. 705			
			702 Theophylact 710

LOMBARD KINGS.	KINGS OF FRANCE.			CALIPHS.
A.D. A.D.	*Burgundy.*	*Austrasia.*	*Neustria.*	A.D.
590 Agilulf 616	A.D. 601 Thierri II.	Theodebert II.	A.D. Chlotaire II.	
	614 Chlotaire II. alone 628.			
616 Theodelinda and Adelwald 626				622 Mohammed
		Part of Aquitaine.		
626 Arivald 638	628 Dagobert	Charibert 630		
	Dagobert, alone 637.			632 Abubeker 634 Omar
638 Rotharis 654	*Austrasia.*	*Neustria.*		
	637 Sigebert II. 654	Clovis II. 655		
				644 Othman
654 Rodoald 659	654 Childeric II.			
		656 Chlotaire III. 668 (Queen Bathildis guardian.)		656 Ali
659 Aribert 662				660 Moawiiah
662 Gondibert 663 663 Grimoald 672	668 Childeric II. alone			
		Part of Austrasia.		
672 Garibald. Pertharit 680	673 Thierri III.	672 Dagobert II.		
	679 Thierri III. alone 691			679 Yezid
680 Cunibert with Pertharit 691				
				685 Abdulmelek
	(687 Pepin, Mayor of the Palace 714) 690 Clovis III. 695			
691 Cunibert alone 701				
	695 Childebert III. 711			
701 Liutprand 702 Aribert II. 712				
				705 Walid I.
	711 Dagobert III.			
712 Ansprand 713				

POPES.	PATRIARCHS OF CONSTANTINOPLE.	EMPERORS OF THE EAST.	EXARCHS OF RAVENNA.
A.D. A.D.	A.D. A.D.	A.D. A.D.	A.D. A.D.
		704 Justinian II., restored 711	
705 John VII. 707	705 Cyrus, deposed 712		
708 Sisinnius			
708 Constantine I. 715		711 Philippicus 713	710 John Rizocopus 713
	712 John VI., deposed 715	713 Anastasius II. 715	713 Scholasticus 725
715 Gregory II. 731	715 Germanus, deposed 731	715 Theodosius III. 717	
		717 Leo the Isaurian 741	
			725 Paul the Patrician 727
731 Gregory III. 741	731 Anastasius 753 " deposed 746 " died 754		727 Eutychius the Eunuch 752
741 Zacharias 742		741 Constantine Copronymus 775	Conquered by Lombards.
742 Stephen II.			
743 Stephen III. 757	754 Constantine, banished —beheaded 766		
757 Paul I. 767			
767 Constantine II. 768	766 Nicetas the Eunuch 780		
768 Philip			
768 Stephen IV. 772			
772 Hadrian I. 795			
		775 Leo IV. 780	
	780 Paul IV., deposed 784	780 Constantine Porphyrogenitus, with Irene 797	
	784 Tarasius 806		
795 Leo III. 816			
	806 Nicephorus, deposed 815	797 Irene	
	815 Theodorus Cassiteras 821		

A.D.	LOMBARD KINGS.	A.D.	A.D.	KINGS OF FRANCE.	A.D.	A.D.	CALIPHS.
713	Liutprand	743					
						714	Suleiman
			716	Chilperic II. Chlotaire IV.			
						717	Omar II.
						719	Yezid II.
			720	Thierri IV.			
						723	Hidjam
			(736	Charles Martel, Mayor of Palace)			
			742	Childeric III.	751	742	Walid II.
743	Hildebrand	743				743	Yezid III.
744	Rachis Duke of Friuli					744	Ibrahim
						745	Merwan
						749	Abdalla the Abbasside
750	Astolphus	756					
			751	Pepin		753	Abugyafar Al-mansor
756	Desiderius	774					
			768	Charlemagne and Carloman			
			772	Charlemagne, alone			
						775	Mohammed Manades
						785	Musa
						786	Haroun Al-raschid

BOOK IV.

CHAPTER I.

MOHAMMED.

The seventh century of Christianity was destined to behold a new religious revolution, only inferior in the extent of its religious and social influence to Christianity itself. Christianity might seem, notwithstanding her internal dissensions, while slowly subduing the whole of Europe, to be still making gradual encroachments in Asia, and at least to apprehend no formidable invasion within her own frontier. The conflict which had raged on the eastern boundaries of the Roman world, in which at one time the Persians had become masters of Syria and plundered the religious treasures of Jerusalem, was a war of the two empires of Rome and Persia, not of Christianity and Fire-worship. The danger which threatened the Byzantine empire, and which, if unaverted, would have yielded up Asia, and even Constantinople, to the followers of Zoroaster, had been arrested by the great military ability and enterprise of Heraclius, the successor of the tyrant Phocas on the throne. But though Persian conquest, had it spread over Asia Minor and Syria and into Europe, might have brought on a dan-

Roman East at commencement of seventh century.

War of Persia.

gerous collision with the religion of the conquerors, yet the issue could not eventually have been fatal, even to the dominance of Christianity. Zoroastrianism had failed to propagate itself with any great success in the parts of Christian Armenia which it had subjugated: nor can we imagine that religion, even when advancing under the victorious banner of its believers, as likely to obtain any firm hold on the inhabitants of Western Asia or Europe, still less as tending to extirpate the deep-rooted Christianity of those regions.

Mohammedanism in appearance.

In the meantime, in an obscure district of a country esteemed by the civilized world as beyond its boundaries, a savage, desert, and almost inaccessible region, suddenly arose an antagonist religion, which was to reduce the followers of Zoroaster to a few scattered communities, to invade India, and tread under foot the ancient Brahminism, as well as the more wide-spread Buddhism, even beyond the Ganges; to wrest her most ancient and venerable provinces from Christianity; to subjugate by degrees the whole of her Eastern dominions, and Roman Africa from Egypt to the Straits of Gibraltar; to assail Europe at its western extremity; to possess the greater part of Spain, and even to advance to the banks of the Loire; more than once to make the elder Rome tremble for her security, and finally to establish itself in triumph within the new Rome of Constantine. Asiatic Christianity sank more and more into obscurity. It dragged on its existence within the Mohammedan empire as a contemptuously tolerated religion; in the Byzantine empire it had still strength to give birth to new controversies — that of Iconoclasm, and even still later that concerning the divine light. It was not without writers, in learning, perhaps, and theologic argument, superior to any in the West—John of Damascus, Eustathius of Thessalonica. Yet its aggressive vigor had entirely departed, and it was happy to be allowed inglorious repose, to take no part in that great war waged by the two powers, now the only two living, active, dominant powers, which contested the dominion of the world—Mohammedanism and Latin Christianity. These implacable adversaries might appear to divide mankind into two unmingling, irreconcilable races. Like the Iran and Touran of the remoter East, the realm of light and the realm of darkness, each is constantly endeavoring to push forward its barriers, appearing on every side, or advancing into the heart of the hostile territory. The realm of darkness, as regards civilization, at times might seem to be the realm of light, the realm of light that of darkness; till eventually Mohammedanism sank back into its primeval barbarism, Latin Christianity, or, rather, the Christianity of later Europe, emerged into its full, it may be hoped, yet growing authority, as the religion, not only of truth, but of civilization.

Arabia.

Arabia, the parent of this new religion, had been a world within itself; the habits and character of the people might seem both to secure them from the invasion of foreign conquerors and to prohibit them from more than a desultory invasion of other countries. Divided into almost countless petty kingdoms, an aggregate of small, independent, and immemorially hostile tribes, they had no bond of union to blend them into a powerful confederacy. The great empires of the East, of Greece and of Rome, had aspired to universal sovereignty, while these wandering tribes of the desert, and even the more settled and flourishing kingdoms of Southern Arabia had pursued unknown and undisturbed their intestine warfare. A nominal and precarious sovereignty had been exercised by some of the Asiatic conquerors over the frontier tribes; but the poverty and irreclaimable wandering habits of most of these, with the impracticable nature of the country, had protected from the ambition of the conquerors the southern regions, of which the wealth and fertility had been greatly exaggerated, and which were supposed to produce all those rich commodities, in fact, transmitted to them from India. Arabia formed no part of the great eastern monarchies. Alexander passed on from Egypt and Syria, to the remoter East. His successors in Egypt and in Syria, the Ptolemies and Seleucidæ, were in general content with commercial relations, carried on with Arabia or through Arabia. The Romans, who might seem to scrutinize the world in order that nothing might escape their ambition, had once or twice turned their arms towards the fabled wealth of Arabia.[1] The unsuccessful, if not ignominious, result of the expedition of Ælius Gallus had taught how little was to be gained, how much hazarded, in such a warfare. The Romans contented themselves with the acquisition of Petra, a city not strictly Arabian, but Edomite in its origin, though for some centuries occupied by the Nabatean Arabs, a commercial emporium, as a station between the East and the Roman world, of the greatest importance, and adorned, during the age of the Antonines, with

[1] The "*intactis* nunc Arabum invides gazis" of Horace, shows the relation in which Arabia stood to the rapacity and to the arms of Rome.

magnificent buildings in that colossal half-barbarous Roman style with which at that time they built temples in so many of the great cities of Syria, Asia Minor and Egypt.

If Arabia offered no great temptation to the foreign invader from the civilized world, the civilized world had as little dread of any dangerous irruption from these wild and disunited tribes. Here and there, perhaps, beyond the proper limits of Arabia, in districts, however, which seemed to belong to their marauding habits rather than to the settled cultivation of more advanced nations, upon the eastern frontier of Syria and towards the Euphrates, had arisen Arabian kingdoms. The Nabatean Petra had attained to some power during the first period of Christianity, had waged an aggressive war against Rome, and even gained possession of Damascus. This territory, however, had become a Roman province; but down to the reign of Justinian petty Saracenic chieftains who assumed the name of kings were engaged on either side in the interminable wars between Rome and Persia. Yet while the prolific North and East were periodically discharging their teeming hordes upon Asia and Europe, Arabia might seem either not gifted with this overflow of population, or to consume it within her own limits. The continual internal wars; polygamy, which became more unfavorable to the increase of the population from the general usage of destroying female infants;[1] the frugal, nomadic, and even the imaginative character of the race, which seemed to attach them to their own soil, and to suppress all desire of conquest in softer, less open, more settled regions,

[1] Weil, p. 19.

conspired to maintain the immutable character of Arabia and of the Arab people; their national and tribal pride, their ancient traditions, their virtues, their polity, and even their commerce, which absorbed the activity of the more enterprising, might appear to coop within itself this peculiar people, as neither destined nor qualified to burst the limits of their own peninsula, or to endanger the peace, the liberties, or the religion of the world.

On a sudden, when probably only vague rumors had reached the courts of Persia or of Constantinople of the religious revolution which had taken place in Medina and Mecca (a revolution which might seem to plunge the whole region in still more desperate internal hostility), Arabia appeared in arms against mankind. A religious fanaticism, almost unexampled in its depth and intensity, had silenced all the fierce feuds of centuries; the tribes and kingdoms had become one; armies, seemingly inexhaustible, with all the wild courage of marauding adventure and the formidable discipline of stubborn unity of purpose, poured forth, one after another, from the desert; and at their head appeared, not indeed the apostle himself (he had discharged his mission in organizing this terrible confederacy), but a military sovereign who united in himself the civil and spiritual supremacy, whose authority rested on the ardent attachment of a clan towards its chief, and the blind and passive obedience of a sect to a religious leader. The reigning Caliph was king and pontiff, according to the oriental theory of sovereignty the father of his people, but likewise the successor of the Prophet, the delegate of God.

Mohammedanism appeared before the world as a

stern and austere monotheism, but it was a practical not a speculative monotheism.[1] It had nothing abstract, indistinct, intellectual in its primary notion of the Godhead. Allah was no philosophic first cause, regulating the universe by established laws, while itself stood aloof in remote and unapproachable majesty. It was an ever-present, ever-working energy, still accomplishing its own purposes.[2] Its predestinarianism was not a fixed and predetermined law wrought out by the obedient elements of the human world, but the actual, immediate operation of the Deity, governing all things by his sole will,[3] and through his passive ministers.[4] It threw aside with implacable and disdainful aversion all those gradations as it were of divinity which approximated man to God and God to man — the Asiatic or Gnostic Æons and Emanations; the impersonated Ideas of the later Platonism, with their all-comprehending Logos; above all, the coequal Persons of the Christian Trinity. Nothing existed but the Creator and the Creation: the Creator one in undistinguished, undivided Unity, the Creation, which comprehended every being intermediate between God and man: an-

[1] One of the sublimest descriptions of God may be found in the second chapter of the Korân, Sale's translation, i. p. 47.

[2] See the fine passage, ch. vi. vol. i. p. 166, &c.

[3] "It is he who hath created the heavens and the earth in truth; and whenever he saith unto a thing, Be, it is." This whole chapter is full of striking passages. "And whomsoever God shall please to direct, he will open his breast to receive the faith of Islam; but whomsoever he shall please to lead into error, he will render his breast strait and narrow, as though he were climbing up to heaven (*i.e.* attempting an impossibility). Thus does God inflict a terrible punishment on those who believe not." — p. 178.

[4] "Though men and angels and devils conspire together to put one single atom in motion, or cause it to cease its motion without his will and approbation, they would not be able to do it." — Creed of orthodox Mohammedans in Ockley, vol. ii. p. li.

gels, devils, genii, all owed their being to almighty power, and were liable to death or to extinction.

Mohammedanism, in more respects than one, was a republication of Mosaic Judaism, with its strong principle of national and religious unity (for wherever it went it carried its language), with its law simplified to a few rigid and unswerving observances, and the world for its land of Canaan; the world which it was commissioned to subdue to the faith of Islam, and to possess in the right of conquest.

Mohammedanism.

Yet nothing was less simple than the popular Mohammedanism. It rationalized, if it might be called Rationalism, only in its conception of the Deity. It had its poetic[1] element, its imaginative excitement, adapted to the youthful barbarianism of the state of society, and to the Oriental character. It created, or rather acknowledged, an intermediate world, it dealt prodigally in angelic appearances, and believed in another incorporeal, or, rather, subtly-corporeal race, between angels and men; the genii, created out of a finer substance, but more nearly akin to man in their weaknesses and trials.[2] The whole life of man was passed under the influence, sometimes in direct communion with these half-spiritual beings.[3] Mohammedanism

1 They (the idolaters) say the Korân is a confused heap of dreams; nay, he has forged it; *nay, he is a poet.* — ch. xxii. v. ii. p. 152.

2 "He created men of dried clay, like an earthen vessel, but he created the genii of fire, clear from the smoke." — Ch. lv. v. ii. p. 209: compare vi. i. p. 178.

3 Mohammedan tradition adopts for the genii the definition of the dæmons in the Talmud. They have three qualities of angels: I. They have wings. II. They pass from one end of the world to the other. III. They know future events, but not certainly: they only hear them from behind the curtain. They have three human qualities. I. They eat and drink. II. They have carnal appetites. III. They die. — Geiger, Was hat Mohammed, p. 83.

borrowed its poetic machinery from all the existing religions — from Magianism, Orientalism, Judaism, Christianity. No religion was less original.[1] Its assertion of the divine unity was a return to Judaism, a stern negation at once of the vulgar polytheism which prevailed among the ruder Arab tribes, and of the mysterious doctrines of Trinitarian Christianity. As to the intermediate world it only popularized still further the popular belief. Its angels were those already familiar to the general mind through Talmudic Judaism and Christianity; its genii were those of the common Eastern superstition. The creation, as affirmed in Islam, was stictly biblical;[2] the history of man was that of the Old Testament, recognized in the New, though not without a large admixture of Jewish legend. The forefathers of the Mohammedan, as of the Jewish and Christian religions, were Adam, Noah, Abraham; and to the older prophets of God, among whom were included Moses and Jesus, were only added two local prophets, sent on special missions to certain of the Arab tribes, to Ad and to Thamud.[3] Even Moham-

[1] In this respect, how different from Christianity! The religion of Christ, on its first promulgation, had to introduce into the world new conceptions of the Deity, new forms of worship, its sacraments of Baptism and the Eucharist, new vices, and new virtues; a new history of man, both as to his creation and his destiny; new religious ancestors, Adam, Noah, Abraham, Moses, David, the Jewish prophets, besides the divine author of the religion and his apostles. All these names were almost strange to the Roman world, and were to supersede those already sacred and familiar to the thoughts of all the Christian converts.

[2] Compare Geiger, p. 64; but Mohammed was impatient of the ascribing *rest* to God on the seventh day. The strictness of the Jewish Sabbath was enforced upon them for their obstinacy in preferring the day of the supposed *rest* of the Almighty to Friday, the proper day of divine worship. — ch. xvi. v. ii. p. 94.

[3] These were no doubt the mythic forms of some historic events; the impersonated memorials of some fearful calamities ascribed to the hand of God; and still living in Arabic tradition.

medan fable had none of the inventive originality of fiction. There is scarcely a legend which is not either from the Talmud, or rather the source of most of the Talmud, the religious tradition of the Jews [1] or the spurious (not the genuine) Gospels of Christianity. The last day, the judgment, the resurrection, hell, and paradise, though invested in a circumstantiality of detail, much of it foreign, as far as we can judge, to the Pharisaic notions of our Saviour's day, and singularly contrasting with the modest and less material images of the New Testament, were already parts of the common creed. The Korân has scarcely surpassed the grosser notions of another life which were already received by the Talmudic Jews and the Judaizing Christians, the Chiliasts of the early ages. It only adapted this materialism to the fears and hopes of a Bedouin and a polygamous people. It may be doubted whether it goes beyond the terrific imaginations of the Talmudists in those minute and particular effects of hellfire which glare in all its pages.[2] In its paradise it dwelt on that most exquisite luxury to a wanderer in the

1 Sale has traced in his notes many of the fables in the Korân to their Talmudic or Rabbinical sources. A prize Essay, on a theme proposed by the University of Bonn, "Was hat Mohammed aus dem Judenthum genommen," by Abraham Geiger, Rabbi of Wiesbaden, is modest, sensible, and contains much curious information. The names for Paradise and Hell, the garden of Eden, and Gehenna, are Hebrew: and he gives twelve other words in the Korân, including Shechinah, all taken from Rabbinical Judaism.

2 Korân passim, *e. g.* "And they who believe not shall have garments of fire fitted unto them, boiling water shall be poured upon their heads, their bowels shall be dissolved thereby, and also their skins, and they shall be beaten with maces of iron. So often as they shall endeavor to get out of hell because of the anguish of their torments, they shall be dragged into the same, and their tormentors shall say unto them, 'Taste ye the pains of burning.'" — ch. xxii. v. ii. p. 169.

desert, perennial rivers of cool pure water; and it added a harem to the joys of the blessed.[1]

In the rites and ceremonial of Islam there was nothing which required any violent disruption of religious habits: its four great precepts only gave a new impulse and a new direction to established religious observances. I. *Prayer*, is the universal language of all religions; and the sense of the perpetual presence, the direct and immediate agency of God in all human things, enforced by the whole Mohammedan creed, as well as the concentration of all earthly worship on one single, indivisible God, has maintained a strict and earnest spirit of adoration throughout the Mohammedan world. II. The natural sympathies of man; the narrower, yet impressive, humanity of the Old Testament, which had bound the Jew to relieve the distressed of his brethren with a generosity which, contrasting with his apparent hostility to the rest of mankind, had moved the wonder of the heathen; the more beautiful, the prodigal, the universal charity of the Christian; perhaps the hospitable habits of the Arabs, had already consecrated *Almsgiving* as among the highest of religious virtues; and Mohammedanism did not degenerate in this respect from what may be called her religious parents. III. As to *Fasting*, the Ramadan was but Lent under another name. IV. The Christianity of the Gospel had in vain abrogated the peculiar sanctity of places. The nature of man, yet imperfectly spiritualized, had sunk back to the old excitements of devotion; the grave of the Redeemer

[1] For Paradise, ch. xlviii. ii. p. 377. "The rivers of incorruptible water, of milk, of wine, of clarified honey, and all kinds of fruits." Still more fully, lv. ii. 411.

had become to the Christian what the site of the Temple was to the Jew; and the Korân, by turning the hearts of all its votaries to the Holy Cities, to Medina and Mecca, availed itself of the universal passion for *pilgrimages*.[1]

The six great articles in the faith of Islam were in like manner the elemental truths of all religions: though peculiarly expressed, they were neither repugnant to human reason nor to prevalent habits of thought. Most men, in some form, believed — I. In God. II. In his Angels. III. In his Scriptures (in divine revelation). IV. In his Prophets. V. In the Resurrection and Day of Judgment. VI. In God's absolute decree and predetermination of good and evil, though this was softened in most creeds into a vague acknowledgment of God's providential government.

The one new and startling article in the creed of Islam was the divine mission of the prophet Mohammed, the apostle of God. Yet Mohammed was but the successor of other prophets; the last of the long and unfailing line of divine messengers to man. Mankind in general might demand miraculous and supernatural proofs of a prophetic mission. The Jew might sullenly disclaim a prophet sprung from the bastard race of Ishmael; the Christian might assume the gospel to be the final and conclusive message to man; but Mohammed averred that his mission was vouched by the one great miracle, the Korân; that he was foreshown both in the Law and in the Gospel, though these prophecies had been obscured or falsified by the jealousy of the dominant party among the Jews and

[1] Gregory the Great mentions pilgrimages to Mount Sinai as still performed in his day, and by women. — Epist. iii. 44.

Christians. Mohammed himself remains, and must remain, an historic problem: his character, his motives, his designs are all equally obscure. Was the Prophet possessed with a lofty indignation at the grovelling idolatry of his countrymen? Had he contrasted the sublime simplicity of the Mosaic unity of God with the polytheism of the Arabs; or, that which appeared to him only the more subtle and disputatious polytheism of the Christians? Had he the lofty political ambition of uniting the fierce and hostile tribes into one confederacy, of forming Arabia into a nation, and so of becoming the founder of a dynasty and an empire; and did he imagine his simple religion as the bond of the confederacy? Did he contemplate from the first foreign conquest or foreign proselytism? or did his more pliant ambition grow out of and accommodate itself to the circumstances of the time, submit to change and modification, and only fully develop itself according to existing exigencies? At this distance of time, and through the haze of adoring and of hostile tradition, it is difficult to trace clearly the outward actions of the Prophet, how much more the inward impulses, the thoughts and aspirations of his secret spirit. To the question whether Mohammed was hero, sage, impostor, or fanatic, or blended, and blended in what proportions, these conflicting elements in his character? the best reply is the favorite reverential phrase of Islam, "God knows."[1]

Mohammed.

[1] Maracci wrote of Mohammed with the learning, but in the spirit, of a monk. With Prideaux he is a vulgar impostor. Spanheim began to take a higher view of his character. Sale and Gagnier, while vindicating him from the coarse invectives of former writers, kindled into admiration, which was accused of approaching to belief. With Boulanvilliers, he rose into a benefactor of the human race; with White and his coadjutors he became

The Korân itself is not above suspicion, at least as far as its absolute integrity and authenticity. The Korân. It was put together some time after the death of Mohammed,[1] avowedly not in the exact order of its delivery. It is not certain whether it contains all that the

the subject of some fine pulpit declamation. Gibbon is brilliant, full, on the whole fair; but his brilliancy on the propagation of Mohammedanism singularly contrasts with his cold, critical view of that of Christianity. Passing over Savary, Volney, in our own times we have the elaborate biography of Dr. Weil, whom scarcely anything has escaped, and Caussin de Perceval's Histoire des Arabes (Paris, 1848), a work of admirable industry and learning, which, with the history and genealogy of the early tribes, embraces the time of Mohammed and his two successors. Major Price, whose contributions to the history of Mohammedanism, from the Shiite (the Persian) traditions (all which we had before were Sunnite and Arabic), are invaluable, of Mohammed himself gives us nothing new. But Col. Vans Kennedy furnishes some extracts from Tabari, a writer some centuries earlier than any of the known biographers of the Prophet, Elmacin, and Abulfeda. Tabari wrote within three centuries of the Hejira, and his account is at once the most striking and most credible which has appeared in Europe. Col. Vans Kennedy's own appreciation of the Prophet (which may be overlooked in a criticism on Voltaire's Mahomet) is the most just with which I am acquainted. — See Bombay Transactions, vol. iii. This passage appears to have escaped the notice of Dr. Weil, whose recent "Mohammed der Prophet" is not only laborious, but also candid and comprehensive. Now, however (1855), the life of Mohammed (part I.), by Dr. Sprenger (Allahabad, 1851) has greatly enlarged our knowledge of, and enabled us to appreciate the earlier traditions of Islam. Still while duly grateful for these valuable accessions to our knowledge, and with all respect for the great learning and industry of Dr. Sprenger, I must demur to some of his conclusions. Islam, he asserts, was long anterior to Mohammed, believed by many before he preached it, "It was begotten by the spirit of the time; it was the inevitable birth of the age and people, the voice of the Arabic nation (pp. 44, 165, 175). True, as far as the first article of the faith, there is but one God:" but it was the second, Mohammed is his Prophet; it was this, forced as a divine revelation into the belief of so large a part of mankind, which was the power, the influence, the all-subduing energy of Islam; the principle of its unity, of its irresistible fanaticism, its propagation, its victories, its empire, its duration.

[1] In the reign of Abubeker, who employed Mohammed's secretary, Zeid Abu Thabit, Zeid collected every extant fragment which was in different hands, written on parchment, on leather, on palm leaves, on bones, or stones. — Weil, Mohammed der Prophet. p. 349; Caussin de Perceval, Histoire des Arabes.

Prophet revealed, or those revelations in their original and unaltered form.[1]

Mohammed[2] was an orphan of a noble family; after the death of his parents he was maintained, first by his grandfather, afterwards by his father's brother. The first twenty-five years of his life passed in obscurity, which the earlier and more authoritative tradition has not ventured to embellish with wonders ominous of his future greatness.[3]

Chadijah, a wealthy widow of his kindred, chose Mohammed *the faithful* (his character had gained him that honorable appellation) to conduct her commercial affairs. He travelled with this charge to Syria,[4] and his success was so great in comparison with that of the former agents of Chadijah, that on his return the grateful widow, moved, according to the simpler account, by

[1] My own judgment is in favor of the authenticity of the Korân (but I know it only from translations). The evident suggestion of the different chapters by the exigencies of different events, and the manifest contradictions, are proofs of its antiquity. The convenient doctrine of abrogation, by which a later sentence annuls a former, and which seems to have been admitted from the first, implies the general integrity of the book.* Dr. Weil believes that though the Korân must not be considered without omission or interpolation, there is no *important* change, addition, or omission. But see on Othman's revision — Weil. die Chalifen, note, i. p. 168. Dr. Sprenger says, "Though not free from interpolation, yet there seems no reason to doubt its authenticity," p. 63.

[2] Mohammed, born April, 570; April, 13, 571, or May 13, 569. Sprenger, p. 75.

[3] For the later traditions, wild and fantastic enough, see Dr. Weil, p. 23, note 6, and 26, note 1.

[4] Bosra is named as the mart to which Mohammed conducted the caravan of Chadijah. The admiration of ships (as one of the most wonderful gifts of God), which perpetually occurs in the Korân, leads me to suspect that the writer had seen more of maritime scenes, in one of the ports of Syria perhaps, than what he may have gathered from accidental glimpses of the navigation of the Red Sea.

* There are 225 verses which contain doctrines or laws recalled by later revelations. — Weil, p. 355.

the prosperity of her trade in his hands, according to the more marvellous, by wonders which took place on his journey, bestowed herself and her wealth on the young and handsome merchant.[1]

Twelve more years, from his marriage at the age of twenty-eight, passed away. In his fortieth year, that eventful period in oriental life,[2] the Prophet began to listen to the first intimations of his divine mission.

The caves of mount Hira, in the immediate neighborhood of Mecca, were already hallowed, it is said, by Arabian superstition. During one of the holy months[3] men were accustomed to retire to a kind of hermitage, built or scooped out of the rocks, for devout meditation: that meditation which, in an imaginative people, is so apt to kindle into communion with the unearthly and invisible. It was in one of these caves that Mohammed received his first communication from heaven.[4] But the form assumed by the vision, the illusion, or the daring conception of Mohammed, showed plainly in what school he had received his religious impressions. It was none of the three hundred and sixty-six deities of the old Arabian religion, or the astral influences of the dominant Tsabaism, it was Gabriel, the divine messenger, hallowed in the Jewish and the Christian scriptures, who appeared as a mighty and

[1] For the description of Mohammed's person, See Dr. Weil, p. 340; Caussin de Perceval, iii. 332, and on his habits at great length, Sprenger, 84, 94.

[2] Some intended analogy with the life of Moses might be suspected; but 40, it is well known, is the indefinite number in the East, and no doubt in many cases it has been assumed to cover ignorance of a real date.

[3] The four holy months, when peace reigned through Arabia, were the first, the seventh, the eleventh, the twelfth. Islam afterwards annulled the holy months as far as war *with unbelievers.*

[4] Each family had its hermitage; that of Hashem, to which Mohammed belonged, was peculiarly disposed to this kind of devotion.

majestic figure, with his feet upon the earth and his head in the heavens.[1] After this solemn interview, as Mohammed walked along (so fully was his mind wrapt in its vision), the stones and clods seemed to exclaim, "Prophet of God."[2] By day the inanimate works of God thus summoned him to his office, by night the angel of God perpetually haunted his slumbers, and renewed his call. The incredulous Mohammed suspected that these were but the awful workings of insanity. His faithful wife consoled him with the praise of his virtues, which could not be so cruelly tried by God. Chadijah at length put these revelations to a singular and characteristic test. They were alone in their chamber when the figure appeared. Chadijah was sitting, as became a chaste matron, shrouded in her veil.[3] She took the Prophet in her arms and said, "Dost thou now see it?" The Prophet said, "I do." She cast off her veil, her head and face were uncovered: "Dost thou now see it?" "I do not." "Glad tidings to thee, O Mohammed," exclaimed Chadijah, "it is not a divi, but an angel; for had it been a divi it would not have disappeared and respected my unveiled face." The visions became more frequent and

[1] Chadijah is represented as altogether ignorant of Gabriel; and it was only from the information she obtained from a relative (Warkeh ben Nussul), a learned Christian, that she learned the name and rank of the angel. Yet she is afterwards said to have been well acquainted with the Pentateuch and the Evangelists.

[2] Tabari, as quoted by Vans Kennedy. — Bombay Transactions, iii. p. 421.

[3] There is a curious passage in Tertullian contrasting the modesty of the Arabian women of his day with the Christian virgins, who shamelessly showed their faces. "Judicabunt nos Arabiæ fœminæ ethnicæ, quæ non caput sed faciem quoque ita totam tegunt, ut uno oculo liberato contentæ sint dimidiam frui lucem, quam totam faciem prostituere." — De Virg. Vel. c. 17.

distinct. At length, on the mountain of Hira, the angel stood before Mohammed in defined and almost human form. Mohammed, still suspecting his own insanity, fled to the summit of the mountain to cast himself headlong from it. The angel caught him under his wing, and as he reposed on his bosom commanded him to read. "I cannot read,"[1] replied Mohammed. "Repeat then!" And the angel communicated to the Prophet the revelation of Islam. Mohammed on his return to his house related to his wife the personal appearance of the angel, and spoke of his mysterious communication. A short time after he lay down,[2] cold and weary, to repose. His wife had covered him. The angel again appeared. "Arise, thou wrapped up." "Why should I arise?" "Arise and preach," said Gabriel; "cleanse thy garments, and flee every abomination." Mohammed imparted to his wife his *divine mission*. "I," said Chadijah, "will be the first believer." They knelt in the appointed attitude of prayer; by the command of Gabriel they performed their ablutions. The child Ali, but seven years old, beheld them, and inquired the reason of this strange conduct. Mohammed replied that he was the chosen prophet of God; that belief in Islam secured salvation in earth and heaven. Ali be-

Mohammed's divine mission.

1 On the translation of these words depends the question whether Mohammed was absolutely illiterate. Those who deny it explain the phrase as confined to that which the angel then ordered him to read. Sprenger, p. 95, gives a different version: "but it is certain that no Mussulman will admit the sense which I give to these verses of the Korân." — Sprenger, 77, 111.

2 On the subject of Mohammed's epilepsy, consult the long note of Dr. Weil, p. 42. It is difficult to resist the evidence which he adduces. Dr. Weil concludes: "I do not think, with Theophanes, that he alleged the apparition of Gabriel to conceal his malady, but that the malady itself was the cause of his belief in these apparitions."

lieved, and became the second of the faithful. Thus was Mohammed the prophet of his household.[1] Slowly, however, did he win proselytes, even among his own kindred.[2] Three years elapsed before the faith received the accession of Abubeker and of Othman, the future caliphs. Mohammed at length is accepted as the prophet of his family, of the noble and priestly house of Hashem. Abu Talib, his uncle, remains almost alone an unbeliever. And now Mohammed aspires to be the prophet of his *Tribe*.[3] That tribe, the Koreishite, was a kind of hierarchy, exercising religious supremacy, and the acknowledged guardians of the Caaba, the sacred stone of Mecca, with its temple. The temple of the Caaba was at once, as is usual among Oriental nations, the centre of the commerce and of the religion of Arabia. Tradition, even in the days of Mohammed thought immemorial, had associated this holy place with the names of Adam, of Seth, and of Abraham; and worshippers from all quarters, idolaters who found each his peculiar idol, the Jew and the Christian, looked with awful reverence on this mysterious spot. The pilgrim of every creed, the merchant from every part of the peninsula, met at Mecca: almost all joined in the ceremonial of visiting the sacred mountain, kissing the black stone, approaching the holy well of Zemzem, each seven times, the mystic number with Arab as with Jew; and sacrifices were offered with devout prodigality. Arabian poetry hung up its most popular songs in the temple of the Caaba. It is

[1] Compare throughout Sprenger who arranges these events differently.

[2] See on the slave converts, specially Zaid, Sprenger, 159.

[3] It was not till the fourth or fifth year after his own conversion that he came forth as a public preacher. — Sura xv. v. 94–99; Sale, ii. p. 75. Compare xxvi. p. 218. He preached on the hill Safa.

not clear to what peculiar form of idolatry the Koreishite adhered, whether to the primitive and Arabian worship, which had enshrined in the temple of Caaba her three hundred and sixty deities; or to the later Tsabaism, a more refined worship of the planetary bodies.[1] But the intractable Koreish met him with contemptuous unbelief. They resisted the new prophet with all the animosity of an established priesthood trembling for their dignity, their power, and their wealth; they dreaded the superiority which would be assumed by the family of Hashem. In that family Abu Talib, though he resisted the doctrines, protected the person of Mohammed, as did all his kindred, except the implacable Abu Lahab. Like other hierarchies the Koreish had been tolerant only so long as they were strong. The eloquence, the virtue, the charity of Mohammed only made him more dangerous; his proselytes increased; the conversion of Hamza, another of his uncles, one of the most obstinate of unbelievers, drove them to madness. A price was set upon his secret assassination, a hundred camels and a thousand ounces of silver. Omar, now twenty-six years old, undertook the deed.[2] He was accosted on his way by the convert Nueim. "Ere thou doest the deed," said Nueim, "look to thine own near kindred." Omar rushed to the house of his sister Fatima, to punish her apostacy: he found some sentences of the Korân, he read them, and believed. Yet the Koreishites abated not in their hostility. The life

Persecution of Mohammed.

[1] The uncle of Mohammed, Abu Talib, was strenuous for the worship of *two* female deities, and the adoration of the "daughters of God" is reprobated in the Korân as one of the worst, probably therefore one of the most prevalent, forms of idolatry: compare Sprenger, 170.

[2] Weil, p. 59; Sprenger, 188.

of Mohammed was a struggle to enforce his creed on an obstinate and superstitious people; of threatened martyrdom for the unity of God and for his own prophetic mission. He was at length placed under a solemn interdict by the two ruling families of the Koreishites. Some of his humbler followers fled to Abyssinia, where they were protected by the sovereign of that land.[1] Mohammed submitted to personal insult. He allowed himself to be abused, to be spit upon, to have dust thrown upon him, and to be dragged out of the temple by his own turban fastened to his neck: he beheld his followers treated with the same ignominy. At times his mind was so depressed as to need the consolations of the angel Gabriel. He constantly changed his bed to elude the midnight assassin. For three years Mohammed was under this interdict,[2] dwelling in a castle of his uncle Abu Talib's, situated in a deep and unassailable ravine, and came to Mecca only during the holy months. The death of Chadijah broke one of the prophet's ties to Mecca: that of Abu Talib, who died an unbeliever, left him only the valor and vigilance of his disciples to shield him against the implacable and deepening hatred of the Koreishites. The Prophet must fly from his native city; and the hopes of making Mecca the national religious metropolis, the centre of his new spiritual empire, seemed to have failed utterly and forever. Miracle or craft alone saved him from the hands of his enemies, who surprised him, nearly alone, in the house of Abubeker. During his flight he only escaped assassination by the faithful Ali

[1] Sprenger, p. 189.

[2] The interdict was suspended in the temple, according to Dr. Weil, in the seventh year of Mohammed's mission.

taking his place in the tent; and, so ran the legend, when he slumbered in a cave, the spider wove its web over the entrance, and a pigeon laid two eggs to show that its solitude had been undisturbed.[1]

Flight. Hegira.

Medina (Yathrib[2]) at once accepted the dignity which had been spurned by Mecca. Six of her most distinguished citizens had already embraced at Mecca the cause of the Prophet. The idolatry of Medina had not the local strength of that of Mecca; it had not the same strongly organized hierarchy. Some rivalry with the commercial importance of Mecca, so closely connected with her religious supremacy, entered, no doubt, into the minds of the Medinese when they thus allied themselves with the chief of the new religion. The proselytes to Islam had prepared the whole city, and Mohammed did not leave Mecca till a deputation from Medina had sworn fealty to their new sovereign.[3] The form of the oath showed the Prophet under a new character. "If,' said these Ansarii (the assistants), "we are slain in your cause, what is our reward?" "Paradise," replied the Prophet.[4]

In Medina appear manifest indications of more direct advances to the Jews. The Arabian Jews in the

1 Era of the Hegira or flight, April 19, 622. According to Caussin de Perceval, the true date of Mohammed's flight from Mecca was the 18th or 19th June, 622. — iii. 17. Weil makes it 20th September. The question is, whether the intercalated year was in use at this time.

2 Yathrib now took the name of Medina (the city). — C. de P. iii. 21.

3 This was the second or great oath of Acaba. — Caussin de Perceval, iii. 8.

4 In the 2d Sura, Mohammed appears to forbid all but defensive warfare: "And fight for the religion of God, against those who fight against you; but transgress not by attacking them first, for God loveth not the transgressors." He was as yet too weak for aggressive war. — Sur. ii. p. 34.

neighborhood of the two great cities were numerous and powerful, formed whole tribes, occupied strong fortresses, and evidently, from the Talmudic character of the Korân, exercised a most extensive religious influence over the central part of Arabia. The widespread expectation of the Messiah among the Jews was mingled, no doubt, with the suggestive movements in the mind of Mohammed; and this fanaticism enlisted in his cause would have placed him at once at the head of a most formidable confederacy.[1] Jerusalem suddenly becomes the centre of the Islamite system instead of Mecca; it is the Kiblah of all prayer. The Prophet is transported to its walls. His journey, to the more refined and spiritual minds, might appear to have taken place in a heaven-sent vision; to the ruder he was described as riding bodily on the mysterious horse El Borak, and lighting from his aërial voyage on the site of the temple of Jerusalem.[2]

[1] Tabari, according to Col. Vans Kennedy, ascribes the ready acquiescence of the Medinese in the views of the Prophet to their fear lest they should be anticipated by their neighbors the Jews. On their return these men first recited the passages of the Korân which they had learned from Mohammed, and then said, "This is that Prophet whose name the Jews daily invoke, and whose coming they so anxiously expect: should they therefore receive him, and be obedient to him, you will be reduced to the greatest difficulties; it is therefore expedient that you should hasten to anticipate the Jews, and receive Mohammed before they can unite with him." Compare Caussin de Perceval, iii. 8. Bombay Trans. p. 430.

[2] On the Kiblah, see Korân, Sur. ii. p. 26, 27, with Sale's note; Abulfeda, ch. xxvi.; Geiger, p. 19. A certain Imam says, that whilst Mohammed was in Mecca, he used the Caaba as his Kiblah, but whilst in Medina he used the holy house as his Kiblah, and there also made a general change; so that one period was abrogated by another. In a certain exposition it is said that he first prayed in Mecca towards the Caaba, and then changed to the Baitu i Mahaddos, which also his followers did at Medina for their pilgrimages, or even sacred processions: but that afterwards the Kiblah was transferred to the Caaba. Hist. of the Temple of Jerusalem, by Jelal

But the Jews repelled the overtures of the Prophet sprung from the race of Ismael. They scoffed at his pretensions, they provoked his terrible vengeance.[1] Tribe after tribe was defeated ; their castle-fastnesses could not sustain the assaults of the impetuous warriors who now went forth under the banner of Islam. First the Jews of Kainoka, then those of Al Nadher, then those of Koraidha and of Khaibar were forced to submission. The remorseless massacre of the Koraidha after the great battle of the Ditch, in which Mohammed watched the slaughter of seven hundred and ninety Jews in cold blood, whom the Korân pursues to the fires of hell, shows the implacable resentment of the Prophet.[2] On other occasions the Prophet was not wanting in clemency; here his deliberate recklessness may be traced to the disappointment of high-wrought hopes.

Progress of Islam.

At length, after a war of some years between the rival cities and the followers of the rival religions, after two bloody battles, that of Beder, in which the Mussulmans were victorious,[3] that

Addin al Jebal, translated by F. Reynolds. — Orient. Fund Translat. p. 109. Jelal Addin is disposed to glorify the temple at Jerusalem, but there is no reason to question his citations from early Mohammedan writers. See also Weil, p. 90. Sprenger, p. 123; he places it a year before the flight. Sprenger gives at some length the wild legend by the Borak, or when he rode not to Jerusalem, but to the Seven Heavens. The voyage was called the Nuraj, p. 126.

1 At different periods many Jews of note embraced Islamism: Waraka, the cousin of Chadijah, Halib ben Maleh, a Jewish prince, and Abdallah ibn Sallaam. — Geiger, page 24.

2 See in "History of the Jews," the successive wars with these Jewish tribes, v. iii. p. 249 *et seq.* For their dates (some years intervened), compare Caussin de Perceval, vol. iii.

3 See the vivid description of the battle of Beder in Caussin de Perceval, iii. 49–65; of Ohud, 89–104: in this battle Mohammed was wounded in the face, and in great danger.

of Ohud, won by the Koreishites, after Medina had been twice besieged by the warriors of Mecca, and after a short truce, violated by the Koreishites, a sudden awe of Islam seized the obstinate unbelievers. In a few years an expedition, which at first bore the appearance of a peaceful pilgrimage and encountered but feeble resistance, made the Prophet master of Mecca.[1] The Caaba opened its unresisting gates; the three hundred and sixty idols fell without resistance on the part of their worshippers. "The truth hath come, let lies disappear." They were dashed to pieces. The Mouedhim proclaimed from the roof, "There is one God, and Mohammed is his prophet." No contumacious voice is heard in denial. The con-
11 Jan. 630. quest was almost without bloodshed, except that of a few from old hereditary hostility. The most powerful of the Prophet's adversaries became proselytes to the faith; the whole population swore allegiance. From that time Mecca becomes again the capital city of Islam; the divine edict in favor of Jerusalem is abrogated; the Prophet is sternly and exclusively Arabian; pilgrimages to the Caaba, now purified of its idols, become an essential part of the religion; the whole energy of Mohammedanism flows from and circulates back to the centre of the system.

Lord of Mecca, Mohammed stands supreme and alone; the Arabian mind and heart are his; the old idolatry has sunk at once before the fear of his arms and the sublimity of his new creed. He can disdain the alliance of those whom before he might stoop to conciliate; he can express hatred and contempt for the Jew and for the Christian, at least within the Arabian

[1] VIII. of the Hegira. — Caussin de Perceval, iii. p. 21, &c.

peninsula; he may pursue them with fierce and implacable hostility. But more than this, and herein is the great debt of gratitude which Arabia owes to Mohammed, the old hereditary feuds of the tribes and races are hushed in awe or turned into one impetuous current against the infidels. What on the whole was the influence of Mohammedanism on the world, we pause not now to inquire, or whether human happiness paid dear for the aggrandizement of the Arab race. But Arabia is now a nation; it takes its place among the nations of the earth; it threatens to become the ruling nation of the world.[1]

It was the policy of Mohammed first to secure the absolute religious unity of Arabia. In Arabia Islam at once declares irreconcilable war with all forms of unbelief: they are swept away or retire into ignominious obscurity. The only dangerous antagonists of Mohammedanism after the death of Mohammed are rival prophets. Moseilama for a time seems to arrest or to divert the current of religious conquest. But even the religious unity of Arabia, much less that of the conquered world, dawns but by degrees upon the mind of Mohammed; his religious ambition expands

1 See in Tabari, ii. 276–8; Ibn Khaldun, 194, the remarkable conversation attributed to Yezdegerd and the ambassadors of Omar: "Who are you to attack an empire? Of all the nations of the world, the poorest, most disunited, most ignorant, most stranger to the arts which are the source of power and wealth." "What you have said of our poverty, our divisions, or barbarism, *was* true indeed." . . . The ambassador describes their misery, their superstition, their idolatry. "Such were we. Now we are a new people. God has raised up among us a man . . . his envoy and true prophet. Islamism, his religion, has enlightened our minds, extinguished our hatreds, made us a society of brothers under laws dictated by divine wisdom. He has said, Consummate my work; spread the empire of Islam over the whole world; the earth is the Lord's, he has bestowed it on you."

with his success; his power is the measure of his intolerance; hence the strong contradictions in the Korân, the alternating tone of hatred and of tolerance, of contempt and of respect, with which are treated the authors and the votaries of other religions. He is a gentle preacher until he has unsheathed the sword:[1] the sword once unsheathed is the one remorseless argument. The convenient principle of abrogation annuls all those sentences of the Korân which speak in a milder tone to unbelievers.[2] At one time we find the broad principle of Eastern toleration explicitly avowed; the diversity of religion is ascribed to the direct ordinance, and all share in the equal favor of God.[3]

But the Korân gradually recants all these gentler sentences, and assumes the language of insulting superiority or undisguised aversion. Even in the Sura which contains the loftiest and most tolerant sentences,

[1] There is a passage in the 29th Sura (revealed at Mecca) commanding Islamites "to dispute mildly with those who receive the Scriptures." But this verse is thought to be abrogated by the chapter of the Sword. — Compare Sale *in loco.*

[2] This principle was early asserted in the Korân. "Whatever verse we shall abrogate or cause thee to forget, we will bring a better than it, or one like unto it." — ch. ii. p. 21.

[3] "Surely those who believe, and those who Judaize, and Christians and Sabeans, whoever believeth in God and the last day, and doth that which is right, they shall have their reward with their Lord; there shall come no fear on them, neither shall they be grieved." — ch. ii. p. 12. This and the parallel passage in the 5th chapter are said to be abrogated, or are explained by commentators whom Reland follows, as meaning that they will previously embrace Mohammedanism. But nothing less than abrogation can remove another passage: "Unto every one of you were given a law and an open path, and if God had pleased he had surely made you one people: but he hath thought fit to give you different laws, that he might try you in that which he hath given you respectively. Therefore strive to equal each other in good works. Unto God shall ye all return, and then will he declare unto you that concerning which ye have disagreed." — ch. v. In another place is the broad axiom, "Let there be no violence in religion." — ch. ii. p. 48.

their spirit is abrogated by the repeated assertion that Jew and Christian have been alike unfaithful to their own law, and that the same disobedience which instigates them to rebel against their own religion is the cause of their unbelief in Islam.[1] The Jews from the earliest ages had been the murderers of the prophets.[2] The murder of the prophet Jesus is among their darkest crimes. What wonder that they now turn a deaf ear to the prophet Mohammed? They had falsified their scriptures; they had erased or perverted the predictions concerning Mohammed; they were enemies, therefore, to all true religion, and, as enemies, to be pursued with unmitigated enmity. They are guilty of a worse impiety (strange, no doubt, was the charge to their own ears), an infringement of the unity of God, which would demand the vengeance of all true believers. "They hold Ezra to be the Son of God."[3]

The Koran becomes intolerant.

To Jews.

Towards the Christians these early tolerant maxims of religious freedom were still further neutralized by the collision of the first principle of Mohammedanism with that of the dominant Christianity. In one milder passage the Korân intimates that the Christians were less irreconcilable enemies to the Prophet than the Jew and the idolater, and this is attributed to the influence of the priests and the monks.[4] The

To Christians.

1 "Thou shalt surely find the most violent of all men in enmity against the true believers, to be the Jews and the idolaters." — ch. v. p. 147.

2 "They dislocate the words of the Pentateuch from their places, and have forgotten part of that which they were admonished." — ch. v. p. 131.

3 Ch. ix. p. 243. Sale quotes one of the commentators (Al Biedawi), who says that this imputation must be true, because it was read to the Jews and they did not contradict it.

4 "Thou shalt surely find those among them to be the most inclinable to entertain friendship for the true believers who say, 'We are Christians.'

sense and the occasion of this sentence are manifest. The idolaters and Jews were in arms against the Prophet, and defending their religion with desperate valor. The only Christians with whom he had then come in contact were a peaceful people, probably monastic communities. But as its views and its conquests expand, in the Korân the worship of Christ becomes the worst impiety: the assertion of his divinity involves the guilt of infidelity.[1] The worshipper of the Christian Trinity denied the Unity of God, and however the contemptuous toleration of a mighty Mohammedan empire might give indulgence to such errors among the lower orders of its subjects, the vital principles of the two religions stood opposed in stubborn antagonism. The Christian would not be soothed by the almost reverential admission of Jesus into the line of heaven-commissioned prophets, or even the respectful language concerning the Virgin Mary. The Mohammedan would not endure with patience the slightest imagined impeachment on the divine Unity. The rude and simple Arab had as yet no turn to or comprehension of metaphysical subtlety: he could not, or would not, conceive the Trinity but as three Gods.

It was indeed but a popular and traditionary Juda-

This cometh to pass because there are priests and monks among them; and because they are not elated with pride." — ch. v. vol. i. p. 147.

1 "Verily Christ Jesus, the son of Mary, is the apostle of God, and his word which he conveyed unto Mary, and a spirit proceeding from him. Believe, therefore, in God and his apostles, and say not there are three Gods: forbear this, it will be better for you. God is but one God. Far be it from him that he should have a son. . . . Christ doth not proudly disdain to be a servant unto God: neither the angels who approach near to his presence." — ch. iv. p. 126. Passages might be multiplied from almost every Sura.

ism,[1] a popular and traditionary Christianity — neither the Judaism of the Law, nor the Christianity of the Gospel — which Mohammed encountered in Arabia. The Prophet may have exaggerated his own ignorance in order to heighten the great standing miracle of the faith, the composition of the exquisite and unrivalled Korân by an unlettered man.[2] But throughout he betrays that he has no real knowledge either of the Old or New Testament: the fables blended up with the genuine Jewish history, though Talmudic, are not drawn from that great storehouse of Jewish learning, but directly from the vulgar belief.[3] The Jews of Arabia had ever been held in contempt, and not without justice, by their more polished brethren of Babylon or Tiberias, as a rude and barbarous people; they had revolted back to old Arabian habits; they are said not even to be noticed in the Talmud.

The Prophet's notions of Christianity were from equally impure sources, if, as no doubt they were, drawn from the vulgar creed of the Arabian Christians. They also must have dwelt apart, as well from the more rigid orthodoxy, as from the intellectual condition of the Church in the more civilized part of the world. They were Trinitarians, indeed, and at least almost worshippers of the Virgin Mary. They are distinctly charged with her deification.[4] But the spu-

1 Geiger, p. 29.

2 "Thou couldst not read any book before this, neither couldst thou write it with thy right hand; then had the gainsayers justly doubted of the divine original thereof." — Sur. 29, ii. p. 250.

3 See the whole account of Moses in the 2d Chapter.

4 "And when God shall say unto Jesus at the last day, O Jesus, son of Mary! hast thou said unto men, Take me and my mother for two Gods, beside God? he shall answer, Praise be unto thee! it is not for me to say that which I ought not." — ch. v. i. p. 156.

rious gospels of the Infancy[1] and of Barnabas[2] contribute far more to the Christianity shown in the Korân than the writings of the Evangelists. Their Gnostic tendencies are shown by the Docetism[3] or unreality of the Saviour's crucifixion, supposed by Mohammed to be the common belief of all Christians.[4] To monastic Christianity Islam stood even in more direct opposition. Marriage in the Korân appears to be the natural state of man.[5] Chastity, beyond a prudent temperance in connubial enjoyments and the abstinence from unlawful indulgences, is a virtue unknown in the Korân; it belongs neither to saints in earth nor in heaven. Even in the respect shown to the Virgin Mary she is spoken of, not under the appellation which sanctified her to Christian ears, but as the *mother* of Jesus. The Korân admits none of the first principles of monasticism, or, rather, directly repudiates them. It disdains the Pantheistic system in all its forms; the Emanation theory of India, the Dualism of Persia, the Mysticism of monkery. God stands alone in his nature, remote, unapproachable; in his power dominant throughout all space, and in all time, but divided by a deep and impassable gulf from created things. The absorption into, or even

1 See in ch. xxx. the account of the birth of Christ. It is difficult to acquit Mohammed of confounding the Virgin Mary with Miriam the Prophetess, the sister of Moses. — vol. ii. p. 133.

2 These works exist in Arabic in more than one form. Compare Thilo, Codex Apoc. N. T.

3 This Docetic notion was formed to favor the Gnostic (not the Catholic) view of the divinity of Christ. — Hist. of Christianity.

4 See the very curious extract from Tabari (Weil, die Chalifen, i. 103), on the substitution of a Jewish youth for Jesus on the cross, and the ascension of Jesus to heaven.

5 Mohammed was aware that the monastic system was later than Christianity. It was not ordained by God. — ch. lvii. p 421.

the approximation towards the Deity by contemplation in this life or perfection in the life to come, are equally foreign to the Korân. The later Sufism, which mingled this Orientalism with the religion of the Prophet, is more absolutely at variance with its original spirit, even than with that of the Gospel. Mohammed raised no speculative or metaphysical questions about the origin of evil: he took the world as it was, and denounced the vengeance of God against sin. To sin, angels, genii, and man were alike liable: they were to be judged at the final resurrection, and either condemned to one of the seven hells, or received into one of the seven heavens. And these seven hells and seven heavens are eternal, immutable. There is no reabsorption of the universe into the Deity. The external world and God will maintain throughout eternity the same separate, unmingling, unapproximating existence.

Creed of Islam.

Such then was the new religion which demanded the submission of the world. As a sublime Monotheism entitled to disdain the vulgar Polytheism of Arabia, of the remoter East, perhaps the Fire-worship of Persia, or even the depraved forms of Judaism and Christianity — yet at the highest it was but the republication of a more comprehensive Judaism; in all other respects its movement was retrograde. The habits of the religion, if it may be so said, were those of the Old Testament, not of the New; the Arabs had hardly attained the point in civilization at which the Jews stood in the time of the Mosaic dispensation.[1] Mohammedanism triumphant

[1] There were some distinctive usages, which are said to have been studiously introduced in order to show aversion and contempt for the Jews. —

over the world would have established the Asiatic form of society: slavery and polygamy would have become the established usages of mankind.

Islamism recognizes slavery to its fullest extent; it treats it as one of the ordinary conditions of society; none of the general principles tend even remotely to its extinction, or, except in the general admonitions to clemency and kindness, towards its mitigation. The Korân, as the universal revelation, would have been a perpetual edict of servitude.

Slavery.

Polygamy was the established usage of Arabia, and Mohammed limited, perhaps, rather than enlarged its privilege. The number of lawful wives is fixed, and with the permission of polygamy[1] are mingled some wise and humane provisions against its evils.[2] But as concubinage with female captives was recognized hardly with any limit, unbounded license became the reward of brilliant valor, and the violation of women or the appropriation of all female captives to the harem became one of the ordinary laws of war.[3]

Polygamy.

Pocock, Not. Miscel. c. 9, p. 369; Geiger, p. 198. Of these the most important is the total abolition of the distinction of meats, with the exception of those prohibited to the Jewish converts to Christianity — that which died a natural death, blood, swine's flesh, and meat sanctified to idols. — Korân, c. ii. p. 30, v. p. 128, vi. 181.

[1] All other license was forbidden. True believers keep themselves from carnal knowledge of any women except their wives, or the captives which their right hands possess (for as to them they shall be blameless); but whoever coveteth any woman beyond these, they are transgressors.

[2] The laws of divorce and of prohibited degrees, &c., are chiefly from the Old Testament. — ch. ii. and iv.

[3] The heaven-sanctioned indulgence of Mohammed in the violation of his own laws, by which he assumed and exercised a right to fifteen or more wives (the number is not quite certain), is perhaps not unjustly charged to the unbridled lust of the Prophet. Yet another at least concurrent cause may be suggested — the anxiety for male issue. Mohammed

The Korân was a declaration of war against mankind. The world must prepare at once for a new barbarian invasion and for its first great universal religious war. This barbarian invasion was not, like that of the Teutons, the Huns, or even the later Monguls of the North and East, wave after wave of mutually hostile tribes driving each other upon the established kingdoms of the civilized world, all loose and undisciplined; it was that of an aggregation of kindred tribes, bound together by the two strong principles of organization, nationality and religious unity. The Arab had been trained in a terrible school. His whole life was a life of war and adventure. The Arabians were a nation of marauders, only tempered by some commercial habits; the Arab was disciplined in the severest abstemiousness and endurance; bred in utter recklessness of human life. The old romance of Antar may show that the Arabs had already some of the ruder elements of chivalry—valor which broke out in the most extraordinary paroxysms of daring, the fervid and poetic temperament, the passion for the marvellous: their old poetry displays their congeniality both with the martial life and the amatory paradise opened by the Korân to true believers.[1] For to all this was now superadded the

Korân war against mankind.

bitterly felt the death of his four sons by Chadijah, who died in their infancy; and that of one by Maria the Egyptian. This was not only a fatal blow to his ambition, which doubtless would have led to the foundation of an hereditary religious dynasty, but was a reproach among his people, and threw some suspicion on his preëminent favor with God. Al-as Ebn Wayel who was so cruel and so daring as to insult him on the loss of his favorite boy as "caudâ mutilus," was accursed of heaven, and a special Sura (the 108th) was revealed to console the Prophet.—Abulfeda, c. lxvii., with Gagnier's note.

[1] Antar, translated by Terrick Hamilton, Esq., passim.

religious impulse, the religious object, the pride of religious as of civil conquest. Religious war is the duty, the glory, assures the beatitude of the true believer. The last revealed chapter, the ninth, of the Korân, the legacy of implacable animosity bequeathed to mankind, has deepened to an unmitigated intenseness of ferocity. It directs the extermination of the idolaters of Arabia; it allows them four months for submission to the belief and to the rites of Islam; after that it commands them to be massacred without mercy, and proceeds after death to inflict on them an eternity of hell-fire.[1] If the same remorseless extermination is not denounced against the Jew and the Christian, the true Islamite is commanded to fight against them till they are reduced to subjection and to the payment of tribute; while, to inflame the animosity of his followers, he repeats in the strongest terms what to their ears sounded not less odious than the charge of idolatry: against the Jew the worship of Ezra as the Son of God; against the Christian, not only that of Christ, but, in allusion no doubt to the worship of saints and martyrs, of their priests and monks.[2] The wealth of the priests and monks is temptingly suggested, and their employment of it against true religion sentenced with a particularity which might warrant the most unscrupulous seizure of such ill-bestowed treasures.[3]

[1] "And when the months wherein ye are not allowed to attack them are passed, kill the idolaters wherever ye shall find them, and take them prisoners, and besiege them, and lay wait for them in every convenient place." — ch. ix. p. 238. The works of these men are vain, and they shall remain.

[2] They take their priests and their monks for their lords, besides God and Christ the son of Mary, although they are commanded to worship one God only.

[3] Dante might have borrowed some of these phrases. "In the day of

The Islamites who stood aloof, either from indolence, love of ease, or cowardice, from the holy warfare, were denounced as traitors to God: the souls of more faithful believers were purchased by God: paradise was the covenanted price if they fought for the cause of God: whether they slay or be slain the promise is assuredly due. The ties of kindred were to be burst: the true believer was to war upon the infidel, whoever he might be; the idolater was even excluded from the prayers of the faithful.[1] The sacred months were not to suspend the warfare against unbelievers. Victory and martyrdom are the two excellent things set before the believer. What may be considered the dying words, the solemn bequest of Mohammed to mankind, were nearly the last words of the last-revealed Sura: "O true believers! wage war against such of the infidels as are near you, and let them find severity in you, and know that God is with them that fear him."[2]

Nevertheless, the Mohammedan invasions (and this was still more appalling to mankind) were by no means the inroads of absolute savages; not the outbursts of spoilers who wasted the neighboring kingdoms and retired to their deserts, but those of conquerors governed by a determined policy of permanent subjugation. Not merely was the alternative of Islamism or tribute to be offered, and unbelievers beyond the

judgment their treasures shall be intensely heated in the fire of hell, and their foreheads and their sides and their backs shall be stigmatized therewith: and their tormentors shall say, This is what ye have treasured up for your souls; take therefore that which ye have treasured up."— ch. ix. p. 244.

1 "It is not allowed unto the Prophet, nor those who are true believers, that they pray for idolaters, although they be of them, after it is become known unto them that they are inhabitants of hell." — ch. ix. p. 252.

2 Ch. ix. p. 263.

bounds of Arabia allowed to capitulate on these milder terms, but even their war-law contained provisions which, while they recognized the first principles of humanity, showed that they intended to settle as masters in the conquered territories. After victory they were to abstain from indiscriminate carnage,[1] from that of children, of the old, and of women; they were to commit no useless or vindictive ravage; to destroy no fruit or palm trees; to respect the corn fields and the cattle. They were to adhere religiously to the faith of treaties. Their conduct to the priests or ministers of an opposite religion was more questionable and contradictory. The monks who remained peacefully in their convents were to be respected and their buildings secured from plunder. But, as if conscious of the power of fanaticism in themselves, they wisely dreaded its reaction through the despair, and it might be, heroic faith of the priesthood. Towards them the war-law speaks in a sterner tone, though even they are not excluded from the usual terms of capitulation. "Another sort of people that belong to the synagogue of Satan, that have shaven crowns, be sure you cleave their skulls and give them no quarter till they either turn Mohammedan or pay tribute."[2]

Mohammed himself, if we are to trust the tradition preserved by the best Arabian historians, had not only vaguely denounced war against mankind in the Korân, but contemplated, at least remotely, vast and unlimited conquests. The vision of the great Arabian empire

[1] "When ye encounter the unbelievers, strike off their heads, until ye have made a great slaughter among them; and bind them in bonds; and either give them a free dismission afterwards, or exact a ransom until the war shall have laid down its arms."—ch. xlvii. ii. 376.

[2] The instructions of Abubeker to the Syrian army, in Ockley, vol. i. p. 22.

had dawned upon his mind.[1] Already, even before the conquest of Mecca, he had summoned, not only the petty potentates of the neighboring kingdoms, but the two great powers of the more civilized world, the king of Persia and the emperor of the East, to submit to his religious supremacy. His language, indeed, was courteous, and only invited them to receive the creed of Islam. If there be any foundation for this fact, which was subsequently embellished with mythic fiction, it might seem that the Prophet, either despairing of the subjugation of his intractable countrymen, had turned his mind to foreign conquest; or that he hoped to dazzle the yet hostile Arabs into his great national and religious confederacy by these magnificent pretensions to universal sovereignty. The neighboring princes replied in very different language. The governor of Egypt, Mokawkas, treated the mission with great respect, and sent, among many valuable presents, two beautiful girls, one of whom, Mary, became a special favorite. The king of Bahrein, Mondar Ebn Sawa, embraced Islam with almost all his people. The king of Ghassan, Al Harith Ebn Ali Shawer, answered, that he would go himself to Mohammed. For this supposed menace the Prophet imprecated a curse on that kingdom. A more fearful malediction was uttered against Hawdka Ebn Ali, king of Yemen, who had apostatized back from Islamism to Christianity, and returned a contemptuous answer. The Prophet's curse was fulfilled in the speedy death of the king. The king of Persia received with indignant astonishment this invitation from an obscure Arabian adventurer to yield up the faith of his an-

[1] In the 7th year of the Hegira.

cestors. He tore the letter and scattered the fragments. "So," said the Prophet, "shall his empire be torn to pieces."[1] The Mohammedan tradition of Persia still points out the scene of this impious rejection of the Prophet's advances.[2] The account of the reception of the Prophet's letter by the emperor Heraclius bears still stronger marks of Arabian fancy. He is said to have treated it with the utmost reverence, placed it on his pillow, and nothing but the dread of losing his crown prevented the Roman from embracing the faith of Islam. A strange but wide-spread Jewish tradition contrasts strongly with this view of the character of Heraclius. A vision had warned the emperor that the throne of Byzantium would be overthrown by a circumcised people.[3] So ignorant was Heraclius of any people so distinguished, but the Jews, that he commenced a violent persecution of the race, and persuaded the kings of France and Spain to join in his merciless hostility to the Israelites.

The Korân itself, the only trustworthy authority as

[1] Later Arabian poetry is full of the omens and prophecies which at the birth of Mohammed foreshowed the fall of the Persian empire. The palace of the sovereign fell, the holy fires went out, and a seer uttered a long poetic prediction concerning the final ruin of the race and empire of Chosroes. — Abulfeda, Vit. Moham. c. i. p. 3, &c.

[2] Khoosroo Purveez was encamped on the banks of the Karasoo river when he received the letter of Mohammed. He tore the letter, and threw it into the Karasoo. For this action the moderate author of the Zeenut ul-Tuarikh calls him a wretch, and rejoices in all his subsequent misfortunes. These impressions still exist. "I remarked to a Persian, when encamped near the Karasoo, in 1800, that the banks were very high, which must make it difficult to apply its waters to irrigation." "It once fertilized the whole country," said the zealous Mohammedan, "but its channel shrunk with horror from its banks, when that madman, Khoosroo, threw our holy Prophet's letter into the stream; which has ever since been accursed and useless." — Malcolm's Persia, vol. i. p. 126.

[3] See Hist. of Jews, iii.: compare Basnage and Jost.

to the views of Mohammed, shows that he watched not without anxiety the strife which, during his own rise, was raging between the Roman and the Persian empires. He rejoiced in the unexpected discomfiture of the Persians, who under Khoosroo Purveez seemed rising to a height of power formidable to the independence of the East, and fatal to the extension of his own meditated empire. The Greeks like the Mohammedans, people of the Book, were less irreconcilably opposed to Islam than the Persians, whom they held to be rank idolaters.[1] Persia, when Mohammed was assuming the state of an independent prince in Medina, was the threatening and aggressive power. Syria, Jerusalem itself, had been wrested from the Roman empire; and Syria and Jerusalem were the first conquests which must pave the way for an Arabian empire. Before the death of Mohammed they had been reconquered by Heraclius, who seemed suddenly to have revived the valor and enterprise of the Roman armies. The Roman empire, therefore, was the first and only great foreign antagonist encountered by the Islamites during the life of the Prophet. The event was not promising: in the battle of Muta some of the bravest of the followers of the Prophet had fallen;[2] the desperate valor and artifice of Khaled, the Sword of God, and the panic of the Roman army, had with difficulty retrieved the day. The war of Tabuc, for which Mohammed made such threatening preparations, ended in failure and

1 Ch. xxx. p. 253. Entitled the Greeks, or al Rum. It announces the defeat of the Greeks by the Persians, and prophesies the final victory of the Greeks.

2 Abulfeda, ch. xliv.

disappointment. The desert seemed to protect the Roman empire on this first invasion from the sons of the desert.[1]

[1] Abulfeda, ch. lvii.; Gagnier, l. vi. ch. xi. Gibbon describes this war with spirited brevity. Korân, 9. The Moslems were discouraged by the heat. "Hell is much hotter," said the indignant Prophet. "Les Musulmans s'avancent vers la Syrie; tout à coup le Prophète reçoit du ciel l'ordre de faire halte. Il revient à Medinah, et la raison de ce mouvement rétrograde n'a jamais été bien expliquée." — Oelsner, Des Effets de la Religion de Mohammed, p. 43. Oelsner supposes the progress of the rival Prophet Moseilama to have been the cause.

CHAPTER II.

SUCCESSORS OF MOHAMMED.

THE death of Mohammed[1] appeared at first the signal for the dissolution of the great Arabian confederacy. The political and religious empire might seem to have been built on no solid foundation. The death of the Prophet could not but be a terrible blow to the faith of the believers. He had never, indeed, pretended to any exemption from the common lot of mortality. He had betrayed his suspicions that he had been poisoned by a Jewish woman. His death had nothing majestic or imposing. It was caused by a fever, and at times his mind wandered. The accounts as to his firmness or feebleness in his last hour are very discrepant. He was said, on one hand, to have edified his followers by an appeal to his own severe justice and virtue. He was prepared to redress wrong: to make restitution for any injustice committed during his life. He actually did make restitution of three drachms of silver claimed by some humble

[1] June 7 or 8, 632. Compare, however, Weil, Leben Mohammed, 351, and Geschichte der Chaliphen, i. p. 2; also p. 16, and note p. 15. He ascribes to Abubeker the publication or forgery of the verses which declared the Prophet mortal. This work of Dr. Weil as summing up, with the same careful industry as in his Life of Mohammed, the labors of all his predecessors, will be among my chief authorities in the few following pages.

person from whom he had withheld it wrongfully. But his impatience under suffering moved the wonder, almost the contempt, of his wife Ayesha. Such weakness he had rebuked in a woman. The Prophet excused himself by declaring that God afflicted him with anguish poignant in the proportion with which he had distinguished him by glory above all mankind.[1] At the death of Mohammed it might seem that, the master-hand withdrawn, all would return to the former anarchy of tribal independence and of religious belief.[2]

His death, on the contrary, after but a short time, was the signal of the most absolute unity; of a concentrated force, which first controlling all the antagonistic elements of disunion in Arabia, poured forth in one unbroken torrent on the world. The great internal schism as to the succession to the caliphate, the proud inheritance of the Prophet, was avoided until Mohammedanism was strong enough to bear the division, which might have been fatal at an earlier period. The rightful heir, the heir whose succession was doubtless intended by the Prophet, and more or less distinctly declared, was set aside; and yet no dissension, at least none fatal to the progress of their arms, paralyzed the counsel or divided the hearts of the Islamites. Three caliphs, Abubeker, Omar, Othman, ascended, in due order, the sacred throne, and organized the first foreign conquests of Islam. Those first foreign conquests, Syria, Persia, Egypt, part of Africa, were achieved before the fierce conflict for

1 Price, History of Mohammedanism, i. p. 13.

2 See on the vain attempt of the Medinese to wrest the succession from the Koreishites, Weil, i. 3.

the caliphate between Ali and Moawija. It is impossible not to admire the singular beauty of the character of Ali. Three times on the point of ascending the throne, each time supported by a formidable host of followers, each time he was supplanted through the boldness or the intrigues of the more turbulent chieftains, each time he submitted with grace and dignity to the exclusion,[1] remained strenuously faithful to the cause, repressed the ambition in which he was by no means wanting, condescended to the condition and zealously discharged the duties of a loyal subject. This he did though the nearest male relation of the Prophet, the son of his uncle, and the husband of a violent woman, the Prophet's daughter, and the father of sons who might have looked forward to the great inheritance.[2] The tragedy of the death of these sons casts back even a more powerful interest on the gentle but valiant Ali.[3]

Never was disunion so perilous to the cause of Mohammedanism; never would a contested succession have produced such disastrous consequences. The dangerous swarm of rival prophets were multiplying in different parts of Arabia; it required the collective force of Islam to crush them; but they fell before the arms and the authority of the caliphs. Moseila-

[1] Dr. Weil seems to think not so willingly, on the first submission, i. p. 6; on the last, p. 153-155. Ali, by general tradition, is exculpated from all share in the murder of Othman. Dr. Weil is throughout very unfavorable to Ali.

[2] Ali, during the lifetime of Fatima the Prophetess, took no second wife: he had altogether fifteen sons and eighteen daughters. — Weil, p. 253.

[3] Hasan and Hussein. Dr. Weil, pitilessly critical, is dead to all the pathetic circumstances of the death of Hussein. Even Tabari's striking account he throws into a note. — p. 317.

ma, the most formidable of all, whose extraordinary influence, subtlety, and valor, seemed at one time to balance the rising fortunes of Mohammedanism, to render it doubtful under the banner of which religion, that of Moseilama or of Mohammed, would go forth the great Arab invasion of the civilized world, lost at length his power and his life before the Sword of God, the intrepid Khaled.[1] The effect of this, no doubt, was not merely to suppress these hostile sects, but to centre the enthusiasm, which was now burning in diverging lines, into one fiery torrent; to crowd the ranks of Islam with new warriors, who had joined it rather from the restless love of enterprise than from any strong conviction as to the relative truth of either creed, and were ready to transfer their allegiance, as success and glory were the only true tests of the divine favor, to the triumphant cause. They became at once earnest and zealous proselytes to a religion which actually bestowed such higher successes upon earth, and promised rewards, guaranteed by such successes, in the life to come. Soldiers, marauders by birth and habit, they had become followers of either prophet by the accidents of local or tribal connection, by the excitement of the imagination and the passion of sect. Their religion was a war-cry, and so that it led to conquest they cared little what name it might sound.[2]

That war-cry was now raised against all who refused faith or tribute to the creed and to the armies of the

[1] Dr. Weil treats the intrigue of Moseilama with the Prophetess Ladjah and the obscene verses quoted with such coarse zest by Gibbon, as fictions of the Mussulman. Moseilama was then 100, if not 150, years old. I confess the latter sounds to me most like fiction. — On Moseilama, p. 21–26.

[2] For the wars of Khaled in Persia under Abubeker, see Weil, 31 *et seq.*

Caliph. The first complete foreign conquest of Mohammedanism was Syria, the birthplace of Christianity. Palestine, the hallowed scene of the Saviour's life and death, was wrested by two great battles,[1] and by the sieges of a few great cities, Bosra, Damascus, and Jerusalem, from the domain of Christendom. It was an easy conquest, fearfully dispiriting to the enemies of Islam, to the believers the more intoxicating, as revealing their irresistible might: the more it baffled calculation the more it appalled the defeated, and made those who found themselves invincible, invincible indeed. On the one side had at first appeared numbers, discipline, generalship, tactics, arms, military engines, the fortifications of cities; on the other, only the first burst of valor, which from its very ignorance despised those advantages. The effete courage of the Roman legionaries had been strengthened by the admission of barbarians into their ranks; and the adventurous campaigns of Heraclius against the Persians had shown that the old intrepidity of the Roman armies was not quite worn out, and under a daring and skilful general might still be aggressive as well as defensive. But now the Emperor and the armies seem alike paralyzed by the suddenness and impetuosity of the Arab movements. The Emperor stands aloof and does not head his armies. The armies melt away before the uncontrollable onset of the new enemies. At Adjnadein and at Jarmuk the slaughter of the Roman armies was counted by tens of thousands, that of the Mohammedans hardly by hundreds. But it was the religious

[1] Adjnadein, July 30, 634. — Weil, p 40, note. Jarmuk, after the death of Abubeker, August 22, 634. — Weil, 46, probably the following day Aug. 23.

impulse which made the inequality of the contest. Religious warfare had not yet become a Christian duty; it atoned for no former criminality of life; it had no promise of immediate reward; it opened not instantaneously the gate of heaven. The religious feeling might blend itself with patriotism and domestic love. The Christian might ardently desire to defend the altar of his God, as well as the freedom of his country and the sanctity of his household hearth. But, even if the days of heroic martyrdom were not gone by, the martyrs whose memory he worshipped had been distinguished by passive endurance rather than active valor. The human sublimity of the Saviour's character consisted in his suffering. According to the monastic view of Christianity, the total abandonment of the world, with all its ties and duties, as well as its treasures, its enjoyments, and objects of ambition, advanced rather than diminished the hopes of salvation. Why should they fight for a perishing world from which it was better to be estranged? They were more highly purified by suffering persecution than by triumphing over their adversaries. It is singular, indeed, that while we have seen the Eastern monks turned into fierce undisciplined soldiers, perilling their own lives and shedding the blood of others without remorse, in assertion of some shadowy shade of orthodox expression, hardly anywhere do we find them asserting their liberties or their religion with intrepid resistance. Hatred of heresy was a more stirring motive than the dread or the danger of Islamism. After the first defeats the Christian mind was still further prostrated by the common notion that the invasion of the Arabs was a just and heaven-commissioned visitation for their sins. Submission was humble acquiescence in the will of God; resistance a vain, almost an impious, struggle to avert inevitable punishment. God was against them; hereafter he might be propitiated by their sufferings, but now (such was their gloomy predestinarianism) they were doomed to drink the lees of humiliation.

On the other hand, the young fanaticism of the Mussulman was constantly fed by immediate promises and immediate terrors. He saw hell with its fires blazing behind him if he fled, paradise opening before him if he fell.[1] The predestined was but fulfilling his fate, accomplishing the unalterable will of God, whether in death or victory. God's immutable decree was the guardian of his unassailable life, or had already appointed his inevitable death. The battle-cry of Khaled, the Sword of God, was "Fight, fight! Paradise! Paradise!" "Methinks" (cried the youthful cousin of Khaled in the heat of battle) "I see the black-eyed girls looking upon me, one of whom, if she should appear in this world, all mankind would die for the love of her. And I see in the hand of one of them a handkerchief of green silk, and a cap made of precious stones, and she beckons me, and calls out, Come hither quickly, I love thee!"[2] Contrast this as a motive to the heart of a ruder, a grosser race, with the Christian's calm, vague, trembling anticipations of a beatitude, of which that which was most definite was exemption from the sorrows and sins of life, the com-

[1] The exhortation of the generals was brief and forcible (at the battle of Jarmuk): "Paradise is before you; the devil and hell-fire in your rear." — Gibbon, c. xli. ix. 405.

[2] Ockley, i. p. 267.

panionship of saints and martyrs, or even of the Redeemer himself; or perhaps some indistinct vision of angelic presence, sweet and solemn but unimpassioned music, a wilderness of dazzling light.

But Christianity did not even offer a stubborn passive resistance.[1] The great cities, which, in the utter inexperience of the Arabs in the art of siege, might have been expected to be inexpugnable, except by famine, fell one after another: Bosra, Damascus, Jerusalem became Mohammedan. The first great conquest, before either of the decisive battles which lost Syria, showed that the religion as well as the arms of Islam was formidable to Christendom. The strong city of Bosra fell not merely by an act of treachery, but of apostasy, and that in no less a person than the governor, the base Romanus. In the face of the people, thus reduced to the yoke of the Saracens, the unblushing renegade owned his treason. He reproached the Christians as enemies of God, because enemies of his apostle; he disclaimed all connection with his Christian brethren in this world or the next, and he pronounced his new creed with ostentatious distinctness. "I choose God for my Lord, Mohammedanism for my religion, the temple of Mecca for the place of my worship, the Mussulmans for my brethren, and Mohammed for my prophet and apostle."

Feeble resistance of Christianity.

At Damascus the valiant Thomas, who had assumed

[1] The complete conquest of Syria occupied about five years. — Weil, i. 82. Abubeker's instructions to the first army which invaded Christian Syria were in these terms: "Fight valiantly. . . . Mutilate not the vanquished; slay not old men, women, or children; destroy not palm-trees; burn not fruit-trees; kill not cattle, but for food. You will find men in solitude and meditation, devoted to God; do them no harm. You will find others with their heads tonsured, and a lock of hair upon their shaven crowns; them smite with your sabres, and give them no quarter." — Caussin de Perceval, iii. 343.

Fall of Damascus.

the command of the city, attempted to encounter the fanaticism of the Mussulmans by awakening as strong fanaticism on his own side. The crucifix was erected at the gate from which Thomas issued forth to charge the enemy. The bishop with his clergy stood around, the New Testament was placed near the crucifix. Thomas placed his hand on the book of peace and love, and solemnly appealed to Heaven to decide the truth of the conflicting religions. "O God, if our religion be true, deliver us not into the hands of our enemies, but overthrow the oppressor. O God, succor those which profess the truth and are in the right way."[1] The prayer was interpreted by the apostate Romanus to Serjabil, the Mohammedan general. "Thou liest, thou enemy of God; for Jesus is of no more account with God than Adam. He created him out of the dust, and made him a living man, walking upon the earth, and afterwards raised him to heaven." But Christianity in the East was not yet a rival Mohammedanism; it required that admixture of the Teutonic character which formed chivalry, to combat on equal terms with the warriors of the Korân. Latin Christianity alone could be the antagonist of the new faith. The romantic adventure of Jonas the Damascene, who to save his life abandoned his religion, in his blind passion led the conquering Moslemins in pursuit of the fugitives from Damascus, and was astonished that his beloved Eudocia spurned with contempt the hand of a renegade, may suggest that Christianity had no very strong hold on many of the bravest of the Roman soldiers.[2]

1 Ockley, i. 87.

2 This story, the subject of Hughes's Siege of Damascus, is told at length by Ockley and Gibbon: Dr. Weil treats it as fiction.

Of Jerusalem. A.D. 636.

The capitulation of Jerusalem shows the terms imposed by the conqueror on his subjects who refused to embrace Islamism, and the degraded state to which the Christians sank at once under the Mohammedan empire. The characteristic summons of the city was addressed to the chief commanders and inhabitants of Ælia. If they admitted at once the unity of God, that Mohammed was the Prophet of God, and the resurrection and the last judgment, then it would be unlawful for the Mohammedans to shed their blood or violate their property. The alternative was tribute or submission; "otherwise I shall bring men against you who love death better than you do the drinking of wine or eating hog's-flesh.[1]" He declared that he would not leave the walls till he had slain the garrison and made slaves of the people. During four months Jerusalem held out in gallant resistance; even then it refused to surrender but to the Caliph in person. The sternly frugal Omar arrived before the walls. On the part of the Romans the negotiation was conducted by the Bishop Sophronius; and Sophronius was constrained to submit to the humiliating function of showing the Holy Places of the city to the new Lord of Jerusalem;[2] to point out the site of the temple in order that the Caliph might erect there his stately mosque for the worship of Islam. In the secret bitterness of his

[1] Ockley, from the author of the History of the Holy Land.

[2] The Arabian traditions mention various artifices of Sophronius to divert Omar from the real holy place, but its true site had been described by the Prophet to Omar. The Prophet had seen it, as will be remembered, in his mysterious journey. One curious account states that Omar crept on his hands and knees till he came to the great sewer. He then stood upright, and proclaimed it to be the place described by the Prophet. — Hist. of Temple of Jerusalem, p. 176.

heart the bishop said, "Now indeed is the abomination of desolation in the holy of holies."

Treaty of capitulation.

By the terms of the treaty the Christians sank at once to an inferior and subject people,[1] Christianity to a religion permitted to exist by the haughty disdain of the conqueror; it submitted to the ignominy of toleration. Christianity was to withdraw from the public gaze, to conceal itself in its own modest sanctuary, no longer to dazzle the general mind by the pomp of its processions or the solemnity of its services.[2] The sight of the devout Mussulman was not to be offended by the symbols of the faith; the cross was no longer to be exhibited on the outside of the churches. The bells were to be silent; the torches no longer to glitter along the streets. The Christians were to wail their dead in secrecy; they were, at the same time, though their ceremonies were not to be insulted by profane interruption, not to enjoy the full privilege of privacy. Their churches were at all times to be open, if the Mussulman should choose to enter; but to attempt to convert the Mussulman was a crime. They were interdicted from teaching their children the Korân, lest, no doubt, it should be profaned by their irreverent mockery; even the holy language (the Arabic) was prohibited: they were not to write or engrave their signet-rings with Arabic letters.

The monasteries were allowed to remain, and the

[1] The capitulation is in the History of the Temple, above cited. It is quoted from the work of Abderrahman Ibn Tamin. It pretends that these were terms submitted of their own accord by the Christians, but the language of the conquering Mussulman is too manifest.

[2] They were not publicly to exhibit the *associating* religion, that is, which associated other gods with the one God.

Mussulman exacted the same hospitality within those hallowed walls which was wont to be offered to the Christian. The monks were to lodge the wayfaring Mussulman, as other pilgrims, for three nights and give him food. No spy was to be concealed in church or monastery.

The whole people was degraded into a marked and abject caste. Everywhere they were to honor the Mussulmans, and give place before them. They were to wear a different dress; not to presume to the turban, the slipper, or girdle, or the parting of the hair. They were to ride on lowly beasts, with saddles not of the military shape. The weapons of war were proscribed, the sword, the bow, and the club. If at any time they carried a sword, it was not to be suspended from the girdle. Their foreheads were to be shaved, their dress girt up, but not with a broad girdle. They were not to call themselves by Mussulman names; nor were they to corrupt the abstemious Islamite by selling wine; nor possess any slave who had been honored by the familiarity of a Mussulman. Omar added a clause to protect the sanctity of the Mussulman's person, it was a crime in a Christian to strike a Mussulman.

Such was the condition to which the Christian inhabitants of Jerusalem fell at once; nearly the same terms, no doubt, were enforced on all the Christians of Syria. For neither Antioch nor Aleppo, nor any of the other great towns, made any vigorous or lasting resistance. The Emperor Heraclius withdrew his troops, and abandoned the hopeless contest. Syria, from a province of the Roman empire, became a province of Islamism, undisturbed by any serious aggression of the Christians till the time of the Crusades.

The Christian historian is not called upon to describe the Mohammedan conquest of Persia. The religion of the fire-worshippers, and the throne of the Sassanian dynasty, occupied the arms of the Mohammedans less than twenty years. Yezdegird, the last of the Sassanians, perished in his flight by an ignoble hand. The Caliph was master of all the wealth, the territory, and the power of that Persian kingdom which had so long contested the East with the Byzantine empire.

Conquest of Persia.

From 632 to 651.

At the same time the tide of conquest was flowing westward with slower but as irresistible force.[1] In less than three years the Saracens were masters of Egypt. Egypt fell an easy prey, betrayed by the internal hostility of the conflicting Christian sects. The Monophysite religious controversy had become a distinction not of sect only but of race. The native Egyptian population, the Copts, were stern Monophysites; the Greeks, especially those of Alexandria, adhered to the Council of Chalcedon. Mokawkas, by his name a native Egyptian, had attained to great power and influence; he is called Governor of Egypt under Heraclius. Mokawkas, according to the tradition, had been among the potentates summoned by Mohammed himself to receive the doctrine of Islam. He had returned a courteous refusal, accompanied with honorable gifts. Now, on the principle that religious hatred is more intense against those who differ the least in opinion, Mokawkas and the whole Coptic popula-

Of Egypt.

[1] The invasion of Amrou is dated June, 638; the capture of Alexandria, December 22, A.D. 640 (641, Weil).

tion, perhaps groaning under some immediate tyranny, preferred to the rule of those who asserted two natures in Christ, that of those who altogether denied his divinity. They acquiesced at once in the dominion of Amrou; they rejoiced when the proud Greek city of Alexandria, the seat of the tyrannical patriarch, who would enforce upon them the creed of Chalcedon, fell before his arms; they were only indignant that the contemptuous toleration of the Mohammedans was extended as well to those who believed in the two natures, as to those who adhered to the Monophysitic creed.[1]

Of Africa. 647 to 698.

The complete subjugation of Africa was less rapid; it was half a century before the fall of Carthage. The commencement of the eighth century saw the Mohammedans masters of the largest and most fertile part of Spain. Latin Christianity has lost the country of Cyprian and Augustine; the number of extinguished bishoprics is almost countless.

The splendor of these triumphs of the Mohammedan arms has obscured the progress of the Mohammedan religion. In far less than a century, not only has the Caliph become the sovereign, but Islamism the dominant faith in Persia, Syria, Egypt, Africa, and part of Spain.[2] But how did the religion, though that of the ruling power, become that of the subject people? In Arabia alone the Korân had demanded the absolute extirpation of all rival modes of belief, of Judaism and Christianity, as well as of the older idolatries. Though vestiges both of Judaism and Christianity might remain, to Omar is attributed the glory of having fulfilled the Prophet's injunctions. But the earlier con-

[1] Compare Weil, p. 105-114.

[2] Ockley, vol. i. p. 318.

Progress of Mohammedanism.

quests do not seem, like those of a later period, that of the Ghaznevides in India, and of the Turks in Europe, the superinduction of an armed aristocracy in numbers comparatively small; of a new and dominant caste into an old society, which in the one case remained Brahminical or Buddhist, in the other Christian. Mohammedanism in most of the conquered countries becomes the religion of the people. In Persia the triumph of the religion was as complete as that of the arms. The faithful worshippers of fire, the hierarchy of Zoroaster, dwindled away, and retired either into the bordering and more inaccessible districts, or into India. On the south of the Caspian, on Mount Elbourz, the sacred fire continued to burn in solitary splendor, after it had been extinguished or had expired on the countless temples, which, under the Sassanian dynasty, had arisen from the Tigris nearly to the Indus. The sacred books of Zoroaster, or at least those of the revived Zoroastrianism under Ardeschir Babhegan, were preserved by the faithful communities, who found an hospitable reception in India. Soon after the conquest the followers of Magianism seem to have become so little dangerous, that the Caliphs gave to them the privilege of the same toleration as to the Christians and Jews; they became what the Korân denied them to be, a third people of the Book. The formation of a new national language, the modern Persian, from the admixture of the old native tongue with the Arabic, shows the complete incorporation of the two races, who have ever since remained Mohammedan. But in the countries wrested from Christianity the case was different. With the remarkable exception of Northern Africa, perhaps of Southern Spain, Christianity, though in degradation and subjection, never ceased to exist. There was no complete change wrought like the slow yet total extinction of Paganism in the Roman world by Christianity. In all the Christian countries, in Syria, and other parts of Asia, and in Egypt, of the three fearful alternatives offered by the Arabian invader — Islam, the sword, or tribute — the Christians, after a vain appeal to the sword, had quietly acquiesced in the humiliating tribute. They had capitulated on the payment of a regular poll-tax, and that not a very heavy one, imposed on the believers in every religion but that of the Korân. So the Nestorian and Jacobite Christians in Persia and Syria, the Copts in Egypt, and a few waning communities for a certain time even in Africa, maintained their worship. Still the relative numbers of the Mohammedans increased with great rapidity. But as, for the achievement of these immense conquests, spread over so vast a surface, the Arabian armies must have been very inconsiderable (little confidence can be placed in the statement of numbers in Oriental writers), so also looking, in a general way, to the population of Arabia, and supposing that the enthusiasm of conquest and religion swept forth a very large part of it in these armed migrations to foreign lands, they must still have borne but a small proportion to the conquered races. In most countries the Arabic language became not merely that of the state but of the people.

Our information is singularly deficient as to this silent revolution in the Christian part of the Mohammedan conquests. We have seen, though not so distinctly, perhaps, as we might wish, primitive Christianity gradually impregnating the mind and heart of the

Roman world; the infant communities are found settling in all the great cities, and gradually absorbing into themselves a large portion of the people; minds of all orders, orators, philosophers, statesmen, at length emperors, surrender to the steady aggression of the Gospel. In some cases may be traced the struggles of old religious belief, the pangs and throes of the spiritual regeneration. We know the arguments which persuaded, the impulses which moved, the hopes and fears which achieved, the religious victory.

But the moral causes, and moral causes there must have been, for the triumph of Islamism, are altogether obscure and conjectural. Egypt has shown how the mutual hostility of the Christians advanced the progress of the Mohammedan arms; it is too probable that it advanced likewise the progress of the Mohammedan faith. What was the state of the Christian world in the provinces exposed to the first invasion of Mohammedanism? Sect opposed to sect, clergy wrangling with clergy, upon the most abstruse and metaphysical points of doctrine. The orthodox, the Nestorians, the Eutychians, the Jacobites, were persecuting each other with unexhausted animosity; and it is not judging too severely the evils of religious controversy to suppose that many would rejoice in the degradation of their adversaries under the yoke of the unbeliever, rather than make common cause with them in defence of their common Christianity. In how many must this incessant disputation have shaken the foundations of their faith! It had been wonderful if thousands had not, in their weariness and perplexity, sought refuge from these interminable and implacable controversies in the simple,

Causes obscure.

intelligible truth of the Divine Unity, though purchased by the acknowledgment of the prophetic mission of Mohammed.

Effects of polygamy.

Mohammed, when he sanctioned one of the old Arabian usages, Polygamy, foresaw not how powerful an instrument this would be for the dissemination of his religion. This usage he limited, indeed, in the Korân, but claimed a privilege in himself of extending to the utmost. His successors, and most of the more wealthy and powerful Mohammedans, assumed the privilege and followed the example of the Prophet, if not in direct violation, by a convenient interpretation of the Law.

Polygamy, on the whole, is justly considered as unfavorable to population, but while it diminishes in one class, it may proportionately tend to rapid and continual increase in another. The crowding together of numerous females in one harem, unless they are imported from foreign countries, since the number of male and female births are nearly equal, must withdraw them from the lower and poorer classes. While then the wealthy and the powerful would have very large families, the poor would be condemned to sterile celibacy, to promiscuous concubinage, or worse. In this relation stood the Christian to the Mohammedan population. There can be no doubt that the Christian females were drawn off in great numbers by violence, by seduction, by all the means at the command of the conqueror, of the master, of the purchaser, into the harems of the Islamites. Among the earliest questions suggested to the Caliph by the chiefs of the Syrian army, was the lawfulness of intermarriage with Grecian women, which had been prohibited by the severe Abu Obeidah. The more indulgent Caliph Omar, though himself the most abstemious of men, admitted the full right of the brave Mohammedans to those enjoyments which they had won by their valor. Those who had no families in Arabia, might marry in Syria; and might purchase female slaves to the utmost of their desires and of their abilities.[1] The Christian, on the other hand, confined by his religion to one wife, often too degraded or too poor to desire or to maintain one; with a strong and melancholy sense of the insecurity of his household; perhaps with the monastic feeling, already so deeply impressed on many minds, now strengthened by such dismal calamities, might, if of a better class, shrink from being the parent of a race of slaves; or impose upon himself as a virtue that continence which was almost a necessity.

But all the children of Christian women by Mohammedans, even if the mothers should have remained faithful to the Gospel, would, of course, be brought up as Mohammedans; and thus, in the fresh and vigorous days of the early Arabian conquerors, before the harem had produced its inevitable eventual effects, effeminacy, feebleness, premature exhaustion, and domestic jealousies, polygamy would be constantly swelling the number of the Mohammedan aristocracy, while the Christians were wasting away in numbers, as in wealth and position. Nor would it be the higher ranks of the conquerors alone which would be thus intercepting, as it were, the natural growth of the Christian population, and turning it into Mohammedan. The Arab invasions were not, like the Teutonic, the migrations of tribes and nations, but the inroad of

1 Ockley, i. 275.

armies. Some might return to their families in Arabia; a few, when settled in foreign lands, might be joined by their household; but by far the larger number of the warriors, whether married or unmarried, would assert the privilege of conquest sanctioned by the Korân, and by the Caliph, the expounder of the Korân. As long as there were women, the hot Arab would not repress his authorized passions; he would not wait for Paradise to reward his toils. The females would be the possession of the strongest; and he would not permit his offspring, even if the mother should be a fervent Christian, and retain influence over her child (in most cases she would probably be indifferent, if not a convert), to inherit the degradation of an inferior caste, but would assert for him all the rights of Islamitish descent. It would be difficult to calculate the effect of this constant propagation of one race, and diminution of the other, even in a few generations.

Extent of Mohammedan conquests.

So grew the Mohammedan empire into a multitude of Mohammedan nations, owning, notwithstanding contested successions, at least a remote allegiance to the Caliph, the heir and representative of the Prophet, but with their religious far more formidable to Christendom than their political unity. Christendom was not only assailed in front and on its more immediate borders; not only reduced to but a precarious and narrow footing in Asia; endangered, so soon as the Arabs became a naval as well as a military power, along the whole of the Mediterranean, in all its islands and on all its coasts: but it was flanked, as it were, by the Mohammedans of Spain, who crossed the Pyrenees, and penetrated into the very heart of the Frankish empire.

Religious consequences

But the most important consequence of the outburst of Mohammedanism in the history of the world and of Christianity was its inevitable transmutation of Christianity into a religion of war, at first defensive, afterwards, during the Crusades, aggressive. Religious wars, strictly speaking, were as yet unknown. Christian nations had mingled in strife, religious animosities had imbittered, or even been a pretext for wars between the Arian Goths or Vandals, and the Trinitarian Romans or Franks. Local persecutions, as among the Donatists of Africa, had been enforced and repelled by arms; perhaps in some instances bishops, in defence of their native country, had at least directed military operations. In ancient history the gods of conflicting nations had joined in the contest. But the world had not yet witnessed wars of which religion was the avowed and ostensible motive, the object of conquest the propagation of an adverse faith, the penalty of defeat the oppression, if not the extirpation, of a national creed. The appearance of the Crescent or of the Cross, not so much over the fortresses or citadels, as over the temples of God, the churches, or the mosques, was the conclusive sign of the victory of Christian or Islamite. Hence sprung the religious element in Christian chivalry; and happily, or rather mercifully for the destinies of mankind in which Christianity and Christian civilization were hereafter to resume, or, more properly, to attain their slow preponderance (it may be hoped, their complete and final triumph), was it ordained that the ruder barbarian virtues, strength, energy, courage, endurance, enterprise, had been infused into the worn-out and decrepit Roman empire; that kings of Teutonic descent, Franks, Germans, Normans, had inherited the dominions of the Western empire, and made, in some respects, until the late conquest of Constantinople by the Turks, common cause with the Christian East. Christendom thus assailed along its whole frontier, and threatened in its very centre, in Rome itself, and even in Gaul, was compelled to emblazon the Cross on its banner, and to heighten all the impulses of freedom and patriotism by the still stronger passion of religious enthusiasm. Christianity had subdued the world by peace, she could only defend it by war. However foreign then and adverse to her genuine spirit; however it might tend to promote the worst and most anti-Christian vices, cruelty, licentiousness, pride, hatred, and to establish brute force as the rule and law of society; however the very virtues of such a period might harmonize but doubtfully with the Gospel; it was an ordeal through which it must pass. The Church must become militant in its popular and secular sense; it must protect its altars, its temples, its Gospel itself by other arms than those of patient endurance, mild persuasion, resigned and submissive martyrdom.

Christianity warlike.

The change was as complete as inevitable. Christianity in its turn began to make reprisals by the Mohammedan apostleship of fire and sword. The noblest and most earnest believers might seem to have read the Korân rather than the Gospel. The faith of Christ or the sword is the battle-word of Charlemagne against the Saxons; the Pope preaches the Crusades; and St. Louis devoutly believes that he is hewing his way to heaven through the bleeding ranks of the Saracens.

Mohammedan civilization.

Nor indeed, in some other respects, was Mohammedanism altogether an unworthy antagonist of Christianity. Not less rapid and wonderful than the expansion of the Mohammedan empire, and the religion of Islam, was the growth of Mohammedan civilization — that civilization the highest, it should seem, attainable by the Asiatic type of mankind. Starting above six centuries later, it has nearly reached its height long before Christianity. The barbarous Bedouins are become magnificent monarchs; in Damascus, in Bagdad, in Samarcand, in Cairo, in Cairoan, in Fez, in Seville, and in Cordova, the arts of peace are cultivated with splendor and success. The East had probably never beheld courts more polished than that of Haroun al Raschid. Cairo, in some points at least, rivalled Alexandria. Africa had not yet become a coast of pirates. In Spain cultivation had never been carried to such perfection; Andalusia has never recovered the expulsion of the Moors. In most of the Mohammedan cities the mosques were probably, in grandeur and decoration (so far as severe Islamism would allow), as rich as the Christian cathedrals of those times. Letters, especially poetry, were objects of proud patronage by the more enlightened caliphs; the sciences began to be introduced from Greece, perhaps from India. Europe recovered the astronomy of Alexandria, even much of the science of Aristotle, from Arabic sources. Commerce led her caravans through the whole range of the Mohammedan dominions; the products of India found their way to the court of Cordova. Mohammedanism might seem in danger of decay, from the progress of its own unwarlike magnificence and luxury. But it was constantly finding on its borders, or within its territories, new fierce and often wandering tribes. New Arabs, as it were, who revived all its old adventurous spirit, embraced Islamism with all the fervor of proselytes, and either filled its thrones with young dynasties of valiant and ambitious kings, or propagated its empire into new regions. The Affghans overran India, and established the great empire of the Ghaznevides. The Turks, race after race, Seljukians and Osmanlies, seized the falling crescent, and, rivalling in fanaticism the earliest believers, perpetuated the propagation of the faith.

The expansion of Islamism itself, the enlargement of her stern and narrow creed, is even more extraordinary. The human mind, urged into active and vigorous movement, cannot be restrained within close and jealous limits. The Korân submits to a transmutation more complete than the Gospel under the influences of Asiatic Gnosticism and Greek philosophy. Metaphysical theology, if it does not tamper with the unity of God, discusses his being and attributes. The rigid predestinarianism is softened away, if not among the soldiery, in the speculative schools. The sublime, unapproachable Deity is approached, embraced, mingled with, by the Divine Love of Sufi. Monachism enslaves the Mohammedan, as it had the Christian mind. The dervish rivals the Christian anchorite, as the Christian anchorite the Jewish Essene or the Indian Fakir.

CHAPTER III.

CONVERSION OF ENGLAND.

CHRISTIANITY had thus lost the greater part of her dominion in two continents. Almost the whole of Asia had settled down under what might seem a more congenial form of civil and religious despotism; it became again Asiatic in all its public and social system. Northern Africa was doomed to exchange her Roman and Christian civilization for Arabic religion, manners, and language, which by degrees, after some centuries, partly from the fanatic and more rude Mohammedanism of the savage native races, the Berbers and others, sunk back into utter barbarism. In Europe, in the meantime, Christianity was still making large acquisitions, laying the foundations of that great federation of Christian kingdoms, which by their hostility, as well as their intercourse, were to act upon each other: until at length that political and balanced system should arise, out of which and by means of which, our smaller continent was to take the lead in the fuller development of humanity; and Christian Europe rise to a height of intellectual and social culture, unexampled in the history of mankind, and not yet, perhaps, at its full and perfect growth. For it was Christianity alone which maintained some kind of combination among the crumbling fragments

Europe Christian.

of the Roman empire. If the Barbaric kingdoms had two associating elements, their common Teutonic descent and their common religion, far the weaker was the kindred and affinity of race. Their native independence was constantly breaking up that affinity into separate, and, erelong, hostile tribes. No established right of primogeniture controlled the perpetual severance of every realm, at each succession, into new lines of kings. Thus Christianity alone was a bond of union, strong and enduring. The Teutonic kingdoms acknowledged their allegiance to the ecclesiastical supremacy of Rome; Rome was the centre and capital of Western Christendom.

Conquests of Western Christianity.

Western Christendom was still aggressive. Its first effort was to reclaim Britain, which had been almost entirely lost to pagan barbarism: and next advancing beyond the uncertain boundary of the old Roman empire, to plant all along the Rhine, and far beyond, among the yet unfelled forests and untilled morasses of Germany, settlements which gradually grew up into great and wealthy cities. Slowly, indeed, but constantly in advance, after the repulse of the Saracenic invasion by Charles Martel, Christianity remained, if not undisputed, yet the actual sovereign of all Europe, with the exception of the Mauro-Spanish kingdom and some of the Mediterranean islands; and so compensated by its conquests in the North for its losses in the East and South. Till many centuries later, a new Asiatic race, the Seljukian Turks, a new outburst, as it were, with much of the original religious fanaticism, precipitated itself upon Europe, and added the narrow remnant of the Greek empire to Islamism and Asiatic influence.

Christianity in Britain.

Britain was the only country in which the conquest by the Northern barbarians had been followed by the extinction of Christianity. Nothing certain is known concerning the first promulgation of the Gospel in Roman Britain. The apostolic establishment by St. Paul has not the slightest historical ground; and considering the state of the island, a state of fierce and perpetual war between the advancing Roman conquerors and the savage natives, may be dismissed as nearly impossible. The Roman legionary on active service, the painted Briton, in stern resistance to the Roman and under his Druidical hierarchy, would offer few proselytes, even to an apostle. The conversion of King Lucius is a legend. There can be no doubt that conquered and half-civilized Britain, like the rest of the Roman empire, gradually received, during the second and third centuries, the faith of Christ. The depth of her Christian cultivation appears from her fertility in saints and in heretics. St. Helena, the mother of Constantine, probably imbibed the first fervor of those Christian feelings, which wrought so powerfully on the Christianity of the age, in her native Britain. St. Alban, from his name and from his martyrdom, which there seems no reason to doubt, was probably a Roman soldier.[1] Our legendary annals are full of other holy names; while Pelagius, and probably his companion Celestine, have given a less favorable celebrity to the British Church.[2]

1 This will account for St. Alban's death in the persecution of Dioclesian, which did not extend, in its extreme violence at least, to the part of the empire governed by Constantius. Yet the doubtful protection of that emperor may neither have been able nor willing to prevent zealous officers from putting the military test to their soldiers. The persecution began with the army. — See Hist. of Christianity, vol. ii. p. 270.

2 St. Germain, Bishop of Auxerre, is said to have been sent into Britain to

Christianity retires before the Saxons.

But all were swept away, the worshippers of the saints and the followers of the heretics, by the Teutonic conquest. The German races which overran the island came from a remote quarter yet unpenetrated by the missionaries of the Gospel. The Goths, who formed three kingdoms in Italy, Spain, and Southern France, were already Christians; the Lombards partially converted; even among the Franks, Christianity was known, and perhaps had some proselytes before the victories of Clovis. But the Saxons and the Anglians were far more rude and savage in their manners; in their religion unreclaimed idolaters. They knew nothing of Christianity, but as the religion of that abject people whom they were driving before them into their mountains and fastnesses. Their conquest was not the settlement of armed conquerors amidst a subject people, but the gradual expulsion — it might almost seem, at length, the total extirpation — of the British and Roman British inhabitants. Christianity receded with the conquered Britons into the mountains of Wales, or towards the borders of Scotland, or took refuge among the peaceful and flourishing monasteries of Ireland. On the one hand, the ejection, more or less complete, of the native race, shows that the contest was fierce and long; the reoccupation of the island by paganism is a strong confirmation of the complete expulsion of the Britons. The implacable hostility engendered by this continuous war, prevented that salutary reaction of the Christianity of the conquered races on the barbarian conquerors, which took

extirpate Pelagianism, which had spread to a great extent. But this, considering how early the monk left his native land, must be very doubtful.— The authority is Prosper.

place in other countries. The clergy fled, perhaps fought, with their flocks, and neither sought nor found opportunities of amicable intercourse, which might have led to the propagation of their faith; while the savage pagans demolished the churches and monasteries (which must have existed in considerable numbers) with the other vestiges of Roman civilization.[1] They were little disposed to worship the God of a conquered people or to adopt the religion of a race whom they either despised as weak and unwarlike, or hated as stubborn and implacable enemies.

A century — a century of continued warfare[2] — would hardly allay the jealousy with which the Anglo-Saxons would have received any attempt at conversion from the British churches. Nor was there sufficient charity in the British Christians to enlighten the paganism of their conquerors. They consoled themselves (they are taunted with this sacrifice of Christian zeal to national hatred) for the loss of their territory, by the damnation of their conquerors, which they were not generous enough to attempt to avert; they would at least have heaven to themselves, undisturbed by the intrusion of the Saxon.[3] Happily Christianity appeared in an opposite quarter. Its missionaries from Rome were unaccompanied by any of

[1] The fine legend of the Halleluiah Victory, in which St. Germanus, at the head of an army of newly baptized Christians (at Easter), marched against the Saxons, chanting Alleluia, and ŏverwhelming them with rocks and trees in a difficult pass of the Welsh mountains, is one of the brightest episodes in the war.

[2] The first Saxon invasion was A.D. 476. Augustine came to England, A.D. 597.

[3] "Qui inter alia inerrabilium scelerum facta, quæ historicus eorum Gildas flebili sermone describit, et hoc addebant, ut nunquam genti Saxonum sive Anglorum, secum Britanniam incolenti, verbum fidei prædicando committerent." — Bede, H. E. i. c. 22.

these causes of mistrust or dislike. It came into that part of the kingdom the farthest removed from the hostile Britons. It was the religion of the powerful kingdom of the Franks; the influence of Bertha, the Frankish princess, the wife of King Ethelbert, wrought no doubt more powerfully for the reception of the faith than the zeal and eloquence of Augustine.

Gregory the Great.

Gregory the Great, it has been said, before his accession to the Papacy, had set out on the sublime though desperate mission of the reconquest of Britain from idolatry. It was Gregory who commissioned the monk Augustine to venture on this glorious service. Yet so fierce and savage, according to the common rumor, were the Anglo-Saxon inhabitants of Britain, that Augustine shrunk from the wild and desperate enterprise; he hesitated before he would throw himself into the midst of a race of barbarous unbelievers, of whose language he was ignorant. Gregory would allow no retreat from a mission which he had himself been prepared to undertake, and which would not have appalled, even under less favorable circumstances, his firmer courage.

Augustine.

The fears of Augustine as to this wild and unknown land proved exaggerated. The monk and his forty followers landed without opposition on the shores of Britain. They sent to announce themselves as a solemn embassage from Rome, to offer to the King of Kent the everlasting bliss of heaven, an eternal kingdom in the presence of the true and living God. To Ethelbert, though not unacquainted with Christianity (by the terms of his marriage, Bertha, the Frankish princess, had stipulated for the free exercise of her religion), there must have been something strange and imposing in the landing of these peaceful missionaries on a shore still constantly swarming with fierce pirates, who came to plunder or to settle among their German kindred. The name of Rome must have sounded, though vague, yet awful to the ear of the barbarian. Any dim knowledge of Christianity which he had acquired from his Frankish wife would be blended with mysterious veneration for the Pope, the great high-priest, the vicar of Christ and of God upon earth. With the cunning suspicion which mingles with the dread of the barbarian, the king insisted that the first meeting should be in the open air, as giving less scope for magic arts, and not under the roof of a house. Augustine and his followers met the king with all the pomp which they could command, with a crucifix of silver in the van of their procession, a picture of the Redeemer borne aloft, and chanting their litanies for the salvation of the king and of his people. "Your words and offers," replied the king, "are fair; but they are new to me, and as yet unproved, I cannot abandon at once the faith of my Anglian ancestors."[1] But the missionaries were entertained with courteous hospitality. Their severely monastic lives, their constant prayers, fastings, and vigils, with their confident demeanor, impressed more and more favorably the barbaric mind. Rumor attributed to them many miracles. Before long the King of Kent was an avowed convert; his example was followed by many of his noblest subjects. No compulsion was used, but it was manifest that the royal favor inclined to those who received the royal faith.

1 All this must have gone on through the cold process of interpretation, probably by some attendants of the queen. Augustine knew no Teutonic language. Latin to the Anglo-Saxons was as unknown.

Augustine, as the reward of his triumph, and as the encouragement of his future labors, was nominated to preside over the infant Church. He received a Metropolitan pallium, which made him independent of the bishops of Gaul. The choice of the see wavered for a short time between Canterbury and London, but it was eventually placed at Canterbury. The Pope already contemplated the complete spiritual conquest of the island, and anticipated a second metropolitan see at York. Each metropolitan was to preside in his province over twelve bishops. So deliberately did the ardent Gregory partition this realm, which was still divided into conflicting pagan kingdoms. Augustine was in constant correspondence with Rome; he requested and received instructions upon some dubious points of discipline. The questions and the replies are deeply tinged with the monastic spirit of the times.[1] It might seem astonishing that minds capable of achieving such great undertakings, should be fettered by such petty scruples; but unless he had been a monk, Augustine would hardly have attempted, or have succeeded in the conversion

The connection with Rome.

[1] Some of the strange questions submitted to the Papal judgment have been the subject of sarcastic animadversion.* But the age and system were in fault, not the men. There are functions of our animal nature on which the less the mind dwells the better. It was the vital evil of the monastic system, that it compelled the whole thoughts to dwell upon them. The awfulness of the religious rites, which it was the object of this system to guard by the most minute provisions as to personal purity, was in all probability much more endangered. But on the whole it is impossible not to admire the gentleness, moderation, and good sense of Gregory's decisions. It is remarkable to find him shaking off the fetters of a rigid uniformity of ceremonial. "Ex singulis ergo quibusque ecclesiis, quæ pia, quæ religiosa, quæ recta sunt, elige, et hæc quasi in fasciculum collecta, apud asylum mentis in consuetudinem depone." — Bede, i. c. 27.

* Hume, Hist. ch. i.

of Britain. With this monkish narrowness singularly contrasts the language of Gregory. On the more delicate question as to the course to be pursued in the conversion of the pagans, whether that of rigid, uncompromising condemnation of idolatry with all its feelings and usages, or the gentler though somewhat temporizing plan of imbuing such of the heathen usages, as might be allowed to remain, with a Christian spirit; whether to appropriate the heathen temples to Christian worship, and to substitute the saints of the Church for the deities of the heathen — was it settled policy, or more mature reflection which led the Pope to devolve the more odious duty, the total abolition of idolatry with all its practices, upon the temporal power, the barbarian king; while it permitted the milder and more winning course to the clergy, the protection of the hallowed places and usages of the heathen from insult by consecrating them to holier uses? To Ethelbert the Pope writes, enjoining him, in the most solemn manner, to use every means of force as well as persuasion to convert his subjects; utterly to destroy their temples, to show no toleration to those who adhere to their idolatrous rites. This he urges by the manifest terrors of the Last Day, already darkening around; and by which, believing no doubt his own words, he labors to work on the timid faith of the barbarian. To Mellitus, now bishop of London, on the other hand, he enjoins great respect for the sacred places of the heathen, and forbids their demolition. He only commands them to be cleared of their idols, to be purified by holy-water for the services of Christianity. New altars are to be set up, and relics enshrined in

Policy of Gregory.

the precincts. Even the sacrifices were to be continued under another name.[1] The oxen which the heathen used to immolate to their gods were to be brought in procession on holy days. The huts or tents of boughs, which used to be built for the assembling worshippers, were still to be set up, the oxen slain and eaten in honor of the Christian festival: and thus these outward rejoicings were to train an ignorant people to the perception of true Christian joys.

British Church.

The British Church, secluded in the fastnesses of Wales, could not but hear of the arrival of the Roman missionaries, and of their success in the conversion of the Saxons. Augustine and his followers could not but inquire with deep interest concerning their Christian brethren in the remote parts of the island. It was natural that they should enter into communication: unhappily they met to dispute on points of difference, not to join in harmonious fellowship on the broad grounds of their common Christianity. The British Church followed the Greek usage in the celebration of Easter; they had some other points of ceremonial, which, with their descent, they traced to the East: and the zealous missionaries of Gregory could not comprehend the uncharitable inactivity of the British Christians, which had withheld the blessings of the Gospel from their pagan conquerors. The Roman and the British clergy met, it is said, in solemn synod. The Romans demanded submission to their disci-

Meeting of Roman and British clergy.

1 "Quia si fana eadem bene constructa sunt, necesse est, ut a cultu dæmonum in obsequio veri Dei debeant commutari; ut dum gens ipsa eadem fana sua non videt destrui, de corde errorem deponat, et Deum verum cognoscens ac adorans ad loca, quæ consuevit, familiarius concurrat." — Greg. M. Epist. ad Mellit.: quoted also in Bede, i. 30.

pline, and the implicit adoption of the Western ceremonial on the contested points. The British bishops demurred; Augustine proposed to place the issue of the dispute on the decision of a miracle. The miracle was duly performed, — a blind man brought forward and restored to sight. But the miracle made not the slightest impression on the obdurate Britons. They demanded a second meeting, and resolved to put the Christianity of the strangers to a singular test, a moral proof with them more convincing than an apparent miracle. True Christianity, they said, "is meek and lowly of heart. Such will be this man (Augustine), if he be a man of God. If he be haughty and ungentle, he is not of God, and we may disregard his words. Let the Romans arrive first at the synod. If on our approach he rises from his seat to receive us with meekness and humility, he is the servant of Christ, and we will obey him. If he despises us, and remains seated, let us despise him." Augustine sat, as they drew near, in unbending dignity. The Britons at once refused obedience to his commands, and disclaimed him as their Metropolitan. The indignant Augustine (to prove his more genuine Christianity) burst out into stern denunciations of their guilt, in not having preached the Gospel to their enemies. He prophesied (a prophecy which could hardly fail to hasten its own fulfilment) the divine vengeance by the arms of the Saxons. So complete was the alienation, so entirely did the Anglo-Saxon clergy espouse the fierce animosities of the Anglo-Saxons, and even imbitter them by their theologic hatred, that the gentle Bede relates with triumph, as a manifest proof of the divine wrath against the refractory Britons, a great victory over that wicked race, preceded by a massacre of twelve hundred British clergy (chiefly monks of Bangor), who stood aloof on an eminence praying for the success of their countrymen.[1]

Relapse into heathenism.

During the lifetime of Augustine Christianity appeared to have gained a firm footing in the kingdom of Kent. A church arose in Canterbury, with dwellings for the bishop and his clergy; and a monastery without the walls, for the cœnobites who accompanied him. Augustine handed down his see in this promising state to his successor, Laurentius. The king of the East Saxons (Essex) had followed the example of the King of Kent. Two other bishoprics, at London and at Rochester, had been founded, and intrusted to Mellitus and Justus. But Ethelbert, the Christian King of Kent, died, and was buried by the side of his wife, Bertha. About the same time died also Sebert, the King of Essex. The successors to both kingdoms fell back to paganism. Both nations, at least the leading men, joined as readily in the rejection, as they had in the acceptance of Christianity. The new King of Kent was pagan in morals as in creed. He was inflamed with an unlawful passion for his father's widow. The rudeness and simplicity of the men of Essex show how little real knowledge of the religion had been disseminated; they insisted on partaking of the fine white bread which the bishops were distributing to the faithful in the Eucharist: and when the clergy refused, unless they submitted to be baptized, they cast them out of the land.

1 "Itaque in hos primum arma verti jubet, et sic cæteras *nefandæ* militiæ copias . . . delevit." — H. E. ii. 2.

It was a sad meeting of the three Christian bishops, who saw all their pious labors frustrated; and so desperate seemed the state of things, that the bishops of London and of Rochester fled into France. Laurentius determined on one last effort; it was prompted, as he declared, by a heavenly vision. He appeared one morning before the king, and, casting off his robe, showed his back scarred and bleeding from a recent and severe flagellation. The king inquired who had dared to treat with such indignity a man of his rank and character. The bishop averred that St. Peter had appeared to him by night, and had inflicted that pitiless but merited punishment for his cowardice in abandoning his heaven-appointed mission. The king was struck with amazement, bowed at once before the awful message, commanded the reinstatement of Christianity in all its honors, and gave the best proof of his sincerity in breaking off his incestuous connection. The fugitive bishops were recalled; Justus resumed the see of Rochester, but the obstinate idolaters of London refused to receive Mellitus. That prelate, on the death of Laurentius, succeeded to the Metropolitan see of Canterbury.

Laurentius.

The powerful kingdom of Northumberland was opened to the first teachers of Christianity by the same influence which had prepared the success of Augustine in Kent. Edwin the king married a daughter of Ethelbert, the Christian sovereign of Kent. The same stipulation was made as in the case of Bertha, for the free exercise of her religion. The sanctity attributed to their females by the whole German race, the vague notion that they were often gifted with prophetic powers, or favored with divine revela-

Christianity in Northumberland.

tions; with something, perhaps, of a higher cultivation and commanding gentleness, derived from a purer religion, increased the natural ascendency of birth and rank. Ethelberga was accompanied into Northumberland by the saintly Paulinus. Already, in the well-organized scheme of Gregory for the spiritual affairs of this island, York had been designated as the seat of a northern Metropolitan. Paulinus was consecrated before his departure bishop of that see. But Paulinus labored long in vain; his influence reached no further than to prevent the family of the queen from relapsing into paganism.

Personal danger, the desire of revenge, and paternal feeling, opened at length the hard heart of Edwin. An assassin, in the pay of his enemy the King of Wessex, attempted his life: the blow was intercepted by the body of a faithful servant. At that very time his queen was brought to bed of her first child, a daughter. Paulinus, who was present, in sincerity no doubt of heart, assured the king that he owed the safety of his life, and the blessing of his child, to the prayers which the bishop had been offering up to the God of the Christians. "If your God will likewise grant me victory over my enemies, and revenge upon the King of Wessex, I will renounce my idols, and worship him." As a pledge that he was in earnest, he allowed the baptism of the infant.

Conversion of King Edwin.

Edwin was victorious in his wars against Wessex. But, either doubting whether after all the God of the Christians was the best object of worship for a warlike race, or mistrusting his own authority over his subjects, he still hesitated, notwithstanding the urgent remonstrances of Paulinus, to fulfil his promise. He ceased to worship his idols, but did not accept Christianity. Even letters from the Pope to Edwin and his queen had but little effect. Paulinus now perhaps first obtained knowledge of Edwin's wild and romantic adventures in his youth, and of a remarkable dream, which had great influence on his future destiny. An exile from the throne of his fathers, Edwin had at length found precarious protection in the court of Redwald, king of the East Anglians. Warned that his host meditated his surrender to his enemies, he was abandoning himself to his desperate fate, when an unknown person appeared to him in a vision, not only promised to fix the wavering fidelity of Redwald, but his restoration likewise to the throne of his ancestors, in greater power and glory than had ever been obtained by any of the kings of the island.

Of the Northumbrians.

Paulinus, however he obtained his knowledge, seized on this vision to promote his holy object. He boldly ascribed it to the Lord, who had already invested Edwin in his kingdom, given him victory over his enemies, and, if he received the faith, would likewise deliver him from the eternal torments of hell. Edwin summoned a conference of his pagan priesthood; this meeting gives a striking picture of the people and the times. To the solemn question, as to which religion was the true one, the High Priest thus replied: — "No one has applied to the worship of our gods with greater zeal and fidelity than myself, but I do not see that I am the better for it; I am not more prosperous, nor do I enjoy a greater share of the royal favor. I am ready to give up those ungrateful gods; let us try whether these new ones will reward us better." But there were others of more reflective minds.

A thane came forward and said, "To what, O King, shall I liken the life of man? When you are feasting with your thanes in the depth of winter, and the hall is warm with the blazing fire, and all around the wind is raging and the snow falling, a little bird flies through the hall, enters at one door and escapes at the other. For a moment, while within, it is visible to the eyes, but it came out of the darkness of the storm, and glides again into the same darkness. So is human life; we behold it for an instant, but of what has gone before, or what is to follow after, we are utterly ignorant. If the new religion can teach this wonderful secret, let us give it our serious attention." Paulinus was called in to explain the doctrines of the Gospel. To complete the character of this dramatic scene, it is not the reflective thane, but the high priest who yields at once to the eloquence of the preacher. He proposed instantly to destroy the idols and the altars of his vain gods. With Edwin's leave, he put on arms and mounted a horse (the Anglian priests were forbidden the use of arms and rode on mares), and, while the multitude stood aghast at his seeming frenzy, he spurred hastily to the neighboring temple of Godmundingham, defied the gods by striking his lance into the wall, and encouraged and assisted his followers in throwing down and setting fire to the edifice. The temple and its gods were in an instant a heap of ashes.[1]

Edwin, with his family and his principal thanes, yielded their allegiance to Christianity. York was chosen as the seat of Paulinus the Metropolitan. In both divisions of the great Northumbrian kingdom,

[1] Bede, ii. c. xiii.

the archbishop continued for six years, till the death of Edwin, to propagate the Gospel with unexampled rapidity. For thirty-six consecutive days he was employed, in the royal palace of Glendale, in catechizing and baptizing in the neighboring stream; and in Deira the number of converts was equal to those in Bernicia. The Deiran proselytes were baptized in the river Swale, near Catterick.

The blessings of peace followed in the train of Christianity. The savage and warlike people seemed tamed into a gentle and unoffending race. So great are said to have been the power and influence of Edwin as Bretwalda,[1] or Sovereign of all the kings of Britain, that a woman might pass, with her new-born babe, uninjured from sea to sea. All along the roads the king had caused tanks of water to be placed, with cups of brass, to refresh the traveller. Yet Edwin maintained the awfulness of military state; wherever he went he was preceded by banners; his rigorous execution of justice was enforced by the display of kingly strength.

But the times were neither ripe for such a government nor such a religion. A fierce pagan obtained, not at first the crown, but a complete ascendency in yet un-Christianized Mercia. The savage Penda entered into a dangerous confederacy with Ceadwalla the Briton, King of Gwyneth, or North Wales. Ceadwalla was a Christian, but the animosity of race was stronger than the community of religion.

Penda.

[1] I leave the question as to the real existence of a Bretwalda to Mr. Kemble, and those, if there still are those, who resist his arguments. If no Bretwalda, as is most probable, he had great power. Much of this history, so striking in many scenes, trembles on the verge of legend.

The ravages of the Briton were more cruel and ruthless than those of Penda himself, who was thought ferocious even among a ferocious and pagan people.

A.D. 633. Edwin fell in the great battle of Hatfield Chase, near Doncaster; and with Edwin seemed to fall the whole noble but unstable edifice of Christianity in the north of the island. The queen of Edwin fled with Paulinus to the court of her brother, the King of Kent.[1]

Fall of Edwin and of Christianity.

The successors to the Northumbrian kingdom, which was now again divided, Osric and Eanfrid, the sons of the former usurper, and enemies of Edwin, made haste to disclaim all connection with the fallen king by their renunciation of Christianity. Both, however, were cut off, one in war, the other by treachery. Oswald was now the eldest surviving prince of the royal house of Edelfrid; and Oswald set up the Cross as his standard, appealed, and not in vain, to the Christian's God, and to the zeal of his Christian followers. After ages reverenced the Cross, to which was ascribed the victory of Oswald over the barbarous Ceadwalla, and the reëstablishment of the kingdom; portions of the wood were said to be endowed with miraculous powers. The Roman clergy had fled with Paulinus after the fall of Edwin; and the gratified Oswald, eager to lose no time in the restoration of Christianity, looked to his nearest neighbors in Scotland for missionaries to accomplish the holy work. The peaceful monastic establishments of Ireland had spread into Scotland, and made settle-

Monasteries of Scotland and Ireland.

[1] Paulinus, who had received the pall of the archbishopric of York, as Honorius that of Canterbury, from the Pope Honorius, undertook the administration of the vacant bishopric of Rochester. — Bede, ii. 18.

ments in the Western Isles. Of these was Hii, or Iona, the retreat of the holy Columba; and in this wild island had grown up a monastery far renowned for its sanctity. From this quarter Oswald sought a bishop for the Northumbrian Church. The first who was sent was Corman, a man of austere and inflexible character, who, finding more resistance than he expected to his doctrines, in a full assembly of the nation, sternly reproached the Northumbrians for their obstinacy, and declared that he would no longer waste his labors on so irreclaimable a race. A gentle voice was heard: "Brother, have you not been too harsh with your unlearned hearers? Should you not, like the apostles, have fed them with the milk of Christian doctrine, till they could receive the full feast of our sublimer truths?" All eyes were turned on Aidan, an humble but devout monk; by general accla- Aidan. mation that discreet and gentle teacher was saluted as bishop. The Episcopal seat was placed at Lindisfarne, which received from a monastery, already established and endowed, the name of Holy Island. In this seclusion, protected by the sea from sudden attacks of pagan enemies, lay the quiet bishopric; and on the wild shores of the island the bishop was wont to sit and preach to the thanes and to the people who crowded to hear him. Aidan was yet imperfectly acquainted with the Saxon language, and the king, who as an exile in Scotland had learned the Celtic tongue, sat at the bishop's feet, interpreting his words to the wondering hearers. From the Holy Island, Aidan and his brethren, now familiar with the Saxon speech, preached the Gospel in every part of the kingdom;[1] they would

[1] Compare the high character of Aidan in the Saxon, and as to ritual

receive no reward from the wealthy, only that hospitality required by austere and self-denying men; all gifts which they did receive were immediately distributed among the poor, or applied to the redemption of captives. Churches arose in all quarters, and Christianity seemed to have gained a permanent predominance throughout Northumbria.

Christianity in Wessex.

Oswald might enjoy the pious satisfaction of assisting in the conversion of the most pagan of the Saxon kingdoms, that of Wessex.[1] The Bishop Birinus had been delegated by the Pope (Honorius) on this difficult enterprise. His success, if not altogether, was in great part due to the visit of Oswald, to demand in marriage the daughter of Cynegils, the king. The king, his whole family, and his principal thanes, received baptism at the hands of Birinus, for whose residence was assigned the city of Dorchester, near Oxford.

Death of Oswald.

But paganism was still unbroken in Mercia, and at the head of the pagan power stood the aged but still ferocious and able Penda, who had already once overthrown the kingdom of Northumbria and killed in battle the Christian Edwin. A second invasion by Penda the Mercian was fatal to Oswald; he, too, fell in the field. His memory lived long in the grateful reverence of his people. His dying thoughts were said to have been of their eternal welfare; his dying words "The Lord have mercy on their souls." A miraculous power was attributed to the dust of the field where his blood had flowed. The places,

observance, Roman, Bede, iii. 5. Bede even excuses Aidan's error as to the time of keeping Easter. — iii. 17.

1 "Paganissimos." — Bede.

where his head and arms had been exposed on high poles by the insulting conqueror till they were laid to rest by the piety of his successor, were equally fertile in wonders.

That successor, his brother Oswio, followed the example of Oswald's Christian devotion with better fortune. But the commencement of his reign was sullied by a most unchristian crime. While Oswio was placed on the throne of Bernicia, Oswin, of the race of Edwin, was raised to that of Deira. Oswin was beautiful in countenance and noble in person, affable, generous, devout. The attachment of the good Bishop Aidan to Oswin was scarcely stronger than that of his ruder subjects. Jealousies soon arose between the two kingdoms which divided Northumbria. The guileless Oswin was betrayed and murdered by the more politic Oswio. On the spot where the murder was committed, Gelling near Richmond, a monastery was founded, at once in respect for the memory of the murdered and as an atonement for the guilt of the murderer.

Oswio and Oswin.

The ability of Penda and the unmitigated ferocity of the old Saxon spirit gave him an advantage over his more gentle and civilized neighbors. This aged chief now aspired to the nominal, as he had long possessed the actual, sovereignty over the island. He had dethroned the King of Wessex; East Anglia was subservient to his authority; his influence named the King of Deira, and when he laid waste Bernicia as far as Bamborough, Oswio had neither the courage nor the power to resist the conqueror of Edwin and of Oswald. The influence of the gentler sex at length brought Mercia within the pale of Christianity. Alchfrid, the son of Oswio, had married the daughter of Penda. The son of Penda, Peada, visited his sister. Alchfrid, partly by his own influence, partly by the beauty of his sister Alchfleda, of whom Peada became enamoured, succeeded in winning Peada to the faith of Christ. Peada returned to the court of his father a baptized Christian, accompanied by four priests. With that indifference which belongs to all the pagan systems, especially in their decline, even Penda, though he adhered to his war-god Woden, did not oppose the free promulgation of Christianity; but with much shrewdness he enforced upon those who professed to believe the creed of the Gospel the rigorous practice of its virtues. They were bound to obey the God in whom they chose to believe.[1]

Penda himself maintained to the end his old Saxon and pagan privilege of ravaging his neighbors' territories and of enforcing the payment of an onerous tribute. His plunder and his exactions drove Oswio at length to despair. He promised a richer offering to God than he had ever paid to the Mercian Bretwalda, if he might obtain deliverance from the enemy of his family, his country, and his religion. The terrible battle which decided the fate of Northumbria, and led to the almost immediate reception of Christianity throughout the great kingdom of Mercia, was fought on the banks of the Aire[2] near Leeds. Penda fell, and with Penda fell paganism. According to the Saxon proverb, the death of five kings was avenged in the waters of Win-
A.D. 655. wed — the death of Anna, of Sigebert, and of Egene, East Anglians, of Edwin and of Oswald.

Oswio, by this victory, became the most powerful

[1] Bede, iii. 21. [2] At Winwĕd field.

king in the island. Immediately after the death of Penda he overran Mercia and East Anglia; his authority was more complete than had ever been exercised by any Bretwalda or supreme sovereign. The Christianity of the island was almost coextensive with the sovereignty of Oswio. In all the kingdoms, except by some singular chance, that of Sussex, it had been preached with more or less success. Everywhere episcopal sees had been founded and monasteries had arisen. In Kent, perhaps, alone, the last vestiges of idolatry had been destroyed by the zeal of Ercombert. Essex, almost the first to entertain, was one of the last to settle down into a Christian kingdom. Redwald, who had first embraced the faith, had wanted power or courage to establish it throughout his kingdom. He attempted a strange compromise. A temple subsisted for some time, in which the king had raised an altar to Christ, by the side of another which reeked with bloody sacrifices to the god of his fathers. But the zeal of his successors made up for the weakness of Redwald. Sigebert, the brother of Erpwald, Redwald's successor, abandoned the throne for the peaceful seclusion of a monastery. From this retreat he was forced in order to join in battle against the terrible Penda. He refused to bear arms, but not the less perished by the sword of the pitiless Mercian. But from that time Christianity prevailed in Essex, as well as throughout East Anglia, though perhaps less deeply rooted than in other parts of the island: for in the fatal pestilence which not long after ravaged both England and Ireland, many of the East Anglians, ascribing it to the wrath of their deserted deities, returned to their

Power of Oswio.

East Anglia. A.D. 627.

A.D. 665.

former idolatry. The episcopal seat of Essex was in London; that of East Anglia, first at Dunwich, afterwards at Thetford.

Division in the Anglo-Saxon Church

But triumphant Christianity was threatened with an internal schism; one half of the island had been converted by the monks from Scotland, the other by those of Rome. They were opposed on certain points of discipline, held hardly of less importance than vital truths of the Gospel.[1] The different period at which each, according to the Eastern or the Roman usage, celebrated Easter, became not merely a speculative question, in which separate kingdoms or separate Churches might pursue each its independent course, but a practical evil, which brought dispute and discord even into the family of the king. The queen of Oswio, Eanfled, followed the Roman usage, which prevailed in Kent; Oswio, the king, cherished the memory of the holy Scottish prelate Aidan, and would not depart from his rule. So that while the queen was fasting with the utmost rigor on what in her calendar was Palm Sunday, the commencement of Passion week, the king was holding his Easter festival with conscientious rejoicings.

A synod was assembled at Whitby, the convent of the famous Abbess Hilda, at which appeared, on the Scottish side, Colman, the Bishop of Lindisfarne; on the other, Wilfrid, afterwards Archbishop of York, who had visited Rōme, was firmly convinced of the Roman supremacy, and exercised great influence over Alchfrid, the heir to the throne. With Wilfrid was Agilbert, afterwards Bishop of Paris, and other dis-

[1] It is curious to find Greek Christianity thus at the verge of the Roman world maintaining some of its usages and coequality.

tinguished men. Colman urged the uninterrupted descent of their tradition from St. John; the authority of Anatolius, the ecclesiastical historian; and that of the saintly Columba, the founder of Iona. Wilfrid alleged the supreme authority of St. Peter and his successors, and the consent of the rest of the Catholic world. "Will he," concluded Wilfrid, "set the authority of Columba in opposition to that of St. Peter, to whom were given the keys of heaven?" The king broke in, and, addressing the Scottish prelates, said, "Do you acknowledge that St. Peter has the keys of heaven?" "Unquestionably!" replied Colman. "Then, for my part," said Oswio, "I will hold to St. Peter, lest, when I offer myself at the gates of heaven, he should shut them against me." To this there was no answer.

A second question, that of the tonsure, was agitated, if with less vehemence, not without strong altercation. The Roman usage was to shave the crown of the head, and to leave a circle of hair, which represented the Saviour's crown of thorns; the Scottish shaved the front of the head in the form of a crescent, and allowed the hair to grow behind. Here likewise the Roman party asserted the authority of St. Peter, and taunted their adversaries with following the example of Simon Magus and his followers! Gradually the Roman custom prevailed on both these points: the Scottish clergy and monks in England by degrees conformed to the general usage; those who were less pliant retired to their remote monasteries in Iona or in Ireland.

In no country was Christianity so manifestly the parent of civilization as among our Anglo-Saxon ancestors. The Saxons were the fiercest of the Teutonic race. Roman culture had not, more than the Gospel, approached the sandy plains or dense forests which they inhabited in the north of Germany. On the rude manners of the barbarian had been engrafted the sanguinary and brutalizing habits of the pirate. Every vestige of the Roman civilization of the island had vanished before their desolating inroad, and the Britons, during their long and stubborn resistance, had become as savage as their conquerors. The religion of the Anglo-Saxons was as cruel as their manners; they are said to have sacrificed a tenth of their principal captives on the altars of their gods.[1] A more settled residence in a country already brought into cultivation may in some degree have mitigated their ferocity, at all events weaned them from piratical adventure; but the century and a half which had elapsed before the descent of Augustine on their coasts had been passed in constant warfare, either against the Britons or of one kingdom against another.

Anglo-Saxon Britain had become again a world by itself, occupied by hostile races, which had no intercourse but that of war, and utterly severed from the rest of Europe. The effect of Christianity on Anglo-Saxon England was at once to reëstablish a connection both between the remoter parts of the island with each other, and of England with the rest of the Christian world. They ceased to dwell apart, a race of warlike, unapproachable barbarians, in constant warfare with the bordering tribes, or occupied in their own petty feuds or inroads; rarely, as in the case of Ethel-

1 Sidon. Apoll. vii. 6. Compare Amm. Marc. xxviii. p. 526; Procop. Hist. Goth. iv.; Julian, orat. i. in laud. Constant. p. 34; Zosimus, iii.; Orosius, vii. p. 549. See Lingard, Hist. of England, ch. ii. p. 62–3.

bert, connected by intermarriage with some neighboring Teutonic state. Though the Britons were still secluded in their mountains, or at extremities of the land, by animosities which even Christianity could not allay, yet the Picts and Scots, and the parts of Ireland which were occupied by Christian monasteries, were now brought into peaceful communication, first with the kingdom of Northumbria, and, through Northumbria, with the rest of England. The intercourse with Europe was of far higher importance, and tended much more rapidly to introduce the arts and habits of civilization into the land. There was a constant flow of missionaries across the British Channel, who possessed all the knowledge which still remained in Europe. All the earlier metropolitans of Canterbury and the bishops of most of the southern sees were foreigners; they were commissioned at least by Rome, if not consecrated there; they travelled backwards and forwards in person, or were in constant communication with that great city, in which were found all the culture, the letters, the arts, and sciences which had survived the general wreck. But the nobler Anglo-Saxons began soon to be ambitious of the dignity, the influence, or the higher qualifications of the Christian priesthood. Nor were the Roman clergy or monks so numerous as to be jealous of those native laborers in their holy work; if there was any jealousy, it was of the independent Scottish missionaries, their rivals in the north, and the opponents of their discipline. A native clergy seems to have grown up more rapidly in Britain than in any other of the Teutonic kingdoms. But they were in general the admiring pupils

Intercourse with Rome.

of the Roman clergy. To them Rome was the centre and source of the faith: a pilgrimage to Rome, to an aspirant after the dignity or the usefulness of the Christian priesthood, became the great object and privilege of life. Every motive which could stir the devout heart or the expanding mind sent them forth on this holy journey: piety, which would actually tread a city honored by the residence, and hallowed by the relics of apostles; awful curiosity, which would behold and kneel before the vicar of Christ on earth, the successor of that Pope who had brought them within the pale of salvation; perhaps the desire of knowledge, and the wish to qualify themselves for the duties of their sacred station. Nor was this confined to the clergy. Little more than half a century after the landing of Augustine, Alchfrid, the son of the King of Northumbria, had determined to visit the eternal city. He was only prevented by the exigencies of the times, and the authority of his father. He was no doubt excited to this design by the accounts of the secular and religious wonders of the city, which already filled the mind of the famous Wilfrid, to whom his father, Oswio, had intrusted his education. Wilfrid had already, once at least, visited Rome; his friend Benedict Biscop several times.

The life of Wilfrid, the first highly distinguished of the native clergy, is at once the history of Anglo-Saxon Christianity in Britain to its complete establishment, and a singular illustration of the effects of this intercourse with the centre of civilization in Italy on himself and on his countrymen.[1]

[1] Eddii, Vit. S. Wilfridi apud Gale X. Scriptores compared with the Ecclesiastical History of Bede.

Wilfrid was the son of a Northumbrian thane. The sanctity of his later life, as usual, reflected back a halo of wonder around his infancy. The house in which his mother gave him birth shone with fire, like the burning bush in the Old Testament. In his youth he was gentle, firm, averse to childish pursuits, devoted to study. A jealous step-mother seconded his desire to quit his father's house; she bestowed on him arms, a horse, and accoutrements, such as might beseem the son of a nobleman, when he should present himself at the court of his king. The beauty and quickness of the youth won the favor of the queen, Eanfled, who, discerning no doubt his serious turn of mind, intrusted him to the care of a cœnobite, with whom he retired to the monastery of Lindisfarne. After a few years he was seized with an earnest longing to visit the seat of the great apostle, St. Peter. Eanfled listened favorably to his design, gave him letters to her kinsman Ercombert, King of Kent; and, accompanied by another youth, Benedict Biscop, he crossed, in a ship provided and manned by King Ercombert, into France, and found his way to Lyons. In that city he was hospitably received by Delfinus, the rich and powerful prelate of the see. Delfinus was so captivated by his manners and character that he made him an offer of splendid secular employment, proposed to adopt him as his son, to marry him to his niece, and put him at the head of the government over great part of Gaul.[1] But Wil-

Wilfrid.

A.D. 654.

In Lyons.

[1] Eddius, the biographer, and Bede agree in this statement. But there are great difficulties in the story. Smith, in his notes on Bede, observes that there is no Delfinus in the list of bishops of Lyons. (Could he be a prelate so called from being a native of Dauphiny?) And in those troubled

frid was too profoundly devoted to his religious views, too fully possessed with the desire of accomplishing his pilgrimage to Rome; he declined the dazzling offer of the noble virgin bride and her dowry of worldly power. He arrived at Rome; and if his mind, accustomed to nothing more imposing than the rude dwelling of a Northumbrian thane, or the church of wood and wattels, expanded at the sight of the cities, which probably, like Lyons, still maintained some of the old provincial magnificence, with what feelings must the stranger have trod the streets of Rome, with all its historical and religious marvels! In Rome the Archdeacon Boniface, one of the council of the Pope, kindly undertook the care of the young Saxon. He instructed him in the four Gospels, in the Roman rule of keeping Easter, and other points of ecclesiastical discipline, unknown or unpractised in the Anglo-Saxon Church. He was at length presented to the successor of St. Peter, and received his blessing. Under the protection of certain relics, one of the inestimable advantages which often rewarded a pilgrimage to Rome, Wilfrid returned to his friend the Bishop of Lyons. There he resided three years; and now, tempted no more by secular offers, or acknowledged to be superior to them, he received, at his earnest request, the tonsure according to the Roman form. But Delfinus (so runs the legend) had incurred the animosity of the Queen Bathildis. With eight other bishops he was put to death. Wilfrid stood prepared to share the glorious martyrdom of his friend. His beauty arrested the

In Rome.

and lawless times in France, how could a bishop dispose of a civil government of such extent?

arm of the executioner; and when it was found that he was a stranger he was permitted to depart in peace.[1]

The young Saxon noble, who had seen so many distant lands — had been admitted to the familiarity of such powerful prelates — had visited Rome, received the blessing of the Pope, and travelled under the safeguard of holy relics — was welcomed by his former friend Alchfrid, now the pious king of Northumbria, with wondering respect. He obtained first a grant of land at a place called Æstanford; afterwards a monastery was founded at Ripon, and endowed with xxx manses of land, of which Wilfrid was appointed abbot. He was then admitted into the priesthood by Agilbert, the Bishop of Wessex. Colman, the Scottish bishop of Lindisfarne, after his discomfiture in the dispute concerning Easter, retired in disgust and disappointment to his native Iona. Tuta, another Scot, was carried off by the fatal plague, which at this time ravaged Britain. Upon his decease, the Saxon Wilfrid was named by common consent to the Northumbrian bishopric. But the plague had swept away the greater part of the southern prelates. Wina alone, the West-Saxon bishop, was considered by Wilfrid as canonically consecrated; the rest were Scots, who rejected the Roman discipline concerning Easter and the tonsure. Wilfrid went over to France; the firm champion of the Catholic discipline was received with the highest

In Northumbria.

1 Here is a greater difficulty. The Queen Bathildis is represented by the French historians, not as a Jezebel who slays the prophets of the Lord (as she is called by Eddius), but as a princess of exemplary piety, a devout servant of the church, and the foundress of monasteries. Ebroin too, the Mayor of the Palace, in this legend is drawn in very dark colors. But on Bathildis and Ebroin more hereafter.

Consecrated at Compiegne.

honors. No less than twelve bishops assembled for his consecration at Compiegne: he was borne aloft on a gilded chair, supported only by bishops — no one else was allowed to touch it. He remained some time (it is said three years) among his friends in Gaul.[1] On his return to England a wild adventure on the shores of his native land showed how strangely the fiercest barbarism still encountered the progress of civilization — paganism that of Christianity. The kingdom of Sussex was yet entirely heathen.

Sussex.

Wilfrid was driven by a storm on its coast. The Saxon pirates had become merciless wreckers; they thought everything cast by the winds and the sea on their coasts their undoubted property, the crew and passengers of vessels driven on shore their lawful slaves. They attacked the stranded bark with the utmost ferocity: the crew of Wilfrid made a gallant resistance. It was a strange scene. On one side the Christian prelate and his clergy were kneeling aloof in prayer; on the other a pagan priest was encouraging the attack, by what both parties supposed powerful enchantments. A fortunate stone from a sling struck the priest on the forehead, and put an end to his life and to his magic. But his fall only exasperated the barbarians. Thrice they renewed the attack, and thrice were beaten off. The prayers of Wilfrid became more urgent, more needed, more successful.[2] The tide came in, the wind shifted; the vessel got to sea, and reached Sandwich. At a later

[1] There may be some confusion in his two periods of residence in Gaul.

[2] Eddius compares the pagan priest to Balaam, the slayer to David, the resistance of this handful of men to that of Gideon, the prayers of Wilfrid to those of Moses and Aaron when Joshua fought with Amalek.

period of his life Wilfrid nobly revenged himself on this inhospitable people by laboring, and with success, in their conversion to Christianity.

On Wilfrid's return to Northumbria, after his long unexplained absence, he found his see preoccupied by Ceadda, a pious Scottish monk, a disciple of the venerated Aidan.[1] Wilfrid peaceably retired to his monastery at Ripon. He was soon summoned to more active duties: he obeyed the invitation of Wulfhere, King of Mercia, to extend Christianity in his kingdom. In the south he must have obtained high reputation. On the death of Deus-dedit, the Archbishop of Canterbury, Wilfrid was intrusted with the care of the vacant diocese. On the arrival of Theodorus, who had been invested in the metropolitan dignity at Rome, almost his first act was to annul the election of Ceadda, and to place Wilfrid in the Northumbrian see at York. Ceadda made no resistance; and as a reward for his piety and his submission, was appointed to the Mercian see of Lichfield.

The Christianity of the Anglo-Saxon kingdoms, whether from Rome or Iona, was alike monastic. That form of the religion already prevailed in Britain, when invaded by the Saxons, with them retreated into Wales, or found refuge in Ireland. It landed with Augustine on the shores of Kent; and came back again, on the invitation of the Northumbrian king, from the Scottish isles. And no form of Christianity could be so well suited for its high purposes at that time, or tend so powerfully to promote civilization as well as religion.

[1] Perhaps after all Wilfrid was only nominated by the Roman party, who, diminished by the plague, may not have been able to support their choice.

Monasticism of the Church.

The calm example of the domestic virtues in a more polished, but often, as regards sexual intercourse, more corrupt state of morals, is of inestimable value, as spreading around the parsonage an atmosphere of peace and happiness, and offering a living lesson on the blessings of conjugal fidelity. But such Christianity would have made no impression, even if it could have existed, on a people who still retained something of their Teutonic severity of manners, and required therefore something more imposing — a sterner and more manifest self-denial — to keep up their religious veneration. The detachment of the clergy from all earthly ties left them at once more unremittingly devoted to their unsettled life as missionaries, more ready to encounter the perils of this wild age; while (at the same time) the rude minds of the people were more struck by their unusual habits, by the strength of character shown in their labors, their mortifications, their fastings, and perpetual religious services. All these being, in a certain sense, monks, the bishop and his clergy cœnobites, or if they lived separate only less secluded and less stationary than other ascetics, wherever Christianity spread, monasteries, or religious foundations with a monastic character, arose. These foundations, as the religion aspired to soften the habits, might seem to pacify the face of the land. They were commonly placed, by some intuitive yearning after repose and security, in spots either themselves beautiful by nature, by the bank of the river, in the depth of the romantic wood, under the shelter of the protecting hill; or in such as became beautiful from the superior care and culture of the monks, — the draining of the meadows, the planting of trees, the home circle of garden or orchard, which employed or delighted the brotherhood. These establishments gradually acquired a certain sanctity: if exposed like other lands to the ravages of war, no doubt at times the fear of some tutelary saint, or the influence of some holy man, arrested the march of the spoiler. If the growth of the English monasteries was of necessity gradual, the culture around them but of slow development (agricultural labor does not seem to have become a rule of monastic discipline), it was not from the want of plentiful endowments, or of ardent votaries. Grants of land and of movables were poured with lavish munificence on these foundations;[1] sometimes tracts of land, far larger than they could cultivate, and which were thus condemned to sterility. The Scottish monks are honorably distinguished as repressing, rather than encouraging, this prodigality.[2] The Roman clergy, if less scrupulous, might receive these tributes not merely as offerings of religious zeal to God, but under a conviction that they were employed for the improvement as well as the spiritual welfare of the people. Nor was it only the sacred mysterious office of ministering at the altar of the new God, it was the austere seclusion of the monks, which seized on the religious affections of the Anglo-Saxon convert. When Christianity first broke upon their rude but earnest minds, it was embraced with the utmost fervor, and under its severest forms. Men were eager to escape the awful pun-

1 Bede calls some of these donations, "stultissimos."

2 "Aidanus, Finan et Colmannus, miræ sanctitatis fuerunt et parsimoniæ. Adeo enim sacerdotes erant illius temporis ab avaritiâ immunes ut nec territoria, nisi coacti, acceperunt." — Henric. Hunting. apud Gale, lib. iii. p. 333.

ishments, and to secure the wonderful promises of the new religion by some strong effort, which would wrench them altogether from their former life. As the gentler spirit of the Gospel found its way into softer hearts, it made them loathe the fierce and rudely warlike occupations of their forefathers. To the one class the monastery offered its rigid course of ceremonial duty and its ruthless austerities, to the other its repose. Nobles left their halls, queens their palaces, kings their thrones, to win everlasting life by the abandonment of the pomp and the duties of their secular state, and, by becoming churchmen or monks, still to exercise rule, or to atone for years of blind and sinful heathenism.

CHAPTER IV.

WILFRID — BEDE.

Wilfrid's buildings.

WILFRID, the type of his time, blended the rigor of the monk with something of prelatic magnificence. The effect of his visit to more polished countries — to Gaul and Italy — soon appeared in his diocese. He who had seen the churches of Rome and other Italian cities, would not endure the rude timber buildings,[1] thatched with reeds — the only architecture of the Saxons — and above which the Scottish monks had not aspired.[2] The church of Paulinus at York had been built of stone, but it was in ruins; it was open to the wind and rain, and the birds flew about and built their nests in the roof and walls. Wilfrid repaired the building, roofed it with lead, and filled the windows with glass. The transparency of this unknown material excited great astonishment. At Ripon he built the church from the ground of smoothed stones; it was of great height, and supported by columns and aisles.[3] All the chieftains and thanes of the kingdom were invited to the consecration of this church. Wilfrid read from the altar

1 Lappenberg observes that the Anglo-Saxons have no other word for building but getimbrian, to work in wood. — Geschichte Engl., i. 170.

2 Eddius, c. xvi.

3 "Polito lapide a terrâ usque ad summum, ædificatam variis columnis et porticibus suffultam in cultum erexit et consummavit." — Eddius, xviii.

the list of the lands which had been bestowed by former kings, for the salvation of their souls, upon the church, and those which were offered that day; and also of the places once dedicated to God by the Britons, and abandoned on their expulsion by the Saxons. This act was meant for the solemn recognition of all existing rights, the encouragement of future gifts, and, it seems, the assertion of vague and latent claims.[1] After this Christian or sacerdotal commemoration, there was something of a return to heathen usage, during three days and three nights uninterrupted feasting. But the architectural wonder of the age was the church at Hexham, which was said to surpass in splendor every building on this side of the Alps. The depth to which the foundations were sunk, the height and length of the walls, the richness of the columns and aisles, the ingenious multiplicity of the parts, as it struck the biographer of Wilfrid, give the notion of a building of the later Roman, or, as it is called, Byzantine style, aspiring into something like the Gothic.[2]

Benedict Biscop.

The friend and companion of Wilfrid at Rome, Benedict Biscop, (a monk of Holy Island), was introducing, in a more peaceful and less ostentatious way, the arts and elegancies of life. When about to build his monastery at Wearmouth, he crossed into Gaul to collect masons skilled in working stone after the Roman manner; when the walls were finished, he sent for

1 Eddius, c. xvii.

2 "Cujus profunditatem in terrâ cum domibus mirificè politis lapidibus fundatam, et super terram multiplicem domum, columnis variis et multis porticibus suffultam, mirabilique altitudine et longitudine murorum ornatam, et variis linearum anfractibus viarum aliquando sursum, aliquando deorsum per cochleas circumductam." — Eddius, c. xxii.

glaziers, whose art till this time was unknown in Britain.[1] Nor was architecture the only art introduced by the pilgrims to Rome. Benedict brought from abroad vessels for the altar, vestments which could not be made in England, and especially two palls, entirely of silk, of incomparable workmanship.[2] Books, embellished if not illuminated manuscripts, and paintings, came from the same quarter. Wilfrid's offering to the church of Ripon was a copy of the Gospels, written in letters of gold, on a purple ground.[3] Other manuscripts were adorned with gold and precious stones. On each of his visits to Rome Benedict brought less ornamented books; on one occasion a large number: and he solemnly charged his brethren, among his last instructions, to take every precaution for the security and preservation of their library. The pictures, which he brought from Rome, were to adorn two churches, one at Wearmouth, dedicated to St. Peter; one at Yarrow, to St. Paul. These were no doubt the earliest specimens of Christian painting in the country. In the ceiling of the nave at Wearmouth were the Virgin and the twelve apostles; on the south wall subjects from the Gospel history; on the north from the Revelations. Those in St. Paul's illustrated the agreement of the Old and New Testament. In one compartment was

A.D. 676.

1 Painted glass seems to have been known at an early period in Gaul, —

> "Sub versicoloribus figuris vernans herbida crusta,
> Sapphiratos flectit per prasinum vitrum capillos."
>
> *Sidon. Apollin.*

This, however, seems a kind of mosaic.

2 "Vasa sancta, et vestimenta quia domi invenire non poterat . . oloserica."

3 "Auro purissimo in membranis depurpuratis, coloratis." — Eddius, c xvii.

Isaac bearing the wood for sacrifice, and below the Saviour bearing his cross.[1]

So far Wilfrid rises to his lofty eminence an object of universal respect, veneration, and love. On a sudden he is involved in interminable disputes, persecuted with bitter animosity, degraded from his see, an exile from his country, and dies at length, though at mature age, yet worn out with trouble and anxiety. The causes of this reverse are lost in obscurity. It was not the old feud between the Roman and the Scottish clergy, for Theodorus, the Archbishop of Canterbury, the head of the Roman party, joins the confederacy against him. As yet the jealousies between the secular and the regular clergy, the priests and monks, which at a later period, in the days of Odo and Dunstan, distracted the Anglo-Saxon Church, had not begun. The royal jealousy of the pomp and wealth of the bishop, which might seem to obscure that of the throne, though no doubt already in some strength, belongs in its intensity to other times. Egfrid, now King of Northumbria, had been alienated from Wilfrid, through his severe advice to the Queen Ethelreda to persist in her vow of chastity. The first husband of Ethelreda had respected the virginity which she had dedicated to God. When compelled to marry Egfrid, she maintained her holy obstinacy, and took refuge, by Wilfrid's connivance, in a convent, to escape her conjugal duties. A new Queen, Ercemburga, instead of this docile obedience to

[1] Bede, after describing the pictures, proceeds: "Quatenus intrantes ecclesiam omnes etiam literarum ignari, quaquaversum intenderent, vel semper amabilem Christi, sanctorumque ejus, quamvis in imagine contemplarentur aspectum: vel Dominicæ Incarnationis gratiam vigilantiore mente recolerent, vel extremi discrimen examinis quasi coram oculis habentes, districtius se ipsi examinare meminerint." — Smith's Bede, p. 295.

Wilfrid, became his bitterest enemy.[1] She it was who inflamed her husband with jealousy of the state, the riches, and the pride of the bishop, his wealthy foundations, his splendid buildings, his hosts of followers. Theodorus, the Archbishop of Canterbury, eagerly accepted the invitation of the King of Northumbria, to assist in the overthrow of Wilfrid.

Theodorus was a foreigner, a Greek of Tarsus, and might perhaps despise this aspiring Saxon. After the death of Archbishop Deus-dedit, the see of Canterbury had remained vacant four years. The kings of Kent and Northumbria determined to send a Saxon, Wighard, to Rome, to receive consecration. Wighard died at Rome; the Pope Vitalian was urged to supply the loss. His choice fell upon Theodorus, a devout and learned monk. Vitalian's nomination awoke no jealousy, but rather profound gratitude.[2] It was not the appointment of a splendid and powerful primate to a great and wealthy church, but a successor to the missionary Augustine. But Theodorus, if he brought not ambition, brought the Roman love of order and of organization, to the yet wild and divided island; and the profound peace which prevailed might tempt him to reduce the more than octarchy of independent

Theodorus Archbishop of Canterbury.

A.D. 664.

A.D. 668.

1 The language ascribed to Ercemburga might apply to a later archbishop of York, the object of royal envy and rapacity. "Enumerans ei . . . omnem gloriam ejus secularem, et divitias, nec non Cœnobiorum multitudinem, et ædificiorum magnitudinem, innumerumque sodalium exercitum, *regalibus* vestimentis et armis ornatum." This is not Wolsey, but Wilfrid.

2 "Episcopum quem petierant a Romano Pontifice." There is a violent dispute (compare Lingard, Anglo-Sax. Antiq., and note in Kemble's Anglo-Saxons, ii. 355) upon the nature of this appointment; all parties, except Mr. Kemble, appear to me to overlook the state of Christianity in England at the time.

bishops into one harmonious community. As yet there were churches in England, not one Church. Theodorus appears to have formed a great scheme for the submission of the whole island to his metropolitan jurisdiction. He summoned a council at Hertford, which enacted many laws for the regulation of the power of the bishops, the rights of monasteries, on keeping of Easter, on divorces, and unlawful marriages. Archbishop Theodorus began by dividing the great bishoprics in East Anglia and in Mercia, and deposed two refractory prelates. He proceeded on his sole spiritual authority, with the temporal aid of the king, to divide the bishopric of York into three sees; so, by the appointment of three bishops, Wilfrid was entirely superseded in his diocese.[1] Wilfrid appealed to Rome, and set out to lay his case before the Pope.[2] So deep was the animosity, that his enemies in England are said to have persuaded Theodoric, King of the Franks, and Ebroin, mayor of the palace, to seize the prelate on his journey, and to put his companions to the sword. Winfred, the ejected Bishop of Mercia, was apprehended in his stead, and thrown into prison.

Wilfrid appeals to Rome.

The wind was fortunately adverse to Wilfrid, and drove him on the coast of Friesland. The barbarous and pagan people received the holy man with hospitality; their fisheries that year being remarkably successful, this was attributed to his presence; and the king, the nobles, and the people, were alike more disposed to listen to the Gospel, first preached among

In Friesland.

[1] Eddius compares Egfrid and Theodorus to Balak and Balaam.—Wilkins, Concil.

[2] Eddius says that he left England amid the tears of *many thousands of his monks.*

them with Wilfrid's power and zeal. The way was thus prepared for his disciple, Willibrod, and for that remarkable succession of missionaries from England, who, kindred in speech, converted so large a part of Germany to Christianity.

After nearly a year passed in this pious occupation in Friesland, Wilfrid ventured into Gaul, and was favorably received by Dagobert II. Two years elapsed before he found his way to Rome. The Pope (Agatho) received his appeal, submitted it to a synod, who decided in his favor. Agatho issued his mandate for the reinstatement of Wilfrid in his see.

A.D. 679. October.

Though the Papal decree denounced excommunication against the layman, degradation and deprivation against the ecclesiastic, who should dare to disobey it, it was received by the King of Northumbria with contempt, and even by Archbishop Theodorus with indifference. Wilfrid, on his return, though armed with the papal authority, which he was accused of having obtained by bribery,[1] was ignominiously cast into prison, and kept in solitary confinement. The queen, with the strange mixture of superstition and injustice belonging to the age, plundered him of his reliquary, a talisman which she kept constantly with her, in her own chamber and abroad. Wilfrid's faithful biographer relates many miracles, wrought during his imprisonment. The chains of iron, with which they endeavored to bind him, shrunk or stretched, so as either not to admit his limbs, or to drop from them. The queen fell ill, and attributed her sick-

In Northumbria.

[1] See Eddius for this early instance of the suspected venality of the Roman curia. "Insuper (quod execrabilius erat), defamaverant in animarum suarum perniciem, ut *pretio* dicerent redempta esse scripta, quæ ad salutem observantium ab apostolicâ sede destinata sunt." — c. xxxiii.

ness to the stolen reliquary. She obtained his freedom, and was glad when the dangerous prelate, with his relics, was safe out of her kingdom.

He fled to Mercia, but the Queen of Mercia was the sister of Egfrid; to Wessex, but there the queen was the sister of Ercemburga; he found no safety. At length he took refuge among the more hospitable pagans of Sussex — the only one of the Saxon kingdoms not yet Christian. The king and the queen, indeed, had both been baptized; the king, Ethelwach, at the persuasion of Wulfhere, King of Mercia, who rewarded his Christianity with the prodigal grant of the Isle of Wight; Eabba, the queen, had been admitted to the sacred rite in Worcestershire. Yet, till the arrival of Wilfrid, they had not attempted to make proselytes among their subjects. They had rested content with their own advantages. A few poor Irish monks at Bosham (near Chichester) had alone penetrated the wild forests and jungles which cut off this barbarous tribe from the rest of England. But their rude hearts opened at once to the eloquence of Wilfrid. He taught them the arts of life as well as the doctrines of the Gospel. For three years this part of the island had suffered by drought, followed by famine so severe, that an epidemic desperation seized the people. They linked themselves by forties or fifties hand in hand, leaped from the rocks, were dashed in pieces, or drowned.[1] Though a maritime people,

Flight of Wilfrid.

[1] The South Saxons are thus described:

"Gens igitur quædam scopulosis indita terris
Saltibus incultis, et densis horrida dumis
Non facilem propriis aditum præbebat in arvis,
Gens ignara Dei, simulacris dedita vanis."

Fredegard, p. 191.

on a long line of sea-coast, they were ignorant of the art of fishing. Wilfrid collected a number of nets, led them out to sea, and so provided them with a regular supply of food. The wise and pious benefactor of the nation was rewarded by a grant of the peninsula of Selsey (the isle of seals). There he built a monastery, and for five years exercised undisturbed his episcopal functions.

Conquest of Sussex by Ceadwalla.

A revolution in the west and south of the island increased rather than diminished the influence of Wilfrid. Ceadwalla, a youth of the royal house of Wessex, had lived as an outlaw in the forests of Chiltern and Anderida. He appeared suddenly in arms, seized the kingdom of the West Saxons, conquered Sussex, and ravaged or subdued parts of Kent. Some obscure relation had subsisted between Ceadwalla (when an exile) and the Bishop Wilfrid.[1] Wilfrid's protector, Adelwalch, fell in battle during the invasion of the stranger. After Ceadwalla had completed his conquests by the subjugation of the Isle of Wight, Wilfrid became his chief counsellor, and was permitted by the king, still himself a doubtful Christian, if not a heathen, to convert the inhabitants; and Ceadwalla granted to the Church one third of the Isle of Wight.

Conversion of Ceadwalla.

The conversion of Ceadwalla is too remarkable to be passed over. It has been attributed to his horror of mind at the barbarous murder of his brother in Kent.[2] It was no light and

Eddius admits that the South Saxons were *compelled* by the king to abandon their idolatry. According to Bede, they understood catching eels in the rivers. — H. E. iv. 13.

[1] "Sanctus antistes Christi in nonnullis auxiliis et adjumentis sæpe anxiatum exulem adjuvavit et confirmavit." — Eddius, c. 41.

[2] According to Henry of Huntingdon, Ceadwalla was not a Christian

politic conviction, but the deep and intense passion of a vehement spirit. The wild outlaw, the bloody conqueror, threw off his arms, gave up the throne which he had won by such dauntless enterprise and so much carnage. He went to Rome to seek that absolution for his sins, from which no one could so effectually relieve him as the successor of St. Peter. At Rome he was christened by the name of Peter. At Rome he died, and an epitaph, of no ordinary merit for the time, celebrated the first barbarian king, who had left his height of glory and of wealth, his family, his mighty kingdom, his triumphs and his spoils, his thanes, his castles, and his palaces, for the perilous journey and baptism at the hands of St. Peter's successor. His reward had been an heavenly for an earthly crown.[1]

when he invaded Kent. Wolf (his brother), a savage marauder, was surprised and burned in a house, in which he had taken refuge, by the Christians of the country. "Post hæc Ceadwalla Rex West Saxoniæ, de his et aliis sibi commissis pœnitens, Romam perrexit." — Apud X. Script. p. 742.

[1] "Culmen, opes, sobolem, pollentia regna, triumphos,
Exuvias, proceres, mœnia, castra, Lares,
Quæque patrum virtus et quæ congesserat ipse
Cædwal armipotens liquit amore Dei.
Ut Petrum sedemque Petri rex cerneret hospes,
Cujus fonte meras sumeret almus aquas,
Splendificumque jubar radianti sumeret haustu,
Ex quo vivificus fulgor ubique fluit.
Percipiensque alacer redivivæ præmia vitæ
Barbaricam rabiem, nomen et inde suum
Conversus, convertit ovans, Petrumque vocari,
Sergius Antistes jussit, ut ipse Pater
Fonte renascentis, quem Christi gratia purgans
Protinus ablutum vexit in arce poli.
Mira fides regis! clementia maxima Christi,
Cujus consilium nullus adire potest!
Sospes enim veniens supremo ex orbe Britanni,
Per varias gentes, per freta, perque vias,
Urbem Romuleam vidit, templumque verendum
Aspexit Petri, mystica dona gerens.

Archbishop Theodorus was now grown old, and felt the approach of death; he was seized with remorse for his injustice to the exiled bishop of York. Wilfrid met his advances to reconciliation in a Christian spirit. In London Theodorus declared publicly that Wilfrid had been deposed without just cause; at his decease intrusted his own diocese to his charge, and recommended him as his own successor. Wilfrid either declined the advancement, or, more probably, was unacceptable to the clergy of the South. After a vacancy of two years, the Abbot of Reculver, whose name, Berchtwald, indicates his Saxon descent, was chosen. He was the first native who had filled the see.[1]

Wilfrid reinstated in York.

Wilfrid was again invested in his full rights as Bishop of York. The king, Egfrid, had fallen in battle against the Picts. His successor was Aldfrid, who had been educated in piety and learning by certain Irish monks. This, though an excellent school for some Christian virtues, had not taught him humble submission to the lofty Roman pretensions of Wilfrid. The feud between the king and the bishop broke out anew. Wilfrid pressed some antiquated claims on certain alienated possessions of the Church; the king proposed to erect Ripon into a bishopric independent of York. Wilfrid retired to the court of Mercia.

A general synod of the clergy of the island was held

Candidus inter oves Christi sociabilis ivit,
  Corpore nam tumulum, mente superna tenet;
Commutâsse magis sceptrorum insignia credas,
  Quem regnum Christi præmeruisse vides."

Bede, *H. E.* v. 7.

[1] According to the Saxon chronicle and others. Bede calls him a native of Wessex

at a place called Eastanfeld. The synod demanded the unqualified submission of Wilfrid to certain constitutions of Archbishop Theodorus. Wilfrid reproached them with their contumacious resistance, during twenty-two years, to the decrees of Rome, and tauntingly inquired whether they would dare to compare their archbishop of Canterbury (then a manifest schismatic) with the successors of St. Peter.[1] However the clergy might reverence the spiritual dignity of Rome, the name of Rome was probably less imposing to the descendants of the Saxons than to most of the Teutonic tribes. The Saxons had only known the Romans in their decay, as a people whom they had driven from the island. The name was perhaps associated with feelings of contempt rather than of reverence. The king and the archbishop demanded Wilfrid's signature to an act of unconditional submission. Warned by a friendly priest that the design of his enemies was to make him surrender all his rights and pronounce his own degradation, Wilfrid replied with a reservation of his obedience to the canons of the fathers. They then required him to retire to his monastery at Ripon, and not to leave it without the king's permission; to give up all the papal edicts in his favor; to abstain from every ecclesiastical office, and to acknowledge the justice of his own deposition. The old man broke out with a clear and intrepid voice into a protest against the iniquity of depriving him of an office held for forty years. He recounted his services

Expulsion of Wilfrid.

[1] "Interrogavit eos quâ fronte auderent statutis apostolicis ab Agathone sancto et Benedicto electo, et beato Sergio sanctissimis papis ad Britanniam pro salute animarum directis præponere, aut eligere decreta Theodori episcopi quæ in discordiâ constituit." So writes Eddius, no doubt present at the synod.

to the Church. The topics were singularly ill-chosen for the ear of the king. He had extirpated the poisonous plants of Scottish growth, had introduced the true time of keeping Easter, and the orthodox tonsure; he had brought in the antiphonal harmony: and "having done all this" (of his noble apostolic labors, his conversion of the heathen, his cultivation of arts and letters, his stately buildings, his monasteries, he said nothing), "am I to pronounce my own condemnation? I appeal in full confidence to the apostolic tribunal." He was allowed to retire again to the court of Mercia. But his enemies proceeded to condemn him as contumacious. The sentence was followed by his excommunication, with circumstances of more than usual indignity and detestation. Food which had been blessed by any of Wilfrid's party was to be thrown away as an idol offering; the sacred vessels which he had used were to be cleansed from the pollution.

But the dauntless spirit of Wilfrid was unbroken, his confidence in the rightful power of the pope unshaken. At seventy years of age he again undertook the dangerous journey to Italy, again presented himself before the pope, John V. A second decree was pronounced in his favor. On his return, the archbishop, overawed, or less under the influence of the Northumbrian king, received him with respect. But the king, Aldfrid, refused all concession. "I will not alter one word of a sentence issued by myself, the archbishop, and all the dignitaries of the land, for a writing coming, as ye say, from the apostolic chair." The death of Aldfrid followed; it was attributed to the divine vengeance; and it was also given out that, on his deathbed, he had expressed deep contrition for the wrongs of Wilfrid. On the accession of Osred a new synod was held on the banks of the Nid. The A.D. 705. archbishop Berchtwald appeared with Wilfrid, and produced the apostolic decree, confirmed by the papal excommunication of all who should disobey it. The prelates and thanes seemed disposed to resist; they declared their reluctance to annul the solemn decision of the synod at Eastanfeld. The abbess Alfreda, the sister of the late king, rose, and declared the deathbed penitence of Aldfrid for his injustice. She was followed by the ealdorman, Berchfrid, the protector of the realm during the king's minority, who declared that, when hard pressed in battle by his enemies, he had vowed, if God should vouchsafe his deliverance, to espouse Wilfrid's cause. That deliverance was a manifest declaration of God in favor of Wilfrid. Amity was restored, the bishops interchanged the kiss of peace; Wilfrid reassumed the monasteries of Ripon and Hexham. The few last years of his life (he lived to the age of 76) soon glided away. He died in another monastery, which he had founded at Oundle; his remains were conveyed with great pomp to Ripon.

Death of Wilfrid. A.D. 709.

So closes the life of Wilfrid, and the first period of Christian history in England. The sad scenes of sacerdotal jealousy and strife, which made his course almost a constant feud and himself an object of unpopularity, even of persecution, are lost in the spectacle of the blessings conferred by Christianity on our Saxon ancestors. Even the wild cast of religious adventure in this life was more widely beneficial than had been a more tranquil course. As the great Prelate of the North, as a missionary, his success showed his unrivalled qualifications. As a bishop, he provoked hostility by an ecclesiastical pomp which contrasted too strongly with the general poverty, and his determination to enforce strict conformity to the authority of Rome offended the converts of the Scottish monks. His banishment into wild pagan countries and his frequent journeys to Rome, were advantageous, though in a very different manner, the former among the rude tribes to whom he preached the Gospel, the latter to his native land. He never returned to England without bringing something more valuable than Papal edicts in his own favor.[1]

The hatred of the churchmen of this time might seem reserved for each other; to all besides their influence was that of pure Christian humanity. Their quarrels died with them; the civilization which they introduced, the milder manners, the letters, the arts, the sciences survived. On the estates which the prodigal generosity of the kings, especially when they gained them from their heathen neighbors, bestowed on the Church, with the immediate manumission of the slaves, could not but tend to mitigate the general condition of that class. Some of these were probably of British descent, and so Christianity might allay even that inveterate national hostility. Nor were their own predial slaves alone directly benefited by the influence of the Churchmen. The redemption of slaves was one of the objects for which the canons allowed the alienation of their lands. Among the pious acts by which a wealthy penitent might buy off the corporal austerities demanded by the discipline of the

[1] Compare Kemble's Anglo-Saxons, ii. 432 *et seq.* I was glad to find that I had anticipated the high authority of Mr. Kemble.

Church, was the enfranchisement of his slaves. The wealth which flowed into the Church at that time in so full a stream was poured forth again in various channels for the public improvement and welfare.[1] The adversaries of Wilfrid, as well as his friends, like Benedict Biscop, were his rivals in this generous strife for the advancement of knowledge and civility. Theodorus, the archbishop, was a Greek by birth; perhaps his Greek descent made him less servilely obedient to Rome. While the other ecclesiastics were introducing the Roman literature with the Roman service, Theodorus founded a school in Canterbury for the study of Greek. He bestowed on this foundation a number of books in his native language, among them a fine copy of Homer.

Bede born 673, died 735.

The rapid progress of Christianity and her attendant civilization, appears from the life and occupations of Bede. Not much more than seventy years after the landing of Augustine on the savage, turbulent, and heathen island, in a remote part of one of the northern kingdoms of the Octarchy, visited many years later by its first Christian teacher, a native Saxon is devoting a long and peaceful life to the cultivation of letters, makes himself master of the whole range of existing knowledge in science and history as well as in theology; and writes Latin both in prose and verse, in a style equal to that of most of his contemporaries. Nor did Bede stand alone; the study of letters was promoted with equal activity by Archbishop Theodorus, and by Adrian, who having declined the

[1] Burke observes, "They extracted the fruits of virtue even from crimes, and whenever a great man expiated his private offences, he provided in the same act for the public happiness." — Abridgment of Eng. Hist. Works, x. p. 268.

archbishopric, accompanied Theodorus into the island. Aldhelm[1] of Malmesbury was only inferior in the extent of his acquirements, as a writer of Latin poetry far superior to Bede.

The uneventful life of Bede was passed in the monastery under the instructor of his earliest youth, Benedict Biscop. Its obscurity, as well as the extent of his labors, bears witness to its repose.[2] Bede stood aloof from all active ecclesiastical duties, and mingled in none of the ecclesiastical disputes. It was his office to master, and to disseminate through his writings, the intellectual treasures brought from the continent by Benedict.

Even if Bede had been gifted with original genius, he was too busy in the acquisition of learning to allow it free scope. He had the whole world of letters to unfold to his countrymen. He was the interpreter of the thoughts of ages to a race utterly unacquainted even with the names of the great men of pagan or of Christian antiquity.

The Christianity of the first converts in the Anglo-Saxon kingdoms was entirely ritual. The whole theology of some of the native teachers was contained in the Creed and the Lord's Prayer. Some of them were entirely ignorant of Latin, and for them Bede himself translated these all-sufficient manuals of Chris-

1 Aldhelm was born about 656, died 709.

2 The Pope Sergius is said to have invited Bede to Rome in order to avail himself of the erudition of so great a scholar. This invitation is doubted. — See Stevenson's Bede, on another reading in the letter adduced by William of Malmesbury. I agree with Mr. Wright (Biograph. Lit. p. 265), that it is more probable the Pope should send for Bede than for a nameless monk from the monastery at Wearmouth. It is nearly certain that Bede did not go to Rome. The death of Pope Sergius accounts very naturally for Bede's disobedience to the papal mandate, or courteous invitation.

tian faith into Anglo-Saxon.[1] Bede was the parent of theology in England. Whatever their knowledge, the earlier foreign bishops were missionaries, not writers; and the native prelates were in general fully occupied with the practical duties of their station. The theology of Bede flowed directly from the fountain of Christian doctrine, the sacred writings. It consists in commentaries on the whole Bible. But his interpretation is that which now prevailed universally in the Church. By this the whole volume is represented as a great allegory. Bede probably did little more than select from the more popular Fathers, what appeared to him the most subtle and ingenious, and therefore most true and edifying exposition. Even the New Testament, the Gospels, and Acts, have their hidden and mysterious, as well as their historical, signification. No word but enshrines a religious and typical sense.[2]

The science as the theology of Bede was that of his age — the science of the ancients (Pliny was the author chiefly followed), narrowed rather than expanded by the natural philosophy, supposed to be authorized and established by the language of the Bible.[3] Bede

[1] See the letter of Bede to Bishop Egbert, in which he enjoins him to enforce the learning these two forms by heart: "Quod non solum de laicis, id est, in populari vitâ constitutis, verum etiam de clericis sive monachis, qui Latinæ sunt linguæ expertes, fieri oportet." He urges their efficacy against the assaults of unclean spirits. — Smith's Bede, p. 306.

[2] "De rerum natura," in Giles, vol. vi.

[3] It is this Christian part of Bede's natural philosophy which alone has much interest, as showing the interworking of the biblical records of the creation, now the popular belief, into the old traditionary astronomy derived by the Romans from the Greeks; and so becoming the science of Latin Christendom. The creation by God, the creation in six days, is of course the groundwork of Bede's astronomical science. The earth is the centre and primary object of creation. The heaven is of a fiery and subtile nature, round, equidistant in every part, as a canopy, from the centre of the earth. It turns round every day, with ineffable rapidity, only moderated by the

had read some of the great writers, especially the poets of antiquity. He had some familiarity with Virgil, Ovid, Lucan, Statius, and even Lucretius. This is shown in his treatises on Grammar and Metre. His own poetry is the feeble echo of humbler masters, the Christian poets, Prudentius, Sedulius, Arator, Juvencus, which were chiefly read in the schools of that time. It may be questioned, however, whether many of the citations from ancient authors, often adduced from mediæval writers, as indicating their knowledge of such authors, are more than traditionary, almost proverbial, insulated passages, brilliant fragments, broken off from antiquity, and reset again and again by writers borrowing them from each other, but who had never read another word of the lost poet, orator, or philosopher.

resistance of the seven planets, — three above the sun: Saturn, Jupiter, Mars, then the Sun; three below: Venus, Mercury, the Moon. The stars go round in their fixed courses; the northern perform the shortest circle. The highest heaven has its proper limit; it contains the angelic virtues, who descend upon earth, assume ethereal bodies, perform human functions, and return. The heaven is tempered with glacial waters, lest it should be set on fire: the inferior heaven is called the firmament, because it separates these superincumbent waters from the waters below. These firmamental waters are lower than the spiritual heavens, higher than all corporeal beings, reserved, some say, for a second deluge, others more truly, to temper the fire of the stars. The rest of Bede's system on the motions of the planets and stars, on winds, thunder, light, the rainbow, the tides, belongs to the history of philosophy. His work on the Nature of Things is curious as showing a monk, on the wild shores of Northumberland, so soon after the Christianization of the island, busying himself with such profound questions, if not observing, recording the observations of others on the causes of natural phenomena; learning all that he could learn, teaching all he had learned, in the Latin of his time; promoting at least, and pointing the way to these important studies. Bede's chronological labors (he was a strenuous advocate for the shorter Hebrew chronology of the Old Testament, in order to establish his favorite theory, so long dominant in theology, of the six ages of the world) implied and displayed powers of calculation rare at that time in Latin Christianity, in England probably unrivalled, if not standing absolutely alone. — Epist. ad Pleguin., Giles, i. p. 145.

The works of Bede were written for a very small intellectual aristocracy. To all but a few among the monks and clergy, Latin was a foreign language, in which they recited, with no clear apprehension of its meaning, the ordinary ritual.[1]

But even at this earlier period, Christianity seized and pressed into her service the more effective vehicle of popular instruction, the vernacular poetry. No doubt from the first there must have been some rude preaching in the vulgar tongue, but the extant Anglo-Saxon homilies are of a later date. Cædmon, however, the greatest of the Anglo-Saxon poets, flourished during the youth of Bede. So marvellous did the songs of Cædmon (pouring forth as they did the treasures of biblical poetry, the sublime mysteries of the Creation, the Fall, the wonders of the Hebrew history, the gentler miracles of the New Testament, the terrors of the judgment, the torments of hell, the bliss of heaven) sound to the popular ear, that they could be attributed to nothing less than divine inspiration. The youth and early aspirations of Cædmon were invested at once in a mythic character like the old poets of India and of Greece, but in the form of Christian miracle.

The Saxons, no doubt, brought their poetry from their native forests. Their bards were a recognized order: in all likelihood in the halls of the kings of the Octarchy, the bard had his seat of honor, and while he quaffed the mead, sang the victories of the thanes

[1] See above, quotation from Epist. to Egbert. Bede adds, that for this purpose he had himself translated the Creed and Lord's Prayer into the vernacular Anglo-Saxon. "Propter quod et ipse multis sæpe sacerdotibus idiotis, hæc quoque utraque, et symbolum videlicet, et Dominicam orationem, in linguam Anglorum translata obtuli." — Epist. ad Egbert. His birth is uncertain; he died about 680.

and kings over the degenerate Roman and fugitive Briton. Of these lays some fragments remain, earlier probably than the introduction of Christianity, but tinged with Christian allusion in their later tradition from bard to bard: such are the Battle of Conisborough, the Traveller's Song, and the Romance of Beowulf.[1] The profoundly religious mind of Cædmon could not endure to learn these profane songs of adventure and battle, or the lighter and more mirthful strains. When his turn came to sing in the hall, and the harp was handed to him, he was wont to withdraw in silence and in shame.[2] One evening he had retired from the hall; it was that night his duty to tend the cattle; he fell asleep. A form appeared to him in a vision and said, "Sing, O Cædmon!" Cædmon replied, "that he knew not how to sing, he knew no subject for a song." "Sing," said the visitant, "the Creation." The thoughts and the words flashed upon the mind of Cædmon, and the next morning his memory retained the verses, which Bede thought so sublime in the native language as to be but feebly rendered in the Latin.

The wonder reached the ears of the famous Hilda, the abbess of Whitby: it was at once ascribed to the grace of God. Cædmon was treated as one inspired. He could not read, he did not understand Latin. But when any passage of the Bible was interpreted to him, or any of the sublime truths of religion unfolded, he sat for some time in quiet rumination, and poured it

[1] Kemble's Beowulf, with preface.

[2] "Unde nonnunquam in conviviis, cum esset lætitiæ causâ, et omnes per ordinem cantare deberent, ille ubi appropinquare sibi citharam cernebat, surgebat a mediâ cœnâ, et egressus ad suam domum repedabat." — Bede, H. E. iv. c. 24.

all forth in that brief alliterative verse, which kindled and enchanted his hearers. Thus was the whole history of the Bible, and the whole creed of Christianity, in the imaginative form which it then wore, made at once accessible to the Anglo-Saxon people. Cædmon's poetry was their bible, no doubt far more effective in awakening and changing the popular mind than a literal translation of the Scriptures could have been. He chose, by the natural test of his own kindred sympathies, all which would most powerfully work on the imagination, or strike to the heart, of a rude yet poetic race.

The Anglo-Saxon was the earliest vernacular Christian poetry, a dim prophecy of what that poetry might become in Dante and Milton. While all the Greek and Latin poetry labored with the difficulties of an uncongenial diction and form of verse; and at last was but a cold dull paraphrase of that which was already, in the Greek and in the Vulgate Bible, far nobler poetry, though without the technical form of verse; the Anglo-Saxon had some of the freedom and freshness of original poetry. Its brief, sententious, and alliterative cast seemed not unsuited to the parallelism of the Hebrew verse; and perhaps the ignorance of Cædmon kept him above the servility of mere translation.[1]

Aldhelm of Malmesbury was likewise skilled in the vernacular poetry; but though he used it for the purpose of religious instruction, it does not seem to have

[1] The poetry of Cædmon may be judged by the admirable translations in the volume on Anglo-Saxon poetry by J. J. Coneybeare. The whole has been edited, with his fulness of Anglo-Saxon learning, by Mr. Thorpe; London, 1832. Mr. Coneybeare may to a certain degree have Miltonized the simple Anglo-Saxon; but he has not done more than justice to his vigor and rude boldness.

been written verse, though one of his songs survived in the popular voice for some time.[1] What he no doubt considered the superior majesty or sanctity of the Latin was alone suited for such mysterious subjects. Of Aldhelm it is recorded that he saw with sorrow the little effect which the services of religion had on the peasantry, who either listened with indifference to the admonitions of the preacher, or returned home utterly forgetful of his words. He stationed himself therefore on a bridge over which they must pass, in the garb of a minstrel, and when he had arrested the crowd and fully inthralled their attention by the sweetness of his song, he gradually introduced into his profane and popular lay some of the solemn truths of religion. Thus he succeeded in awakening a deeper devotion and won many hearts to the faith, which he would have attempted in vain to move by severer language, or even by the awful excommunication of the church. What he himself no doubt despised, his vernacular verse, in comparison with the lame stateliness of his poor hexameters, ought to have been his pride.

Among a people accustomed to the association of music, however rude, with their poetry, the choral ser-

[1] "Nativæ quippe linguæ non negligebat carmina, adeo ut teste libro Elfredi, de quo superius dixi, nullâ unquam ætate par ei fuerat uspiam poesin Anglicam posse facere, tantum componere, eadem appositè vel canere vel dicere. Denique commemorat Elfredus carmen triviale Adhelmum fecisse; adjiciens causam qua probet rationaliter tantum virum his quæ videntur frivola institisse. Populum eo tempore semibarbarum, parum divinis sermonibus intentum, statim cantatis missis domos cursitare solitum: ideoque sanctum virum, super pontem qui rura et urbem continuat, abeuntibus se opposuisse obicem, quasi artem cantandi professum. Eo plus quam semel facto, plebis favorem et concursum emeritum hoc commento, sensim inter ludicra verbis scripturarum insertis, cives ad sanitatem reduxisse, qui si severè et *cum excommunicatione* agendum putasset, profecto profecisset nihil." — W. Malmesb. Vit. Adhelm.; Wharton, Anglia Sacra, p. 4.

vice of the church must have been peculiarly impressive. The solemn Gregorian system of chanting was now established in Rome, and was introduced into England by the Roman clergy and by those who visited Rome, with zealous activity. Here, though opposed on some points, Archbishop Theodorus and Wilfrid acted in perfect amity.[1] In Kent the music of the church had almost from the first formed a part of the divine worship, and James the Deacon, the companion of Paulinus, had taught it in Northumbria. It is recorded to the praise of Theodorus that on his visitation throughout the island he introduced everywhere that system of chanting which had hitherto been practised in Kent alone; and among the important services to the church, of which Wilfrid boasted before the synod of Eastrefield, is the introduction of antiphonal chanting.[2] So much importance was attached to this part of the service, that Pope Agatho permitted John, the chief of the Roman choir, to accompany Benedict Biscop to England[3] in order to instruct the monks of Wearmouth in singing: John gave lessons throughout Northumbria.

Even at this early period the Anglo-Saxon laws are strongly impregnated with the dominant Christianity: they are the laws of kings, whose counsellors, if not their co-legislators, are prelates. In those of King Ina of Wessex, either the parent or the priest is bound to bring, or force to be brought, the infant to holy bap-

[1] Bede, H. E. iv. 2.

[2] "Aut quomodo juxta ritum primitivæ ecclesiæ consono vocis modulamine binis astantibus choris persultare, responsoriis antiphonisque reciprocis instruerem." — Eddius, c. 45.

[3] Bede, H. E. iv. 18. On this and on the pictures brought from Rome on more than one occasion, compare Wright, Biographia Literaria, Life of B. Biscop.

tism within thirty days under a penalty of thirty shillings;[1] if he should die unbaptized, the wehrgeld of this spiritual death is the whole possessions of the guilty person. Spiritual relationship was placed in the same rank with natural affinity. The godfather claimed the wehrgeld for the death of his godson, the godson for that of the godfather. Sunday was hallowed by law. The slave who worked by his lord's command was free, and the lord paid a fine; if by his own will, without his lord's knowledge, he suffered corporal chastisement. If the free man worked on the holy day without his lord's command, he lost his freedom or paid a compensation of sixty shillings.

Already the awful church had acquired a recognized right of sanctuary. The nature of kirk shot, a payment of certain corn and seed as first fruits, is somewhat obscure, whether paid to the church as the church, or to the church only from lands held of the church. The laws of Kent, during the archiepiscopate of Berchtwald, protect the Sabbath, punish certain immoralities, and guarantee all grants of lands to the church: there are even exemptions from secular imposts.

Thus, then, in less than a century and a half from the landing of Augustine to the death of Bede, above half a century before the conflicting kingdoms were consolidated into one monarchy, every one of these kingdoms had become Christian. Each had its bishop or bishops. Kent had its metropolitan see of Canterbury and the bishopric of Rochester; Essex, London; East Anglia, Dunwich, afterwards under Archbishop Theodorus Elmham, removed later to Nor- A.D. 597-735.

[1] Thorpe, vol. i. p. 103; Kemble, ii. 490 *et seq.* et append. D.

wich: late-converted Sussex had Selsey; Wessex, Winchester, afterwards also Sherburn. The great kingdom of Mercia at first was subject to the single Bishop of Lichfield; Leicester, Worcester, Hereford, and Sidmanchester in Lindesay were severed from that vast diocese. The province of York, according to Archbishop Theodorus's scheme, was to comprehend York, Hexham, and Lindisfarne. Hexham fell in the Danish invasions; Lindisfarne was removed to Durham; a see at Ripon saw but one bishop; the modern bishopric of Carlisle may be considered the successor of the bishopric of Whitherne in Galloway. Above these rose the Metropolitan of Canterbury; after some
A.D. 785. struggle for its independence that of York. As in all the Teutonic kingdoms the hierarchy became a coördinate aristocracy, taking their seats as representatives of the nation in the witenagemote,[1] counsellors of the king as great territorial lords, sitting later as nobles with the earls, as magistrates with the ealdermen. Besides their share in the national councils, as a separate body they hold their own synods, in which they enact laws for all their Christian subjects — at Hertford, at Hatfield, at Cloveshoo probably near Tewkesbury (Cloveshoo was appointed as the place of meeting for an annual synod), later at Calcuith supposed to be in Kent. Peaceful monasteries arise in all quarters; monasteries in the strict sense, and also conventual establishments, in which the clergy dwell together, and from their religious centres radiate around and dissem-

[1] As in all the Teutonic kingdoms, the province of the Witan, or parliament, and the synod, were by no means distinctly comprehended or defined. The great national council, the Witan, in its sovereign capacity, passed laws on ecclesiastical subjects; the synods at least occasionally trenched on the civil laws.

inate Christianity through the land. Each great church, certainly each cathedral, had its monastery, the priests of which were not merely the officiating clergy of the church, but the missionaries in all the surrounding districts. Christianity became the law of the land, the law underwent the influence of Christianity. The native Teutonic religion, except in a few usages and superstitions, has absolutely disappeared. The heathen Danes, when they arrive, find no vestige of their old kindred faith in tribes sprung not many centuries before from the same Teutonic races. The Roman arts, which the fierce and savage Jutes and Angles had obliterated from the land, revive in another form. Besides the ecclesiastical Latin, a Teutonic literature has begun; the German bards have become Christian poets. No sooner has Anglo-Saxon Britain become one (no doubt her religious unity must have contributed, if imperceptibly, yet in a great degree to her national unity) than she takes her place among the confederation of European kingdoms.

CHAPTER V.

CONVERSION OF THE TEUTONIC RACES BEYOND THE ROMAN EMPIRE.

While the early Christianity of these islands retired before the Saxon conquerors to Wales, to the Scottish Hebrides, and to Ireland, and looked on the heathen invaders as hopeless and irreclaimable Pagans, beyond the pale of Christian charity, and from whom it was a duty, the duty of irreconcilable hatred, to withhold the Gospel, that faith was flowing back upon the continent of Europe in a gentle but almost continuous tide. In Anglo-Saxon England it was only after a century, that, on the invitation of the Northumbrian king already converted by Roman missionaries, the monks from Iona, and from some, perhaps, of the Irish monasteries, left their solitudes, and commenced their mission of love.

Conversion of Germans.

But already, even before the landing of Augustine in England, an Irish monk has found his way to the continent, and is commencing the conversion of German tribes in a region, if within the older frontier of the Roman territory, reduced again to the possession of heathen Teutonic tribes: and from that time out of these islands go forth the chief apostles of Germany. Columban is the forerunner, by at least a century, of the holy Boniface.[1]

[1] Columban lived at the end of the sixth and the beginning of the seventh century.

It is difficult to conceive the motives which led forth these first pious wanderers from their native land. Columban, at his outset, was no missionary, urged by a passionate or determined zeal to convert Pagan nations to the Cross of Christ; nor was he a pilgrim, lured forth from his retreat by the unconquerable desire of visiting the scenes of apostolic labors, the spiritual wonders of Rome, or to do homage to the relics of Saints or Apostles. He and his followers seemed only to seek a safe retreat in which he might shroud his solitary devotion; or, if his ascetic fame should gather around him an increasing number of disciples, form a cœnobitic establishment. They might have found, it might be supposed, retirement not less secure against secular intrusion, as wild, as silent, as holy, in the yet peaceful Ireland, or in the Scottish islands, as in the mountains of the Vosges or the valleys of the Alps.[1]

St. Columban

But the influence of Columban, as the parent of so many important monasteries on the borders and within the frontier of Teutonic Paganism, as well as the reverence with which his holy character was invested, and which enabled him to assert the moral dignity of Christianity with such intrepidity, are events which strongly mark the religious history of this age. The stranger monk issues from his retreat to rebuke the vices of kings, confronts the cruel Brunehaut, and such is the fearful sanctity which environs the man of God, that even her deadly hostility can venture nothing beyond his banishment.

Columban was born in Leinster, at the period when Ireland is described as a kind of Hesperian elysium of

[1] Mabillon, Ann. Benedict., vol. i. p. 191.

His birth. peace and piety. His early aspirations after monastic holiness were fostered in the convent of Banchor, on the coast of Ulster. He became a proficient in the mystic piety of the day. But he was suddenly seized with the desire of foreign travel; he wrung an unwilling consent to his departure from his spiritual father, Comgal, abbot of Banchor. He just touched on, but shrunk from, the contaminated shores of Paganized Britain, and landed in Gaul. The fame of his piety reached the ears of one of the kings of the land: all that Columban requested was permission to retire into some unapproachable wilderness.

The woody mountains of the Vosges rose on the frontiers of the kingdoms of Austrasia and of Burgundy. Tribes of Pagan Suevians then occupied that part of Switzerland which bordered on those kingdoms. War and devastation had restored as solitudes to nature districts which had been reclaimed to culture and fertility by the industry of Roman colonists. It was on the site of ancient towns that hermits now found their wildernesses. Columban, with his twelve followers, first settled among the ruins of a small town called Anegratis. The woods yielded herbs and roots and the bark of trees for food, the streams water and probably fish. But the offerings of piety were not wanting; provisions were sent by those who were desirous of profiting by the prayers of these holy men. But the heart of Columban yearned for still more profound solitude. In the depths of the wild woods, about seven miles off, as he wandered with his book, he found a cave, of which the former inhabitant, a bear, gave up quiet possession to the saint — for the wild beasts, wolves as well as bears and the Pagan

In Alsace, about A.D. 590.

Suevians, respected the man of God. Miracle as usual arose around the founder of a monastery. The fame of the piety and wonder-working powers of Columban gathered a still increasing number of votaries; the ruins of Anegratis could no longer contain the candidates for the monastic life.

About eight miles distant lay the more extensive ruins of a fortified Roman town, Luxovium,[1] now overgrown with the wild forest jungle, but formerly celebrated for its warm springs. Amid the remains of splendid baths and other stately buildings, Columban determined to establish a more regular monastery. The forest around is said to have been strewn with marble statues, and magnificent vestiges of the old Pagan worship. On this wreck of heathenism rose the monastery of Luxeuil. Neophytes crowded from all parts; the nobles of the court threw off their arms, or fled from the burdensome duties of civil life to this holy retreat. A second establishment became necessary, and in a beautiful spot, watered by several streams, rose the succursal abbey of Fontaines. Columban presided as abbot over all these institutions. His delight was ever to wander alone in the woods, or to dwell for days in his lonely cave. But he still exercised strict superintendence over all the monasteries of the Rule which he had formed; he mingled in and encouraged their useful labors in husbandry, it was thought, with more than human wisdom and sagacity.

1 "Invenitque castrum firmissimo munimine olim fuisse cultum, a supradicto loco distans plus minus octo millibus quem prisca tempora Luxovium appellabant: ibique aquæ calidæ cultu eximio extructæ habebantur. Ibi imaginum lapidearum densitas vicinos saltus densabat, quas cultu miserabili rituque profano vetusta paganorum templa honorabant." — Jonas, Vit. Columb. c. 9.

But peace was not to be found even in the lonely forests of the Vosges. After twelve years of undisturbed repose, religious disputes invaded the quiet shades of Luxeuil. Columban was arraigned before a synod of Gaulish bishops for his heterodox usage about keeping Easter, in which he adhered to the old British discipline. Columban answered with a kind of pathetic dignity, "I am not the author of this difference. I came as a stranger to this land for the sake of our common Lord and Saviour Christ. I beseech you by that common Lord who shall judge us all, to allow me to live in silence, in peace, and in charity, as I have lived for twelve years, beside the bones of my seventeen departed brethren. Let Gaul receive into her bosom all those who, if they deserve it, will be received into the kingdom of heaven."

Dispute with Gaulish bishops.

Columban had to wage a nobler strife against the vices of the neighboring court. The famous Brunehaut had fled from the kingdom of the elder of her royal grandchildren, Theodebert of Austrasia, and taken refuge with the younger, Thierri, King of Burgundy. She ruled the realm by the ascendency of that strong and unscrupulous mind which for above forty years had raised her into a rival of that more famous Fredegonde, her rival in the number of her paramours, and in the number of murders which she had perpetrated.[1] She ruled the king through his vices. Thierri had degenerated, like the

Queen Brunehaut and King Thierri.

About A.D. 606.

[1] It was not till 613 that she met with a death horrible as her own crimes. Exposed on a camel to the derision of the camp of her enemy, King Chlotaire, she was tied to the tail of a wild horse, and literally torn to shreds. — H. Martin, p. 139. What wonder that in such days men sought refuge in the wilderness, and almost adored hermits like Columban!

rest of the race of Clovis, from the old Teutonic virtues, and plunged headlong into Roman license. In vain his subjects had attempted to wean him from his countless mistresses by a marriage with the daughter of the Visigothic king. Neglected, mortified, persecuted by the arts of Brunehaut, the unhappy princess returned to her home. Already Brunehaut had resisted the remonstrances of Didier, Bishop of Vienne, who had rebuked the incontinence of Thierri and his ill-usage of his wife. Didier was murdered on his road from Lyons to Vienne. The fame of Columban induced Thierri to visit his saintly retirement. Columban seized the opportunity to reproach him for his adulteries, and to persuade him that the safety of his realm depended on his having a legitimate heir. Thierri listened with awe to the man of God ; he promised to act according to his wise counsels. Even Brunehaut, the murderer of bishops, dared not lay her hand on him. Brunehaut saw her power in danger. Whether she sought the interview in the vain hope of softening him by her blandishments, or whether he came of his own accord, Columban visited the queen in her palace. The stern virtue of the saint was not to be moved. Brunehaut approached him, and entreated his blessing on two illegitimate sons of Thierri. (The benediction of the saint seems to have had some connection with their hopes of succession to the throne ; to which, according to Frankish usage, legitimacy was not indispensable.) "These bastards, born in sin," replied Columban, "shall never inherit the kingdom." He passed away unmolested through the awe-struck court. Brunehaut began a petty and vexatious warfare, by cutting off the supplies from the monasteries, and stirring up jealousies with other neighboring convents. Either to remonstrate, or to avert the royal anger, Columban again approached the court, then held at the village of Epaisses,[1] but he refused to enter under the roof. Thierri ordered a royal banquet to be prepared and sent out to the saint at the door. "It is written," said Columban, "that God abhors the offerings of the wicked; his servants must not be polluted with food given by those who persecute his saints." He dashed the wine on the earth and scattered about the other viands. The affrighted king again promised amendment, but abstained not from his notorious adulteries. Columban then addressed to him a letter, in which he lashed his vices with unsparing severity, and threatened him with excommunication.[2] The king could bear no more; he appealed to his nobles, he appealed to his bishops, knowing no doubt their jealousy of the stranger monk and their dislike of some of his usages. He demanded free ingress and egress for his servants into the monastery. Columban haughtily replied, "that if he dared thus to infringe the monastic rule, his kingdom would fall, and his whole race be cut off." When Thierri himself attempted to enter the refectory, he shrunk before the intrepid demeanor and terrible language of the abbot. Yet with some shrewdness he observed, "Do not think that I will gratify your pride by making you a martyr." To a sentence of banishment the stranger monk replied, that he would not be driven from his monastery but by force. At length a man was found who did not quail before the saint. Columban was arrested, and carried

[1] The villa Brocarica, Bourcheresse, between Châlons and Autun. — H. Martin, Histoire de la France, ii. 160.

[2] Jonas describes the letter as "verberibus plenas."

to Besançon; but even there his guards, from awe, performed their duty so negligently that he escaped and returned to Luxeuil. Again he was seized, not without difficulty, and carried off amid the lamentations of his faithful followers. Two or three Irish monks alone were permitted to accompany him. He was hurried in rude haste toward Nantes; at Orleans he was not allowed to enter the church, hardly permitted to visit the shrine of St. Martin at Tours; and embarked on board a vessel bound to Ireland.

Columban banished.

During all this journey the harsh usage of the royal officers was mitigated by the wondering reverence of the people: it is described as a continued scene of miracle. The language attributed to Columban by his admiring biographer shows not only the privilege assumed by the monastic saints of that day, of dispensing with the humble tone of meekness and charity, but also the fearless equality, or rather superiority, with which a foreign monk thus addresses the kings of the land. "Why are you retiring hitherward?" said the Bishop of Tours. "Because that dog Thierri has driven me away from my brethren." To another he said, "Tell thy friend Thierri that within three years he and his children shall perish, and God will root up his whole race." In those days such prophecies concerning one of the royal families of the Franks was almost sure of its fulfilment.

Journey through France.

Columban was justified in the estimation of men, even of kings, in taking this lofty tone. The vessel in which he was embarked was cast back on the coast of Neustria. The King Clothaire II. humbly solicited the saint to hallow his kingdom by making it his residence. Columban declined the offer,

Return to France.

and passed into Austrasia, where King Theodebert received him with the same respectful deference.

The monks from Luxeuil flocked around their beloved master; but Columban declined likewise the urgent entreaties of Theodebert to bless his kingdom by the establishment of a monastery. He yearned for wilder solitudes. With his followers he went to Moguntiacum (Mentz), and embarked upon the Rhine. They worked their way up the stream till they reached the mouth of the Limmat, and followed that river into the lake of Zurich. From the shores of the lake they went by land to Tugium (the modern Zug). Around them were the barbarous heathen Suevians. Columban and his disciples had little of the gentle and winning perseverance of missionaries; they had been accustomed to dictate to trembling sovereigns. Their haughty and violent demeanor, which overawed those who had been brought up in Christianity, provoked the Pagans, instead of weaning them from their idolatries. A strange tale is told of a huge vat of beer, offered to the god Woden, which burst at the mere breath of Columban. St. Gall, his companion,[1] set their temples on fire, and threw their idols into the lake. The monks were compelled to fly; and Columban left the Pagans of that district with a most unapostolic malediction, devoting their whole race to temporal misery and eternal perdition.[2] They retreated to Arbon, on the lake of Constance; there, from

Zug.

[1] The history of St. Gall is related in more than one form in Pertz, tom. ii. p. 1–34.

[2] "Fiant niti eorum in interitum; ergo ad mediam ætatem cum pervenerint stupor ac dementia eos apprehendant, ita ut alieno ære oppressi, ignominiam suam agnoscant conversi." — Vita S. Galli, apud Pertz, ii. p. 7.

a Christian priest, named Willimar, they heard of a ruined Roman city at the end of the lake, named Brigetium (Bregenz). At Brigetium Columban found a ruined church dedicated to St. Aurelia, which he rebuilt. But the chief objects of worship in the re-Paganized land were three statues of gilded brass. St. Gall preached to the people in their own language. He then broke their idols in pieces, and threw them into the water: part of his hearers applauded, but some departed in undisguised anger.

Bregenz.

In this remote spot they built their monastery. St. Gall was a skilful fisherman, and supplied the brethren with fresh fish from the lake. One silent night, when he was fishing, he heard (it is said), from the highest peak, the voice of the Spirit of the Mountains calling on the Spirit of the Waters in the depth of the lake. "I am here," was the reply. "Arise, then, to mine aid against these strangers who have cast me from my temple; let us expel them from the land." "One of them is even now busied in my waters, but I cannot break his nets, for I am rebuked by the prevailing name, in which he is perpetually praying."[1]

St. Gall.

The human followers of the Pagan deities were not so easily controlled. After two or three years the monks found a confederacy formed against them, at the head of which was a neighboring chieftain, the savage Cunzo.[2] Columban determined to retire. He

1 This story is too picturesque and striking to be omitted. It is characteristic, too, to find the divinities to which the Greeks would have attributed such sights and sounds, turned into malignant spirits. Two naked girls were bathing in a stream in which St. Gall was fishing. Of old they would have passed for nymphs; with him they were devils in that enticing shape. Sounds which they hear on the mountains, when catching hawks, are voices of devils.

2 Cunzo's daughter is said to have been betrothed to King Thierri.

had some thoughts of attempting the conversion of the Slavi and the Veneti; but an angel, perhaps the approach of age, admonished him to seek a quiet retreat in Italy. He was honorably received by Agilulf, King of Lombardy. After some time spent in literary labors, in confutation of the Arianism which still lingered in that part of Italy, he founded the famous monastery of Bobbio.[1]

St. Gall, from real or simulated illness, remained behind. He withdrew with his boat and fishing nets to Arbon; he was accompanied by some of the Irish monks, and in that neighborhood founded the monastery, not less celebrated, which bore his name.

Founders of monasteries.

Thus these Irish monks were not merely reinvigorating the decaying monastic spirit, which perhaps was languishing from the extreme severity of the rule of Cassianus chiefly followed in the monasteries of Gaul, but they were winning back districts which had been won from Roman civilization by advancing barbarism. Monasteries replaced ruined Roman cities. From them issued almost a race of saints, the founders of some of the most important establishments within or on the borders of the old Roman territory: Magnus and Theodorus, the first abbots

[1] I follow the early life of St. Gall in Pertz, from which was derived that of Walafrid Strabo. Jonas, the biographer of Columban, represents him as still persecuted by Brunehaut and Thierri, who may indeed have excited the confederacy against him. Jonas also carries Columban back to the court of Theodebert, King of Austrasia, whom, when in the height of his power, he endeavors to persuade to take the clerical habit. "When was it heard," was the indignant reply, "that a Merovingian on the throne stooped to become a clerk?" "If you become not one voluntarily," said the prophetic monk, "you will so by compulsion!" Theodebert afterwards, defeated by Brunehaut and the King of Burgundy, was forced to take orders, and then put to death. The history probably produced the prophecy.—Jonas, c. 27. Columban died about A.D. 615.

of Kempten and of Fussen; Attalus of Bobbio; St. Romaric of Remiremont; St. Omer, St. Bertin, St. Amand, the apostles of Flanders; St. Wandrille, the founder of Fontenelle, in Normandy.[1] Gradually the great establishments, founded on the rule of Columban, dropped the few peculiarities of discipline which distinguished them from the Roman Church; they retained those of their rule which differed from that of St. Benedict which was now beginning to prevail throughout western Christendom. Yet there was nothing of great importance to distinguish them from the Benedictine foundations; their rule, habits, studies (all, perhaps, but their dress) were those of western monasticism.[2]

English missionaries.

Columban and his immediate followers had hardly extended the influence of Christianity beyond the borders of the old Roman empire. But, important as outposts on the verge of Christendom, or even in districts which had reverted to barbarism, gradually encircling themselves with an enlarging belt of cultivation and of Christianity, they were only thus gradually and indirectly aggressive. Another century had nearly elapsed when the Apostle of Germany came forth from a different part of the British Isles. Those Saxon conquerors whom Columban, when he touched the shores of Britain, left behind as irreclaimable heathens, had now become Christians from one end of the land to the other. In their turn they were to send out their saintly and more adventurous missionaries into their native German forests. Wilfrid of York had already made some progress in

1 Michelet, Hist. de France, i. 275.
2 Mabillon, Hist. Ordin. Benedict., i. p. 195.

the conversion of the Frisians on the lower part of the Rhine; but almost all beyond the Rhine, when Boniface undertook the conversion of Germany, was the undisputed domain of the old Teutonic idolatry.

St. Boniface.

Boniface (his proper Saxon name was Winfrid) was born near Crediton, in Devonshire. From his infancy he is said to have displayed a disposition to singular piety; and in his youth the influence of his father could not repress his inclination to the monastic life. The father, alarmed by a dangerous illness, yielded to the wishes of the boy, who was received into a monastery at Exeter; afterwards he moved to Netley. Having completed his studies, he was ordained priest at thirty; and a confidential mission on which he was employed between a synod of the clergy and the Archbishop Berchtwald shows the estimation in which he was already held. But Boniface was eager for the more adventurous life of a missionary. His first enterprise was discouraging, and might have repressed less earnest zeal. With the permission of his superiors he embarked at London, landed on the coast of Friesland, and made his way to Utrecht. But Radbold, King of Frisia, at war with one of the Frankish kings, had commenced a fierce persecution of the Christians; everywhere he had destroyed the churches, and rebuilt the temples. Boniface found his eloquence wasted on the stubborn heart of the pagan, and returned to England.

About A.D. 700.

In Friesland. About A.D. 716.

But his spirit was impatient of repose. He determined to visit Rome, perhaps to obtain the sanction of the head of Western Christendom for new attempts to propagate the Gospel in Germany. He

About A.D. 718.

crossed the sea to Normandy, and with a multitude of other pilgrims journeyed through France, paying his adorations in all the more famous churches; escaped the dangers of the snowy Alps, the Lombards, who treated him with unexpected humanity, and the predatory soldiery, which were prowling about in all directions. He found himself, at length, on his knees in the Church of St. Peter. He was received, on the presentation of recommendatory letters from his bishop, with condescending welcome.

In Rome.
A.D. 717-8.

The Pope, Gregory II. (our history will revert to the intermediate succession of popes; we are now in the eighth century), entered into all the views of Boniface, and sanctioned his passionate wish to ascertain how far the most savage tribes of Germany would receive the Gospel. Gregory bestowed upon him ample powers, but exacted an oath of allegiance to the Roman see. He recommended him to all the bishops and to all orders of Christians, above all to Charles Martel,[1] who, as mayor of the palace exercised royal authority in that part of France. He urged Charles to assist the missionary by all means in his power in the pious work of reclaiming the heathen from the state of brute-beasts.[2] And Charles Martel faithfully fulfilled the wishes of the Pope. "Without the protection of the prince of the Franks," writes the grateful Boniface, "I could neither rule the people, nor defend the priests, the monks, and the handmaids of God, nor prevent pagan and idolatrous rites in Germany."[3] The Pope attributes the spiritual subjugation

Gregory II.
A.D. 715-730.

A.D. 719.

1 See the letter in which Charles takes him under his mundebund or defence.—Apud Giles, i. 37.

2 Gregor. II., Epist. iv. v. vi.

3 Bonifac., Epist. xii., apud Giles, to Daniel, Bishop of Winchester.

of a hundred thousand barbarians by the holy Boniface to the aid of Charles.[1]

Armed with these powers, and with a large stock of relics, Boniface crossed the Alps and entered into Thuringia. This province was already in part Christian; but their Christianity required much correction (they were probably Arians), and the clergy were in no way disposed to that rigid celibacy now required of their order. Boniface did all in his power, but, notwithstanding the urgent addresses of the Pope himself to the Thuringians, by no means with complete success; they still resisted the monastic discipline. When he left Thuringia he heard of the death of Radbold? the pagan king of Friesland. He immediately embarked on the Rhine, in the hope of renewing, under better auspices, his attempts on that country. For three years he labored there with great success, as the humble assistant of the Bishop Willibrod. Again the temples fell, and the churches rose. Willibrod felt the approach of age, and desired to secure as his coadjutor, as the future successor to his bishopric, a youthful teacher of so much zeal and wisdom. The humility of Boniface struggled against the offers, the arguments, the earnest entreaties of the Prelate. He pleaded that he was not yet fifty, the canonical age of a bishop. At length he declared that he had been employed on a special service by the Pope to propagate the Gospel in Germany; he had already delayed too long in Friesland; he dared not decline, without the direct mandate of the Pope, his more imperative and arduous duties as a missionary.

In Thuringia.

In Friesland. A.D. 719.

Our curiosity, and higher feelings, are vividly ex-

[1] Sirmond. Concil. ii. p. 527.

cited by the thought of the earliest preachers of Christianity plunging into the unknown depths of the German forests, addressing the Gospel of peace to fierce and warlike tribes, encountering the strange and perhaps appalling superstitions of ages, penetrating into hallowed groves, and standing before altars reeking with human blood.[1] We expect the kindling adventure of romance to mingle with the quiet and steady course of Christian benevolence and self-sacrifice; at least perpetually to meet with incidents which may throw light on the old Teutonic character, the habits, manners, institutions of the various tribes. The biographers of the saints are in general barren of this kind of information; they rarely enter into details on the nature or the rites of the old religions; they speak of them in one sweeping tone of abhorrence; they condemn the gods under the vague term of idols, or adopt the Roman usage of naming them after the deities of Greece and Rome. On the miracles of their own saints they are diffuse and particular; but on the power, attributes, and worship of the heathen gods, except on a few occasions, they are almost silent. Boniface, it is said, on his first expedition among the Saxons and Hessians, baptized thousands, destroyed the heathen temples, and set up Christian churches. As a faithful servant he communicated his wonderful successes to Rome; he was sum-

Silence of Christian writers about Paganism.

Boniface invited to Rome, 722. In Rome, 723. Ordained bishop, 723.

[1] Read (it is however on this subject quite vague) the counsel given to his countrymen, as to the mode of arguing with the heathen, by Daniel, Bishop of Winchester, as seen from his letters, in which he advises Boniface to keep on good terms even with the wicked clergy of France. It is curious, that he was to contrast the fertile lands of the Christians, flowing with oil and wine, and abounding in wealth, with the cold and dreary deserts left to the pagans and their gods. — Epist. xiv. i. 48.

moned to the metropolis of Christianity, and, after a profession of faith in the Trinity, which would bear the searching inquisition of Rome,[1] he was raised to the dignity of a bishop. On his return to Germany, Boniface found but few of his Hessian proselytes adhering to pure Christianity. They had made a wild mixture of the two creeds; they still worshipped their sacred groves and fountains; some yet offered sacrifices on their old altars. The wizards and soothsayers still maintained their influence; the trembling worshippers still acknowledged the might of their charms and the truth of their omens.

The oak of Geismar.

Boniface determined to strike a blow at the heart of the obstinate Paganism. There was an old and venerable oak,[2] of immense size, in the grove of Geismar, hallowed for ages to the Thunderer. Attended by all his clergy, Boniface went publicly forth to fell this tree. The pagans assembled in multitudes to behold this trial of strength between their ancient gods and the God of the stranger. They awaited the issue in profound silence. Some, no doubt, expected the axe to recoil on the sacrilegious heads of the Christians. But only a few blows had been struck, when a sudden wind was heard in the groaning branches of the tree, and down it came toppling with its own weight, and split into four huge pieces. The shuddering pagans at once bowed before the superior might of Christianity. Boniface built out of the wood a chapel to St. Peter. After this churches everywhere arose; and here and there a monastery was settled. But the want of laborers

[1] This was usual, or we might suppose that they dreaded another Ulphilas among these new German converts.

[2] Near Fritzlar. The oak is called robur Jovis.

was great; and Boniface sent to his native land for a supply of missionaries. A number of active and pious men flocked from England to his spiritual standard; and many devout women obeyed the impulse, and either founded or filled convents, which began to rise in the districts beyond the Rhine. The similarity of language no doubt qualified the English missionaries for their labors among the Teutonic races; Italians had been of no use.

Boniface had won a new empire to Christianity; and was placed over it as spiritual sovereign by the respectful gratitude of the Pope. He received the pall of a Metropolitan, and was empowered as primate to erect bishoprics throughout Germany. Again he visited Rome, and was invested by Gregory III., the new Pope, with full powers as representative of the Apostolic see.

Boniface Metropolitan of Mentz. A.D. 745.

The Metropolitan throne was fixed on the Rhine, at Mentz. This city had formerly been a bishop's see. In the wars of Carloman, the Frank, against the Saxons, the Bishop Gerold went out to battle with his sovereign and was slain. He was succeeded by his son, Gewelib, a man of strict morals, but addicted to hawks and hounds. Gewelib cherished the sacred hereditary duty of revenging his father's death.[1] He discovered the man by whose hand Gerold had fallen, lured him to an amicable interview in an island on the river, and stabbed him to the heart. Neither king nor nobles thought this just exaction of blood for blood the least disqualification for a

[1] From the Life of Boniface by a presbyter of Mentz. — Pertz, p. 354. Episcopus autem a cæde regressus, rudi populo, rudis adhuc præsul, licet ætate maturus, tamen fide . . . præficitur; non computantibus nec rege, nec cæteris optimatibus, vindictam patris crimen esse, dicentibusque "Vicem reddidit patris morti."

Christian bishop. But the Christianity of Boniface was superior to the dominant barbarism. The blood-stained bishop was deposed by the act of a council, and on the vacancy the Metropolitan see erected at Mentz. From his Metropolitan see of Mentz, Boniface ruled Christian Germany with a parental hand. He exercised his power of establishing bishoprics by laying the foundations of some of those wealthy and powerful sees, which long possessed so commanding an influence in Germany. On his return from his third visit to Rome he passed through Bavaria; there he found but one solitary bishopric, at Passau. He founded those of Salzburg, of Freisingen, and of Ratisbon. In Thuringia the episcopal see was fixed at Erfurt; in Hesse, at Buraberg, which was afterwards removed to Paderborn: for Franconia he founded that of Wurtzburg. Besides these churches, those of Utrecht, Cologne, Eichstadt, Tongres, Worms, Spires, Augsburg, Constance, and Coire owned their allegiance to the supremacy with which the Metropolitan of Mentz had been invested by the successor of St. Peter.[1]

Condemns heretics.

Boniface ruled the minds of the clergy, the people, and the kings. He held councils, and condemned heretics: one, an impostor named Adalbert, who pretended to work miracles; the other, Clement, a Scot, who held some unintelligible doctrines on Christ's descent into hell, and on predestination.[2] The obsequious Frankish Sovereign of Neus-

1 The acts of Boniface in the reformation of the clergy of France will be related in a subsequent chapter.

2 I cannot in these very obscure persons discern with some Protestant writers of Germany, even my friend M. Bunsen, sagacious prophets and resolute opponents of Papal domination which was artfully and deliberately established by Boniface; a premature Luther and Calvin. Neither the

tria, who claimed dominion over the whole of Christian Germany, punished the delinquents with imprisonment. Carloman, himself, who had risen from the post of Mayor of the Palace to that of Sovereign, was so wrought on by the pious eloquence of Boniface, that he abandoned his throne, bequeathed his son to the perilous guardianship of his brother Pepin, went to Rome, and retired into a monastery.

Boniface even resisted within his own diocese, the author of his greatness. The Pope Stephen, on his visit to Pepin, presumed to ordain a Bishop of Mentz. Boniface resisted this encroachment, and it was only at the earnest representation of Pepin, who urged the unreasonableness of such a quarrel between the heads of the Church, that the feud was allayed.[1]

Resists the Pope.

But power and dignity were not the ruling passions of Boniface. He threw off all the pomp and authority of the Primate of Germany to become again the humble apostle. He surrendered his see to Lul-

A.D. 753.

jealousies nor the politic schemes belong to the time. The respect of Boniface for Rome was filial not servile. The tenets of Adalbert and Clement were doubtless misunderstood or misrepresented, but they are to me altogether indistinct and uncertain.

1 There is something remarkable in the simplicity with which Boniface remonstrates against certain unchristian practices at Rome. He asks Pope Zacharias if it can be true that heathen usages, such as feasts at the kalends of January, phylacteries worn by the women, enchantments and divinations, are allowed at Rome. He even ventures on one occasion to make more delicate inquiries as to simoniacal practices, especially that of selling metropolitan palls. "Quod talia a te nobis referantur, quasi nos corruptores sumus canonum, et patrum rescindere traditiones quæramus, ac per hoc, quod absit, cum nostris clericis in simoniacam hæresim incidamus, accipientes et compellentes, ut hi quibus pallia tribuimus, nobis præmia largiantur." — Zachariæ Epist. ad Bonifac. Labbe, Conc. "Non oportet ut qui caput ecclesiæ estis, cæteris membris exempla contentionis præbeatis." — Vit. Bonifac. apud Pertz, vol. ii. p. 336.

lus, one of the Englishmen whom he had invited to Germany, and set forth, if not to seek, not to shrink from martyrdom among the savage pagans. He obtained that last glorious crown of his devoted life. In Friesland he had made numerous converts; the day was appointed on which he was to administer the rite of confirmation to a multitude of these neophytes. The morn had begun to dawn on the open country where the tents had been pitched, when they were suddenly attacked by a band of armed heathens. The converts of Boniface rose up in self-defence, but the saint discouraged their vain efforts, and exhorted them to submit in peace and joy to their heaven-appointed martyrdom. All met their doom; but their assailants quarrelled about the spoil; made themselves drunk with the wine, and so fell upon each other, and revenged the Christian martyrs. The body of St. Boniface was conveyed to the monastery of Fulda.

Death of Boniface. A.D. 754.

This renowned monastery had owed its foundation to Boniface. These great conventual establishments were of no less importance in German history than the bishoprics. The history of Fulda, illustrates the manner in which these advanced posts of Christianity and civilization were settled in the midst of the deep Teutonic forests.

Monasteries. Fulda.

Sturmi was the son of noble Christian parents in Noricum; the enthusiasm of youthful piety led him to follow Boniface into Germany. He was ordained priest, and labored successfully under the guidance of his master. He was seized with the dominant passion for the monastic state; and Boniface encouraged rather than repressed his ardor. With a

Sturmi.

few companions he entered into the forest solitude, and fixed at first at Hertzfeld. But this retirement was at once too near the frontier and exposed to danger from the pagan Saxons. Boniface urged them to strike deeper into the wilderness. Though their impulse was so different, their adventures resembled those of the backwoodsmen in America, exploring the unknown forests. They tracked in their boats along some of the rivers; but their fastidious piety, and, not perhaps altogether unworldly sagacity, could find no place which united all the requisites for a flourishing monastery; profound seclusion, salubrious and even beautiful situation, fertile soil, abundant water.[1] With the tone, and, in their belief, with the authority of a prophet, Boniface declared, on their report, that the chosen site would be revealed at length. Sturmi set out alone upon an ass, and with a small stock of food plunged fearlessly into the wilderness. He beguiled the way with psalms, at the same time he surveyed the country with a keen and curious observation. At night he lit a circular fire, to scare away the wild beasts, and lay down in the midst of it. His ass was one day startled by a number of wild Sclavonians bathing in a stream, and the saint perceived the offensive smell which proceeded from them.[2] They mocked him, probably by their gestures, but did him no harm. At

[1] "Tunc avidus locorum explorator ubique sagaci obtutu montuosa atque plana perlustrans loca, montes quoque et colles vallesque adspiciens, fontes et torrentes atque fluvios perlustrans, pergebat." — Vita S. Sturmii, Pertz, ii. 368.

[2] "Et ipse vir Dei eorum fœtorem exhorruit." This seems to be meant literally, though the words which follow, "qui more Gentilium servum Dei subsannabant," might perhaps lead to another sense. If I am right in my translation, it is a curious illustration of the antipathy of races. — Apud Pertz, ibid.

length he arrived at a spot on the banks of the Fulda, where he was so delighted with the situation, the soil, the water, that having passed the whole day in exploring it, he determined that this must be the site predicted by Boniface. He returned to his companions. Boniface not merely approved of the choice, but also obtained a grant of the site, with a demesne extending four miles each way, from the pious Carloman, who, whatever his own title, gave it to God with as much facility as lands are now granted in Canada or Australia. Boniface himself went to visit the place, and watched the clearing of the forest and the preparations for building with unfailing interest. The monks of Fulda adopted the rule of St. Benedict; the multitude of candidates for admission was so great, that accommodation could not be found fast enough. Of all the gifts of Boniface, the most valuable was that of his body, which refused to repose anywhere but in the abbey of Fulda.

The abbots of Fulda were not perpetually employed in the peaceful and legitimate Christian Apostleship of Boniface for the conversion of Germany. At a later period they were summoned to attend Charlemagne on his Mohammedan mission for the conversion of the heathen Saxons by the sword. On his first campaign, the aged Sturmi was one of the flock of bishops, and abbots, and clergy who followed in the train of war.

England, meantime, had been still supplying the more peaceful warriors of the Cross, who endeavored in vain by preaching the Gospel to subdue the fierce and exasperated Saxons. Willibald, the Apostle of Friesland, was a Northumbrian. Adalbert, Bishop of

Utrecht, and Leofwin, who was martyred by the Saxons, with many others, came from our island. St. Ludger, though a Frisian by descent, had studied under Alcuin at York.[1] In this singular manner the Anglo-Saxon invasion of England flowed back upon the continent; and Gregory the Great, by his conversion of England, gave the remote impulse to the conversion of large parts of Germany.

[1] Vita S. Ludgeri, printed in Bede's works.

CHAPTER VI.

THE PAPACY FROM THE TIME OF GREGORY THE GREAT TO GREGORY II.

	A.D.		A.D
Gregory the Great, died	604	Adeodatus	672
Sabinianus	604, 606	Domnus	677
Boniface III.	607	Agatho	679
Boniface IV.	608	Leo II.	682
Deus-dedit	615, 618	Benedict	684
Boniface V.	618, 625	John V.	685
Honorius I.	625, 638	Conon	686
Severinus (2 months and 4 days)	639	Sergius	687, 701
John IV.	640	John VI.	702
Theodorus I.	642	John VII.	705, 707
Martin I.	649, 655	Sisinnus	708
Eugenius I.	654	Constantine	708
Vitalianus	657	Gregory II.	716

All these conquests of Christianity were, in a certain sense, the conquests of the Roman See. Augustine had been a Roman missionary, and though the ancient British Church had raised up something of an intractable spirit in some of the English kingdoms, and passing to the continent with Columban and his followers, had asserted some independence, and for a time had maintained usages which refused to conform to the Roman discipline; yet reverence for Rome penetrated with the Gospel to the remotest parts. Germany was converted to Latin

The Teutons converted to Latin Christianity.

Christianity. Rome was the source, the centre, the regulating authority recognized by the English apostles of the Teutons. The clergy were constantly visiting Rome as the religious capital of the world, to do homage to the head of Western Christendom, to visit the shrines of the apostles, the more devout to obtain relics, the more intellectual, knowledge, letters, arts. The Pontificate of Gregory the Great had been the epoch at which had commenced at least both this great extension of Latin Christianity, and the independence of the Roman See. But the impulse had been much stronger towards the subjugation of these new dominions, than towards emancipation from the secular power of the Eastern emperors. While the Papal influence was thus spreading in the West, and bishops from the remotest parts of the empire, and of regions never penetrated by the Roman arms, looked to Rome as the parent of their faith, — if not to an infallible, at least to the highest authority in Christendom — the Pope, in his relation to the Eastern empire, has sunk again into a subject. He is the pontiff of a city within a conquered province, that province arbitrarily governed by an officer of the sovereign. He is consecrated only after the permission of the Emperor, is expected to obey the imperial mandate even on religious matters, exposed to penalties for contumacy, in one case arrested, exiled, and with difficulty saved from capital punishment.

Popes subordinate to the Eastern Emperors.

In the century, or but few years more, after the death of Gregory the Great, down to the accession of Gregory II.,[1] a rapid succession of twenty-four popes filled the Apostolic See. Few of

Successors of Gregory I.

[1] Gregory the Great died 604. Gregory II. Pope 716.

them stand forth out of the obscurity of the times. The growth or rather the maintenance of the papal power is to be ascribed more to the circumstances of the age than to the character or ability of the popes. Many of them were of Roman, most of Italian birth; few, even if they had been greater men, ruled long enough to achieve any great acts. Two of those, whose reign was most protracted, were distinguished, the one, Honorius I., only for his errors; the other, Martin, for his misfortune.

Sabinianus. A.D. 604. Sept. 13.

Sabinianus, the successor of Gregory, has the character of a hard and avaricious man. He was a native of Volterra, and had been employed as the envoy and representative of Gregory at Constantinople.[1] The admirers of Gregory describe Sabinianus as a bitter enemy to the fame of his holy predecessor. Gregory's unbounded liberality to the poor, Sabinianus reproached as a prodigal waste of the treasures of the Church, a vain ostentation, a low art to obtain popularity. A dreadful famine followed the accession of the new pontiff: he sold the corn, which Gregory was wont to distribute freely, at exorbitant prices;[2] and laid the fault of the parsimony, to which he said that he was compelled, on the prodigality of Gregory. But the people, some of whom are said to have perished with hunger before the eyes of the unpitying pope, could not comprehend what might have been necessary, or even wise, economy.

Sabinianus seems to have struck on a chord of popular Roman feeling, which answered more readily to his

[1] The Apocrisiarius was the title of the papal envoy at the Byzantine court.

[2] 30 solidi a bushel.

touch. The populace listened greedily to the charge, first said to have been made by Sabinianus, of the wanton destruction made by the late pope of the public buildings and other monuments of the city. Gregory was accused as having defaced with systematic Christian iconoclasm, and demolished the ancient temples, and of having thrown down and broken to pieces the statues which still adorned the city.[1] The revenge suggested by the malice of Sabinianus was the public destruction of the works of Gregory. The pious mendacity of Peter the Deacon, as it had saved the mortal remains of his master from insult, now protected his works. He assured the populace that himself had seen the Holy Ghost, in the shape of a dove, whispering into the ear of Gregory. Whatever be the truth of these old traditions, they betray the existence of two unscrupulous hostile factions, one adoring, the other bitterly persecuting the fame of Gregory; and exhibit a singular, yet not unnatural, state of feeling in the

[1] Platina (de Vit. Pontif.) connects these two rumors. The iconoclasm of which Gregory is accused has given rise to a long controversy. Platina indignantly rejects the charge of wantonly destroying the public edifices, and assigns very probable reasons for their decay. "Absit hæc calumnia a tanto Pontifice Romano, præsertim cui certè post Deum patria quam vita charior fuit. Multa profecto ex collapsis ædificiis exedit vetustas. Multa præterea demoliuntur homines ædificandi gratiâ, ut *quotidiè cernimus.* Impacta illa foramina, quæ tum in concavo fornicum, tum in conjuncturis marmorum, quadratorumve lapidum videntur, non minus a Romanis quam a barbaris avellendi æris causâ crediderim. In fornicibus enim, quo levior esset moles, ollas cum numismatibus collocabant. Lapides vero quadratos æneis clavis firmabant." The statues, he proceeds, fell of themselves, their marble or bronze pedestals being objects of plunder. The heads, the necks being the slenderest part, were knocked off in the fall. This is in answer to the accusation that Gregory caused the statues to be beheaded. I am not sure that Gregory's more religious contemporaries would have thought these charges calumnious: the period was not passed when the hatred of idolatry would predominate over the love of art.

Roman populace. The old Roman attachment to their majestic edifices, and even to the stately images of their ancient gods, is struggling successfully against their Christian reverence for their pontiff, but yielding to the most credulous Christian superstition. Superstition triumphed the more easily over a hard and avaricious prelate; and, on the Pope's refusal to allow the sainted Gregory the quiet enjoyment of Christian peace in heaven, brought him down to punish his guilty successor, and avenge his own wrongs. Thrice Gregory appeared to rebuke Sabinianus — thrice he appeared in vain; the fourth time the spirit struck the pontiff a violent blow on the head, of which he died. So exasperated were the people against Sabinianus, that his funeral procession was conducted by a long circuit without the city, from the Lateran palace to St. Peter's, to escape the insults of the Romans. A vacancy of nearly a year ensued after the death of Sabinianus. The brief pontificate of Boniface III. is marked by the assumption of that awful title before which Christendom bowed for so many centuries, that of Universal Bishop. The pious humility of Gregory had shuddered at the usurpation of this title by the Patriarch of Constantinople. No language could express the devout abhorrence of this impious, heretical, diabolic, anti-Christian assertion of superiority. Boniface then represented the pope at the Imperial Court, and succeeded not merely in wresting this title from the rival prelate of Constantinople, but in obtaining an acknowledgment of the su-

A.D. 606. Feb. 22, to A.D. 607. Feb. 19.[1]

Boniface III.

[1] I would observe that in many of these dates, it is that of the consecration and burial which are recorded, not the accession and death of the Pope.

premacy of St. Peter's successor.[1] Neither the motive of the donor of this magnificent privilege, nor the donor himself, commend the gift. It was the tyrant Phocas, who hated the Patriarch of Constantinople for his humanity, in protecting, as far as he had power, the widow and the three helpless daughters of the murdered emperor Maurice from his vengeance; and this hatred of the Patriarch of Constantinople, rather than the higher respect for the Bishop of Rome, still less any mature deliberation on the justice of their respective claims, awarded the superiority to the old Rome. On the death of Phocas the Patriarch of Constantinople resumed, if he had ever abandoned, the contested title.

Even greater obscurity hangs over the decision of a synod held by Boniface at Rome, which is thought to have invested the papal see in more substantial and immediate power. Seventy-two bishops, thirty-three presbyters, and the whole assembled clergy, passed a canon that, under the penalty of anathema, no one should form a party for the succession to a bishopric; three days were to elapse before the election, and all bribery and simoniacal bargaining were strictly forbidden. No election was to be good unless made by the clergy and people, and ratified by the prince. A later and more doubtful authority subjoins, not till approved by the pope, under the solemn form, "We will and we ordain."[2]

1 The early authorities for this fact are Anastasius Bibliothecarius in Vit. Bonifac. IV, and Paulus Diaconus, Hist. Longobard. Schroëck (Chr. Kirch. Gesch., xvii. 73, and xix. 488) is disposed to question the whole, to which perhaps too much importance has been given by modern controversialists. Baronius and Pagi have added, without any authority, that Phocas forbade the Patriarch of Constantinople to call himself Universal Bishop.

2 This sentence rests only on the late and doubtful authority of Platina, in Vit. Pontif.

Boniface IV., a Marsian, is celebrated for the conversion of the Pantheon into a Christian Church. With the sanction of the emperor, this famous temple, in which were assembled all the gods of the Roman world, was purified and dedicated to the new tutelar deities of mankind, the Virgin, and all the martyrs.

Boniface IV. Nov. 607. A.D. 608. Sept. 15. died A.D. 615. May 25.

Deus-dedit and Boniface V. occupied the papal throne for ten years of peace, unbroken by any hostile collision, either with the Exarch or the Lombard kings, and even undisturbed by any important controversy.

Deus-dedit. A.D. 615. Oct. 19. died A.D. 618. May 25. Boniface V. A.D. 618–625. Oct. 25.

But the fatal connection with the Eastern empire drove the succeeding popes into the intricacies and feuds of a new theological strife. While Mohammedanism was gathering in her might on its borders, and the stern assertors of the Divine Unity had already begun to wrest provinces from the Roman empire, the bishops in all the great sees of the East, the emperors themselves, were distracting their own minds, persecuting their subjects, and even spreading strife and bloodshed through their cities on the question of the single or the double Will in Christ. Honorius I. incurred a condemnation for heresy, his more orthodox successors suffered persecution, and one of them exile and death.

Honorius I.

It might have been supposed that Nestorianism, with its nâtural offspring, Eutychianism, had exhausted or worn out the contest concerning the union of the Godhead and the manhood in the Saviour. The Church had asserted the coexistence of the two natures — man with all his perfect properties — God with all His perfect attri-

Controversy about the two wills in Christ.

butes: it had refused to keep them in almost antagonistic separation with the Nestorian — to blend them into one with Eutyches. The Nestorian and the Monophysite had been alike driven away from the high places of the Church; though still formidable sects, they were but sects.

But the Godhead and the manhood, thus each distinct and complete in itself, yet so intimately conjoined — where began the divergence? where closed the harmony? Did the will, not merely the consentient, but absolutely identical will, and one unconflicting operation of that will, having become an active energy, perform all the works of the Redeemer, submit to and undergo his passion? or did each nature preserve its separate independence of will, and only by the concordance of these two at least theoretically conflicting wills, produce the harmonious action of the two natures? At what point did the duality terminate — the unity begin?

Sergius, the Patriarch of Constantinople, first, it might seem almost inadvertently, stirred this perplexing question. He discovered a writing of his holy predecessor, Mennas, which distinctly asserted that the Christ was actuated by but one will. He communicated it to some of the Eastern bishops, to Theodorus of Pharan, who had a high name as a theologian, and to Cyrus, then Bishop of Phasis; both bowed before the authority, and accepted the doctrine of Mennas.

The Emperor Heraclius, though he did not aspire to the character of a distinguished theologian, like his predecessor Justinian, could not, even occupied as he was with his adventurous and successful campaigns in the East, keep himself aloof from religious A.D. 626.

controversy.[1] In a suspension of arms during his war of invasion against the Lazians he encountered at Phasis the Bishop Cyrus whom he consulted on the
A.D. 622. important question of the single or double will, the single or double operation in Christ. Cyrus appealed to the Patriarch of Constantinople, who on his own authority, and that of his predecessor, Mennas, decided in favor of the Monothelitic view. This doctrine had already offered itself under the captivating aspect of an intermediate term, which might conciliate the Monophysites with the Church. In Armenia, four years before, Heraclius had an interview with Paul, a follower of Severus, who, taken with the notion of one operation in Christ, was disposed to accede (with this explanation) to the Council of Chalcedon. At a later period, a more important personage, the Jacobite Patriarch, Anastasius, consented to remain, on these terms, with the Catholic Church. He was to be rewarded with the patriarchate of Antioch. Anastasius, it is said
A.D. 628. by his enemies, a man of consummate craft, had overreached the unsuspecting emperor; the Jacobites mocked the simplicity of the Catholics, who, by this concession, instead of winning converts, had gone over to the doctrines of their adversaries. Monothelitism was but another form of Monophysitism.

Sergius of Constantinople addressed a letter to Honorius I. Honorius, in distinct words, declared himself a Monothelite. Yet Honorius, it is manifest, entirely misapprehended the question, and seemed not in the least to understand its subtle bearings on the contro-

[1] Walch has assigned the dates adopted in the text, for the various incidents in the history of the Monothelitic controversy. — Ketzer-Geschichte, t. ix.

versies of the East. The unity which he asserted was not an identity, but a harmony. His main argument was, that the sinless human nature of Christ, being ignorant of that other law in the members, warring against the law of the mind, there could be no conflicting or adverse will in the God-Man.[1] But this plainer and more practical conception of the question betrayed the unsuspecting Pope into words, to which the Monothelites, proud of their important partisan, as well as the stern polemic resentment of his adversaries, bound him down, with inexo- A.D. 633, 634.
rable rigor. Notwithstanding the charitable attempt of one of his successors, John IV., to interpret his words in this wider meaning, Honorius I. was branded by the Council of Constantinople with the name of heretic.

The whole church might seem in danger of falling into the same condemnation. All the prelates of the great sees of Rome, of Constantinople, of Alexandria (now occupied by Cyrus, formerly Bishop of Phasis) and of Antioch, had asserted the one indivisible will in Christ. In Egypt this reconciling tenet had wrought wonders. On this basis had been framed certain chapters, which the followers of Dioscorus and of Severus, all the Jacobite sects, received with eager promptitude. For once the whole people of Alexandria became one flock; almost all Egypt, Libya, and the adjacent provinces, with one voice and one spirit, obeyed the ortho-

[1] Ὅθεν καὶ ἓν θέλημα ὁμολογοῦμεν τοῦ κυρίου Ἰησοῦ Χριστοῦ· ἐπειδὴ προδήλως ὑπὸ τῆς θεότητος προσελήφθη ἡ ἡμετέρα φύσις, οὐκ ἁμαρτία ἐν ἐκείνῃ, δηλαδὴ ἡ φύσις πρὸ τῆς ἁμαρτίας κτισθεῖσα, οὐκ ἥτις μετὰ τὴν παράβασιν ἐφθάρη. — Honor. Epist., Labbe, 930. The metaphysical and practical character of the two letters contrast singularly. Honorius reproves the introduction of terms not recognized by the Scriptures.

dox Patriarch of Alexandria.[1] Sophronius alone, who during the controversy became Bishop of Jerusalem, the same Sophronius who afterwards signed the humiliating capitulation of Jerusalem to the Mohammedans, boldly asserted and elaborately defended the doctrine of the two wills. So deeply impressed was Sophronius with the vital importance of this question, that long after, when the Saracens were masters of the Holy City, he took Stephen, Bishop of Dora, to the spot which was supposed to be the Golgotha, the place of the Lord's crucifixion. "To that God," he said, "who on this very place was crucified for thee, at his second coming to judge the quick and the dead, thou shalt render thine account, if thou delayest or art remiss in the defence of his imperilled faith; go thou forth in my place. As thou knowest, on account of this Saracen invasion, now fallen upon us for our sins, I cannot bodily strive for the truth, and before the world proclaim, to the end of the earth, to the apostolic throne at Rome, the tenets of orthodoxy." Sophronius protested, appealed, wrote large volumes; and the religious peace which seemed descending on the afflicted East, gave place again to strife, and feud, and mutual anathema.

But in the Byzantine empire, the creed to its nicest shades and variations was an affair of state: it was fixed, or at least defined, by imperial authority. Heraclius, while he looked with miscalculating or awestruck apathy on the progress of the Mohammedan arms, could not refrain from interference with this question of metaphysic theology. In his name appeared the famous Ecthesis,[2] or Exposition of the

[1] Sergii ad Honor. Epist. apud Concil. Const. III., Labbe, p. 921.
[2] Ecthesis Heraclii apud Labbe, p. 200.

Faith, drawn in all probability by the Patriarch Sergius, but which, as professed by the emperor, his subjects were bound to receive in humble and unquestioning obedience. The Ecthesis declared the two wills in Christ to be a heresy, which even the impious Nestorius had not dared to promulgate. It was affixed, as the proclamation of the imperial creed, on the gates of the great church at Constantinople. The publication of the Ecthesis was followed, or immediately preceded, by the death of Sergius of Constantinople and that of Honorius of Rome.

A.D. 638. Oct. 12.

The Popes who succeeded Honorius amply retrieved by their resolute opposition to Monothelitism what was considered the delinquency of that prelate. On the death of Honorius, Severinus was elected to the papal throne; but the confirmation of his election was long delayed at Constantinople, and only conceded on the promise of his envoys that he would accede to the creed of Heraclius. Severinus, however, repudiated the Monothelitic doctrine. In the interval between the election and confirmation of Severinus, the plunder of the treasures of the Roman Church by the Exarch of Ravenna showed the unscrupulous and irreverent character of the Byzantine government. Maurice, the Chartulary, harangued the soldiers. While they were defrauded of their pay, the Church was revelling in wealth. The Exarch's officer occupied the Lateran palace, and sealed up all the accumulated riches which Christian emperors, patricians, consuls had bestowed for their souls' health, for the use of the poor, and the redemption of captives. The rapacious Exarch Isaac hastened to Rome. The plunder was divided, the Emperor propitiated by his

Severinus Pope A.D. 638 (?), not confirmed till 640.

share, which was transmitted to Constantinople. The more refractory of the clergy, who presumed to remonstrate, were sent into banishment.

Severinus died after a pontificate of two months and four days. He was succeeded by John IV., a Dalmatian by birth.[1] John not only condemned the Monothelite doctrine, but piously endeavored to vindicate the memory of his predecessor Honorius from the imputation of heresy. Honorius had denied only the two human wills, the conflicting sinful will of fallen man, and the impeccable will, in the person of Christ.[2] But the apology of John neither absolved the memory of Honorius before the Council of Constantinople, nor did the religious reverence of his successors, whose envoys were present at that Council, interpose in his behalf. The apology of John was addressed to the Emperor Constantine, whom it did not reach. For the death of Heraclius was followed by a rapid succession of revolutions at Constantinople. The later years of that Emperor had contrasted unfavorably with the glorious activity of his earlier administration. The conqueror of Persia seemed to look on the progress of Mohammedanism with the apathy of despair. He had deeply wounded the religious feelings of his subjects by an incestuous marriage with his niece Martina. It was the object of his dying wishes, of his last testament, that his son by Martina, Heracleonas, should share the

A.D. 640. Aug. 2. John IV. consecrated Dec. 25.

Death of Heraclius. Revolution in Constantinople.

[1] Anastasius in vitâ.

[2] "Decessor meus, docens de mysteriis incarnationis Christi, dicebat non fuisse in eo, sicut in nobis peccatoribus, mentis et carnis contrarias voluntates; quod quidam ad proprium sensum convertentes, divinitatis ejus et humanitatis unam eum voluntatem docuisse suspicati sunt."—Epist. Joan., Labbe or Mansi, sub ann. 641.

empire with his elder brother, Constantine. The two sons of Heraclius were proclaimed coequal Cæsars, under the sovereignty of the Empress Martina. But even Constantinople would not submit to the sway of an incestuous female. Martina was compelled to descend from the throne, and was succeeded by the feeble Constantine, whose decaying health broke down after a reign of but a hundred days. The enemies of Martina ascribed his death to poison administered by his stepmother and by Pyrrhus the Patriarch. Martina indeed again assumed the empire; but Constantine on his death-bed had taken measures to secure the protection of the army for his children, the legitimate descendants of Heraclius. He had been assured that Heraclius had placed vast sums of money in the hands of the Patriarch to maintain the interests of Martina and her son. He, therefore, before he expired, sent a large donative to Valentinus, who commanded the army in the suburb of Chalcedon. Valentinus imperiously demanded the punishment of the guilty usurpers, of the assassins of Constantine. The citizens of Constantinople mingled with the ferocious soldiery. In the church of St. Sophia, Heracleonas was compelled to mount the pulpit, holding by the hand Constans, the elder of the sons of Constantine. With one voice the people, the soldiers, saluted Constans sole Emperor. A wild scene of pillage ensued; the barbarian soldiers, the Jews, and other lawless partisans desecrated the holy edifice by every kind of outrage. The Patriarch Pyrrhus, after depositing a protest on the high altar, fled. The Senate condemned Martina to the loss of her tongue, Heracleonas to the mutilation of his nose; these wretched victims were sent to die in exile.

A.D. 641.

Constans was sole Emperor, and would brook no rival. His own brother Theodosius was compelled to incapacitate himself for sovereignty by holy orders. Yet even so the jealousy of Constans felt no security. Nothing was indelible to the imperial will at Constantinople; a successful usurper would have shaken off even that disqualification. Nearly twenty years after, Theodosius, the deacon, was assassinated by the command of his brother, whom the indignant people drove from his throne.

In the meantime religious war continued without abatement between Rome and Constantinople. The Monothelite Paul succeeded the Monothelite Pyrrhus. The Ecthesis kept its place on the doors of the great church. But in the West, and in the whole of the African churches yet unsubdued by the Mohammedans, all Latin Christianity adhered to the doctrine of the two Wills. The monk Maximus, the indefatigable adversary of Monothelitism, travelled through the East and through Africa, denouncing the heresy of Sergius, and exciting to the rejection of the imperial Ecthesis. In

A.D. 645.

Africa he held a long disputation, still extant, with the exile Pyrrhus. Theodorus I. had succeeded after the short popedom of John IV. to the pontifical throne of Rome. Theodorus rejected Monothelitism with the utmost zeal. During his pontificate, Pyrrhus of Constantinople came to Rome. Whether or not he acknowleged himself confuted by the unanswerable metaphysics of Maximus, he presented a memorial recanting all his errors on the single Will in Christ.[1] The Pope Theodorus had received

Pope Theodorus, A.D. 642, Nov. 24.

[1] "Præsente cuncto clero et populo, condemnavit omnia, quæ a se vel a decessoribus suis scripta vel acta sunt adversus immaculatam fidem." — Vit. Thedor.

with courtesy from Paul, the successor of Pyrrhus, the communication of his advancement to the see of Constantinople; he had expressed some cautious doubts as to the regularity of the deposition of Pyrrhus, yet he had given his full approbation, he had expressed his joy on the elevation of Paul.[1] But Paul was a Monothelite, Pyrrhus at his feet a penitent convert to orthodoxy. Pyrrhus was received with all A.D. 646. the honors which belonged to the actual patriarch of Constantinople.

But Pyrrhus, from what motive appears not, retired to Ravenna, recanted his recantation, and declared himself a conscientious Monothelite.[2] The indignant Pontiff was not content with the ordinary ter- A.D. 648. rors of excommunication against this double renegade. In a full assembly of the clergy of Rome, and of the neighboring bishops, he heaped the most vehement anathemas on the head of the new Judas, and calling for the consecrated wine on the altar, poured some drops into the ink, and so signed the excommunication with the blood of Christ. Is it to be supposed that the blood of the Redeemer was reverenced in a less appalling sense than in later ages, or that the passion of the Pope triumphed not only over Christian moderation, but over the strongest religious awe?[3] Theodorus was not satisfied with the excommunication of Pyrrhus, he excommunicated Paul also. Paul revenged

1 "Et quidem gavisi super hujus sumus ordinatione." — Epist. Theodori ad Episcop. Constantin, apud Labbe, sub ann.

2 He may have hoped for his reinstatement in the patriarchate by the recommendation of the Exarch, and have found that his reconciliation with Rome stood in his way.

3 Theophanes, p. 509, ed. Bonn.; Anastas., p. 163, ibid.; Vit. Maximi; Epist. Synodal.

himself by suppressing the religious worship of the Papal envoys at the Court, maltreating, and even causing to be scourged some of their attendants.

Martin I., the successor of Theodorus, plunged more deeply, and with more fatal consequences, into this religious strife, or rather this revolt of the Western Province against the religious supremacy of the Emperor. Constans had withdrawn the obnoxious Ecthesis; Paul the Patriarch had himself ordered it to be removed from the gates of the great Church. The Ecthesis of Heraclius was replaced by the Type of Constans. The Type spoke altogether a different language; it aspired to silence by authority this interminable dispute. It presumed not to define the Creed, further than all parties were agreed, or beyond the decisions of the former councils. It stated the question with perspicuity and fairness, and positively prohibited the use of the phrase either of the single or the double Will and Energy.[1] The penalties for the infringement of the Imperial decree were severe: against the ecclesiastic, deposition and deprivation; against the monk seclusion and banishment from his monastery; against the public officer, civil or military, degradation; against the private man of rank, confiscation of goods; against the common people, scourging and banishment.

Martin I. June, 649.

Martin summoned a council in the Lateran, which was attended by 105 bishops, chiefly from Italy and the adjacent islands. After five sessions, in which the whole West repudiated Monothelitism with perfect unanimity, twenty canons were framed condemning that heresy with all its authors.

A.D. 649. Oct. 5.

[1] The Type in Labbe or Mansi, sub ann.

But Pope Martin was not content with anathematizing the erroneous doctrine of the Single Will, with humbling the rival prelate of Constantinople by excommunication in full council, with declaring the edict of the deceased Emperor Heraclius, the Ecthesis, absolutely impious; he denounced as of equal impiety the Type of the reigning Emperor. Its exhortation to peace he scorned as a persuasive to unholy acquiescence in heresy; silence on such doctrines was a wicked suppression of divine truth.

Nor was Martin wanting in activity to maintain his bold position. He published the decrees of the Lateran Council throughout the West; he addressed letters to the Frankish kings, entreating them to send representatives of their churches to join a solemn spiritual embassy to Constantinople. He despatched other missives to Britain, to Spain, and to Africa. He even appointed a Legate in the East to supersede the Monothelite patriarchs of Antioch and Jerusalem. His letter to Paul of Thessalonica is in a tone of condemnatory haughtiness which had hardly yet been assumed by a successor of St. Peter.[1]

But to the Emperor of the East the Pope was a refractory subject and no more. In Constantinople the person of the bishop had never been invested in that

[1] See a curious specimen of the logic of anathema. The Bishop of Thessalonica, because he refuses to join Martin in anathematizing the Monothelites, is confirming all the errors of Pagans, Jews, and heretics:—"Ut per hoc non solum eos etiam quos anathematisamus, nempe ipsas hæreticorum personas, anathematisare recuses . . . . sed ut etiam omnem omnium errorem Paganorum, Judæorum, hæreticorum in te confirmes. Si enim omnia omnium horum dogmata condemnamus, ut contraria et inimica veritati, tu vero omnia una nobiscum voce non anathematisas quæ anathematisamus, consequens est, te horum omnium errorem confirmasse, qui a nobis sive ab ecclesiâ catholicâ anathematisatur."—Ad Paul. Epist. Thessal. apud Labbe, sub ann. 649.

sanctity which shielded it from law, or that which was law in the East, the imperial will. Even the natural reverence for the holy office had been disturbed by the perpetual feuds, the mutual anathemas and excommunications, the depositions, the degradations, the expulsions, fatal to that unhappy see: and as old Rome was now a provincial city, her bishop would not command greater respect than the prelate of the Imperial Capital.

The Exarch Olympius received orders to seize the Pope if he persisted in his contumacy to the imperial edict, and to send him prisoner to Constantinople. But Olympius found the people of Rome prepared to take up arms in defence of their bishop. He attempted to obtain his end by more peaceful means. Later writers have protected the Pope by miracle from an attempted assassination,[1] and bowed the awestruck Exarch before the feet of Martin. But Olympius was hastily summoned from Rome to repel an invasion of Sicily by the Saracens, and died of fatigue in that island.

The new Exarch Theodorus, named Calliopas, was more resolute in the execution of his orders. He marched to Rome, and summoned the Pope to surrender to the Imperial authority. Some delay took place from the apprehensions of the Exarch, that soldiers, and means of defence, stones, and other weapons, were concealed in the Church. But Martin shrunk from bloodshed, and refused the offers of his partisans,
A.D. 653. June 15. headed by many of the clergy, to resist the Exarch. Martin had ordered his bed to be

1 The swordsman of Olympius was employed to stab the Pope while administering the communion to the Exarch; he was struck with blindness. —Anastas. in Vit.

strewed before the high altar in the Lateran. The Exarch and his troops entered the Church, the light of the candles flickered on the armor of the soldiery. Martin obeyed the summons of the Exarch to accompany him to the Lateran palace; there he was permitted to see some of the clergy. But suddenly he was hurried into a litter, the gates of Rome closed June 19.
to prevent his partisans from following him, he was carried to the harbor of Portus, embarked and landed at Messina. Thence to Avidos, on the island July 1.
of Naxos, where he was first permitted the use of a bath. The pious clergy crowded with their votive presents: the presents were seized, and the donors beaten back by the soldiery: "he who is a friend to Pope Martin is an enemy to the State." From Avidos a messenger was sent to Constantinople, to announce the arrival of the heretic and rebel, the enemy and disturber of the whole Roman empire. On the 17th of September he arrived at Constantinople; he was left lying on a bed on the deck of the ship the whole day, the gaze of curious or hostile spectators. At sunset he was carried on a litter under a strong guard Pope Martin in Constantinople.
to Prandearia, the chief guard-house. There he was imprisoned, and forbidden to make known who he was. After ninety-three days of this im- Dec. 20.
prisonment he was conveyed, on account of his weakness, upon a litter before the Senate. He was commanded to stand, but being unable, was supported by two guards. "Wretch," said the chief minister, "what wrong has the Emperor done to thee? has he deprived thee of anything, or used any violence against thee?" Martin was silent. Twenty witnesses were examined in order to connect him with some treason

against the Emperor.[1] Troilus demanded why he had not prevented, but rather consented to the rebellion of the Exarch Olympius. "How could I oppose the rebellion of Olympius, who had the whole army of Italy at his command? Did I appoint him Exarch?" The Pope was carried out to be exposed in a public place, where the Emperor could see him from a window. He was then half stripped of his clothes, which were rent down, amid the anathemas of the people. The executioner fixed an iron collar round his neck, and led him through the city to the Prætorium, with a sword carried before him. He was then cast, first into a dungeon, where murderers were confined, then into another chamber, where he lay half naked and shivering with cold. The order for his execution was expected every moment. The next day the Patriarch Paul was lying

A.D. 654. on his death-bed, and besought the Emperor to show mercy to the persecuted Martin.[2] Martin, who hoped for speedy martyrdom, heard this with regret. On the death of Paul, Pyrrhus, who had returned from Italy, resumed the throne of Constantinople. A long examination of Martin took place on the conduct of Pyrrhus at Rome. For eighty-five days Martin languished in prison: he was at length taken away, and embarked for the inhospitable shores of

A.D 655. Cherson. At Cherson he died. Such was the end of a Pope of the seventh century, who dared to resist the will of the Emperor. The monk Maxi-

[1] He denied that he had sent money to the Saracens; he had only given some moderate sums to certain destitute servants of God. He repudiated the charge of having disdained the worship of the Virgin. — Ad Theodor. Epist.; Sirmond. iii. 320; Mansi sub ann.

[2] All this curious detail is furnished by two letters of Martin himself, and a long account by one of his followers. — Apud Labbe, pp. 63–75.

mus and some of his followers were treated even with greater cruelty. Maximus refused to deny the two Wills in Christ; his tongue and his right hand were cut off, and so mutilated he was sent into exile.[1]

A.D. 657.

While Martin was yet living, Eugenius was elected to the see of Rome. His short rule[2] was followed by the longer but uneventful Pontificate of Vitalianus. The popes, warned by the fate of Martin, if they did not receive, did not condemn the Type of Constans. They allowed the question of the two Wills in Christ to slumber. Eugenius received from the new Patriarch of Constantinople, Peter, the account of his elevation, with a declaration of faith, silent on the disputed point. During the pontificate of Vitalianus Rome was visited by the Byzantine emperor. Constans had withdrawn from the Eastern Rome forever. He dared not confront the hatred of the people on account of the murder of his brother the Deacon Theodosius, whom not even the tonsure could protect from his jealousy.[3] He was pursued by the curses of mankind; and by the avenging spectre of his brother, which constantly offered to his lips a cup of blood: "Drink, brother, drink!" Yet in his restless wanderings he at times proclaimed a

Pope Eugenius I.

A.D. 657. July 30.

1 Collatio S. Maxim. cum Theodoro, apud Labbe; Theophan. Cedrenus, Vit. Maximi. — Libellus Synod.

2 If reckoned from the banishment of Martin, 2 years, 8 months, and 24 days (654–657). If from the death of Martin, only 6 months and 23 days. But the chronology is doubtful. — Binii. Not. in Anastas. Vit. apud Labbe, 432.

3 According to Cedrenus, at the tonsure of Theodosius, he had received the sacrament, it should seem, as a pledge for his brother's future security. *Ἔκειρε πρότερον αὔτον διὰ Παύλου πατριάρχου διάκονον, ὅς καὶ μετέδωκε τῷ βασιλεῖ τῶν ἀχράντων μυστηρίων ἐν ἁγίῳ ποτηρίῳ.*—P. 343.

nobler object, the repression of the Saracens, who now began to command the Mediterranean and threaten Sicily, and of the Lombards, who seemed about to swallow up the Byzantine Exarchate in Italy.[1] It is even said that in his hatred to Constantinople, he proposed to restore the empire to old Rome.[2] But he visited Rome as a plunderer, not as the restorer of her
A.D. 663. power. He was received by the Pope Vita-
July 5. lianus almost with religious honors. The haughty conduct of Constans in Rome, and the timid servility of Vitalianus, contrast with the meetings of the Western Cæsars, fifty years later, with the successors of St. Peter. To the Emperor, the Pope is merely the high priest of the city. To the Pope, the Emperor is his undoubted lord and master. The Emperor has all the unquestioning arrogance of the sovereign, whose word is law, and who commands without scruple the plunder of the public edifices, sacred as well as profane; the Pope the subject, who dares not interpose to protect the property of the city, or even of the
July 17. Church. Constans remained twelve days in Rome; all the ornaments of brass, besides more precious metals, were stripped from the churches, the iron
A.D. 668. roof torn from the Pantheon, now a church, and the whole sent off to Constantinople. Constans retired amid the suppressed execrations of all orders, to die a miserable death at Syracuse.

The Byzantine government did not discourage encroachments even on the spiritual supremacy of Rome in the West. Maurus, Bishop of Ravenna, embold-

[1] Paulus Diacon. lib. v.

[2] Βουλόμενος καὶ τὴν βασιλείαν εἰς τὴν πρεσβυτέραν Ῥώμην μετενέγκειν. — Zonar. l. xiv. 11; Glycas. Theophanes.

ened by his city having become the capital of the Exarchate, asserted and maintained his independence of the Bishop of Rome. The Archbishop of Ravenna boasted of a privilege, issued by the Emperors Heraclius and Constantine, which exempted him from all superior episcopal authority, from the authority of the Patriarch of old Rome.[1] Vitalianus hurled his excommunication against Maurus. Maurus threw back his excommunication against Vitalianus. It was not till the pontificate of Leo II. that the pride of the Archbishop of Ravenna was humbled or self-humiliated, and Maurus, who had been an object of superstitious veneration to the people, deposed from his sanctity. Archbishop Theodorus, involved in a violent contest with his clergy, sacrificed the independent dignity of his see to his own power, and submitted to Rome; he was rewarded with the title of saint.[2]

Adeodatus and Domnus, or Donus, the successors of Vitalianus, have left hardly any record of their actions to Christian history. But the summons to a general council at Constantinople was issued by the successor of Constans, Constantine the Bearded, during the pontificate of Domnus; it arrived after the accession of Agatho, a Sicilian, to the Roman pontificate.

Adeodatus. A.D. 672, April 11; 676, June 16. Donus. A.D. 676, Aug.; 678, April 11. Agatho. A.D. 678, Aug.

Constantine the Bearded was seized apparently with a sudden and an unexplained desire to reunite the East and the West under one creed. Monothelitism may have been more unpopular in the East than outward

[1] "Sancimus amplius securam atque liberam ab omni superiori Episcopali conditione manere, et solum orationi vacare pro nostro imperio, et non subjacere pro quolibet modo patriarchæ antiquæ urbis Romæ, sed manere eam αὐτοκεφάλην." — Agnelli, Vit. Pontif. Ravenn. Apud Muratori, p. 148.

[2] Agnelli, p. 151.

circumstances had shown; the monks may have been of the opposite party; Constantine himself may have felt religious doubts as to the prevailing creed. It was not, however, till fourteen years after his accession that the sixth general council actually assembled

A.D. 680. at Constantinople to decide the question of Monothelitism. They met in a chamber of the imperial palace. The Emperor himself presided, by twelve of his chief ministers. Of the great patriarchs were present George of Constantinople, and Macarius of Antioch. The designated envoys of Pope Agatho were the Bishops Abundantius of Paterneum, John of Portus, John of Rhegium, the sub-deacon Constantine, the presbyters Theodorus and Gregory, and the deacon John. Pope Agatho had entertained a hope of the presence of Theodorus, Archbishop of Canterbury, "the philosopher." He makes something like an ostentatious boast of the Lombard, Slavian, Frank, Gaulish, Gothic, and British bishops, subject to his authority.[1] Two monks, George and Peter, represented the Patriarchs of Jerusalem and of Alexandria. The proceedings were conducted with solemn regularity. On one side were the legates of Pope Agatho, on the other Macarius of Antioch, a determined Monothelite. During the seventh sitting George, the Patriarch of Constantinople, rose and declared that, having carefully compared the passages from the fathers, cited by the Westerns and by Macarius, he had been convinced by the unanswerable

1 "Sperabamus deinde de Britaniâ Theodorum archiepiscopum et *philosophum* ad nostram humilitatem conjungere; et maximè quia in medio gentium, tam Longobardorum, quamque Slavorum, necnon Francorum, Gallorum, et Gothorum, atque Britannorum, plurimi confamulorum nostrorum esse noscuntur." — Apud Mansi, sub ann. 680.

arguments of the Romans; "to them I offer my adhesion, theirs is my confession and belief." The example of George was followed by the Bishops of Ephesus, Heraclea, Cyzicum, Chalcedon, the Phrygian Hierapolis, Byzia in Thrace, Mytilene, Methymna, Selybria, Prusias, and Anastasiopolis. Macarius and his scholar, the monk Stephen, stood alone in open and contumacious resistance to the doctrine of the two wills. Macarius was degraded from his Patriarchal dignity; the monk Stephen condemned as another Eutyches or Apollinaris. The fifteenth session was enlivened by a strange episode. A monk, Polychronius, denounced as an obstinate Monothelite, challenged the council to put the doctrine to the test of a miracle. He would lay his creed on a dead body; if the dead rose not, he surrendered himself to the will of the Emperor. A body was brought into a neighboring bath. The Emperor, the ministers, the whole council, and a wondering multitude, adjourned to this place. Polychronius presented a sealed paper, which was opened and read; it declared his creed, and that he had been commanded in a vision to hasten to Constantinople to prevent the Emperor from establishing heresy. The paper was laid on the corpse; Polychronius sat whispering into its ear, and the patient assembly awaited the issue for some hours. But the obstinate dead would not come to life. An unanimous anathema (all seem to have been too serious for ridicule) condemned Polychronius as a heretic and a deceiver. The Synod returned to its chamber, and endeavored to argue with the contumacious Polychronius, who, still inflexible, was degraded from all his functions.[1]

[1] Concil. sub ann.

The council proceeded with its anathemas. George of Constantinople endeavored to save his predecessors from being denounced by name; the council rejected his motion, and one cry broke forth — Anathema against the heretic Theodorus of Pharan! Anathema against the heretic Sergius! (of Constantinople). Anathema against the heretic Cyrus! Anathema against the heretic Honorius! (of Rome). Anathema against the heretic Pyrrhus; against the heretic Paul; against Peter, Macarius, Polychronius, and a certain Apergius! At the close of the proceedings of this sixth general council, a creed was framed, distinctly asserting the two wills and the two operations in Christ; and at the close of all, amid gratulations to the Cæsar, were again recited the names of the anathematized heretics, commencing with Nestorius, ending with Sergius, Honorius of Rome, and all the more distinguished Monothelites.

The decree of the council of Constantinople, the sixth ecumenic council, was at once a triumph and an humiliation to the see of Rome; a triumph as establishing the orthodoxy of the doctrines maintained in the West by all the Bishops of Rome, excepting Honorius. The Patriarch of Constantinople had been constrained to recant the creed of his predecessors; the whole line after Sergius had been involved in one anathema. The Emperor himself had adopted the creed of Rome. The one obstinate Patriarch, Macarius of Antioch, had been stripped of his pall, and driven, with every mark of personal insult and ignominy, from the assembly. Yet was it an humiliation, for it condemned a Bishop of Rome as an anathematized heretic. But, while the Pope made the most of his triumph, he seemed utterly to disregard the humiliation. The impeccability of the Bishop of Rome was not as yet an article of the Roman creed. The successor of Agatho (who had died during the sitting of the Council) Pope Leo II., announced to the churches of the West the universal acceptance of the Roman doctrine; to the bishops and to the King of Spain he recapitulated the names of the anathematized heretics, among the rest of Honorius, who, instead of quenching the flame of heresy, as became the apostolic authority, had fanned it by his negligence; who had permitted the immaculate rule of faith, handed down by his predecessors, to suffer defilement.[1] The condemned Monothelites of the East were banished to Rome, as the place in which they were most likely to be converted from their errors; and where some of them, weary of imprisonment in the monasteries to which they were consigned, abjured their former creed. Macarius of Antioch alone resisted alike all theological arguments, and all the more worldly temptations of reinstatement in the dignity and honors of his see.

A.D. 682. Sept., Oct.

The names of the Popes Benedict II., of John V., a Syrian by birth, of Conon, and of Sergius, fill up the rest of the seventh century. During this period an attempt was made to remedy the inconvenience of awaiting so long the imperial confirmation of the papal election. Nearly a year elapsed before the consecration of Benedict II. An edict of Constantine,

Popes. Benedict II., A.D. 683–685. John V., A.D. 685, 686. Conon, A.D. 686, 687 Sergius I., A.D. 687.

A.D. 684. Jan. 26.

[1] "Qui flammam heretici dogmatis, non ut decuit apostolicam auctoritatem incipientem extinxit, sed negligendo confovit." — Ad Episcop. Hispan., Labbe, p. 1246. "Honorius Romanus qui immaculatam apostolicæ traditionis regulam quam a prædecessoribus suis accepit maculari consensit." — Epist. ad Ervig. Reg. Hispan., p. 1252.

who still cultivated a close alliance with the Popes, enacted that, on the unanimous suffrage of the clergy, the people, and the soldiery (the soldiery are now assuming in the election of the Pontiff the privilege of the Prætorian Guard in the election of the Emperor), the Pope might at once proceed to his consecration. This regulation, however, demanded that rare occurrence on the election of a Bishop of Rome, unanimity. On the election of Conon, and afterwards of Sergius, strife arose, and contending competitors divided the suffrages. The Exarch of Ravenna resumed his right of interference and of final sanction before the conse-

Theodorus, A.D. 687. Paschalis anti-Pope, A.D. 687–692.

cration of the Pope. On the death of Conon three candidates were proposed by their conflicting partisans. The Archdeacon Paschalis, the Archpresbyter Theodorus, were supported by two rival factions; a third proposed Sergius, of a Syrian family, which had settled at Palermo in Sicily. Each of the other candidates occupied a strong position in the city, when the third party set up Sergius, and carried him in triumph to the Lateran Palace. Theodorus was compelled to surrender his claims, but Paschalis had sent large offers of money to Ravenna, and depended on the support of the Exarch. The Exarch came to Rome, declared in favor of Sergius, but exacted from him a donative at least equal to that offered by the rejected Paschalis.[1] The churches were laid under contribution to satisfy the rapacious Exarch.

Quinisextan Council.

Sergius rejected certain canons of the Quinisextan Council,[2] which assembled at the summons of the Emperor Justinian II. This Council is

[1] Anastas. in Vit. Sergii.

[2] Called also the Council in Trullo, from the chamber in the imperial palace in which it was held.

the great authority for the discipline of the Greek Church. Rigid in its enactments against marriage after entering into holy orders, and severe against those who had married two wives, or wives under any taint as of widowhood, actresses, or any unlawful occupation, it nevertheless deliberately repudiated the Roman canon[1] which forced such priests to give up all commerce with their wives: it asserted the permission of Scripture in favor of a married clergy, married, that is, to virgins and reputable wives previous to taking orders. Sergius disdainfully refused his adhesion to the authority of the Council, and annulled its decrees. Justinian, like his predecessor Constans, endeavored to treat the Pope as a refractory subject. He sent orders for his apprehension and transportation to Constantinople. But Sergius was strong, not only in the affections of the people, but of the army also. The protospatharius, the officer of the Emperor, was driven with insult from the city; the Pope was obliged to interfere in order to appease the tumult among the indignant soldiery. Ere the Emperor could revenge his insulted dignity he was himself deposed. Before his restoration Sergius had been dead several years. Even if the successors of Sergius pursued his contumacious policy, nearer objects of detestation first demanded the revenge of Justinian, who had no time to waste on a distant priest who had only resisted his religious supremacy. But on a later occasion Justinian asserted to the utmost the imperial authority.

Sergius died, A.D. 701. Justinian restored, 705.

The eighth century opened with the pontificate of John VI., in which the papal influence displayed it-

[1] Can. iii. xiii. apud Labbe, pp. 1141–1148.

John VI. A.D. 702–705. self in the becoming character of protector of the peace of the city. The Pope saved the life of the Exarch Theophylact, against whom the soldiery had risen in insurrection: they were calmed by the persuasive eloquence of the Pontiff. Certain infamous persons had made charges against some of the more eminent citizens of Rome, to tempt the Exarch to plunder them of their property. By the Pope's influence they were themselves punished by a heavy fine. He compelled or persuaded the Lombard Duke of Benevento, who had made a predatory incursion into Campania, to withdraw into his own territories. The Pope redeemed all the captives which the Lombard had taken.

During the pontificate of John VII., a Greek, the Emperor Justinian II. resumed the throne of Constantinople. The timid Pope trembled at his commands to receive the decrees of the Quinisextan Council; he endeavored to temporize, but escaped by death from the conflict. Sisinnius, a Syrian, was chosen his successor, but died twenty days after his election.

John VII. 705–707.

A.D. 707.

He was succeeded by Constantine, another Syrian. At the commencement of this pontificate, Felix, the newly-elected Archbishop of Ravenna, came to Rome for his consecration. But Felix refused to sign the customary writing testifying his allegiance to the Roman see, and to renounce the independence of Ravenna. The imperial ministers at Rome took part against him, and, in fear of their power, he tendered an ambiguous act of submission in which he declared his repugnance to his own deed. It was said that this act, laid up in the Roman archives, was in a few days

Constantine.

found black and shrivelled as by fire. But Felix had a more dangerous enemy than Pope Constantine. The Emperor Justinian had now glutted his vengeance on his enemies in the East; he sought to punish those who had either assisted or at least rejoiced in his fall in the more distant provinces. The inhabitants of Ravenna had incurred his wrath. A fleet, with Theodorus the patrician at its head, appeared in A.D. 708 their haven; the city was occupied, the chief citizens seized, according to one account by treachery, transported to Constantinople, and there by the sentence of the Emperor put to death. The Archbishop was beprived of his eyes in the most cruel manner A.D. 709. by the express orders of the Emperor. He was then banished to the Crimea.[1] The terrible Justinian still aimed at reducing the West to obedience to the Quinisextan Council. He summoned Constantine before his presence in Constantinople. The Pope had the courage and wisdom to obey. His obedience conciliated the Emperor. Everywhere he was well A.D. 710, 711. entertained, and he was permitted to delay till the tempestuous winter season was passed. In the spring he arrived in Constantinople, where he was received by Tiberius, son of the Emperor. Justinian was himself at Nicea; he advanced to Nicomedia to meet the Bishop of Rome. It is said by the Western writers that the Emperor knelt and kissed the feet of the Pope — an act neither consonant to Greek usage nor to the character of Justinian. But the Emperor's pride was gratified by the submission of Constantine. How far the Pope consented to the canons of the Quinisextan Council, by what arts he eluded those which were adverse

[1] Anastas. in Vit.; Agnelli, Vitæ Pontif. Ravennat.

to the Roman Discipline, history is silent. But Constantine returned to Italy in high favor with the Emperor, and bearing the imperial confirmation of all the privileges of the Church of Rome. The wisdom of Constantine's conduct became still more manifest. During his absence John Rizocopus, the new Exarch, entered Rome, seized and put to death many of the principal clergy. The Exarch proceeded to Ravenna, where he was slain in an insurrection of the citizens.[1] This insurrection grew to an open revolt. Ravenna and the Pentapolis threw off the imperial yoke, under the command of George, son of Giovannicius, the Emperor's secretary. On the death of Justinian and the change of the dynasty they renewed their allegiance; the blind Archbishop Felix returned from his banishment, and resumed the functions of his see.

Constantine was the last Pope who was the humble
A.D. 716. subject of the Eastern Emperor. With Gregory II. we enter on a new epoch in the history of Latin Christendom.

[1] Anastasius — Agnelli, ut supra.

CHAPTER VII.

ICONOCLASM.

THE eighth century gave birth to a religious contest, in its origin, in its nature, and in its impor- Iconoclasm. tant political consequences entirely different from all those which had hitherto distracted Christendom. Iconoclasm was an attempt of the Eastern Emperor to change by his own arbitrary command the religion of his subjects. No religious revolution has ever been successful which has commenced with the government. Such revolutions have ever begun in the middle or lower orders of society, struck on some responsive chord of sympathy in the general feeling, supplied some religious want, stirred some religious energy, and shaken the inert strength of the established faith by some stronger counter emotion. Whatever the motives of the Emperor Leo the Isaurian (and on this subject, as in all the religious controversies where the writings of the unsuccessful party were carefully suppressed or perished through neglect, authentic history is almost silent), whether he was actuated by a rude aversion to what perhaps can hardly yet be called the fine arts with which Christianity was associating itself, or by a spiritual disdain and impatience of the degrading superstition into which the religion of the Gospel had so long been degenerating, the attempt was as politically unwise and unseasonable as the means employed were despotic and altogether unequal to the end. The time was passed, if it had ever been, when an imperial edict could change, or even much affect, the actual prevailing religion of the empire. For this was no speculative article of belief, no question of high metaphysical theology, but a total change in the universal popular worship, in the spirit and in the essence, if not of the daily ritual, of countless observances and habitual practices of devotion. It swept away from almost all the churches of the Empire objects hallowed by devotion, and supposed to be endowed with miraculous agency; objects of hope and fear, of gratitude and immemorial *veneration*. It not merely invaded the public church, and left its naked walls without any of the old remembrancers of faith and piety; it reached the private sanctuary of prayer. No one could escape the proscription; learned or unlearned, priest or peasant, monk or soldier, clergyman or layman, man, woman, and even child, were involved in the strife. Something to which their religious attachments clung, to which their religious passions were wedded, might at any time be forcibly rent away, insulted, trampled under foot; that which had been their pride and delight could only now be furtively visited, and under the fear of detection.

Nature of the controversy.

Nor was it possible for this controversy to vent itself in polemic writings; to exhaust the mutual hatred which it engendered in fierce invectives, which, however they might provoke, were not necessarily followed by acts of conflict and bloodshed. Here actual, personal, furious collision of man and man, of faction and faction, of armed troops against armed troops, was inevitable. The contending parties did not assail each other with mutual anathemas, which they might despise, or excommunication and counter-excommunication, the validity of which might be questioned by either party. On one side it was a sacred obligation to destroy, to mutilate, to dash to pieces, to deface the objects on which the other had so long gazed with intense devotion, and which he might think it an equally sacred obligation to defend at the sacrifice of life. It was not a controversy, it was a feud; not a polemic strife, but actual war declared by one part of Christendom against the other. It was well perhaps for Christendom that the parties were not more equally balanced; that, right or wrong, one party in that division of the Christian world, where total change would have been almost extermination, obtained a slow but complete triumph.

In all the controversies, moreover, in which the Emperors had been involved, whether they had plunged into them of their own accord, or had been compelled to take a reluctant part, — whether they embraced the orthodox or the erroneous opinions, — they had found a large faction, both of the clergy and the people, already enlisted in the cause. In this case they had to create their own faction; and though so many of the clergy, from conviction, fear, or interest, became Iconoclasts, as to form a council respectable for its numbers; though, among some part of the people, an Iconoclastic fanaticism broke out, yet it was no spontaneous movement on their part. The impulse, to all appearance, emanated directly from the emperor. It was not called forth by any general expression of aversion to the existing superstition by any body of the clergy, or by any single bold reformer: it was announced. it was enacted in that character of Supreme Head of the Empire, which was still supposed to be vested in the Cæsar, and had descended to him as part of his inheritance from his pagan predecessors. This sovereignty comprehended religious as well as temporal autocracy; and of this the clergy, though they had often resisted it, and virtually, perhaps, held it to be abrogated, had never formally, publicly, or deliberately, declined the jurisdiction. It is a proof of the strong will and commanding abilities of the great Iconoclastic Emperors, that they could effect, and so long maintain, such a revolution, by their sole authority, throughout at least their eastern dominions.

And there was this irremediable weakness in the cause of Iconoclasm. It was a mere negative doctrine, a proscription of those sentiments which had full possession of the popular mind, without any strong countervailing religious excitement. There was none of that appeal to principles like those of the Reformation, to the Bible, to justification by faith, to the individual sense of responsibility. The senses were robbed of their habitual and cherished objects of devotion, but there was no awakening of an inner life of intense and passionate piety. The cold naked walls from whence the Scriptural histories had been effaced, the despoiled shrines, the mutilated images, could not compel the mind to a more pure and immaterial conception of God and the Saviour. It was a premature Rationalism, enforced upon an unreasoning age — an attempt to spiritualize by law and edict a generation which had been unspiritualized by centuries of materialistic devotion. Hatred of images, in the process of the strife, might become, as it did, a fanaticism — it could never become a religion. Iconoclasm might proscribe idolatry, but it had no power of kindling a purer faith.

Its consequences.

The consequences of this new religious dissension were of the utmost political importance, both in the East and in the West. In the East, instead of consolidating the strength of Christendom in one great confederacy against invading Mohammedanism, it distracted the thoughts of men from their more pressing dangers, weakened the military energy which, under the Isaurian race of emperors, seemed likely to revive; depopularized, with at least one half of their subjects, sovereigns of such great ability as Leo and Constantine Copronymus (whose high qualities for empire pierce through the clouds which are spread over their names by hostile annalists); and finally by adding a new element of animosity to the domestic intrigues within the palace, interrupted the regular succession, and darkened the annals of the empire with new crimes.

But its more important results were the total disruption of the bond between the East and the West — the severance of the Italian province from the Byzantine Empire; the great accession of Power to the Papacy, which took the lead in this revolution; the introduction of the Frankish king into the politics of Italy; and eventually the establishment of the Western Empire under Charlemagne.

Yet this question, thus prematurely agitated by the Iconoclastic emperors, and at this period of Christianity so fatally mistimed, is one of the most grave, and it should seem inevitable controversies, arising out of our religion. It must be judged by a more calm and profound philosophy than could be possible in times of actual strife between two impassioned and adverse factions. It is a conflict of two great principles, which it is difficult to reconcile. On the one hand, there can be no doubt that with ignorant and superstitious minds, the use, the reverence, the worship of images, whether in pictures or statues, invariably degenerates into idolatry. The Church may draw fine and aërial distinctions between images as objects of reverence and as objects of adoration; as incentives to the worship of more remote and immaterial beings, or as actual indwelling deities; it may nicely define the feeling which images ought to awaken; — but the intense and indiscriminating piety of the vulgar either understands not, or utterly disregards these subtleties: it may refuse to sanction, it cannot be said not to encourage, that devotion which cannot and will not weigh and measure either its emotions or its language. Image-worship in the mass of the people, of the whole monkhood at this time, was undeniably the worship of the actual, material, present image, rather than that of the remote, formless, or spiritual power, of which it was the emblem or representative. It has continued, and still continues, to be in many parts of Christendom this gross and unspiritual adoration; it is a part of the general system of divine worship. The whole tendency of popular belief was to localize, to embody in the material thing the supernatural or divine power. The healing or miraculous influence dwelt in, and emanated from, the picture of the saint — the special, individual picture — it was contained within the relic, and flowed directly from it. These outward things were not mere occasional vehicles of the divine bounty, indifferent in themselves, they possessed an inherent, inalienable sanctity. Where the image was, there was the saint. He heard the prayer, he was carried in procession to allay the pestilence, to arrest the conflagration, to repel the enemy. He sometimes resumed the functions of life, smiled, or stretched his hand from the wall. An image of the same saint, or of the Virgin, rivalled another image in its wonder-working power, or its mild benignity.

On the other hand, is pure and spiritual Christianity — the highest Christianity to which the human mind can attain — implacably and irreconcilably hostile to the Fine Arts? Is that influence of the majestic and the beautiful awakened through the senses by form, color, and expression, to be altogether abandoned? Can the exaltation, the purification of the human soul by Art in no way be allied with true Christian devotion? Is that aid to the realization of the historic truths of our religion, by representations, vivid, speaking, almost living, to be utterly proscribed? Is that idealism which grows out of and nourishes reverential feelings, to rest solely on the contemplation of pure spirit, without any intermediate human, yet superhumanized, form? Because the ignorant or fraudulent monk has ascribed miraculous power to his Madonna or the image of his patron saint, and the populace have knelt before it in awe which it is impossible to distinguish from adoration, is Christianity to cast off as alien to its highest development, the divine creations of Raffaele, or of Correggio. Are we inexorably to demand the same sublime spiritualism from the more or less imaginative races or classes of mankind?

This great question lies indeed at the bottom of the antagonism between those two descriptions of believers; to a certain extent, between the religion of southern and that of northern Europe, between that of the races of Roman and some of those of Teutonic descent; between that of the inhabitants of towns or villages; and rude mountaineers; finally, between Roman Catholicism and Protestantism.

But since, in the progress of civilization, the fine arts will no doubt obtain, if not greater influence, more general admiration, religion must either break off entirely all association with these dangerous friends, and the fine arts abandon the most fertile and noblest field for their development; or their mutual relations must be amicably adjusted. A finer sense of their inherent harmony must arise; the blended feelings which they excite must poise themselves far above the vulgar superstition of idolatry while they retain the force and intensity of devotional reverence. The causes which may be expected to work this sacred reconciliation may be the growing intelligence of mankind, greater familiarity with the written Scriptures; and, paradoxical as it may sound, but as may hereafter appear, greater perfection in the arts themselves, or a finer apprehension of that perfection in ancient as in modern art.

Doubtless, the pure, unmingled, spiritual notion of the Deity was the elementary principle of Christianity. It had repudiated all the anthropomorphic images, which to the early Jews had impersonated and embodied, if it had not to grosser minds materialized, the Godhead, and reduced him to something like an earthly sovereign, only enthroned in heaven in more dazzling pomp and magnificence. Even the localization of the Deity in the temple or the tabernacle, a step towards materialization, had been abrogated by the Saviour himself. Neither Samaria nor Jerusalem was to be any longer a peculiar dwelling-place of the Universal Father.

Throughout the early controversy on image-worship, there was a steadfast determination to keep the Parent and Primal Deity aloof from external form. No similitude of the unseen, incomprehensible Father, was permitted for many centuries;[1] even in a symbolic form, as in the vision of Ezekiel, which Raffaelle and some of the later painters have ventured to represent. It should seem, that even if the artists had been equal to the execution, the subject would have been thought presumptuous or profane.[2]

But if Christianity was thus in its language and in its primal conception so far superior in its spirituality to the religion of the Old Testament, it had itself its peculiar anthropomorphism: it had its visible, material, corporeal revelation of the Deity. God himself, according to its universal theory, had condescended to the human form.[3] Christ's whole agency, his birth, his infancy, his life, and his death, had been cognizable to the senses of his human brethren in the flesh. If, from the language of the Scriptures, descriptive of all those wonderful acts of power, of mercy, and of suffering, the imagination might realize to itself his actual form, motions, demeanor, the patient majesty in death,

[1] "Cur tandem patrem domini Jesu Christi non oculis subjicimus, et pingimus, quoniam quod sit non novimus, Deique natura spectanda proponi non potest ac pingi. Quod si eum intuiti essemus ac novissemus prout filium ejus, illum quoque spectandum proponere potuissemus, ac pingere, ut et illius imaginem idolum appellares." — Greg. II. Epist. i., ad Leon. Imper. p. 14.

[2] See the chapter in the History of Christianity on the Fine Arts, vol. iii. p. 486 *et seq.*, and Didron, Iconographie Chrétienne.

[3] *Οὐ τὴν ἀοράτου εἰκονίζω θεότητα, ἀλλ' εἰκονίζω θεοῦ τὴν ὁραθεῖσαν σάρκα.* — Joann. Damascen, Orat. de Imag. 1.

the dignity after the resurrection, the incipient glory in the ascension, and worship that mental image as the actual incarnate Godhead, why might not that which was thus first embodied in inspired language, and thence endowed with life by the creative faculty of the mind, be fixed in color and in stone, and so be preserved from evanescence, so arrayed in permanent ideal being? Form and color were but another language addressed to the eye, not to the ear. While the Saviour was on earth, the divinity within his human form demanded the intensest devotion, the highest worship which man could offer to God. The Saviour thus revivified by the phantasy, even as he was in the flesh, might justly demand the same homage. When that image became again actual form, did the material accessories — the vehicle of stone or color — so far prevail over the ideal conception, as to harden into an idol that which, as a mental conception, might lawfully receive man's devotions? It seemed to awaken only the same emotions, which were not merely pardonable, but in the highest degree pious, in the former case: why, then, forbidden or idolatrous in the latter? [1]

The same argument which applied to the Saviour, applied with still greater force to those merely human beings, the patriarchs and prophets of the Old Testa-

[1] This argument is urged by Gregory II. in his epistle to Germanus at great length: "Enarrent illa et per voces, et per literas, et per picturas." So Germanus: *ἅπερ διὰ τῆς ἀκοῆς ἀληθῆ πεπιστεύκαμεν ταῦτα καὶ διὰ γραφικῆς μιμήσεως πρὸς βεβαιοτέραν ἡμῶν πληροφορίαν συνιστάνομεν.* — Epist. ad Joann. Episc. Synad. They argued that this was an argument for Christ's real humanity against the Docetic sects. Their favorite authority was Basil: *ἃ γὰρ ὁ λόγος τῆς ἱστορίας διὰ τῆς ἀκοῆς παρίστησι, ταῦτα γραφὴ σιωπῶσα διὰ μιμήσεως δείκνυσι.* So also Joann. Damasc.: *ὅπερ τῇ ἀκοῇ ὁ λόγος, τοῦτο τῇ ὁράσει ἡ εἰκών.*

ment, the apostles, the saints, the martyrs, even to the Virgin herself. Why should not their histories be related by forms and colors, as well as by words? It was but presenting the same truths to the mind through another sense. If they were unduly worshipped, the error was in the hagiolatry or adoration of saints, not in the adoration of the image. Pictures were but the books of the unlearned; preachers never silent of the glory of the saints, and instructing with soundless voice the beholders, and so sanctifying the vision. "I am too poor to possess books, I have no leisure for reading: I enter the church, choked with the cares of the world, the glowing colors attract my sight and delight my eyes, like a flowery meadow; and the glory of God steals imperceptibly into my soul. I gaze on the fortitude of the martyr and the crown with which he is rewarded, and the fire of holy emulation kindles within me, and I fall down and worship God through the martyr, and I receive salvation."[1] Thus argues the most eloquent defender of images, betraying in his ingenious argument the rudeness of the arts, and the uncultivated taste, not of the vulgar alone. It is the brilliancy of the colors, not the truth or majesty of the design, which enthralls the sight. And, so in general, the ruder the art the

[1] *Ὅτι βίβλοι τοῖς ἀγραμμάτοις εἰσίν αἱ εἴκονες, καὶ τῆς τῶν ἁγιῶν τιμῆς ἀσίγητοι κήρυκες, ἐν ἀήχῳ φωνῇ τοῦς ὁρῶντας δίδασκουσαι, καὶ τὴν ὅρασιν ἁγάζουσαι. Οὐκ εὐπορῶ βίβλων, οὐ σχόλην ἄγω πρὸς τὴν ἀνάγνωσιν· εἴσειμι εἰς τὸ κοινὸν τῶν ψυχῶν ἰατρεῖον, τὴν ἐκκλησίαν, ὥσπερ ἀκάνθαις τοῖς λογισμοῖς συνπνιγόμενος, ἕλκει με πρὸς θέαν τῆς γραφῆς τὸ ἄνθος, καὶ ὡς λειμὼν τέρπει τὴν ὅρασιν, καὶ λεληθότως ἐναφίησι τῇ ψυχῇ δόξα θεοῦ. Τεθέαμαι τὴν καρτερίαν τοῦ μάρτυρος, τῶν στεφάνων τὴν ἀνταπόδοσιν, καὶ ὡς πυρὶ πρὸς ξύλον ἐξάπτομαι τῇ προθυμίᾳ, καὶ πίπτων προσκυνῶ θεὸν διὰ τοῦ μάοτυοος, καὶ λαμβάνω τὴν σωτηρίαν.*— Joann. Damascen. de Imag. Orat. ii. ɒ 747.

more intense the superstition. The perfection of the fine arts leads rather to diminish than to promote such superstition. Not merely does the cultivation of mind required for their higher execution, as well as the admiration of them, imply an advanced state; but the idealism, which is their crowning excellence, in some degree unrealizes them, and creates a different and more exalted feeling. There is more direct idolatry paid to the rough and ill-shapen image, or the flat, unrelieved, and staring picture, — the former actually clothed in gaudy and tinsel ornaments, the latter with the crown of gold leaf on the head, and real or artificial flowers in the hand, — than to the noblest ideal statue, or the Holy Family with all the magic of light and shade. They are not the fine paintings which work miracles, but the coarse and smoke-darkened boards, on which the dim outline of form is hardly to be traced. Thus it may be said, that it was the superstition which required the images, rather than the images which formed the superstition. The Christian mind would have found some other fetich, to which it would have attributed miraculous powers. Relics would have been more fervently worshipped and endowed with more transcendent powers, without the adventitious good, the familiarizing the mind with the historic truths of Scripture or even the legends of Christian martyrs, which at least allayed the evil of the actual idolatry. Iconoclasm left the worship of relics, and other dubious memorials of the saints, in all their vigor; while it struck at that which, after all, was a higher kind of idolatry. It aspired not to elevate the general mind above superstition, but proscribed only one, and that not the most debasing, form.

Of the emperors Leo the Isaurian and his son Constantine, the great Iconoclasts, the only historians are their enemies. That the founder of this dynasty was of obscure birth, from a district, or rather the borders, of the wild province of Isauria, enhances rather than detracts from the dignity of his character. Among the adventurers who from time to time rose to the throne of Byzantium, none employed less unworthy means, or were less stained with crime, than Leo. Throughout his early career the inimical historians are overawed by involuntary respect for his great military and administrative qualities. He had been employed on various dangerous and important services, and the jealousy of the ruling emperor, on more than one occasion, shows that he was already designated by the public voice as one capable of empire. Justinian II. abandoned him with a few troops, in an expedition against the Alani; from this difficulty he extricated himself with consummate courage and dexterity. He appears equally distinguished in valor and in craft. In the most trying situations his incomparable address is as prompt as decisive; against treacherous enemies he does not scruple to employ treachery.

Leo the Isaurian. A.D. 717.

His character.

The elevation of an active and enterprising soldier to the throne was imperiously demanded by the times, and hailed with general applause. The first measures of Leo were to secure the tottering empire against her most formidable enemies the Mohammedans, who were encompassing Constantinople on every side. Never had the Byzantine Empire been exposed to such peril as during the siege of Constantinople by Moslemah. Nothing but the indefatigable courage, military skill, and restless activity of Leo, aided by the new invention of the Greek fire, saved the eastern capital from falling five centuries before its time into the hands of the Mohammedans.[1] There can be no greater praise to Leo than that his superstitious subjects saw nothing less than the manifest interposition of the tutelary Virgin throughout their unexpected deliverance.

Leo persecutes Jews and heretics.

Leo had reigned for ten years, before he declared his hostility to image-worship. But his persecuting spirit had betrayed itself in the compulsory baptism of the Jews and the Montanists (probably some Manichean sect called by that ancient name) in Constantinople.[2] The effect of these persecutions was not encouraging. The Jews secretly washed off the contamination of baptism, and instead of fasting before the Holy Communion, polluted its sanctity, if they did not annul its blessings by eating common food. The Montanists burned themselves in their houses. In an orthodox emperor, however, these acts would have passed without reprobation, if not with praise.

Edict against images.

At the close of these ten years in the reign of Leo, Christendom was astounded by the sudden proscription of its common religious usages. The edict came forth, interdicting all worship of images. Leo was immediately asserted and believed to be as hostile to the adoration of the Virgin, to the worship of saints and of relics, as to that of images.[3]

[1] Theophanes passim.

[2] Ib. p. 336.

[3] Οὐ μόνον γὰρ περὶ τὴν σχετικὴν τῶν σεπτῶν εἰκόνων ὁ δυσσεβὴς ἐσφάλλετο προσκύνησιν, ἀλλὰ καὶ περὶ τῶν πρεσβειῶν τῆς παναγίου θεοτόκου, καὶ πάντων τῶν ἁγίων· καὶ τὰ λείψανα αὐτῶν ὁ παμμίαρος, ὡς οἱ διδάσκαλο. αὐτοῦ Ἄραβες, ἐβδελύττετο. — Theoph. p. 625.

In the common ear the emperor's language was that of a Jew or a Mohammedan, and fables were soon current that the impulse came from those odious quarters. It was rumored that while Leo was yet an obscure Isaurian youth named Conon, two Jews met him and promised him the empire of the world if he would grant them one request: this was, to destroy the images throughout Christendom.[1] They bound him by an oath in a Christian church! After the young Conon had ascended the throne, he was called on to fulfil his solemn vow. The prototype of the Christian Emperor in Iconoclasm had been the Sultan Yezid of Damascus. Yezid had been promised by a magician a reign of forty years over the Mohammedan world on the single condition of the destruction of images. God had cut off the Mohammedan in the beginning of his impiety, but Leo only followed this sacrilegious and fatal example. His adviser was said to be a certain Besor, a Syrian renegade from Christianity, deeply imbued with Mohammedan antipathies. The real motives of Leo it is impossible to conjecture. Had the rude soldier been brought up in a simpler Christianity among the mountains of his native Isauria? Had the perpetual contrast between the sterner creed and plainer worship of Mohammedanism and the paganized Christianity of his day led him to inquire whether this was the genuine and primitive re-

[1] And this was the emperor whose first religious act was the persecution of the Jews. Neither Pope Gregory nor any of the Western writers, nor even Theophanes, the earliest Byzantine, knew anything of this story. The first version is in a very doubtful oration ascribed to John of Damascus, passes through Glycas and Constantine Manasses, till the fable attains its full growth in Zonaras and Cedrenus. Theophanes gives the story of the Sultan Yezid.

ligion of the Gospel? Had he felt that he could not deny the justice of the charges of idolatry so prodigally made against his religion by the Jews and Mohammedans, and so become anxious to relieve it from this imputation? Had he found his subjects, instead of trusting, in their imminent danger from the Mohammedan invasion, to their own arms, discipline, and courage, entirely reposing on the intercession of the Virgin and the saints and on the magic influence of crosses and pictures? Did he act as statesman, general, or zealot, he pursued his aim with inflexible resolution, though not in the first instance without some caution.

For the war which the emperor declared against the
A.D. 726. images did not at first command their destruction. The first edict prohibited the worship, but only the worship, of all statues and pictures which represented the Saviour, the Virgin, and the saints. The statues and those pictures which hung upon the walls, and were not painted upon them, were to be raised to a greater height, so as not to receive pious kisses or other marks of adoration.[1]

About this period an alarming volcanic eruption took place in the Ægean. The whole atmosphere was dark as midnight, the sea and the adjacent islands strewn with showers of ashes and of stones. A new island suddenly arose amid this awful convulsion. The emperor beheld in this terrific phenomenon the divine wrath, and attributed it to his patient acquiescence in the idolatry of his subjects. The monks, on the other

[1] Unfortunately, none of the earlier edicts of the Iconoclastic emperors are extant. It is doubtful, and of course obstinately disputed, whether Leo condescended to require the sanction of any council or synod, or of any number of bishops. — Walch, p. 229.

hand, the implacable adversaries of the emperor and the most ardent defenders of image-worship, beheld God's fearful rebuke against the sacrilegious imperial edicts.[1]

The first edict was followed, at what interval it is difficult to determine, by a second of far greater severity. It commanded the total destruction of all images,[2] the whitewashing the walls of the churches. But if the first edict was everywhere received with the most determined aversion, the second maddened the image-worshippers, the mass of mankind, including most of the clergy and all the monks, to absolute fury. In the capital the presence of the emperor did not in the least overawe the populace. An imperial officer had orders to destroy a statue of the Saviour in a part of Constantinople called Chalcopratia. This image was renowned for its miracles. The thronging multitude, chiefly of women, saw with horror the officer mount the ladder. Thrice he struck with his impious axe the holy countenance, which had so benignly looked down upon them. Heaven interfered not, as no doubt they expected; but the women seized the ladder, threw down the officer, and beat him to death with clubs. The emperor sent

1 The chronology of these events is in the highest degree obscure. Baronius, Maimbourg, the Pagis, Spanheim, Basnage, Walch, have endeavored to arrange them in natural and regular sequence. The commencement of the actual strife in the tenth year of Leo's reign gives one certain date, A.D. 726. The death of Pope Gregory II. another, A.D. 731. The great difficulty is the time at which the second more severe edict followed the first. Some place it as late as 731; but it had manifestly been issued before the first epistle of Gregory. It seems to me as clear that it preceded the tumult at Constantinople, which arose from an attempt to destroy an image; but destruction does not seem to have been commanded by the earlier and milder edict.

2 Anastasius adds that they were to be burned in the most public place in the different cities. — Vit. Greg. II.

an armed guard to suppress the tumult; a frightful massacre took place. But the slain were looked upon, some were afterwards worshipped, as martyrs in the holy cause. In religious insurrections that which with one party is suppression of rebellion, with the other is persecution. Leo becomes, in the orthodox histories, little better than a Saracen; the pious were punished with mutilations, scourgings, exile, confiscation; the schools of learning were closed, a magnificent library burned to the ground. This last is no doubt a fable; and the cruelties of Leo were at least told with the darkest coloring. Even his successes in war were ingeniously turned to his condemnation. The failure of the Saracens in an attack on Nicea was, as usual, attributed to the intervention of the Virgin, not to the valiant resistance of the garrison. The Virgin was content with the death of a soldier who had dared to throw down and trample on her statue. She had appeared to him and foretold his death. The next day her prophecy was fulfilled, his brains were beat out by a stone from a mangonel. But the magnanimity of the Virgin did not therefore withdraw her tutelary protection from the city. Nicea escaped, though Leo, besides his disrespect for images, is likewise charged with doubting the intercession of the Mother of God.

Nor did this open resistance take place in Constantinople alone. A formidable insurrection broke out in Greece and in the Ægean islands. A fleet was armed, a new emperor, one Cosmas, proclaimed, and Constantinople menaced by the rebels. The fleet, however, was scattered and destroyed by ships which discharged the Greek fire: the insurrection was suppressed, the leaders either fell or were executed, along with the usurper.[1] The monks here, and throughout the empire, the champions of this as of every other superstition, were the instigators to rebellion. Few monasteries were without some wonder-working image; the edict struck at once at their influence, their interest, their pride, their most profound religious feelings.

But the more eminent clergy were likewise at first almost unanimous in their condemnation of the emperor. Constantine, Bishop of Nacolia, indeed, is branded as his adviser. Another bishop, Theodosius, son of Apsimarus, Metropolitan of Ephesus, is named as entering into the war against images. But almost for the first time the bishops of the two Romes, Germanus of Constantinople, and Pope Gregory II., were united in one common cause. Leo attempted to win Germanus to his views, but the aged patriarch (he was now 95 years old) calmly but resolutely resisted the arguments, the promises, the menaces of the emperor.

But the conduct of Gregory II., as leading to more important results, demands more rigid scrutiny. The Byzantine historians represent him as proceeding, at the first intimation of the hostility of the emperor to image worship, to an act of direct revolt, as prohibiting the payment of tribute by the Italian province.[2] This was beyond the power, probably beyond the courage, of Gregory. The great results of the final separation of the West from the inefficient and inglorious sovereignty of the East might excuse or palliate, if he had foreseen them, the disloyalty of Pope Gregory to Leo. But it would be to estimate his political and religious sagacity too highly to endow him with this gift

1 Theoph. Chronograph. p. 629.

2 Theophanes, followed by the later writers.

of ambitious prophecy, to suppose him anticipating the full development of Latin Christianity when it should become independent of the East. Like most ordinary minds, and, if we are to judge by his letters, Gregory's was a very ordinary mind, he was merely governed by the circumstances and passions of his time without the least foreknowledge of the result of his actions. The letter of Pope Gregory to the emperor is arrogant without dignity, dogmatic without persuasiveness; in the stronger part of the argument far inferior, both in skill and ingenuity, to that of the aged Germanus, or the writer who guided his pen.[1] The strange mistakes in the history of the Old Testament, the still stranger interpretations of the New, the loose legends which are advanced as history, give a very low opinion of the knowledge of the times. As a great public document, addressed to the whole Christian world by him who aspired to be the first ecclesiastic, we might be disposed to question its authenticity, if it were not avouched by the full evidence in its favor and its agreement with all the events of the period. After some praise of the golden promise of orthodoxy, in the declaration of Leo on ascending the throne, and in his conduct up to a certain period, the Pope proceeds, "For ten years you have paid no attention to the images which you now denounce as idols, and whose total destruction and abolition you command. Not the faithful only but infidels are scandalized at your impiety. Christ has condemned those who offend one of his little ones, you fear not to offend the whole world. You say that God has forbidden the worship

Letter of Gregory II. A.D. 729.

[1] Compare the two letters of Germanus to John of Synnada, and to Thomas of Claudiopolis. — Conc. Nic. ii. sess. iv.

of things made with hands; who worships them? Why, as emperor and head of Christendom, have you not consulted the wise? The Scriptures, the fathers, the six councils, you treat with equal contempt. These are the coarse and rude arguments suited to a coarse and rude mind like yours, but they contain the truth." Gregory then enters at length into the Mosaic interdiction of idolatry. "The idols of the Gentiles only were forbidden in the commandment, not such images as the Cherubim and Seraphim, or the ornaments made by Bezaleel to the glory of God." It is impossible without irreverence to translate the argument of the Pope, from the partial vision of God to Moses described in the book of Exodus.[1] What follows, if on less dangerous ground, is hardly less strange. "Where the body is, says our Lord, there will the eagles be gathered together. The body is Christ, the eagles the religious men who flew from all quarters to behold him. When they beheld him they made a picture of him. Not of him alone, they made pictures of James the brother of the Lord, of Stephen, and of all the martyrs; and so having done, they disseminated them throughout the world to receive not worship but reverence." Was this ignorance in Gregory, or effrontery? He then appeals to the likeness of Christ sent to Abgarus, king of Edessa. "God the Father cannot be painted, as his form is not known. Were it known and painted, would you call that an idol?" The pope appeals to

1 "Si videris me, morieris; sed ascende per foramen petræ et videbis posteriora mea." Gregory no doubt understood this in an awfully mysterious sense, but not without a materializing tendency. The whole Godhead was revealed in Christ, "nostrarum generationum ætate in novissimis temporibus manifestum seipsum, et posteriora simul et anteriora perfecte nobis ostendit."

the tears of devotion which he himself has shed while gazing on the statue of St. Peter. He denies that the Catholics worship wood and stone, these are memorials only intended to awaken pious feelings.[1] They adore them not as gods, for in them they have no hope, they only employ their intercession. "Go," he then breaks out in this contemptuous tone, "Go into a school where children are learning their letters and proclaim yourself a destroyer of images, they would all throw their tablets at your head, and you would thus be taught by these foolish ones what you refuse to learn from the wise." (It might be asked what well-instructed children now would say to a pope who mistook Hezekiah (called Uzziah) for a wicked king, his destroying the brazen serpent for an act of impiety, and asserted that David placed the brazen serpent in the *Temple.*) "You boast that as Hezekiah after 800 years cast out the brazen serpent from the temple, so after 800 years you have cast out the idols from the churches. Hezekiah truly was your brother, as self-willed, and, like thee, daring to offer violence to the priests of God." "With the power given me by St. Peter," proceeds Gregory, "I could inflict punishment upon thee, but since thou hast heaped a curse on thyself, I leave thee to endure it." The pope returns to his own edification while beholding the pictures and images in the churches. The passage is of interest, as showing the usual subjects of these paintings. "The miracles of the Lord; the Virgin Mother, with the infant Jesus on her breast, surrounded by choirs of angels; the Last Supper; the Raising of Lazarus; the miracles of giving sight to

1 Οὐ λατρευτικῶς ἀλλὰ σχετικῶς, "non latriâ sed habitudine." This is the invariable distinction.

the blind; the curing the paralytic and the leper; the feeding the multitudes in the desert; the transfiguration; the crucifixion, burial, resurrection, ascension of Christ; the gift of the Holy Ghost; the sacrifice of Isaac, which seems to have been thought, doubtless as typifying the Redeemer's death, a most pathetic subject." The pope then reproaches Leo for not consulting the aged and venerable Germanus, and for listening rather to that Ephesian fool the son of Apsimarus. The wise influence of Germanus had persuaded Constantine, the son of Constans, to summon the sixth council. There the emperor had declared that he would sit, a humble hearer, to execute the decrees of the prelates, and to banish those whom they condemned. "If his father had erred from the faith he would be the first to anathematize him." So met the sixth council. "The doctrines of the Church are in the province of the bishops not of the emperor: as the prelates should abstain from affairs of state, so princes from those of the Church."[1] "You demand a council: — revoke your edicts, cease to destroy images, a council will not be needed." Gregory then relates the insult to the image of the Saviour in Constantinople. "Not only those who were present at that sacrilegious scene, but even the barbarians had revenged themselves on the statues of the emperor, which had before been received in Italy with great honor. Hence the invasion of the Lombards, their occupation of Ravenna, their menaces that they would advance and

[1] "Scis sanctæ ecclesiæ dogmata non imperatorum esse, sed pontificum: idcirco ecclesiis præpositi sunt pontifices a reipublicæ negotiis abstinentes, et imperatores ergo similiter ab ecclesiasticis abstineant, et quæ sibi commissa sunt, capessant." This was new doctrine in the East.

seize Rome. It is your own folly which has disabled you from defending Rome; and you would terrify us and threaten to send to Rome and break in pieces the statue of St. Peter, and carry away Pope Gregory in chains, as Constans did his predecessor Martin. Knowest thou not that the popes have been the barrier-wall between the East and the West — the mediators of peace? I will not enter into a contest. I have but to retire four-and-twenty miles into Campania, and you may as well follow the winds. The officer who persecuted Pope Martin was cut off in his sins; Martin in exile was a saint, and miracles are performed at his tomb in the Chersonese. Would that I might share the fate of Martin. But, for the statue of St. Peter, which all the kingdoms of the West esteem as a *god on earth*, the whole West would take a terrible revenge.[1] I have but to retire and despise your threats; but I warn you that I shall be guiltless of the blood that will be shed; on your head it will fall. May God instil his fear into your heart! May I soon receive letters announcing your conversion! May the Saviour dwell in your heart, drive away those who urge you to these scandals, and restore peace to the world!"[2]

If Gregory expected this expostulatory and defiant epistle to work any change in Leo, he was doomed to

[1] "Quam omnia Occidentis regna, velut Deum terrestrem habent." This looks something like idolatry.

[2] Gregory alludes with triumph to his conquest over the northern kings, who are submitting to baptism from the hands of his missionary, St. Boniface. "Nos viam ingredimur in extremas occidentis regiones versus illos, qui sanctum baptisma efflagitant. Cum enim illuc episcopos misissem, et sanctæ ecclesiæ nostræ clericos, nondum adducti sunt ut capita sua inclinarent et baptizarentur eorum principes, quod exoptent, ut eorum sim susceptor."

disappointment. In a subsequent, but shorter letter, he attempted to appall the emperor by the great names of Gregory the Wonder-worker, Gregory of Nyssa, Gregory the Theologian, of Basil, and of Chrysostom, to whose authority he appealed as sanctioning the worship of images. He held up the pious examples of those obedient sons of the Church, Constantine the Great, Theodosius the Great, Valentinian the Great, and Constantine who held the sixth council. "What are our churches but things made with hands, of stone, wood, straw, clay, lime? but they are adorned with paintings of the miracles wrought by the saints, the passion of the Lord, his glorious mother, his apostles. On these pictures men spend their whole fortunes; and men and women, with newly baptized children in their arms, and grown-up youths from all parts of the world come, and, pointing out these histories, lift up their minds and hearts to God." The pope renews his earnest admonitions to the emperor to obey the prelates of the Church in all spiritual things. "You persecute us and afflict us with a worldly and carnal arm. We, unarmed and defenceless, can but send a devil to humble you, to deliver you to Satan for the destruction of the flesh, and the salvation of the spirit. Why, you ask, have not the councils *commanded* image-worship? Why have they not commanded us to eat and drink?" (Images, Gregory seems to have considered as necessary to the spiritual as food to the corporeal life.) "Images have been borne by bishops to councils; no religious man goes on a pilgrimage without an image." "Write to all the world that Gregory, the Bishop of Rome, and Germanus, Bishop of Constantinople, are in error concerning

Second letter.

images; cast the blame on us, who have received from God the power to bind and to loose."

When Gregory addressed these letters to the Emperor Leo, the tumult in Constantinople, the first public act of rebellion against Iconoclasm, had taken place;

Degradation of Germanus.

but the aged Bishop Germanus was not yet degraded from his see. Germanus, with better temper and more skilful argument, had defended the images of the East.[1] Before his death he was de-

A.D. 731.

posed or compelled to retire from his see. He died most probably in peace, his extreme age may well account for his death. His personal ill-treatment by the emperor is the legend of a later age to exalt him into a martyr.[2]

But these two powerful prelates were not the only champions of their cause, whose writings made a strong impression on their age. It is singular that the most admired defender of images in the East, was a subject not of the emperor but of the Mohammedan Sultan.

John of Damascus.

John of Damascus was famed as the most learned man in the East, and it may show either the tolerance, the ignorance, or the contempt of the Mohammedans for these Christian controversies, that writings which became celebrated all over the East, should issue from one of their capital cities, Damascus.[3]

The ancestors of John, according to his biographer, when Damascus fell into the hands of the Arabs, had almost alone remained faithful to Christianity. They commanded the respect of the conquerors, and were employed in judicial offices of trust and dignity, to

1 Compare his letters in Mansi, in the report of the Second Council of Nicea.

2 Cedrenus, iv. 3.

3 Vit. Joann. Damasceni, prefixed to his works.

administer no doubt the Christian law to the Christian subjects of the sultan. His father, besides this honorable rank, had amassed great wealth; all this he devoted to the redemption of Christian slaves, on whom he bestowed their freedom. John was the reward of these pious actions. John was made a child of light immediately on his birth. This, as his biographer intimates, was an affair of some difficulty and required much courage. The father was anxious to keep his son aloof from the savage habits of war and piracy, to which the youth of Damascus were addicted, and to devote him to the pursuit of knowledge. The Saracen pirates of the sea-shore, neighboring to Damascus, swept the Mediterranean and brought in Christian captives from all quarters. A monk named Cosmas had the misfortune to fall into the hands of these freebooters. He was set apart for death, when his executioners, Christian slaves no doubt, fell at his feet, and entreated his intercession with the Redeemer. The Saracens inquired of Cosmas who he was. He replied that he had not the dignity of a priest, he was a simple monk, and burst into tears. The father of John was standing by, and asked, not without wonder, how one already dead to the world could weep so bitterly for the loss of life? The monk answered, that he did not weep for his life, but for the treasures of knowledge which would be buried with him in the grave. He then recounted all his attainments: he was a proficient in rhetoric, logic, in the moral Philosophy of Aristotle and of Plato, in natural philosophy, in arithmetic, geometry, and music, and in astronomy. From astronomy he had risen to the mysteries of theology, and was versed in all the divinity of the Greeks. He could not but lament that he was to die without leaving an heir to his vast patrimony of science, to die an unprofitable servant who had wasted his talent. The father of John begged the life of the monk from the Saracen governor, gave him at once his freedom, placed him in his family, and confided to him the education of his son. The pupil in time exhausted all the acquirements of his teacher. The monk assured the father of John that his son surpassed himself in every branch of knowledge. Cosmas entreated to be dismissed, that he might henceforth dedicate himself to that higher philosophy, to which the youthful John had pointed his way. He retired to the desert, to the monastery of St. Saba, where he would have closed his days in peace, had he not been compelled to take on himself the Bishopric of Maiuma.

The attainments of the young John of Damascus commanded the veneration of the Saracens; he was compelled reluctantly to accept an office of still higher trust and dignity than that held by his father. As the Iconoclastic controversy became more violent, John of Damascus entered the field against the emperor. His three orations in favor of image-worship were disseminated with the utmost activity throughout Christendom.

The biographer of John brings a charge of base and treacherous revenge against the emperor. It is one of those legends of which the monkish East is so fertile, and cannot be traced, even in allusion, to any document earlier than the life of John. Leo having obtained, through his emissaries, one of John's circular epistles in his own handwriting, caused a letter to be forged, containing a proposal from John of Damascus to betray his native city to the Christians. The emperor, with specious magnanimity, sent this letter to the sultan. The indignant Mohammedan ordered the guilty hand of John to be cut off, a mild punishment for such a treason! John entreated that the hand might be restored to him, knelt before the image of the Virgin, prayed, fell asleep, and woke with his hand as before. The miracle convinced the sultan of his innocence: he was reinstated in his place of honor. But John yearned for monastic retirement. He too withdrew to the monastery of St. Saba. There a severe abbot put his humility and his obedience to the sternest test. He was sent in the meanest and most beggarly attire to sell baskets in the market-place of Damascus, where he had been accustomed to appear in the dignity of office, and to vend this poor ware at exorbitant prices. As a penance for an act of kindness to a dying brother, he was set to clean the filth from all the cells of his brethren. An opportune vision rebuked the abbot for thus wasting the splendid talents of his inmate. John was allowed to devote himself to religious poetry, which was greatly admired, and to his theologic arguments in defence of images.

The fame of this wonder of his age rests chiefly on these writings, of which the extensive popularity attests their power over the minds of his readers. His courage in opposing the emperor, and in asserting the superior authority of the Church in all ecclesiastic affairs, considering that he was secure either in Damascus or in his monastery and a subject of the Saracenic kingdom, is by no means astonishing. The three famous orations repeat, with but slight variations, each after the other, the same arguments; some the

Orations of John.

ordinary and better arguments for the practice, expressed with greater ingenuity and elegance than by the other writers of the day, occasionally with surpassing force and beauty, not without a liberal admixture of irrelevant and puerile matter; the same invectives against his opponents, as if by refusing to worship the images of Christ, his mother, and the saints, they refused to worship the venerable beings themselves. Pictures are great standing memorials of triumph over the devil; whoever destroys these memorials is a friend of the devil; to reprove material images is Manicheism, as betraying the hatred of matter, which is the first tenet of that odious heresy. It was a kind of Docetism, too, asserting the unreality of the body of the Saviour. At the close of each oration occurs almost the same citation of authorities, not omitting the memorable one of the Hermit, who was assailed by the demon of uncleanness. The demon offered to leave the holy man at rest if he would cease to worship an image of the Virgin. The hard-pressed hermit made the rash vow, but in his distress of mind communicated his secret to a famous abbot, his spiritual adviser. "Better," said the abbot, "that you should visit every brothel in the town, than abstain from the worship of the holy image."

The third oration concludes with a copious list of miracles wrought by certain images; an argument more favorable to an incredulous adversary, as showing the wretched superstition into which the worship of images had degenerated and as tending to fix the accusation of idolatry.

From the death of Leo the Isaurian the history of Iconoclasm belongs exclusively to the East, until the

Council of Frankfort interfered to regulate the worship of images in the Transalpine parts of Europe. Gregory III., the successor of Gregory II., whose pontificate filled up the remaining years of Leo's reign, inflexibly pursued the same policy as his predecessor. In the West, all power, almost all pretension to power, excepting over Sicily and Calabria, expired with Leo; [1] and this independence partly arose out of, and was immeasurably strengthened by, the faithful adherence of the West to image-worship; but the revolt or alienation of Italy from the Eastern empire will occupy a later chapter in Christian history.

Constantine Copronymus.

Leo was succeeded by his son Constantine. The name by which this emperor was known is a perpetual testimony to the hatred of a large part of his subjects. Even in his infancy he was believed to have shown a natural aversion to holy things, and in his baptism to have defiled the font. Constantine Copronymus sounded to Greek ears as a constant taunt against his filthy and sacrilegious character.

A.D. 741.

The accession of Constantine, although he had already been acknowledged for twenty years, with his father, as joint-emperor, met formidable resistance. The contest for the throne was a strife between the two religious parties which divided the empire. During the absence of Constantine, on an expedition against the Saracens, a sudden and dangerous insurrection placed his brother-in-law, Artavasdus, on the throne. Constantinople was gained to the party of the usurper by treachery. The city was induced to submit to Artavasdus only by a rumor, industriously prop-

1 Leo died June, 741. Gregory III. in the same year.

agated and generally believed, of the death of Constantine. The emperor on one occasion had been in danger of surprise, and escaped by the swiftness of his horses. In the capital, as throughout Greece and the European part of the Empire, the triumph of Artavasdus was followed by the restoration of the images. Anastasius, the dastard Patriarch of Constantinople, as he had been the slave of Leo, now became the slave of the usurper, and worshipped images with the same zeal with which he had destroyed them. He had been the principal actor in the deception of the people by the forged letters which announced the death of Constantine. He plunged with more desperate recklessness into the party of Artavasdus. The monks, and all over whom they had influence, took up the cause of the usurper; but the mass of the people, from loyal respect for the memory of Leo, or from their confidence in the vigorous character of Constantine and attachment to the legitimate succession, from indifference or aversion to image-worship, still wavered, and submitted, rather than clamorously rejoiced in the coronation of Artavasdus. The Patriarch came forward, seized the crucifix from the altar, and swore by the Crucified that Constantine had assured him that it was but folly to worship Jesus as the Son of God; that he was a mere man, that the Virgin Mother had borne him, but as his own mother Mary had borne himself. The furious people at once proclaimed the deposition of Constantine, no doubt to the great triumph of the image-worshippers. Besor, the renegade counsellor of Leo, to whom popular animosity attributed the chief part in the destruction of the images, fell in the first conflict.

But Constantine Copronymus with the religious

opinions inherited the courage, the military abilities, and the popularity with the army which had distinguished his father Leo. After some vicissitudes, a battle took place near Ancyra, fought with all the ferocity of civil and religious war. The historian expresses his horror that, among Christians, fathers should thus be engaged in the slaughter of their children, brothers of brothers.[1] Constantine followed up his victory by the siege of the capital. After an obstinate resistance, and after having suffered all the horrors of famine, Constantinople was taken. Artavasdus escaped for a short time, but was soon captured, and brought in chains before the conqueror. An unsuccessful usurper risks his life on the hazard of his enterprise. It is difficult to decide whether the practice of blinding, instead of putting to death in such cases, was a concession to Christian humanity. The other common alternative of shutting up the rival for the throne in a monastery and disqualifying him for empire by the tonsure, was not likely to occur to Constantine, nor would it have been safe, considering the general hatred of the monks to the emperor. Artavasdus was punished by the loss of his eyes; it was wanton cruelty afterwards to expose him, with his sons and principal adherents, during the races in the Hippodrome, to the contempt of the people.

Constantine was a soldier, doubtless of a fierce temper; the blinding and mutilation of many, the beheading a few of his enemies, the abandonment of the houses of the citizens to the plunder of his troops, was the natural course of Byzantine revolution; and these cruelties have no doubt lost nothing in the dark representations

[1] Theophanes *in loco.*

of the emperor's enemies, the only historians of the times. But they suffered as rebels in arms against their sovereign, not as image-worshippers. The fate of the Patriarch Anastasius was the most extraordinary. His eyes were put out, he was led upon an ass, with his face to the tail, through the city; and after all this mutilation and insult, for which, considering his tergiversation and impudent mendacity, it is difficult to feel much compassion; he was reinstated in the Patriarchal dignity. The clergy in the East had never been arrayed in the personal sanctity which, in ordi-
A.D. 743. nary occasions, they possessed in the West; but could Constantine have any other object in this act than the degradation of the whole order in public estimation?

For ten years Constantine refrained from any stronger measures against image-worship. The overthrow of Artavasdus no doubt threw that large party of time-servers, the worshippers of the will of the emperor, on his side. His known severity of character would impress even his more fanatical opponents with awe; many images would vanish again, as it were, of their own accord; even the monks might observe some prudence in their resistance. During these ten years Constantine had secured the frontiers of the Empire against the Saracens in the East, and the Bulgarians on the North. His throne had been strengthened by the birth of an heir. A dreadful pestilence, which, contrary to the usual course, travelled from west to east, spread from Calabria to Sicily, and throughout great part of the Empire. The popular mind, and even the government, must have been fully occupied by its ravages. The living, it is said, scarcely sufficed to bury the dead; the gardens within the city, and the vineyards without, were turned into a vast cemetery. The image-worshippers beheld in this visitation the vengeance of God against the Iconoclasts.[1]

In the tenth year of Constantine rumors spread abroad of secret councils held for the total destruction of images. A.D. 746. Either the emperor must have prepared the public mind for this great change with consummate address, or reverence for images must have been less deeply rooted in the East than in the West, otherwise it can scarcely be supposed that so large a number of the clergy as appeared at the Third Council of Constantinople would have slavishly assented to the strong measures of the emperor.

Three hundred and forty-eight bishops formed this synod, which aspired to the dignity of the Seventh Ecumenic Council. Third Council of Constantinople. Its adversaries objected the absence of all the great Patriarchs, especially that of the Pope, who was present neither in person nor by his delegates. The Patriarchs of Alexandria, Antioch, and Jerusalem were now cut off, as it were, from Christendom; they were the subjects of an unbelieving sovereign, perhaps could not, if they had been so disposed, obey the summons of the emperor. The Bishop of Rome was, if not in actual revolt, in contumacious opposition to him, who still claimed to be his sovereign. The Patriarch of Constantinople had lost all weight. The Bishop of Ephesus, occasionally the Bishop of Perga, presided in the council.

Part of the proceedings of this assembly have been

1 Διὰ τὴν ἀσεβῶς γεγενημένην εἰς τὰς ἱερὰς εἴκονας ὑπὸ τῶν κρατούντων κατένεξιν. — Theophanes sub ann. 738, p. 651.

preserved in the records of the rival council, the second held at Nicea. The passages are cited in the original words, followed by a confutation, sanctioned apparently by the Nicene bishops. The confutation is in the tone of men assured of the sympathy of their audience. It deals far less in grave argument than in contemptuous crimination. The ordinary name for the Iconoclasts is the arraigners of Christianity.[1] It assumes boldly that the worship of images was the ancient, immemorial, unquestionable usage of the Church, recognized and practised by all the fathers, and sanctioned by the six General Councils: that the refusal to worship images is a new and rebellious heresy. Every quotation from the fathers which makes against images is rejected as a palpable forgery, so proved, as it is asserted, by its discordance with the universal tradition and practice of the Church.

But the Council of Constantinople had manifestly set the example of this peremptory and unargumentative dictation: it may be reasonably doubted whether it attempted a dispassionate and satisfactory answer to the better reasonings of the image-worshippers. It proscribes the lawless and blasphemous art of painting.[2] The fathers of Constantinople assume, as boldly as the brethren of Nicea their sanctity, that all images are the invention of the devil; that they are idols in the same sense as those of the heathen.[3] Nor do they hesitate to impute community of sentiment with the worst heretics to their opponents. They thought that

[1] *Χριστιανοκατήγοροι* is the term framed for the occasion.

[2] *Τὴν ἀθέμιτον τῶν ζωγράφων τέχνην βλασφημοῦσαν.*

[3] Faith they asserted came by *hearing*, and hearing from the Word of God. — P. 467.

they held the image-worshippers in an inextricable dilemma. If the painters represented only the humanity of Christ, they were Nestorians; if they attempted to mingle it with the Divinity, they were Eutychians, circumscribing the infinite, and confounding the two substances.[1] It was impiety to represent Christ without his divinity, Arianism to undeify him, despoil him of his godhead.

The Council of Nicea admits the perfect unanimity of the Council of Constantinople. These 348 bishops concurred in pronouncing their anathema against all who should represent the Incarnate Word by material form or colors, who should not restrict themselves to the pure spiritual conception of the Christ, as he is seated, superior in brightness to the sun, on the right hand of the Father; against all who should confound the two natures of Christ in one human image, or who should separate the manhood from the godhead in the Second Person of the indivisible Trinity; against all who should not implore the intercession of the Virgin in pure faith, as above all visible and invisible things;[2] against all who should set up the deaf and

1 They made him ἀθεωτὸν. The fathers of Nicea were indignant at the barbarism of this word (p. 443). Their opponents might have retorted the use of the whimsical hybrid φαλσόγραφοι. The most remarkable passage, as regards art, in this part of the controversy, is a description of a painting of the martyrdom of St. Eufemia, from the writings of Asterius, Bishop of Amasia. This picture, or rather series of pictures, must have been of many figures, grouped with skill, and in the judgment of the bishop with wonderful expression; the various passions were blended with great felicity. Asterius compares it with the famous picture of Medea killing her children, which his language, somewhat vague indeed, might lead to the supposition that he had actually seen. The taste of Asterius may be somewhat doubtful, since in one picture he describes the executioner drawing the teeth of the victim: the reality of the blood which flowed from her lips filled him with horror. — Labbe, p. 489.

2 Ὑπερτέραν τε εἶναι πάσης ὁράτης καὶ ἀοράτου κτίσεως.

lifeless images of the saints, and who do not rather paint the living likenesses of their virtues in their own hearts. All images, whether statues or paintings, were to be forcibly removed from the churches; every one who henceforth should set up an image, if a bishop or priest, was to be degraded; if a layman, excommunicated. The one only image of the Redeemer, which might be lawfully worshipped, was in the Holy Sacrament; at the same time, therefore, that all images were to be removed, all respect was to be paid to the consecrated vessels of the Church.

Was then all this host of bishops, the concordant cry of whose anathema rose to heaven (according to the fathers of Nicea, like that of the guilty cities of the Old Testament) only subservient to the Imperial Will?[1] Or had a wide-spread repugnance to images grown up in the East? Were the clergy and the monks in hostile antagonism on this vital question? It appears evident, that the old ineradicable aversion to matter, the constant dread of entangling the Deity in this debasing bondage, which has been traced throughout all the Oriental controversies, lay at the bottom of much of this tergiversation. "We all subscribe," they declared at the close of their sitting, "we are all of one mind, all of one orthodoxy, worshipping with the spirit the pure spiritual Godhead."[2] They concluded with their prayers for the pious emperor, who had given peace to the Church, who had extirpated idolatry, who had triumphed over those who taught that error, and settled forever the true doctrine.

[1] Ἡ *κραυγὴ αὐτῶν τοῦ ἀναθέματοος σοδομικῶς καὶ γομοῤῥιχῶς πεπλήθυνται.* —Labbe, p. 526.

[2] *Πάντες νοερῶς τῇ νοερᾷ θεότητι λατρεύοντες προσκυνοῦμεν.*

They proceed to curse by name the principal assertors of image-worship. "Anathema against the double-minded Germanus, the worshipper of wood! Anathema against George (of Cyprus), the falsifier of the traditions of the fathers! Anathema against Mansar (they called by this unchristian-sounding name the famous John of Damascus), the Saracen in heart, the traitor to the Empire; Mansar the teacher of impiety, the false interpreter of Holy Scripture!"

CHAPTER VIII.

COUNCIL OF NICEA. CLOSE OF ICONOCLASM.

Thus was image-worship proscribed by a council, in numbers at least of weight, in the severest and most comprehensive terms. The work of demolition was committed to the imperial officers; only with strict injunctions, not perhaps always obeyed, to respect the vessels, the priestly vestments, and other furniture of the churches, and the cross, the naked cross without any image.[1]

But if the emperor had overawed, or bought, or compelled the seemingly willing assent of so large a body of the eastern clergy, the formidable monks were still in obstinate implacable opposition to his will. The wretched Anastasius had died just before the opening of the council; and the emperor himself, it is said, ascended the pulpit, and proclaimed Constantine Bishop of Sylæum, ecumenic Patriarch and Bishop of Constantinople. Constantine had been a monk, and this appointment might be intended to propitiate that powerful interest, but Constantine, unlike his brethren, was an ardent Iconoclast.

The emperor was a soldier, and fierce wars with the Saracens and Bulgarians were not likely to soften a

[1] The crucifix was of a later period. — See Hist. of Christianity, iii. p. 515.

temper naturally severe and remorseless. He had committed his imperial authority in a deadly strife for the unattainable object of compelling his subjects to be purer and more spiritual worshippers of God than they were disposed to be; not suspecting that his own sanguinary persecutions were more unchristian than their superstitions. It was now fanaticism encountering fanaticism. Everywhere the monks preached resistance to the imperial decree, and enough has been seen of their turbulent and intractable conduct to make us conclude that their language at least would keep no bounds. Stephen, the great martyr of this controversy, had lived as a hermit in a cave near Sinope for thirty years. The monks in great numbers had taken refuge in the desert, where they might watch in secret over their tutelary images; and not monks alone, but a vast multitude of the devout, crowded around the cell of Stephen to hear his denunciations against the breakers of images. The emperor ordered him to be carried away from his cell, the resort of so many dangerous pilgrims, and to be shut up in a cloister at Chrysopolis. The indignation of the monks was at its height. One named Andrew hastened from his dwelling in the desert, boldly confronted the emperor in the church of St. Mammas, and sternly addressed him— "If thou art a Christian, why dost thou treat Christians with such indignity?" The emperor so far commanded his temper, as simply to order his committal to prison; he afterwards summoned him again to his presence. The mildest term that the monk would use to address the emperor, was a second Valens, another Julian. Constantine's anger got the mastery; he commanded the monk to be scourged in the Hippodrome, and then to be strangled. The sisters of Andrew hardly saved his remains from being cast into the sea.[1]

For several years either the occupation of the emperor by foreign wars, or the greater prudence of the monks, enforced by this terrible example, suspended at least their more violent collisions with the authorities.

The monk Stephen.

Stephen still continued to preach in his cloister against the sin of the Iconoclasts.[2] The emperor sent the Patriarch to persuade him to subscribe the decrees of the Council of Constantinople. The Patriarch's eloquence was vain. The emperor either allowed or compelled the aged monk to retire to the wild rock of Proconnesus, where, to consummate his sanctity, he took his stand upon a pillar. His followers assembled in crowds about him, and built their cells around the pillar of the saint. But the zeal of Stephen would not be confined within that narrow sphere. He returned to the city, and in bold defiance of the imperial orders denounced the Iconoclasts. He was seized, cast into prison, and there treated with unusual harshness. But even there the zeal of his followers found access. Constantine exclaimed, in a paroxysm of careless anger, "Am I or this monk the emperor of the world?" The word of the emperor was enough for some of his obsequious courtiers; they rushed, broke open the prison, dragged out the old man along the streets, with every wanton cruelty, and cast his body at last into the common grave of the public malefactors.

The emperor took now a sterner and more desperate

1 Theophanes *in loc.*

2 Acta S. Stephani, in Analectis Græcis. p. 396.

Persecution of the monks.

resolution. He determined to root out monkery itself. An old grievance was revived. The emperor and the people were enraged, or pretended to be enraged, that the monks decoyed the best soldiers from the army, especially one George Syncletus, and persuaded them to turn recluses.[1] The emperor compelled the patriarch not only to mount the pulpit and swear by the holy cross that he would never worship images, but immediately to break his monastic vows, to join the imperial banquet, to wear a festal garland, to eat meat, and to listen to the profane music of the harpers.

Then came a general ordinance, that the test of signing the articles of Constantinople should be enforced on all the clergy, and all the more distinguished monks.[2] On their refusal the monks were driven from their cloisters, which were given up to profane and secular uses. Consecrated virgins were forced to marry; monks were compelled, each holding the hand of a woman, doubtless not of the purest character, to walk round the Hippodrome among the jeers and insults of the populace. Throughout the empire they were exposed to the lawless persecutions of the imperial officers. Their zeal or their obstinacy was chastised by scourgings, imprisonments, mutilations, and even death. The monasteries were plundered, and by no scrupulous or reverent hands; churches are said to have been despoiled of all their sacred treasures, the holy books

[1] This, according to the martyrologist of Stephen, was a trick of the Emperor, with whom George had a secret understanding, to bring odium on the monks.

[2] *Τόμον συνοδικὸν αὐτὰ καλέσας ὃ ἀσεβέστατος, ἀπῃτεῖ ἀρχιερεῖς τε πάντας, καὶ τῶν μοναζόντων τοὺς περιβοήτους ἐπ' ἀρέτῃ, ταῦτα ὑποσημάνασθαι.* — Compare Concil. Nic. ii. p. 510.

burned, feasts and revels profaned the most hallowed sanctuaries. Multitudes fled to the neighboring kingdoms of the less merciless Barbarians; many found refuge in the West, especially in Rome. The Prefect of Thrace was the most obsequious agent of his master's tyranny. Throughout that Theme the monks were forced to abandon their vows of solitude and celibacy under pain of being blinded and sent into exile. Monasteries, with all their estates and property, were confiscated. Relics as well as images, in some cases no doubt books,[1] and the whole property of the convents, was pillaged or burned by the ignorant soldiery. The personal cruelties against the monks will not bear description; the prefect is said not to have left one in the whole Theme who ventured to wear the monastic habit.

In Constantinople a real or suspected conspiracy against the emperor involved some of the noblest patricians, and some who filled the highest offices of state, in the same persecution. Eight or nine of the more distinguished were dragged, amid the shouts of the rabble, round the Hippodrome, and then put to death. The fate of two brothers, named Constantine, moved general commiseration. The prefect was scourged and deposed for not having suppressed these signs of public sympathy. Others were blinded, cruelly scourged, and sent into exile.[2] The patriarch himself was accused of having used disrespectful language toward the emperor. Already

Degradation of the patriarch. A.D. 759.

[1] Some books were burned as containing pictures. One is mentioned in a statement made to the Council of Nicea: *'Αργυρᾶς πτύχας ἔχει, καὶ ἑκατέρωθεν ταῖς εἰκόσι πάντων τῶν ἁγιῶν κεκόσμηται* — Pictures illuminated on a silver ground! — Conc. Nic., p. 373.

[2] Theophanes, compared with statement before the Nicene Council.

he had been required to acquit himself of imputing Nestorianism to his master; now his accusers swore on the cross that they had heard him hold conference with one of the conspirators. Constantine ordered the imperial seal to be affixed on the palace of the patriarch, and sent him into banishment.

But this miserable slave of the imperial will was not allowed to shroud himself in obscure retirement. He had consented to the consecration of Nicetas, an eunuch of Sclavonian descent, in his place. For some new offence, real or supposed, the exiled patriarch was brought back to the capital, scourged so cruelly that he could not walk, and then carried in a litter, and exposed in the great church before all the people assembled to hear the public recital of the charges made against him, and to behold his degradation. At each charge the secretary of his successor smote him on the face. He was then set up in the pulpit, and while Nicetas read the sentence of excommunication, another bishop stripped him of his metropolitan pall, and calling him by the opprobrious name Scotiopsis, face of darkness, led him backwards out of the church. The next day his head, beard, eyebrows, were shaved; in a short and sleeveless dress he was put upon an ass, and paraded through the circus (his own nephew, a hideous, deformed youth, leading the ass) while the populace jeered, shouted, spat upon him. He was then thrown down, trodden on, and in that state lay till the games were over. Some days after the emperor sent to demand a formal declaration of the orthodoxy of his own faith, and of the authority of the council. The poor wretch acknowledged both in the amplest manner; as a reward he was beheaded,

His death.

while still in a state of excommunication, and his remains treated with the utmost ignominy. The historian adds, as an aggravation of the emperor's ferocity, that the patriarch had baptized two of his children.[1]

This odious scene, blackened it may be by the sectarian hatred of the later annalists, all of whom abhorred Iconoclasm, has been related at length, in order to contrast more fully the position of the Bishop of Rome. This was the second patriarch of Constantinople who had been thus barbarously treated, and seemingly without the sympathy of the people; and now, in violation of all canonical discipline, the imperial will had raised an eunuch to the patriarchate. What wonder that pontiffs like Gregory II. and Gregory III. should think themselves justified in throwing off the yoke of such a government, and look with hope to the sovereignty of the less barbarous Barbarians of the North — Barbarians who, at least, had more reverence for the dignity of the sacerdotal character!

Character and death of Constantine Copronymus.

If the Byzantine historians, all image-worshippers, have not greatly exaggerated the cruelties of their implacable enemy Constantine Copronymus, they have assuredly not done justice to his nobler qualities, his valor, incessant activity, military skill, and general administration of the sinking empire, which he maintained unviolated by any of its formidable enemies, and with imposing armies, during a reign of thirty-five years, not including the twenty preceding during which he ruled as the colleague of his father Leo. Constantine died, during a campaign against the Bulgarians, of a fever which, in the charitable judgment of his adversaries, gave him a

A.D. 775.

[1] Theophanes, p. 681.

foretaste of the pains of hell. His dying lips ordered prayers and hymns to be offered to the Virgin, for whom he had always professed the most profound veneration, utterly inconsistent, his enemies supposed, with his hostility to her sacred images.

Helena and Irene.

A female had been the principal mover in the great change of Christianity from a purely spiritual worship to that paganizing form of religion which grew up with such rapidity in the succeeding centuries; a female was the restorer of images in the East, which have since, with but slight interruption, maintained their sanctity. The first, Helena, the mother of Constantine the Great, was a blameless and devout woman, who used the legitimate influence of her station, munificence, and authority over her imperial son, to give that splendor, which to her piety appeared becoming, to the new religion; to communicate to the world all those excitements of symbols, relics, and sacred memorials which she found so powerful in kindling her own devotion. The second, the Empress Irene, wife to the son and heir of Constantine Copronymus, an ambitious, intriguing, haughty princess, never lost sight of political power in the height of her religious zeal, and was at length guilty of the most atrocious crime against God and womanhood.[1]

Leo IV.

Irene, during the reign of her husband Leo, surnamed the Chazar, did not openly betray her inclination to the image-worship which she had solemnly forsworn under her father-in-law Constantine. Leo was a man of feeble constitution and gentle mind,

1 The Pope Hadrian anticipated a new Constantine and a new Helena in Irene and her son. — Hadrian, Epist. apud Labbe, p. 102.

controlled by the strongest influences of religion. He endeavored to allay the heat of the conflicting parties. His first acts gave some hopes to the image-worshippers that he was favorably disposed to the Mother of God and to the monks (these interests the monks represented as inseparable); he appointed some metropolitans from the abbots of monasteries.[1]

This short reign of Leo IV. is remarkable for the A.D. 775–780. attempt of the emperor to reintroduce a more popular element into the public administration — a kind of representative assembly; — and the general voice, in gratitude to Leo, demanded the elevation of his infant son to the rank of Augustus. The prophetic heart of the parent foresaw the danger. He was conscious of his own feeble health; to leave an unprotected infant on the throne was (according to all late precedent in the Byzantine empire) to doom him to death. Leo assembled not the senate and nobles alone, the chief officers of the army and of the court, but likewise the people of Constantinople. He explained the cause of his hesitation, confessed his fears, and demanded and received a solemn oath upon the cross, that on his death they would acknowledge no other emperor but his son. The next day he proclaimed his son Augustus: the signatures of the whole people to their oath were received and deposited, amid loud acclamations that they would lay down their lives for the emperor, on the table of the Holy Communion.

A few months matured a conspiracy. Nicephorus, the emperor's brother, was designed for the throne.

[1] Ἐδοξεν εὐσεβὴς εἶναι πρὸς ὀλιγον χρόνον, καὶ φίλος τῆς θεοτόκου καὶ τῶν μοναχῶν. — Theophan., p. 695.

Conspiracy repressed.

But again the emperor, instead of putting forth the strong and revengeful arm of despotism, appealed to the people. In a full assembly he produced the proofs of the conspiracy, and left the cause to the popular judgment. The general voice declared the conspirators guilty of a capital crime, and renewed their vows of fidelity to the infant emperor. But the gentle Leo spared his brother; some few of the conspirators were put to death, others incapacitated for future mischief by the tonsure; — thus the greatest honor, that of the priesthood, had become a punishment for crime! The moderation of Leo induced him to appoint as Patriarch of Constantinople, Paul, a Cypriot by birth, as yet of no higher rank than a reader; a man willing to shrink and keep aloof from the controversy of the day. Leo was ill rewarded. The monkish party, watching no doubt his declining health, and knowing the secret sentiments of the empress, introduced some small images, in direct violation of the law, into the palace, and even into her private chamber. Some deeper real or suspected cause of apprehension must have existed in the mind of the emperor to make him depart from his wonted leniency. Many of the principal officers were seized and cast into prison, where one of them died, in the following reign held to be a martyr, the rest became distinguished monks. But from that time so strong was the hatred of the image-worshippers, that Leo was branded as a cruel persecutor; his death was attributed to an act of sacrilege. He was a great admirer of precious stones, and took away and wore a crown, the offering of the Emperor Heraclius to some church. The fatal circle burned into his head, which broke out

Death of Leo. A.D. 780.

into carbuncles, of which he died. There was no need to invent this fable to account for the death of one so infirm as Leo; still less to suggest suspicions, on the other side, that his death was caused by poison.

Irene Empress.

Irene at once seized the government in the name of her son Constantine, who was but ten years old. An attempt was made on the part of Nicephorus, the rebel brother of Leo, to supplant the empress in the regency and in the tutelage of her son. It was suppressed; the chiefs of the faction punished by the scourge and exile, the brothers of the late emperor compelled to undergo ordination and to administer the Eucharist as a public sign of their incapacitation for secular business.

The crafty Irene dissembled for a time her design for the restoration of images. Her ambitious mind (it is not uncommon in her sex) was deeply tinged by superstition; no doubt she thought that she secured the divine blessing, or rather that of the Virgin and the saints, upon her schemes of power, by the honor which she was preparing for their images. Fanaticism and policy took counsel together within her heart. But the clergy of Constantinople were too absolutely committed, as yet, on the other side; the army revered the memory, perhaps chiefly on that account the opinions, of Constantine Copronymus. The Patriarch, an aged and peaceful man, who had sincerely wished to escape the perilous charge of the episcopate, was neither disposed nor fitted to lend himself as an active instrument in such an enterprise. He was not absolutely indisposed to the image-worshippers; and when the empress allowed the laws to fall into disuse, and connived at the quiet restoration of some images, and encouraged the monks with signs of favor, it was bruited abroad that she acted in no discordance with the bishop's secret opinion. The public mind was duly prepared by prodigies in the remoter parts of the Empire for the coming revolution.

A.D. 783. Tarasius Patriarch.

On a sudden the Patriarch Paul disappeared. It was proclaimed that he had renounced his dignity, retreated into a cloister, and taken the habit of a monk. It cannot be known whether he had any secret understanding with the empress, but he who had been so solemnly and publicly pledged to the former emperor against the images would hardly, an old and unambitious man, take a strong part in their restoration. The empress visited his cloister and inquired the cause of his sudden retirement. From the first, said the lowly patriarch, his mind had been ill at ease; that he had accepted a see rejected from the communion of great part of Christendom; should he die in this state of excommunication he would inevitably go to hell.[1] The empress sent the chief persons of the court to hear this confession from the lips of the repentant patriarch. Paul deplored with bitter sorrow that he had concurred in the decrees against images; his mind was now awakened to truth; and he suggested, no doubt the suggestions of others, that nothing could heal the wounds of the afflicted Church but a general council to decide on image-worship. Having made this humiliating declaration he expired in peace.

[1] The Empress states this in the imperial letter read at the opening of the Council of Nicea: — Τὸ *ἀνάθεμα ἔξω ἀπὸ πασῆς τῆς καθολικῆς ἐκκλησίας, ὃ ἀπάγει εἰς τὸ σκοτὸς τὸ ἐξώτερον, τὸ ἡτοιμασμένον τῷ διαβόλῳ καὶ τοῖς ἀγγελοίς αὐτοῦ.* — P. 52.

On the succession to the see of Constantinople might A.D. 784. depend the worship or the rejection of images throughout the East. Among all the clergy Irene could find no one of influence, ability, and resolution equal to cope with the approaching crisis. The appointment of a monk would probably have been the signal for the rallying of the adverse party. Among her privy counsellors [1] was a man who in the world bore the character of profound religion, and of whose ability and ambition Irene had formed a high, and, as events proved, a just estimate. The empress assembled the people; she declared her respect for the memory of Paul; she asserted that she would not have allowed him to abandon his higher duties for monastic seclusion, but God had now withdrawn him from the scene, and it was necessary to appoint a successor of known capacity and holiness. The affair had been well organized; a general acclamation demanded Tarasius; to the demand the empress assented with undisguised satisfaction. Tarasius gave a good omen of his future conduct by the address with which he seemed to decline the arduous honor, on account of the controversies which distracted the Church. In a well-acted scene the empress employed persuasion, influence, authority, to win the reluctant patriarch. Tarasius played admirably the part of humble refusal, of concession of capitulation on his own terms. The condition of his acceptance was the summoning a council to decide the great question of image-worship, which he declared to have been decreed by the sole authority of the emperor Leo, and to that authority the Council of Constantinople had only yielded its assent. Most of

[1] Ασηκρητις — the Grecized Latinism.

the people gave, at least seemingly, their cordial concurrence in the election, though even the admirers of Tarasius admit that there was much secret murmuring, and some open clamor among the lower populace.

Tarasius immediately took measures to consolidate the whole strength of the party. Messengers were sent to Rome to obtain the presence of the Pope (Hadrian) in person or by his legates. Hadrian made some show of remonstrance against the sudden promotion of a layman to so important a see, but acquiesced in it, as demanded by the emergencies of the times. The patriarchs of Alexandria and of Antioch and of Jerusalem were summoned, and certain ecclesiastics appeared as representatives of those prelates.

The Council met in Constantinople; but with the army and a large part of the populace of Constantinople image-worship had lost its power. The soldiery, attached to the memory and tenets of Constantine Copronymus, broke into the assembly, and dispersed the affrighted monks and bishops. The empress in vain exerted herself to maintain order. No one was hurt; but it was manifest that no council of image-worshippers was safe in the capital.

A.D. 785.

Nicea was chosen for the session of the council, no doubt on account of the reverence which attached to that city, hallowed by the sittings of the first great council of Christendom. Decrees issued from Nicea would possess peculiar force and authority; this smaller city, too, could be occupied by troops, on whom the empress could depend, and in the mean time Irene managed to disband the more unruly soldiery. Thus, while the Bulgarians menaced one frontier and the Saracens another, she sacrificed the

Second council of Nicea.

safety of the Empire, by the dissolution of her best army, to the success of her religious designs.

A.D. 787. The council met at Nicea. The number of ecclesiastics is variously stated from 330 to 387. Among these were at least 130 monks or abbots, besides many bishops, who had been expelled as monks from their sees, and were now restored. Tarasius took the lead as virtual, if not acknowledged, president of the assembly. The first act of the Council of Nicea showed the degree of dispassionate fairness with which the inquiry was about to be conducted. After the imperial letters of convocation had been read, three bishops appeared, Basilius of Ancyra, Theodosius of Myra in Lycia, Theodosius of Amorrium; they humbly entreated permission to recant their errors, to be reconciled to the Catholic Church. They recited a creed framed with great care, and no doubt of prearranged orthodoxy, in which they repudiated the so-called Council of Constantinople, as a synod of fools and madmen, who had dared to violate the established discipline of the Church, and impiously reviled the holy images. They showered their anathemas on all the acts, on all the words, on all the persons engaged in that unhallowed assembly.[1]

The council received this humble confession of their sin and misery with undisguised joy; and Tarasius pronounced the solemn absolution. Certain other prelates were then admitted, among them the Bishops of Nicea and Rhodes. They were received after more strict examination, and citation of ecclesiastical prece-

[1] They denounced the prelates who presided in the assembly; among the rest Basil of Pisidia, on whom they inflicted an ecclesiastical nickname. He was fitly named (κακεμφάτως) τρικάκκαβος, or τρίκακος.

dents, from which it appeared that bishops who recanted Ariænism and Nestorianism, having been readmitted into the Church, even Iconoclasts should not be rejected from her bosom on the same terms.[1] The severer monks made vigorous resistance to these acts of lenity, but were overruled at length. It was debated to what class of heretics the Iconoclasts were to be ascribed. The patriarch proposed only to confound them with the most odious of all the Manicheans and the Montanists.[2] The inexorable leader of the monkish party asserted that it was worse than the worst heresy, being absolute renegation of Christ.[3] This was among the preliminary acts of a council, assembled to deliberate, examine, discuss, and then decide this profound theological question.

The whole proceedings of the council, though conducted with orderly gravity, are marked with the same predeterminate character, the same haughty and condemnatory tone towards the adversaries of image-worship. The fathers of Nicea impaired a doubtful cause by the monstrous fables which they adduced, the preposterous arguments which they used, their unmeasured invectives against their antagonists. The Pope Hadrian, in his public letter, related a wild and recent legend of a vision of Constantine the Great,

1 It is worthy of remark that they accuse the Council of Constantinople of asserting the sole authority of Scripture, the insufficiency of Tradition without it: *'Ως εἰ μὴ ἐκ τῆς παλαιᾶς καὶ καινῆς θιαθήκης ἀσφαλῶς διδαχθῶμεν, οὐ ἑπόμεθα ταῖς διδασκαλίαις τῶν ἁγίων πατέρων.* They brand this doctrine as that of Arius, Nestorius, and other heretics.

2 The usual difficulty arose as to ordinations conferred or received by such heterodox bishops.

3 'Η *αἵρεσις αὕτη χεῖρον πάντων τῶν αἱρέσεων κακόν· οὐαὶ τοῖς εἰκονομάχοις, καὶ (κακῶν κακίστη) ὡς τὴν οἰκονομίαν τοῦ Σωτῆρος ἀνατρέπονται.* — P. 78.

in which St. Paul and St. Peter appeared to him, and whom he knew to be the apostles by their resemblance to pictures of them, exhibited to him by Pope Silvester.[1] It is the standing argument against the Iconoclasts: "the Jews and Samaritans reject images, therefore, all who reject them are as Jews and Samaritans."[2] The ordinary appellations of the Iconoclast comprehend every black shade of heresy, impiety, atheism.

The rapidity with which the council executed its work was facilitated by the unanimity of its decisions.[3] The whole assembly of bishops and monks subscribed the creed, in which, after assenting to the decrees of the first six councils, and to the anathemas against the heretics denounced therein, they passed, acting, as they declared, under the guidance of the Holy Spirit, the following canon.

Decree on image-worship.

"With the venerable and life-giving cross shall be set up the venerable and holy images, whether in colors, in mosaic work, or any other material, within the consecrated churches of God, on the sacred vessels and vestments, on the walls and on tablets, on houses and in highways. The images, that is to say, of our God and Saviour Jesus Christ; of the immaculate mother of God; of the honored angels; of all saints and holy men. These images shall be treated as holy memorials, worshipped, kissed, only without that peculiar adoration[4] which is reserved for the Invisible, Incomprehensible God." All who

[1] Labbe, Concil., p. 111.

[2] Ib., p. 358.

[3] There were eight sittings between the 24th Sept. and 23d Oct. — Walch, p. 560.

[4] We have no word to distinguish between προσκύνησις and λάτρεια.

shall violate this, as is asserted, immemorial tradition of the Church, and endeavor, forcibly or by craft to remove any image, if ecclesiastics, are to be deposed and excommunicated, if monks or laymen, excommunicated.

The council was not content with this formal and solemn subscription. With one voice they broke out into a long acclamation, "We all believe, we all assent, we all subscribe. This is the faith of the apostles, this is the faith of the Church, this is the faith of the orthodox, this is the faith of all the world. We, who adore the Trinity, worship images. Whoever does not the like, anathema upon him! Anathema on all who call images idols! Anathema on all who communicate with them who do not worship images! Anathema upon Theodorus, falsely called Bishop of Ephesus; against Sisinnius of Perga, against Basilius with the ill-omened name! Anathema against the new Arius Nestorius and Dioscorus, Anastasius; against Constantine and Nicetas! (the Iconoclast Patriarchs of Constantinople). Everlasting glory to the orthodox Germanus, to John of Damascus! To Gregory of Rome everlasting glory! Everlasting glory to the preachers of truth!"

Our history pauses to inquire what incidental notices of the objects and the state of Christian art transpire during this controversy, more especially in the proceedings of the Council of Nicea. There seem to have been four kinds of images against which the hostility of their adversaries was directed, and which were defended by the resolute attachment of their worshippers. I. Images, properly so called, which were thrown from their pedestals, and broken in pieces. II. Mosaic paintings, which were picked out. III.

Paintings on waxen tablets on the walls, which were smoked and effaced. IV. Paintings on wood, which were burned. There were likewise carvings on the sacred vessels; and books were destroyed on account of the pictures with which they were embellished.[1]

In all the images and paintings there was, as formerly observed, a reverential repugnance to attempt any representation of God the Father. The impiety of this was universally admitted; the image-worshippers protest against it in apparent sincerity, and not as exculpating themselves from any such charge by their adversaries.

The first and most sacred object of art was the Saviour, and next to the Saviour the "Mother of God." The propriety of substituting the actual human form of the Saviour for the symbolic Lamb,[2] or the Good Shepherd, was now publicly and authoritatively asserted. Among the images of various forms and materials some are mentioned of silver and of gold. A certain Philastrius objected to the Holy Ghost being figured in the form of a dove.[3]

A question of the form under which angels and archangels should be represented could not but arise. The fitness of the human form was unhesitatingly asserted; and angels were declared to have a certain corporeity, more thin and impalpable than the grosser body of man, but still not absolute spirit. Severus objected to angels in purple robes: they should be white, no doubt as representing light.[4]

1 Passim, especially address to the Emperor at the close of the Council. — P. 580.

2 P. 123. See curious extract from the Journeying of the Twelve Apostles; a Docetic book, and so ruled to be by the Council.

3 P. 370.

4 P. 373.

The whole of the New Testament is said to have been represented; meaning, no doubt, all the main facts of the history.[1] Among the subjects in the Old Testament, as early as Gregory of Nyssa, a picture is described of the sacrifice of Isaac, in which there must have been an attempt at least at strong expression.[2] Chrysostom is cited for a picture on the sublime but difficult subject of the angel destroying the army of Sennacherib. Images of Moses, of Elijah, of Isaiah, and of Zechariah, are named. Pope Hadrian asserts (but there has been already ground to question his assertion), that Constantine built a church in Rome, in which was painted on one side Adam expelled from paradise, on the other, the penitent thief ascending into it. In Alexandria there was an early painting of the Saviour between the Virgin and John the Baptist.

There is nothing, or hardly anything, to induce the supposition that any one image or painting was distinguished as a work of art; as impressing the minds of its worshippers with admiration of its peculiar grace, majesty, or resemblance to actual life. Art, as art, entered not into the controversy. It was the religious feeling which gave its power to the image or painting, not the happy design, or noble execution, which awakened or deepened the religious feeling. The only exception to this is the description of the picture representing the martyrdom of St. Euphemia, by Asterius Bishop of Amasia. This was painted on linen.[3]

Among the acclamations and the anathemas which closed the Second Council of Nicea, echoed loud salu-

[1] P. 358. [2] P. 203. [3] Ἐν σίνδονι.

tations and prayers for the peace and blessedness of the new Constantine and the new Helena. A few years passed, and that Constantine was blinded, if not put to death, by his unnatural mother, whom religious faction had raised into a model of Christian virtue and devotion.

Irene and Constantine her son.

A long struggle took place, when Constantine reached the age of manhood, between the mother, eager to retain her power, and the son, to assume his rightful authority. All the common arts of intrigue and party manœuvre were exhausted before they came to open hostilities. The principal courtiers, and part of the army, ranged themselves in opposite factions. Irene, anticipating, it was said, her adversaries, struck the first blow, seized, scourged, shaved into ecclesiastics, and imprisoned the chief of her son's adherents. A considerable part of the troops swore solemnly that the son should not reign during the lifetime of Irene; the son was given over to her absolute power, and chastised like a refractory schoolboy. The next year a division of the army revolted, and proclaimed Constantine sole Emperor. The usual fate of the scourge and the tonsure befell the leaders of Irene's faction. The Empress was confined to her palace. But her inexhaustible fertility in intrigue soon restored her power. Constantine, having suffered a shameful defeat by the Bulgarians, through her advice wreaked his vengeance on his uncles, whom he accused of aspiring to the throne; they were blinded, or mutilated by the loss of their tongues. Five years afterwards, on the very same day of the month (a less superstitious age might have beheld in this coincidence the retributive hand of God), Constantine was blinded by his mother.

These five years were years of base intrigue, treachery, outward courtesy and even the familiar intercourse of close kindred, of inward hatred, jealousy, and attempts to mine and countermine each the interest of the other. It was attributed to his mother's advice, with the design of heightening his unpopularity, that Constantine divorced himself from his wife Maria, forced her to retire into a convent, and married a woman of her bedchamber, named Theodota. The rigid monks were furious at the weakness of the Patriarch Tarasius, who had sanctioned the reception of the divorced empress in a monastery. Plato, the most intolerant, and therefore most distinguished of them, withdrew from communion with the Patriarch. The indignant Emperor imprisoned some, and banished others of the more refractory monks to Thessalonica. This at once threw the whole powerful monastic faction into the interests of the Empress, who openly espoused their cause. The Armenian guards, who had now assumed something like the power, insolence, and versatility of the old Prætorian troops, were alienated by the severity of Constantine. Irene wound her toils with consummate skill around her ill-fated victim. There was treachery in his army, in his court, in his palace. He was bitterly afflicted by the loss of his eldest son. At length the plot was ripe; he knew it, and attempted in vain to make his escape to the East. Either fearing, or pretending to fear, lest he should regain his liberty, Irene sent to her secret emissaries around his person, and threatened to betray their treachery if they did not deliver up their master to her hands. Constantine was seized on the Asiatic side of the Bosphorus, conducted

Murder of Constantine.

to the porphyry chamber, in which Irene had borne him — her first-born son. In that very chamber the crime was perpetrated. His eyes were put out, so
A.D. 797. cruelly and so incurably, as to threaten his death.[1] In the East, the conduct of the unnatural mother was seen with unmitigated horror. An eclipse of the sun, accompanied with such darkness, that ships wandered from their courses, was held to be a sign of the sympathy of the heavenly orbs with the suffering Emperor — an expression of divine disapprobation. Among the few instances in the annals of mankind, in which ambition and the love of sway have quenched the maternal feeling — that strongest and purest impulse of human nature — is the crime committed against her son by the Empress Irene. But it is even more awful and humiliating that (so inextinguishable are religious passions!) a churchman of profound learning, of unimpeachable character, should, many centuries after, be so bewildered by zeal for the *orthodox* Empress, as to palliate, extenuate, as far as possible apologize for this appalling deed, in which the sounder moral sense of the old Grecian tragedy would have imagined a divine Nemesis for the accumulated guilt of generations of impious ancestors.[2]

[1] Δεινῶς καὶ ἀνιάτως πρὸς τὸ ἀποθανεῖν αὐτόν. — Theophan., p. 732.

[2] The passage must be quoted: — "Scelus planè execrandum, nisi quod multi excusant, justitiæ eam zelus ad id faciendum excitâsset, quo nomine eadem post hæc meruit commendari. At non fuit matris jussio, ut ista pateretur, sed ut teneretur," (this is directly contrary to Theophanes and the best authorities,) "nec amplius imperaret, tanquam si e manu furiosi gladium auferret. Docuit Christus verbis suis summæ pietatis genus esse in hoc adversus filium esse crudelem, ipso dicente." (The Cardinal here cites our Lord's words, Matt. x. 37, "He that loveth son or daughter more than me is not worthy of me."). "Quum jam olim, Dei præcepto, justæ sint armatæ manus parentum in filios, abeuntes post Deos alienos, illisque necatis, qui hoc fecerint, Moysis ore laudati, ita dicentis, Exod. xxxii. 29.

So completely indeed might the Iconoclastic faction appear to be crushed, that neither during the strife between the mother and the son, though it might have some latent influence, did it give any manifest or threatening sign of its existence; and Irene reigned in peace for five years, and was overthrown by a revolution, in which religion had no apparent concern.

A.D. 797–802.

The controversy slept during the reign of Nicephorus, and that of Michael, surnamed Rhangabes. The monks throughout this period seem to form an independent power (a power no doubt arising out of, and maintained by, their championship of image-worship), and to dictate to the Emperor, and even to the Church. On the other hand, among the soldiery are heard some deep but suppressed murmurs of attachment to the memory of Constantine Copronymus.

Nicephorus emperor. A.D. 802–811.

Michael. A.D. 811–813.

Leo the Armenian ascended the throne, for which Michael Rhangabes felt and acknowledged his incapacity. The weak Michael had courted the friendship of the monks; on his invitation, or with his acquiescence, they settled in increasing swarms within the city. The Armenian was another of those rude soldiers, born in a less civilized part of Christendom, in which image-worship had not taken profound root. But he did not betray his repugnance to the

Leo the Armenian.

Plurimum interest quo quis aliquid animo agat. Si enim regnandi cupidine Irene in filium molita esset insidias, detestabilior Agrippina matre Neronis fuisset . . . Contra vero quod ista, *religionis causâ*, amore justitiæ in filium perpetrata credantur, ab Orientalibus nonnullis, qui facto aderant, *viris sanctissimis!* eadem posthæc præconio meruit celebrari." As if any motive could be assigned but the most unscrupulous ambition; though doubtless she was throughout supported by the image-worshippers. — Baron. Ann. sub ann. DCCXCVI.

popular religious feeling until, like his predecessor the Isaurian Leo, he had secured the north-western and eastern frontiers of the empire. Against the Bulgarians, who were actually besieging Constantinople, he began the war by a base act of treachery, an attempt to assassinate Cromnus, their victorious king, during a peaceful interview; he terminated it by a splendid victory, which for a time crushed the power of these Barbarians. He was equally successful against the Saracens. The firm and prosperous administration of Leo extorted from the exiled Patriarch of Constantinople, Nicephorus, an ample if unwilling acknowledgment. "Impious as he was, he was a wise guardian of the public interests. Firm in civil as in military affairs, superior to wealth, he chose his ministers for their worth, not their riches, and aimed at least at the rigid execution of justice."[1]

But all these virtues were obscured, in the sight of the image-worshippers, by his attempt to suppress that worship. Even on his accession there was some mistrust of his opinions; the name Chameleon can scarcely apply to anything but his suspected religious versatility. The Patriarch at that time tendered him a profession of faith, which he adroitly put by till he should have despatched the more pressing duties of his station. He seemed, however, as he passed the brazen gate, to do homage to an image of the Saviour placed above it.

The enemies of Leo attribute his change to the artifices of a monk, by some strange contradiction a hater of images. The superstitious Leo was addicted to the consultation of self-asserted diviners; he had been designated by this monk, endowed as was supposed

[1] Theophan. Contin., p. 30.

with the prophetic gift, for the throne. As the witch of Endor Saul, so the monk had recognized the future monarch, though shrouded in disguise. At the same time, he was threatened with immediate death if he did not follow the course of Leo the Isaurian; if he did, the empire was to remain in his family for generations.

Against image-worship.

The emperor summoned the Patriarch Nicephorus to his presence before the senate, and proposed the insidious question, whether there were not those who denied the lawfulness of worship to images? The Patriarch was not scrupulous in his reply. He appealed to the holy Veronica, the napkin with the impression of the Saviour's face, the first sacred image not made with hands. He declared that there were images made by the apostles themselves, of the Saviour and the Mother of God; that there was actually in Rome a picture of the transfiguration, painted by the order of St. Peter; he did not forget the statue at Paneas, in Palestine.[1] Another bishop boldly admonished the emperor to attend to his proper business, the army, and not to venture to meddle with the affairs of the Church, in which he had no concern. The indignant emperor banished the two intractable prelates. Euthymus, of Sardis, who had used still more opprobrious language, was corporally punished with blows and stripes. As Irene had promoted Tarasius, so Leo raised an officer of his household, Theodotus Cassiteras, to the patriarchal throne. Image-worship was again proscribed by an imperial edict. The worshippers are said to have been ruthlessly persecuted; and Leo, according to the phraseology of the day, is accused of showing all the bloodthirstiness, without the gener-

[1] Symeon Magister in Theoph. Contin., p. 607.

osity, of the lion. Yet no violent popular tumult took place; nor does the conspiracy which afterwards cut short the days of Leo the Armenian appear to have been connected with the strife of religious factions. He might have escaped his fate but for his scrupulous reverence for the institutions of the Church. Michael the Stammerer had risen, like Leo, to military distinction. He was guilty, or at least suspected, of traitorous designs against the emperor, thrown into prison, and condemned to immediate death. But the next day (the day appointed for his execution) was the feast of the nativity of Christ. The wife of Leo urged him not to profane that sacred season, that season of peace and good-will, by a public execution. Leo, with a sad prophetic spirit, answered that she and her children would bitterly rue the delay; but he could not withstand her scruples and his own. Yet his mind misgave him: at midnight the emperor stole into the dungeon, to assure himself that all was safe. The prisoner was sleeping quietly; but a slave who had hid himself under the bed, recognized the purple sandals of the emperor. Michael instantly sent word to the other conspirators, that unless they struck the blow he would denounce them as his accomplices. The chamberlain of Leo was Michael's kinsman; and on the dawn of the holy day, which Leo had feared to violate, the conspirators mingled with the clergy, who assembled as usual, at the third watch, to hail the birth of Christ. The emperor was famed for the finest voice in the city: he had joined in the beautiful hymn of peace, when the conspirators rushed to the attack. At first, in the fog of the morning, they mistook the leader of the clergy for the emperor, but fortunately he took off his cap and showed his tonsure. Leo, in the mean time, had taken refuge at the altar, seized the great cross, and with this unseemly weapon, grasped in his despair, kept his enemies at bay, till at length a gigantic soldier lifted his sword to strike. Leo reminded him of his oath of allegiance: "'Tis no time to speak of oaths," replied the soldier, "but of death;" and swearing by the divine grace,[1] smote off the arm of his sovereign, which fell with the heavy cross; another struck off his head. Michael was crowned with the fetters of his captivity still on his legs.

Murder of Leo.

Whatever hopes the clergy, at least the image-worshippers, or the monks, might have conceived at the murder of Leo, which they scrupled not to allege as a sign of the divine disfavor towards the Iconoclasts, were disappointed on the accession of Michael the Stammerer. The new emperor was a soldier more rude than the last; he could scarcely read. His birth was ascribed to a Phrygian village, chiefly inhabited by Jews; and he was said to have been educated in a strange creed, which was neither Judaism nor Christianity. He affected a coarse humor; he did not spare the archbishop, who returned without authority, but without rebuke, from his exile, and forced an interview with the emperor. Michael received and dismissed him with civil scorn. Rumors were circulated, that even on more sacred subjects he did not repress his impious sarcasms. His whole conduct seemed tinged with a kind of Sadducizing Judaism. He favored the Jews in the exaction of tribute (perhaps he was

Michael the Stammerer. A.D. 821.

1 Ἔτι τε κατὰ τῆς θείας ὀμόσας χάριτος. This, as a fact, or an embellishment of the historian, is equally characteristic. — Theoph. Contin., p. 39.

guilty of the sin of treating them with justice), he fasted on the Jewish Sabbath, he doubted the resurrection of the dead, and the personality of the devil, as unauthorized by the religion of Moses.[1] Image-worship he treated with contemptuous impartiality. He declared that he knew nothing of these ecclesiastical quarrels; that he would maintain the laws and enforce an equal toleration. To the petitions of the patriarch for the formal restoration to his see, he offered his consent if the patriarch would bury the whole question, alike the decrees of Constantinople and Nicea, in oblivion; and in a great public assembly (assembled for the purpose), he proclaimed the worship of images a matter altogether indifferent. Yet Michael is charged with departing from his own lofty rule of toleration. The calamities of his reign, the danger of the capital and the whole empire from the invasion of the apostate Thomas, the loss of Crete and of other islands to the Saracens, were ascribed to the just vengeance of God for the persecutions of his reign.

But the worst crime of which Michael was guilty, in the sight of the image-worshippers, was the parentage and education of him whom the monkish writers call the new Belshazzar, Theophilus. Michael, in his aversion to the monastic faction, intrusted the education of his son to a man of high character, John the Grammarian, whom Theophilus in after life, having employed
A.D. 829. as his chief counsellor in civil affairs, as ambassador in the most difficult negotiations, advanced at length to the see of Constantinople. Theophilus was an Oriental, his enemies no doubt said, a Mohammedan Sultan on the throne of the Roman Empire. Even his

[1] Theophan. Contin., p. 49.

marriage, though to one wife, had something of the supercilious condescension of the lord of a harem. The most beautiful maidens of the empire were assembled, in order that Theophilus might behold and choose his bride. Of these, Eucasia was the loveliest. Theophilus paused, and as he gazed on her beauty, in a strange moralizing fit he said, with an obvious allusion to the fall, "Of how much evil hath woman been the cause?" The too ready or too devout Eucasia replied, with as evident reference to the Mother of God, "And of how much good?" Startled by her quickness and her theology, Theophilus passed on to the more gentle and modest Theodora. Eucasia retired to shroud her disappointment in a convent. The justice of Theophilus, somewhat ostentatiously displayed, was of that severe, capricious, but equitable character, which prevails where the law being part of the religion, the sovereign the hereditary head of the religion, his word is law. He was accessible to the complaints of his meanest subjects; as he passed on certain days to the church in the Blachernae, any one might personally present a petition, or demand redress. As he rode abroad, he would familiarly inquire the price of the cheapest commodities, and express his strong displeasure at what he thought exorbitant charges. One instance may show, as no doubt it did show to his subjects, the impartiality and capricious rigor of his judgments.[1] Petronas, the brother of the empress, had darkened by a lofty building the dwelling of a poor widow. Once she appealed

[1] One edict, attributed to Theophilus, may remind us of the Emperor Paul of Russia. Himself being inclined to baldness, he ordained that all his subjects should cut their hair short: to let it flow over the shoulders incurred a heavy penalty.

to the emperor, but Petronas, secure as he supposed in his interest, disregarded the imperial command to redress the grievance. On her second complaint, this man, who had filled offices of dignity, was ignominiously, publicly, and cruelly scourged in the market-place. The haughty, rather Roman, contempt of Theophilus for commerce, appears in his commanding a vessel full of precious Syrian merchandise to be burned, though it belonged to the Empress Theodora, reproaching her with degrading the imperial dignity to the paltry gains of commerce.[1] The revenues, which he had in some degree restored by economy or by better administration and increased perhaps by the despised commerce to Constantinople, he expended with Eastern magnificence. He sent a stately embassy to the caliph at Bagdad. John the Grammarian represented his sovereign, and was furnished with instructions and with presents intended to dazzle the Barbarian. Of two vessels of enormous cost, which he was to exhibit at a great feast, one was intentionally lost, that the ambassador might astonish the Saracen with his utter indifference, and produce with greater effect the second and far more splendid vase of silver, full of gold coins. A scene of gorgeous emulation took place. The caliph poured out his gold, which John affected to treat as so much dust; the caliph brought forth a hundred Christian captives, splendidly attired, and offered them to the ambassadors, who refused them till they could repay an equal

Character of Theophilus.

[1] Gibbon (as Schlosser has observed) has exaggerated the cruel punishments of Theophilus. With Schlosser, I find no authority for, "The principal ministers, for some venial offences, for some defect of equity or vigilance, a præfect, a quæstor, a captain of the guard, were banished or mutilated, or scalded with burning pitch, or burned in the Hippodrome."

number of Saracen captives. Yet all this rivalship with the Hagarene, as he is contemptuously called by contemporary history, though it soon gave place to implacable hostility and uninterrupted war, would confirm with the image-worshippers the close alliance between Iconoclasm and Mohammedanism. Even in the other branch of expenditure in which Theophilus displayed his magnificence, the sumptuous buildings with which he adorned Constantinople (a palace built on the model of a Saracenic one, belonging to the caliph, in the same style, and same variety of structure and material), would display a sympathy in tastes, offensive to devout feeling.[1] Though among his splendid edifices churches were not wanting, one especially, dedicated to St. Michael the Archangel, called Tricinatus, from its triple apse.

A character like that of Theophilus, stern and arbitrary even in his virtues, determined in his resolutions, and void of compassion against those who offended against his justice, that is his will, was not likely, when he declared himself an Iconoclast, to conduct a religious persecution without extreme rigor. He was a man of far higher education than the former image-breaking emperors, and saw no doubt more clearly the real grounds of the controversy. Theophilus wrote poetry, if the miserable iambics with which

[1] John the Grammarian, on his return from Syria, persuaded the Emperor *τὰ τοῦ Βρύου ἀνάκτορα πρός τὴν τῶν Σαρακηνῶν κατασκευασθῆναι ὁμοίωσιν. ἐν τε σχήμασι καὶ ποικιλίᾳ μηδὲν ἐκείνων τὸ σύνολον παραλλάττοντα.* — Theophan. Contin., p. 98. Symeon Magister assigns a different period to this palace, which he embellishes with the Eastern luxury of *παράδεισοι*, and tanks of water. This, however, shows that already there was a peculiar Saracenic style of building, new to the Romans, and introduced into Constantinople. The fact is not unworthy of notice in the history of architecture.

he wished to brand the faces of some of his victims may be so called. He composed church music; some of his hymns were admitted into the church service, in which the emperor himself led the choir.[1]

Theophilus could not but perceive the failure, and disdain to imitate his father's temporizing policy, who endeavored to tolerate the monks, while he discouraged image-worship.[2] He avowed his determination to extirpate both at once. Leo the Armenian and Michael the Stammerer had attempted to restrict the honors paid to images; Theophilus prohibited the making new ones, and ordered that in every church they should be effaced, and the walls covered with pictures of birds and beasts. The sacred vessels, adorned with figures, were profaned by unhallowed hands, sold in the public markets, and melted for their metal. The prisons were full of painters, of monks and ecclesiastics of all orders. The monks, driven from their convents, fled to desert places; some perished of cold and hunger, some threw off the proscribed dress, yet retained the sacred character and habits; others seized the opportunity of returning to the pleasures as to the dress of the world.

Persecutes image-worshippers.

Yet in the mass of the monastic faction the fanaticism of the emperor was encountered by a fanaticism of resistance, sometimes silent, sullen and stubborn, sometimes glorying in provoking the wrath of the

1 *Οὐ παρῃτήσατο τὸ χειρονομεῖν*, leading them it should seem by the motion of his hand. The clergy appear to have made the emperor pay for the privilege of indulging his tastes. *Δοὺς τῷ κλήρῳ αὐτῆς λίτρας ὑπὲρ τούτου χρυσοῦ ἑκατὸν.* — Theophan. Contin., p. 107.

2 Theophilus caused to be constructed two organs, entirely of gold, set with precious stones; and a tree of gold, on which sat birds which sang by a mechanical contrivance, the air being conveyed by hidden pipes. — Symeon Magister, p. 627.

persecutor. One whole brotherhood, that of the Abrahamites, presented themselves before the emperor. They asserted on the evidence, as they said, of the most ancient fathers,[1] that image-worship dated from the times of the apostles; they appealed to the pictures of the Saviour by St. Luke, and to the holy Veronica. Irritated by their obstinacy, and not likely to be convinced by such arguments, the emperor drove them with insults and severe chastisements from the city. They took refuge in a church, on an island in the Euxine, dedicated to John the Baptist *the awful*.[2] There they are said to have suffered martyrdom. Another stubborn monk, the emperor, in a more merciful mood, sent to his learned minister, John the Grammarian. The monk, according to the historian, reduced the minister to silence: if discomfited, the Grammarian bore his defeat with equanimity, the successful controversialist was allowed to retire and wait for better times in a monastery.

There was another monk, however, named Lazarus, a distinguished painter, whom the emperor could induce by no persuasion to abandon his idolatrous art. As milder measures failed, Lazarus was cruelly scourged and imprisoned. He still persisted in exercising his forbidden skill, and hot iron plates were placed on his guilty hands. The illness of the empress saved his life; he too took refuge in the church of the Baptist, where, having recovered the use of his hands, he painted "that fearful harbinger of the Lord," and on the restoration of images, a celebrated picture of the Saviour over the gate Chalce.

1 Dionysius (the pseudo Dionysius), Hierotheus, and Irenæus.

2 Τοῦ φοβεροῦ.

Two others, Theophilus, and his brother Theodorus, for presuming to overpower the emperor in argument, and to adduce a passage in the Prophet Isaiah, not, as the emperor declared, in his copy, suffered a more cruel punishment. Their faces were branded with some wretched iambic verses, composed by the emperor; they were then banished; one died, the other survived to see the triumph of image-worship.[1]

This religious war seems to have been waged by the emperor on one side, and the monks on the other, with no disturbance of the general peace of the Empire. No popular tumults demanded the interference of the government. The people, weary or indifferent, submitted in apathy to the alternate destruction and restoration of images. But for the fatal passion of Theophilus for war against the Saracens, in which, with great personal valor, but no less military incapacity, he was in general unsuccessful, he might have maintained the Empire during all the later years of his reign in wealth and prosperity.

Theodora empress.

The history of Iconoclasm has a remarkable uniformity. Another female in power, another restoration of images. After the death of Theophilus his widow Theodora administered the empire, in the name of her youthful son Michael, called afterwards, the Drunkard. Theodora, like her own mother Theoctista, had always worshipped images in private. Twice the dangerous secret had been betrayed to the emperor that the females of his own family practised this forbidden idolatry. On one occa-

[1] All the historians (monks) relate this strange story, but the passage in Isaiah favorable to image-worship, and forged by the monks, is rather suspicious; as well as twelve iambic verses tattooed on their faces.

sion the children prattled about the pretty toys which their grandmother kept in a chest and took out, kissing them herself and offering them to the children's respectful kisses. Another time a dwarf, kept as a buffoon in the palace, surprised the empress taking the images, which he called by the same undignified name, from under her pillow, and paying them every kind of homage. The empress received a severe rebuke; the dwarf was well flogged for his impertinent curiosity. Theodora learned caution, but brooded in secret over her tutelar images.

No sooner was Theophilus dead than the monks, no doubt in the secret of Theodora's concealed attachment to images, poured into Constantinople from all quarters. At this juncture the brave Manuel, the general who had more than once retrieved the defeats of Theophilus, once had actually rescued him from the hands of the Saracens, and who had been appointed under the will of the emperor one of the guardians of the empire, fell dangerously ill. The monks beset his bedside, working at once on his hopes of recovery and his fears of death. Manuel yielded, and threw the weight of his authority into the party of the image-worshippers. Theodora had before feared to cope with the strength of the opposite faction, so long dominant and in possession of many of the more important civil and military dignities. She now ventured to send an officer of the palace to command the patriarch, John the Grammarian, either to recant his Iconoclastic opinions, or to withdraw from Constantinople. The patriarch is accused of a paltry artifice. He opened a vein in the region of his stomach, and showed himself wounded and bleeding to the people. The rumor

spread that the empress had attempted to assassinate the patriarch. But the fraud was detected, exposed, acknowledged. The abashed patriarch withdrew, un-
A.D. 842. pitied and despised, into the suburbs. Methodius was raised to the dignity of the patriarchate. The worshippers of images were in triumph.

But Theodora, still tenderly attached to the memory of her husband, demanded as the price of her inestimable services in the restoration of images, absolution for the sin of his Iconoclasm and his persecution of the image-worshippers. Methodius gravely replied, that the power of the clergy to grant absolution to the living was unbounded, but of those who had died in obstinate sin, they had no authority to cancel or to mitigate the damnation. Even her own friends suspected the empress of a pious lie when she asserted, and even swore, that her husband, in the agony of death, had expressed his bitter repentance, had ascribed all the calamities of his reign to his stubborn heresy, had actually entreated her to bring him the images, had passionately kissed them, and so rendered up his spirit to the ministering angels. The clergy, out of respect to the empress and zeal for their own object, did not question too closely the death-bed penitence of Theophilus; with one consent they pronounced his pardon before God, and gave a written sentence of his absolution to the empress.

All was now easy; the fanaticism of Iconoclasm was exhausted or rebuked. A solemn festival was appointed for the restoration of images. The whole clergy of Constantinople, and all who could flock in from the neighborhood, met in and before the palace of the archbishop, and marched in procession with crosses, torches, and incense, to the church of St. Sophia. There they were met by the empress and her infant son Michael. They made the circuit of the church, with their burning torches, paying homage to every image and picture, which had been carefully restored, never again to be effaced till the days of later, more terrible Iconoclasts, the Ottoman Turks. Feb. 19, 842.

The Greek Church from that time has celebrated the anniversary of this festival with loyal fidelity.[1] The successors of Methodius, particularly the learned Photius, were only zealous to consummate the work of his predecessors, and images have formed part of the recognized religious worship of the Eastern world.

1 Methodius was Patriarch only four years.

CHAPTER IX.

SEVERANCE OF GREEK AND LATIN CHRISTIANITY.

Up to the eighth century Rome had not been absolutely dissevered from the ancient and decrepit civilization of the old Empire. After a short period of subjection to the Ostrogothic kingdom, by the conquest of Justinian she had sunk into a provincial city of the Eastern realm. In the eighth century she suddenly, as it were, burst the bonds of her connection with the older state of things, disjoined herself forever from the effete and hopeless East, and placed herself at the head of the rude as yet, and dimly descried and remote, but more promising and vigorous civilization of the West. The Byzantine Empire became a separate world, Greek Christianity a separate religion. The West, after some struggle, created its own empire: its natives formed an independent system, either of warring or of confederate nations. Latin Christianity was the life, the principle of union, of all the West; its centre, papal Rome.

Eighth century.

Mohammedanism — which was gradually encircling and isolating the Byzantine Empire from its outlying provinces, obtaining the naval superiority in the Mediterranean, and subjecting the islands to her sway; which, with the yet unconverted Bulgarians, fully occupied all the Eastern armies, and left the Emperor without power to protect or even keep in subjection the Exarchate and the Italian dependencies — was the remoter cause of the emancipation of the West. The Korân thus in some degree, by breaking off all correspondence with the East, contributed to deliver the Pope from a distant and arbitrary master, and to relieve him from that harassing rivalry with which the patriarch of Constantinople constantly renewed his pretensions to equality or to superiority; and so placed him alone in undisputed dignity at the head of Western Christendom. But the immediate cause of this disruption and final severance between the East and West was the Iconoclasm of the Eastern emperors. Other signs of estrangement might seem to forebode this inevitable revolution. The line of Justinian, the conqueror of Italy, after it had been deposed and had reassumed the Empire in the person of the younger emperor of that name, was now extinct. Adventurer after adventurer had risen to power, and this continual revolution could not but weaken the attachment, especially of foreign subjects, who might think, or choose to think, succession and hereditary descent the only strong titles to their obedience. Rome and Italy must thus ignominiously acknowledge every rude or low-born soldier whom the rabble of Constantinople, the court, or more powerful army, might elevate to the throne.

Exarchs of Ravenna.

The exarchal government from the first had only been powerful to tyrannize and feeble to protect. The Exarch was like the satrap of an old Eastern monarchy; and this was more and more sensibly felt throughout Italy. Without abandoning any of its inferior demands on the obedience, this rule was becoming less and less able to resist the growing power and enterprise of the Lombards, or even to preserve the peace of the Italian dependencies. The exarchate had still strength to levy tribute, and to enforce heavy taxation, the produce of which was sent to Constantinople. It repaid these burdens but scantily by any of the defensive or conservative offices of government. During the pontificate of John VI., the Exarch Theophylact had only been protected from the resentment of his own soldiery by the interference of the pope. The most unambitious pontiff might wish to detach his country and his people from the falling fortunes of the Byzantine Empire. If he looked to Rome, its allegiance to the East was but of recent date, the conquest of Justinian; if to his own position, he could not but know that the successor of St. Peter held a much higher place, both as to respect and authority, before he had sunk into a subject of Constantinople. Never till this period in the papal annals had a pope been summoned, like a meaner subject, to give an account of his spiritual proceedings in a foreign city; nor had he been seized and hurried away, with insult and cruel ill usage, to Constantinople, and, like the unhappy Martin, left to perish in exile.

Whatever lingering loyalty, under these trying circumstances, might prevail in Italy, or in the mind of the pontiff, to the old Roman government — whatever repugnance to the yoke of Barbarians, which might seem the only alternative when they should cease to be the subjects of the Empire — these bonds of attachment were at once rudely broken when the emperor became an heresiarch; not a speculative heresiarch on some abstract and mysterious doctrine, but the head of a heresy which struck at the root of the popular religion — of the daily worship of the people. In general estimation, an Iconoclastic Emperor almost ceased to be a Christian: his tenets were those of a Jew or a Mohammedan. In the East the emperor, from fear, from persuasion, or from conviction, obtained, at one time at least, a formidable party in his favor, even among the clergy. But for the monks, images might have disappeared from the East. In the West, iconoclasm was met with universal aversion and hostility. The Italian mind had rivalled the Greek in the fertility with which it had fostered the growth of image-worship: it adhered to it with stronger pertinacity. The expressive symbol of the fourth century, and the suggestive picture, which was, in the time of Gregory the Great, to be the book of Scripture to the unlearned, had expanded into the fondest attachment to the images of saints and martyrs, the Virgin, and the Saviour. In this as in all the other great controversies, from good fortune, from sagacity, from sympathy with the popular feeling, its adherents would say from a higher guidance, the papacy took the popular and eventually successful side. The pope was again not the dictator, he was the representative of the religious mind of the age. One of the more recent popes, the timid John VII., a Greek by birth, might seem almost prophetically to have committed the papal see to the support of image-worship, and resistance to an iconoclastic emperor. In a chapel which he dedicated in honor of the Virgin, in the church of St. Peter, the walls were inlaid with pictures of the holy fathers; and throughout

Image-worship in Italy.

John VII.

Rome he lavishly adorned the churches with pictures and statues. Gregory II. had no doubt often worshipped in public before these works of his holy predecessor.

Gregory II. A.D. 715-731.

The character of Gregory II. does not warrant the belief that he had formed any deliberate plan of policy for the alienation of Italy from the Eastern Empire. He was actuated not by worldly but by religious passions — by zeal for images, not by any splendid vision of the independence of Italy. For where indeed could be found the protecting, the organizing, the administrative and ruling power which could replace the abrogated authority of the Empire? The papacy had not yet aspired to the attributes and functions of temporal sovereignty.

In Italy the Lombard kingdom in the north, with its kindred dukedoms of Benevento and Spoleto in the south, alone possessed the strength and vigor of settled government.[1] Under the long and comparatively peaceful reign of Rotharis, it had enjoyed what appears almost fabulous prosperity: it had its code of laws. Liutprand now filled the throne, a prince of great ambition and enterprise. If the papacy had entered into a confederacy of interests with the Lombard kings, and contenting itself with spiritual power, by which it might have ruled almost uncontrolled over Barbarian monarchs, and with large ecclesiastical possessions without sovereign rights, Italy might again perhaps have been consolidated into a great kingdom. But this policy, which the papacy was too Roman to pursue with the Gothic kings, or which was repudiated

[1] From 635 to 651. During all this period Catholic and Arian bishops presided over their separate congregations in most of the cities of Italy. — Le Beau, Bas Empire, lviii. 4.

as bringing a powerful temporal monarch in too close collision with the supreme pontiff, was even less likely to be adopted with the Lombards.[1] Between the papal see and the Lombard sovereigns — indeed between the Lombards and the Italian clergy — there seems almost from first to last to have prevailed an implacable and inexplicable antipathy. Of all the conquerors of Italy, these (according to more favorable historians) orderly and peaceful people are represented as the most irreclaimably savage. The taint of their original Arianism was indelible. No terms are too strong with the popes to express their detestation of the Lombards.

According to the course of events, as far as it can be traced in chronological order, Gregory remained wavering and confounded by these simultaneous but conflicting passions: his determination to resist an iconoclastic emperor, and his dread of the Lombard supremacy in Italy. Up to the tenth year of his pontificate he had been occupied by the more peaceful duties of his station. He had averted the aggressions of the Lombard dukes on the patrimony of St. Peter; he had commissioned Boniface to preach the A.D. 719. Gospel in Germany; he had extended his paternal care over the churches in England. No doubt, even if his more formal epistles had not yet been delivered, he had expostulated with the emperor on the first appearances of his hostility to images[2] repeatedly, fre-

1 Yet the Lombards had more than once defended the Pope against the Exarch. — Epist. Olradi. Episcop. Mediol. ad Carol. M. de Translat. S. Augustin. Olrad says of Liutprand, that he was "protector et defensor fidelis Ecclesiarum Dei . . . . . Christianissimus fuit ac religionis amator."

2 On the first intelligence of the Emperor's open iconoclasm, the Pope sent everywhere letters, "cavere se Christianos, quod orta fuisset impietas." — Vit. Greg. II.

quently, if not by private letters, probably by other missives.

Iconoclastic edict. A.D. 728.

But the fatal edict came to Italy as to one of the provinces subject to the Emperor Leo. The Exarch Scholasticus commanded it to be published in the city of Ravenna. The people broke out in instant insurrection, declared their determination to renounce their allegiance rather than permit their churches to be despoiled of their holiest ornaments, attacked the soldiery, and maintained a desperate conflict for the mastery of the city. Liutprand, the Lombard king, had been watching in eager expectation of this strife to expel the exarch, and to add the whole Roman territory to his dominions. With a large force he sat down before Ravenna. Though the garrison made a vigorous defence, Liutprand, by declaring himself a devout worshipper of images, won the populace to his party; Ravenna surrendered; the troops of Liutprand spread without resistance over the whole Pentapolis.

A.D. 727.

Lombards take Ravenna.

Gregory was alarmed, for if he hated the heretical emperor, he had no less dread and dislike of the conquering Lombard.[1] The establishment of this odious sovereignty throughout Italy, which had been so long making its silent aggressions in the South, with a king of the unmeasured ambition and ability of Liutprand, was even more formidable to the pope than the effete tyranny of Constantinople.[2]

Gregory first discerned, among her islands and

1 "Quia, peccato favente, Ravennatum civitas, quæ caput extat omnium, a *non dicendâ* gente Longobardorum capta est." — Greg. Epist. x.

2 The chronology is so uncertain, that I have been constrained to follow sometimes one authority, sometimes another — Baronius, Pagi, Muratori — and so have endeavored to trace the historical sequence of events.

marshes, the rising power of Venice, equally jealous with himself of the extension of the Lombard power. There the exarch had taken refuge. At the instigation of Gregory a league was formed of the maritime forces of Venice, already of some importance, nominally with the exarch, really with the pope, and the whole Roman or Byzantine troops. Ravenna was retaken while Liutprand was at Pavia, and before he could collect his army to relieve it.

Venice. A.D. 727.

Ravenna retaken.

Gregory was still outwardly a loyal subject of the emperor, but the breach was inevitable. Iconoclasm had now become fanaticism with Leo; and Gregory, whether his celebrated letters had yet been dispatched or were only in preparation, was as resolute in his assertion of image-worship. Rumors spread, and were generally believed, that the Iconoclast had sent orders to seize or to murder the pope. Each successive officer who was sent to retrieve the imperial affairs was supposed to be charged with this impious mission. Leo, no doubt, would have scrupled as little as his predecessors to order the apprehension of the refractory prelate, and his transportation to Constantinople; nor if blood had been shed in resistance to his commands, would he have considered it an inexpiable crime.[1] But the pope believed himself, or declared his belief, that he was menaced with secret assassination. Three persons are named — the Duke Basil, Jordan the Chartulary, and John surnamed Lurion — as meditating this crime, under the sanction first of Marinus, Duke of the city of Rome, afterwards of Paul, who was sent as Exarch to restore the imperial ascendency. Two of these

1 Comp. Muratori sub ann. DCCXXVII.

murderers were killed by the people; the third, Basil, turned monk to save his life.[1] Paul the Exarch occupied Ravenna, which, with the Pentapolis, with Rome and Naples, were the only parts of Italy still in possession of the emperor, though Venice owned a doubtful allegiance. It was announced that the Exarch intended to march to Rome to depose the Pope, and at the same time measures were to be taken to destroy the images in the churches throughout Italy. The whole territory — Venice, the Pentapolis, Rome — at once rose up in defence of the Pope. They declared that they would not recognize the commission of Paul; his generals began to contemplate their separate independence. They were only prevented by the prudence of Gregory from proclaiming a new emperor, and sending him against Constantinople. The crafty Lombards again joined the popular cause. Exhilaratus, Duke of Naples, said to have plotted against the pope's life, was slain with his son. Ravenna was divided between the papal and imperial factions. The Exarch fell in the tumult. The Lombards were the gainers in all these commotions: they occupied all the strong places in the Exarchate and in the Pentapolis.

A new Exarch, the last Exarch of Ravenna, Eutychius, landed at Naples. He is likewise accused of designing to send a band of assassins to Rome, to murder, not only the Pope, but also the chief nobles of the city. But for the intervention of the Pope, they would have retaliated by sending assassins to kill the Exarch. A fearful state of Christian society when such acts, if

[1] Gregory is silent in his letters about these attempts at assassination. But the letters may have been written, even if not delivered, before this date.

not designed, were believed to be designed by both parties!

All Rome pledged itself by a solemn oath to live and die in defence of their Pontiff[1] — the protector of the images in their churches. The Lombards were equally loud in their protestations of reverence for his person. The ban of excommunication was issued against the Exarch, the odious mutilator and destroyer of those holy memorials. Eutychius at first attempted to alienate the Lombards from the papal interest, but it now suited the politic Liutprand to adhere in the closest league to the rebellious Romans. Eutychius had not offered a tempting price for his alliance. Some time after, coveting the independent dukedoms of Spoleto and Benevento, Liutprand entered into secret negotiations with the Exarch. The dukedoms by this treaty were to be the share of the Lombard king, Rome to be restored to its allegiance to the emperor. Liutprand having made himself master of Spoleto, and A.D. 729. thus partly gained his own ends, advanced to Rome, and encamped in the field of Nero.[2] The Pope, like his predecessors, went forth to overawe by his commanding sanctity this new Barbarian conqueror, who threatened the Holy City. It pleased Liutprand to be overawed; he was not too sincere in his design to restore the imperial authority in Rome. He played admirably the part of a pious son of the Church; his conduct, as doubtless he intended, contrasted no little to his advantage with that of the sacrilegious Iconoclast Leo. He cast himself at the feet of the Pope, he

1 "Qui ex scriptis nefandam viri (Exarchi) dolositatem despicientes una se quasi fratres Romani atque Longobardi catenâ fidei constrinxerunt cuncti mortem pro defensione Pontificis sustinere gloriosam." — Olradi. Epist.

2 Anastasius, Vit.

put off his armor and all his splendid dress, his girdle, Liutprand in Rome. his sword, his gauntlets, his royal mantle, his crown of gold, and a cross of silver, and offered them at the tomb of the Apostle. He entreated the Pope (his arguments were not likely to be ineffectual) to make peace with the Exarch. So completely did harmony appear to be restored, that the Pope and the Exarch united in suppressing an insurrection raised by a certain Petasius, who proclaimed himself emperor under the title of Tiberius III. The Exarch, with the aid of the Romans, seized the usurper, and sent his head A.D. 730. to Constantinople. After this the Exarch probably retired to Ravenna, and must at least have suspended all active measures for the suppression of image-worship.

Throughout these transactions the Pope appears actually if not openly an independent power, leaguing with the allies or the enemies of the Empire, as might suit the exigences of the time; yet the share of Gregory II. in the revolt of Italy has been exaggerated by those who boast of this glorious precedent and example for the assertion of the ecclesiastical power, by depriving an heretical subject of his authority over part of his realm, and striking the Imperial Head with the impartial thunders of excommunication; so also by those who charge him with the sin of rebellion against heaven-constituted monarchy. If, as is said, he proceeded to the hostile measure of forbidding the Italian subjects of Leo to pay their tribute; if by a direct excommunication he either virtually or avowedly released the subjects of the Emperor from their allegiance[1] (his

[1] Theophanes, iv. c. 5 (p. 621); after him by Glycas, Zonaras, Cedrenus. See likewise Anastasius.

own language in his letters by no means takes this haughty or unsubmissive tone), his object was not the emancipation of Italy, but the preservation of images, in which Gregory was as fanatically sincere as the humblest monk in his diocese.

No doubt a council was summoned and held at Rome by Gregory II., in which anathemas were launched against the destroyers of images. If, however, the emperor was by name excommunicated by the pope, this was not and could not be, as in later times with the kings and emperors of Western Europe, an absolute and total exclusion from Christian privileges and Christian rites. It was a disruption of all communion with the Bishop of Rome, and his orthodox Italian subjects.[1] No doubt there was a latent assertion that the Roman church was the one true church, and that beyond that church there was no salvation; but the Patriarch of Constantinople recognized no such power in the Roman pontiff, unless himself joined in the anathema; and Anastasius, the present Patriarch, was now an ardent destroyer of images.[2]

Nov. 730. Council at Rome.

Leo revenged himself by severing the Transadriatic provinces, the Illyrica, from the Roman patriarchate, and by confiscating the large estates of the see of Rome in Calabria and Sicily. He appears too to have chosen this unfortunate time for an increase in the taxation of

1 Walch makes two sensible observations; first, that the revolt of Italy and the extinction of the Exarchate was not complete till after the death of both Gregorys; secondly, that the excommunication of the Emperor by the Pope was not an exclusion from all spiritual privileges, but merely a refusal to communicate with him.

2 In the reference to the council in the letter of Pope Hadrian to Charlemagne, p. 1460, he does not mention, though he does not exclude the notion of the excommunication of the Emperor. The council was held in Nov. 730; Gregory died Feb. 731.

those provinces. A new census was ordered with a view to a more productive capitation tax. The discontent at these exactions would no doubt strengthen the general resistance to the measures of Leo; and perhaps Gregory's prohibition of the payment to the imperial revenue may have been but resistance to these unprecedented burdens.

Buried Feb. 11, 731.

Gregory III.

Such was the relation between the see of Rome and the Eastern Empire at the death of Gregory II. His successor, Gregory III., was of Syrian birth. At the funeral of the deceased pope, the clergy and the whole people broke out into a sudden acclamation, and declared Gregory III. his successor. But he was not consecrated till the ensuing month. So far was this election from a deliberate renunciation of allegiance to the Empire, or an assertion of independence on the part of the Pope or the Roman people, that the confirmation of the election by the Exarch at Ravenna was dutifully awaited before the Pope assumed his authority. Nor did Gregory III. break off or suspend his direct intercourse with the seat of government. His first act was a mission to Constantinople to announce his adherence to the doctrines of his predecessor on image-worship; and though his inflexible language was not likely to conciliate the Emperor, this mission and much of the subsequent conduct of Gregory show the separation of Italy from the Empire was, at least, even if remotely contemplated, no avowed object of the papal policy. The first message was intrusted to George the Presbyter, but its language was so sternly and haughtily condemnatory of the emperor's religious proceedings, that the trembling ambassador had hardly begun his journey when he fled back to Rome and acknowledged that he had not courage for this dangerous mission. The Pope was so indignant at this want of sacerdotal daring, that he threatened to degrade the Presbyter, and was hardly persuaded to impose a lighter penance. Once more George A.D. 732. was ordered to set out for the court of Leo; he was arrested in Sicily, and not allowed to proceed. Gregory, finding his remonstrances vain or unheard, assumed a bolder attitude.

The council held by Gregory III. was formed with great care and solemnity. It was intended Nov. 1, 732. to be the declaration of defiance on the subject of images from all Italy. The archbishops of Grado and Ravenna, with ninety-three other prelates or presbyters of the apostolic see, with the deacons and the rest of the clergy, the consuls and the people of Rome, pronounced their decree that, whoever should overthrow, mutilate, profane, blaspheme the venerable images of Christ our God and Lord, of the immaculate and glorious Virgin, of the blessed apostles and saints, was banished from all communion in the body and blood of Christ, and from the unity of the Church.

This solemn edict was sent to Constantinople by Constantine, the defender of the city. Constantine also was arrested in Sicily, his letters taken away, and after an imprisonment of a year, he was allowed to return to Rome to report the bad success of his mission. Another address was sent in the name of the people of Italy, urging their attachment to the images, and imploring the emperor to annul his fatal statute. This, with two expostulatory letters from the pope, got not beyond Sicily. The messengers were seized by Sergius, the commander of the imperial troops, confined for eight months, sent back with every indignity to Rome, and menaced with the punishment of traitors and rebels if they should venture to land again in Sicily.

In Rome Gregory III. set the example of image-worship on the most splendid scale. He had obtained six pillars of precious marble from the Exarch at Ravenna, and arranged them in order with six others of equal value. These he overlaid with the purest silver, on which, on one side, were represented the Saviour and the apostles, on the other the Mother of God with the holy virgins. In an oratory of the same church he enshrined, in honor of the Saviour and the Virgin, relics of the apostles, the martyrs, and saints of all the world. Among his other costly offerings was an image of the Holy Mother of God, having a diadem of gold and jewels, a golden collar with pendent gems, and earrings with six jacinths. In the Church of the Virgin was another image of the Mother, with the Divine Infant in her arms, adorned with pearls of great weight and size. Many other of the churches in Rome and in the neighborhood were decorated with images of proportionate splendor.

The Emperor, about this time, made his last desperate effort to retrieve his fortunes in Italy, to relieve the Exarch Eutychius, who was shut up in powerless inactivity in Ravenna, and to reduce the refractory pope and Italy to obedience. A formidable armament was embarked on board a great fleet, under the command of Manes, one of his bravest and most experienced generals. The fleet encountered a terrible storm in the Adriatic; great part of the ships was lost; and the image-worshippers on the coast of Calabria beheld their shores strewn with the wrecks of the Iconoclastic navy. Henceforth the Eastern Empire

Loss of Emperor's fleet.

almost acquiesced in the loss of the exarchate. Eutychius maintained for a long time his perilous position in Ravenna, temporizing between the pope, the Lombards, and the Franks. Nearly twenty years later he abandoned the seat of government, and took refuge in Naples.

Flight of the Exarch.

Now, however, that the real power of the empire in Italy was extinguished, it might seem that nothing could resist the Lombards. Though King Liutprand and Gregory III., at least for the first eight years of Gregory's pontificate, maintained their outward amity, the Lombards, though not now Arian, were almost equally objects of secret abhorrence to the Catholic and the Roman. Italy must again become a Barbarian kingdom, the Pope the subject of a sovereign at his gates or within his city.

At this juncture the attention of Europe, of all Christendom, is centred upon the Franks. The great victory of Tours had raised Charles Martel to the rank of the protector of the liberties of the religion of the Western world, from the all-conquering Mohammedans. It was almost the first,[1] unquestionably the greatest defeat which that power had suffered, from the time that it advanced beyond the borders of Arabia, and having yet found no limits to its conquests in the East, had swept westward over Africa, Spain, and Southern Gaul, and seemed destined to envelop the whole world.

Charles Martel. A.D. 729.

The Pope was thus compelled, invited, encouraged by every circumstance to look for protection, unless he submitted to the abhorred Lombard, beyond the Alps.[2]

1 The bloody defeat of Toulouse by Count Eudes led to no result.

2 Liutprand marched across the Alps but the year before in aid of Charles

The Franks alone of Barbarian nations had from the first been converted to orthodoxy, and adhered to it with unshaken fidelity. The Franks had dutifully listened to the papal recommendation of Boniface, the Apostle of Germany, had countenanced and assisted his holy designs for the conversion of the Teutonic tribes beyond the Rhine. Already had Gregory II. opened a communication with the Franks; already, before the dissolution of the Byzantine power, had secret negotiations begun to secure their aid against the Lombards.[1] Eight or nine years of doubtful peace, at least of respectful mutual understanding, had intervened; when, almost on a sudden, the Lombards and the Pope are involved in open war, and Gregory III. throws himself boldly on the faith and loyalty of the mighty Frank. He sends the mystic keys of the Sepulchre of St. Peter and filings of his chains as gifts, which no Christian could resist; he offers the significant yet undefined title of Roman Consul. The letter of Gregory in the following year appeals in the most piteous tone to the commiseration and piety of the Barbarian. "His tears are falling day and night for the destitute state of the Church. The Lombard king and his son are ravaging by fire and sword the last remains of the property

A.D. 739.

Gregory appeals to Charles Martel.

Martel against the Saracens, who had again appeared in formidable force in the South of France.

[1] The authority for this important fact is Anastasius in his Life of Stephen III., who, in his dispute with King Astolph, "cernens præsertim, ab imperiali potentiâ nullum esse subveniendi auxilium, tunc quemadmodum prædecessores ejus beatæ memoriæ *dominus Gregorius* et Gregorius alter, et dominus Zacharias, beatissimi pontifices Carolo excellentissimæ memoriæ, Regi Francorum direxerunt, petentes sibi subveniri, propter impressiones ac invasiones quas et ipsi in hâc Romanorum provinciâ a nefanda Longobardorum gente perpessi sunt." Charles Martel was not *king*.

of the Church, which no longer suffices for the sustenance of the poor, or to provide lights for the A.D. 740. daily service. They had invaded the territory of Rome and seized all his farms;[1] his only hope was in the timely succor of the Frankish king. Gregory knew that the Lombards were negotiating with the Frank, and dexterously appeals to his pride. "The Lombards are perpetually speaking of him with contempt, — 'Let him come, this Charles, with his army of Franks; if he can, let him rescue you out of our hands.' O unspeakable grief, that such sons so insulted should make no effort to defend their holy mother the Church![2] Not that St. Peter is unable to protect his successors, and to exact vengeance upon their oppressors; but the apostle is putting the faith of his followers to trial. Believe not the Lombard kings, that their only object is to punish their refractory subjects, the dukes of Spoleto and Benevento, whose only crime is that they will not join in the invasion and the plunder of the Roman see. Send, O my most Christian son! some faithful officer, who may report to you truly the condition of affairs here; who may behold with his own eyes the persecutions we are enduring, the humiliation of the Church, the desolation of our property, the sorrow of the pilgrims who frequent our shrines. Close not your ears against our supplications, lest St. Peter close against you the gates of heaven. I conjure you by the living and true God, and by the keys of St. Peter, not to prefer the alliance of the Lombards to the love of the great apostle, but hasten, hasten to our succor, that we may say with the prophet, 'The Lord hath heard us in

1 In partibus Ravennatum.

2 Fredegar. Contin. apud Bouquet, ii. 457.

the day of tribulation, the God of Jacob hath protected us.'"

The letter of Gregory III. seems rather like the cry of sudden distress than part of a deliberate scheme of policy. He is in an agony of terror at the formidable invasion of the Lombards, which threatens to absorb Rome in the kingdom of Liutprand. Succor from the East is hopeless; he turns to any quarter where he may find a powerful protector, and that one protector is Charles Martel. From the Lombard king he had not much right to expect forbearance, for it is clear that he had encouraged the duke of Spoleto, the vassal, as the ambitious Liutprand asserted, of the Lombard kingdom, in rebellion against his master. Duke Thrasimund had fled for refuge to Rome; and from Rome he had gone forth, not unaided, to reconquer his dukedom. The troops of Liutprand had overrun the Roman territory; they were wasting the estates of the Church. Liutprand had severed four cities, Amelia, Orta, Polymartia, and Blera, from the Roman territory.[1] Some expressions in Gregory's second letter to Charles almost
A.D. 741. imply that he had entered Rome and plundered the Church of St. Peter.[2] So nearly did Rome become a Lombard city.

[1] Ab eodem rege ablatæ sunt e Ducatu Romano quatuor civitates. — Anastasius.

[2] Baronius drew this inference from the words of Gregory. Muratori contests the point, which is not very probable, and is not mentioned by Anastasius. Muratori explains the words "omnia enim lumina in honorem ipsius principis Apostolorum. . . . ipsi abstulerunt. Unde et Ecclesia Sancti Petri denudata est, et in nimiam desolationem redacta," as relating to the devastation of the Church estates; "che servivano alla Luminaria d' essa Chiesa, ed al sovvenimento de' Poveri." But he has omitted the intermediate words, "et quæ a vestris parentibus, et a vobis oblata sunt." The lights or chandeliers, the oblations of former Frankish kings or of Charles, can scarcely be explained but of the actual ornaments of the

These acts of Gregory III. mark the period of transition from the old to the new political system of Europe. They proclaimed the severance of all connection with the East. The Pope, as an independent potentate, is forming an alliance with a Transalpine sovereign for the liberation of Italy, and thus taking the lead in that total revolution in the great social system of Europe, the influence of which still survives in the relations between the Transalpine nations and Italy. The step to papal agrandizement, though yet unpremeditated, is immense. Latin Christendom is forming into a separate realm, of which the Pope is the head. Henceforth the Pope, if not yet a temporal sovereign, is a temporal potentate.

The Pope a temporal power.

Speculation may lead to no satisfactory result, but it is difficult not to speculate on the extent to which the popes may have had more or less distinct conceptions as to the results of their own measures. Was their alliance with the Franks beyond the Alps, even if at first the impulse of immediate necessity, and only to gain the protection of the nearest powerful rival to the hated Lombards, confined to that narrow aim? How soon began to dawn the vision of a spiritual kingdom over the whole West — the revival of a Western Empire beyond the Alps, now that the East had abandoned or lost its authority — or at least of some form of Roman government under which the title of consul or patrician should be borne by a Trans-

Church. St. Peter's may have been plundered without the fall of the whole of Rome. The siege of Rome is mentioned among the military exploits of Liutprand in his epitaph. Compare Gregor. Epist. ii. ad Carol. Martel. Baronius and Muratori, sub ann. DCCXLI. Gretser published the two letters in his volume of the Epistolæ Pontificum.

alpine sovereign thus bound to protect Rome, while the real authority should rest with the pope? Some ambiguous expressions in Gregory's epistle sound like an offer of sovereignty to Charles Martel. He sends him the keys of the tomb of St. Peter as a symbol of allegiance, and appears to acknowledge his royal supremacy.[1] The account of the solemn embassy which conveyed these supplicatory letters asserts that the Pope offered to the Frankish ruler the titles of Patrician and Consul of Rome, thus transferring, if not the sovereignty, the duty and honor of guarding the imperial city, the metropolis of Christendom, to a foreign ruler. According to another statement, he spoke not in his own name alone, but in that of the Roman people, who, having thrown off the dominion of the Eastern empire, placed themselves under the protection of his clemency.[2]

Charles Martel.

Charles Martel had received the first mission of Gregory III. with magnificence, yet not without hesitation. The Lombards used every effort to avert his interference in the affairs of Italy; and some gratitude was due to Liutprand, who had rendered him powerful service (according to the Lombard's epitaph, he had fought in person for the cause of Christendom against the Saracens in Aquitaine.[3]) But Charles returned a courteous answer, sent presents to Rome,

1 "Per ipsas sacratissimas Claves Confessionis Beati Petri, quas vobis ad regnum direximus." — Greg. Epist. ii.

2 Annales Metenses.

3 The lines relating to the siege of Rome (which the poet places first), and to this fact, run thus: —

"Roma suas vires jampridem milite multo
Obsessa expavit, deinde tremuere feroces
Usque Saraceni, quos dispulit impiger, ipsos
Cum premerent Gallos, Karolo poscente juvari."

Note to Paul. Diacon. apud Muratori, c. lviii.

and directed Grimon, abbot of Corbey, and Sigebert, a monk of St. Denys, to proceed with the ambassadors to the imperial city.

Not the least extraordinary part of this memorable transaction is the strangely discrepant character in which Charles Martel appeared to the Pope and to the clergy of his own country. While the Pope is offering him the sovereignty of Rome, and appealing to his piety, as the champion of the church of St. Peter, he is condemned by the ecclesiastics beyond the Alps as the sacrilegious spoiler of the property of the Church ; as a wicked tyrant who bestowed bishoprics on his counts and dukes, expelled his own relative, the rightful Archbishop of Rheims, and replaced him by a prelate who had only received the tonsure. A saint of undoubted authority beheld in a vision the ally of the popes, the designated Consul of Rome, the sovereign at whose feet were laid the keys of St. Peter's sepulchre, tormented in the lowest pit of hell. So completely had this view worked into the Christian mind, that Dante, the faithful recorder of popular Catholic tradition, adopts the condemnatory legend, and confirms the authority of the saint's vision.

CHAPTER X.

HIERARCHY OF FRANCE.

The origin of this hostility between Charles Martel and the hierarchy of France throws us back nearly a century, to the rise of the mayors of the palace, who had now long ruled over the pageant Merovingian kings, the do-nothing kings of that race; and to the enormous accumulation of wealth, territory, and power acquired by the bishops and monasteries of France. The state of this great Church, the first partly Teutonic Church, and its influence on the coming revolution in Latin Christianity and on the papal power, must
A.D. 637. justify the digression. The kingly power of the race of Clovis expired with Dagobert I. In each of the kingdoms, when the realm was divided — above the throne, when it was one kingdom — rose the Mayor of the Palace, in whom was vested the whole kingly power. But the Franks now at least shared with the Romans the great hierarchical dignities: they were bishops, abbots. If they brought into the order secular ambition, ferocity, violence, feudal animosity, they brought also a vigor and energy of devotion, a rigor of asceticism, a sternness of monastic virtue. It was an age of saints: every city, every great monastery boasts, about this time, the tutelar patron of its church; legend is the only history: while at the same time fierce

bishops surpass the fierce counts and barons in crime and bloodshed, and the holiest, most devout, most self-denying saints are mingling in the furious contest or the most subtle intrigue. This Teutonizing of the hierarchy was at once the consequence and the cause of the vast territorial possessions of the Church, and of the subsequent degradation and inevitable plunder of the Church. This was a new aristocracy, not as the Roman hierarchy had been, of influence and superior civilization, but of birth, ability, ambition, mingled with ecclesiastical authority,[1] and transcendent display of all which was esteemed in those times perfect and consummate Christianity. Nor were the bishops strong in their own strength alone. The peaceful passion for monachism had become a madness which seized on the most vigorous, sometimes the fiercest souls. Monasteries arose in all quarters, and gathered their tribute of wealth from all hands. The translation of the remains of St. Benedict to Fleury on the Loire was a national ovation. All ages, ranks, classes, races crowded to the holy ceremony. Of the sons of Dagobert, Sigebert, who ruled in Austrasia, passed his life in peaceful works of piety. The only royal acts which he was permitted to perform were lavish donations to bishops and to monasteries.[2] On the death of his brother, Clovis II. of Neustria,[3] the widow Bathildis was raised to the regency in the name of her infant son, Clotaire III. Bathildis succeeded to some part of the authority,

[1] It is not easy to trace this slow and gradual Teutonizing of the higher clergy. The names are not sure indications of birth: Romans sometimes barbarized their names. — Guizot, Essai V. iii. 2; Hallam, Supplemental note, p. 75.

[2] Vita S. Sigeberti, apud Bouquet, ii. He founded twelve monasteries.

[3] Sigebert and Clovis died about the same time, 654, 655.

to none of the crimes or ambition of Brunehaut or Fredegonde. She was a Saxon captive of exquisite beauty. Erthinwold, the Neustrian mayor of the palace, sacrificing his own honorable passion to his ambition, married her to the king, Clovis II. Queen Bathildis was the holiest and most devout of women; her pious munificence knew no bounds; remembering her own bondage, she set apart vast sums for the redemption of captives. Not a cathedral, not a monastery, but records the splendid donations of Queen Bathildis: not farms or manses, but forests, districts, almost provinces.[1] The high-born Frankish bishop, Leodegar (the St. Leger of later worship), had been raised by the sole power of Bathildis to the great Burgundian bishopric of Autun. Legend dwells with fond pertinacity on the holiness of the saint; sterner but more veracious history cannot but detect the ambitious and turbulent head of a great faction. There was a fierce and obstinate strife for the mayoralty;

[1] "La trace de ses bienfaits se retrouve dans les archives de toutes les grandes abbayes de son temps. Luxeuil et d'autres monastères de Bourgogne en reçurent de grandes sommes et des terres. Dans le voisinage de Troyes, S. Frodoard obtint un vaste terrain marécageux nommé l'Isle Germanique, d'où il fit sortir la florissante abbaye de Moustier-la-belle. Curbion ou Moutier S. Lomer reçut la grande ville de Nogaret, plusieurs talents d'or et d'argent . . . elle accorde beaucoup de présents, une grande forêt, et des pâturages du domaine royal au fondateur de Jumièges, S. Filibert . . . Clotaire, sur les conseils de Bathilde, augmente les vastes domaines de Fontenelle . . . cité modèle où quinze cent travailleurs étaient enrolés avec neuf cent moines. Bathilde eut encore . . . sa part dans la munificence de Clovis II. et de Clotaire III. envers les monastères de Saint Denys en France, de Saint Vincent de Paris, de Fleury sur Loire, et de St. Maur de Fosses." St. Maur had the honor of possessing the bodies of St. Benedict and of St. Maur. — D. Pitra, Vie de St. Léger, p. 141. "Ainsi combla-t-elle de largesses les églises de S. Denys, et de S. Germain de Paris, de S. Médard de Soissons, de S. Pierre de Chartres, de S. Anian d'Orléans, de S. Martin de Tours." — P. 145. See, too, the donations of Dagobert II., p. 356.

France must become a theocracy; the Bishop of Autun, if not in name, in power would alone possess that dignity. His rival Ebroin, the actual mayor, entered into internecine strife with the aspiring hierarchy: none but that hierarchy has handed down the short dark annals of the time, and Ebroin has been chronicled as the most monstrously wicked of men. Under the rule of Ebroin, it was said by his authority, the Bishop of Paris was murdered for his pride; but Ebroin fell before the fiercer aggression of Leodegar, the Burgundian bishop, who was supported by all the forces of Burgundy. It was held to be a splendid effort of Christian virtue that the saint spared the life of Ebroin. He was banished to the monastery of Luxeuil (the foundation of St. Columban), compelled to give up his wife, to submit to the tonsure, and to take the irrevocable vows. Leodegar ruled supreme, and in the highest episcopal splendor, in his cathedral city of Autun. If his poetical biographer is right, he assumed even the title of mayor of the palace.[1] But the haughty Neustrian nobility became weary of the rule of a woman and of bishops; Bathildis surrendered her power, and retired to her convent of Chelles.

By a sudden revolution the Bishop of Autun found himself an exile in the same monastery with his fallen rival, that of Luxeuil.[2] The bishop had sternly condemned the marriage of the King Childeric (Austrasia and Neustria had become again one kingdom) with his cousin-german, Bilihildis. He was accused of a

1 "Quippe domus major penitus, rectorque creatus
Antistes meritis suscepit jura regenda
Aulæ post regem."
MS. printed by M. Pitra, 472.

2 See the pleasing description of Luxeuil — Lucens ovile, apud Pitra.

conspiracy against the life of the king. Affairs again wheeled round; Childeric was murdered; Ebroin and Leodegar, reconciled by their common misfortune, if not by their common religion, set forth together from their convent, erelong to strive with still fiercer animosity for the prize of power. Ebroin, the apostate, another Julian, cast off his religion, that is his monastic vows; his free locks again flowed; he returned to the embraces of his wife.[1] By common consent, Thierry III., the youngest of the sons of Clovis II., brother of Clotaire and of Chilperic, who had been imprisoned in the abbey of St. Denys, if not tonsured, to incapacitate him from the throne, was brought forth to act the part of king. Ebroin aspired to and succeeded in wresting the mayoralty from Leudes, the rival set up by the Bishop of Autun.

No long time elapsed; the bishop is besieged in his cathedral city, and Autun boldly defies, under the command of her bishop, the kingly power, Ebroin ruling in the name of King Thierry III. Leodegar found it necessary to capitulate: he made his capitulation wear the appearance of lofty religious sacrifice; but he escaped not the revenge of Ebroin, who scrupled not to abuse his victory with the most atrocious barbarities against the holy person of the bishop. His eyes were pierced, his lips cloven, his tongue cut out. Two years after (he had taken refuge or had been

1 The poet naturally describes this enforced monachism as the unforgiven crime, which caused the insatiable vindictiveness of Ebroin: —

"Illum propter, compulsus sum perdere crinem,
Depulsus regno, monachalem sumere formam,
Conjugis amplexus dulces et basia liqui,
Oscula nec prolis collo suspensa tenebam."

Pitra, p. 477.

consigned a prisoner to the abbey of Fecamp) he was cruelly put to death. He became a martyr as well as a saint in the annals of the Church — a martyr in the calm and majestic patience with which he submitted to his sufferings: — but a martyr to what Christian truth? To what but the power of the clergy, or to his own power, it is difficult to say.[1] Erelong he became the most potent and popular saint of his prolific age; his relics were disputed by cities, submitted to the ordeal of the divine judgment; distant churches boasted some limb of the holy martyr, his miracles were numberless, and even in the nineteenth century petitions are made for some of the wonder-working bones of St. Leger.[2]

The policy by which Ebroin, the mayor of the palace, retained his power — the depression of the higher nobles, the elevation of the lower — belongs to the history of France, not to that of Christianity. What the higher nobility and some of the bishops

1 Compare (it is neither unamusing nor uninstructive) the Vie de S. Leger, par le R. P. Dom. J. B. Pitra, Paris, 1846. The author has ingeniously interwoven into one all the legends of the period, with much of the patient industry and copious erudition, and with the devout feelings, the prejudices (we must pardon some little of the bitterness of later times) of his spiritual ancestors of St. Maur. M. Pitra looks back with fond reverence to the times when bishops ruled sole and supreme in their cities; when grants of counties were lavished on monasteries: when monastic admiration for monastic virtues created saints by hundreds; when miracle was almost the law, not the exception, in nature. M. Pitra believes that he believes all the supernatural stories of those times, and that with a kind of earnestness differing much from the bravado of belief avouched by some other kindred writers. The life of St. Leger is in truth an excellent religious romance; but, even in these days, will not pass for history in the literature which still boasts the living names of Guizot, the Thierrys, C. Remusat, Ampère, and their rising scholars.

2 See in Pitra, p. 439, the letter from the curé of Evreuil (dated Oct. 4, 1833) to the Bishop of Autun. Conceive such a letter addressed to the Bishop of Autun of the days of the republic!

called rebellious tyranny, his partisans held to be high and rigid justice; yet Ebroin had in his party some of the most holy bishops: saint balanced saint.[1] St. Genesius of Lyons, St. Leger, were his enemies; one his victim. In his party were St. Præjectus (St. Prie) of Auvergne, St. Reol of Rheims, St. Agilbert of Paris, St. Ouen of Rouen.[2] A council of bishops sat in judgment on St. Leger, at Marli, near Paris: it is difficult to believe that they were not consenting to his death.[3]

But Ebroin bore no charmed life: less than a charmed life in those times could not hope duration, not even to attain to good old age. Once he baffled a formidable insurrection; and with the aid of two prelates (Reol, metropolitan of Rheims, and Agilbert of Paris) cut off Martin, one of the grandsons of Pepin the Great, of Landon, who with his brother Pepin aspired to the mayoralty at least of Austrasia. The bishops swore upon certain relics that Martin's life should be secure, but they had withdrawn the holy witnesses, and swore on the empty case.[4] These bishops, afterwards saints, at least did not protest against the death of the deluded youth. Ebroin himself per-

1 "Mulciber in Trojam, pro Trojâ stabat Apollo,
Æqua Venus Teucris, Pallas iniqua fuit."

2 On one occasion, it is said, Ebroin consulted St. Ouen. "Remember Fredegonde," replied the bishop. Ebroin was wise, and understood at once. Fredegonde the example urged by a saint! — Gesta Francorum.

3 "Et cum diu flagitantes," the Synod with Ebroin, "non valuissent elicere — ejus tunicam consciderunt a capite," — a degradation, previous to death, performed by ecclesiastics. — Apud Bouquet.

4 "Nuntios dirigit, Ægilbertum et Reolum Remensis urbis Episcopum, ut fide promissâ in incertum super vacuas capsas sacramenta falsa dederint. Qua in re ille credens *eos* ac Lugduno-Clavato cum sodalibus ac sociis ad Erchrecum veniens, illic cum suis omnibus interfectus est." — Fredegar. Contin., apud Bouquet, ii. p. 451.

ished by the blow of an assassin — perished not in this world only. A monk on the shores of the Saône, who had been blinded by Ebroin, heard a boat rowed furiously down the stream. A terrible voice thundered out, "It is Ebroin, whom we are bearing to the caldron of hell." [1]

Pepin the Short, the heir of Pepin the Great of Landon, (whose daughter had married the son of the famous Arnulf of Metz), rose to the mayoralty, first in one kingdom, at length in the whole of France. Under his vigorous administration France resumed her unity: it ceased to be a theocracy. The bishops retired, it is feared not to their holier offices. Councils, which had been as frequent as diets or malls, ceased. As it ever has been, the enormous wealth and power accumulated by saints, or reputed saints, worked their inevitable consequences. They corrupted their masters, and tempted violent and unworthy men to usurp the high places of the Church. Those who boast the saints, the splendid monasteries, the noble foundations, the virtues, the continence, the wonders of the former generation, as bitterly lament the degradation, the worldliness, the vices, the drunkenness, licentiousness, marriage or concubinage of the succeeding race. It was this state of the clergy which moved the indignation and contempt of St. Boniface, and which the Pope himself hoped to constrain by the holy influence of the German missionary prelate and by the power of Charles Martel.[2]

[1] Adonis Chron. apud Bouquet, ii. p. 670.

[2] "Quidem affirmant (quod plurimum populo nocet) homicidas vel adulteros in ipsis sceleribus perseverantes, fieri tamen posse sacerdotes." So writes Boniface at the court of Charles Martel. — Epist. xii., Giles, i. p. 36.

Such then was the clergy of France, when Charles Martel, after a furious conflict, won the inheritance of his father, Pepin the Short — the mayoralty of France. Even from his birth the clergy had been adverse to Charles. He was the son of Pepin, by Alpaide, whom, in the freedom of royal polygamy, Pepin had married during the lifetime of his former wife, Plectruda. The clergy, not without ground, denied the legitimacy of Charles. Already his patrimony, the royal revenues, being exhausted by his strife for the Mayoralty, Charles had not scrupled to lay his hands on the vast, tempting, misused wealth of the hierarchy.

Erelong, on this kingdom — of which more than one-half of the nobility were bishops or abbots, of which a very large proportion, no doubt the best cultivated and richest land, was in the hands of the monks and clergy — burst the invasion of the unbelieving Saracens. The crescent waved over Narbonne and the cities of the south; churches and monasteries were effaced from the soil. How terrible, how perilous was that invasion, one fact may witness. Autun, in the centre of Burgundy, the city of St. Leger, with all its Gaulish, Roman, Burgundian, hierarchical, monastic splendor, was captured and utterly laid waste. The hierarchy fought not themselves, though the Bishop of Sens did gallantly, and in arms, defend his city. Charles would not be content with the barren aid of their prayers: his exactions, his seizure of their possessions, which they held only through his valor, they still branded as impious and sacrilegious robberies.[1] Hence the extraor-

Compare letter to Pope Zacharias, especially on the lives of certain deacons (Epist. xliv.), and the answer of Zacharias.

[1] Compare M. Guizot's (Essais, xiv.) suggestions as to the mode in which Charles Martel seized and redistributed church property to his warriors.

dinary contradiction: — while the Pope sees in Charles Martel only the conqueror of the Saracens at Poictiers, only the great transalpine power which may control the hated Lombards, the hero of Christendom, the orthodox sovereign; with the hierarchy of France Charles is a Belshazzar who has laid his unhallowed hands on the treasures of the Church, a sacrilegious tyrant doomed to everlasting perdition.

CHAPTER XI.

PEPIN, KING OF FRANCE.

But whatever might have been the result of the negotiations between the pope and Charles Martel, they were interrupted by the death of the two contracting parties. Charles Martel and Gregory III. died within a month of each other.[1]

Pope Zacharias, Dec. 741.

Zacharias, a Greek, succeeded to Gregory III. At his election even the form of obtaining the consent of the Exarch, as representative of the Eastern emperor, was discarded forever. The death of Charles Martel, which weakened his power by dividing it between his sons Carloman and Pepin, left the Pope at the mercy of Liutprand. The exarchate, the Roman territory, Rome itself, was utterly defenceless against the Lombard, exasperated, as he might justly be, at this attempt to mingle up a Transalpine power in the affairs of Italy. At the time of Gregory's death there seems to have been a suspension of hostilities, attributed, though with no historical authority, to the remonstrances or menaces of Charles Martel. But now the terror even of the name of Charles was withdrawn, and the Pope had no protection but in the

[1] Baronius inclines to the damnation of Charles; at least, ascribes his death to his tardiness in not marching to the Pope's succor. How came the Pope also to die at this critical time? Charles Martel died A.D. 741, Oct. 21; Gregory III., Nov. 27.

sanctity of his office. He sent an embassy to Liutprand, who received it with courtesy and respect, granted advantageous terms of peace to the dukedom or territory of Rome, and promised to restore Ameria and the other cities which he had seized, to the Roman territory. Liutprand inexorably demanded that the Pope should abandon the cause of the rebellious Duke of Spoleto. Thrasimund was compelled to submit: he was deposed, and retired into a monastery. Liutprand appointed a more obedient vassal, his own nephew, a dangerous neighbor to Rome, to the dukedom. But Liutprand delayed the restoration of the four cities: his armies still occupied the midland regions of Italy.

The independence of Rome was on the hazard: Italy was again on the verge of becoming a Lombard kingdom. The future destinies of Europe were trembling in the balance. Had the whole of Italy, at least to the borders of Naples (Naples, and even Sicily, could easily have been wrested from the Greek empire), been consolidated under one hereditary rule, and had the Pope sunk back to his spiritual functions, Pepin and his more powerful successor, Charlemagne, might not have been invited into Italy as protectors of the liberties and religion of Rome.

The course of Lombard conquest was arrested by the personal weight and sacerdotal awe which environed the Pope. Since the time of Leo the Great, no pontiff placed such bold reliance on his priestly character and on himself as Zacharias. Other Popes had not mingled in the active life of man with man. They had officiated in the churches, presided in councils of ecclesiastics, issued decrees, administered their temporal affairs through their officers or legates. Zacharias seemed to delight in encountering his most dangerous enemies face to face: he was his own ambassador. Zacharias no doubt knew the character of the Lombard king. With all his ambition and warlike activity, Liutprand, if we are to believe the Lombard historian, blended the love of peace and profound piety. He was renowned for his chastity, his fervency in prayer, his liberality in alms-giving. He was illiterate, yet to be equalled with the sagest philosophers.[1] The strength and the weakness of such a character were equally open to impressions from the apostolic majesty, perhaps the apostolic gentleness, of the head of Christendom.

Interview with Liutprand at Terni. A.D. 742.

The spiritual potentate set forth in his peaceful array, surrounded by his court of bishops, to the camp of Liutprand near Terni. He was met at Cortona by Grimoald, an officer of Liutprand's court, conducted first to Narni, afterwards with great pomp, accompanied by part of the army and by the Lombard nobility, to Terni.[2] The scene of the interview was a church — that of St. Valentine; the Pope thus availing himself of the awfulness by which a religious mind like that of Liutprand would in such a place be already half prostrated before his holy antagonist. There he would listen with deeper emotion to the appalling admonitions of the pontiff on the vanity of earthly grandeur. The Lombard was reminded of the strict, it might be speedy, account which he was to give tc God in whose presence he stood, of all the blood which he had shed in war. He was threatened with

[1] "Castus, pudicus, orator pervigil, eleemosynis largus, literarum quidem ignarus, sed philosophis æquandus." — Paul. Diac.

[2] Anastas. in Vit. Zachariæ.

eternal damnation if he delayed to surrender the four cities, according to his stipulations.

The issue of such a contest could not be doubtful. The appalled Barbarian yielded at once. He declared that he restored the four cities to St. Peter. His generous piety knew no bounds. He gave back all the estates of the Church in the Sabine country, which the Lombards had held for thirty years — Narni, Osimo, Ancona, and towns in the district of Sutri — released unransomed all the Roman prisoners taken in the war, and concluded a peace for twenty years with the dukedom of Rome. The treaty was ratified by a solemn service, at which the Pope (the bishopric of Terni being vacant) officiated; the pious king, the officers of his court and army, attended in submissive reverence. The Pope then entertained him with a great banquet,[1] and returned to Rome. The deliverer of the city from a foreign yoke was received with a religious ovation, as well deserved as one of the Triumphs of older days. The procession passed from the ancient Pantheon, now the church of St. Mary ad Martyres, to St. Peter's.

Treaty of peace.

Yet beyond the immediate circle of the pontiff's magic influence, Liutprand could not resist the temptation offered by the wreck of the defenceless exarchate. Though, according to his treaty with the Pope, he respected the territory of Rome, he suddenly surprised Cesena, and announced his determination to subdue the rest of the exarchate. Ravenna already beheld the formidable conqueror before her walls.

1 "Ubi cum tantâ suavitate esum sumpsit, et cum tantâ hilaritate cordis, ut diceret rex tantum se nunquam meminisse comessatum." — Vit. Zachar.

The only refuge was in the unarmed Pope. Eutychius the Exarch, the archbishop, the people of the city and of the province joined in an earnest petition for the intervention of the pontiff. Zacharias espoused their cause; he sent an embassy to Pavia to dissuade Liutprand from further aggression, and to request the restoration of Cesena. The Lombard refused to receive the ambassadors. The unbaffled Pope determined once more to try the effect of his personal presence: he set forth in state towards Pavia. The importance attached to this journey is attested by the miracles with which it was invested. A cloud, by the special interposition of St. Peter, hovered constantly over the sacred band, to shield them from the violent heats, till they pitched their tents in the evening. At some distance from Ravenna he was met by the Exarch; and, still overshadowed by the faithful cloud, which poised itself at length over one of the churches, he entered the city. He left it followed by the whole population, men and women, in tears, praying for the good pastor who had left his own flock for their protection. A new sign, like a fiery army in the heavens, marshalled him on his way towards Pavia. But he derived greater advantage from other guidance. He had sent forward some of his attendants to Imola, on the Lombard border, from whom he received intelligence of orders issued to stop him on his march. The Pope made a rapid journey and reached the Po. On the banks he was met by some of the Lombard nobles, whom the king, having in vain attempted to elude the reception of the embassy, sent to receive him with due honors. After the arrival at Pavia, a few days were passed in relig-

Second interview at Pavia. A.D. 743.

ious ceremonies, at which the king attended with his wonted devotion. It was St. Peter's day; a day happily chosen for the august ceremony. At length Liutprand consented to admit the pontiff to an interview in his palace. After long and resolute re- June 29. sistance on the king's part, Zacharias extorted the abandonment of his ambitious designs on the exarchate, the restoration of two-thirds of the territory of Cesena.

Thus for a short time longer the wreck of the imperial dominion in Italy was preserved by the sole influence, the religious eloquence and authority, of the unarmed Bishop of Rome. But such was the power of religion in those times, that not merely did it enable the clergy to dictate their policy to armed and powerful sovereigns, to arrest Barbarian invasion, and to snatch, as it were, conquests already in their rapacious hands; in every quarter of Western Europe Kings become monks. kings were seen abdicating their thrones, placing themselves at the feet of the Pope as humble penitents, casting off their pomp, and submitting to the privations and the discipline of monks.

It has been related that when Columban, some years before, endeavored to persuade the Merovingian Theodebert to abandon his throne and become an ecclesiastic, the whole assembly burst out into scornful laughter.[1] "Was it ever heard that a Merovingian king had degraded himself into a priest?" The saint had replied, "He who disdains to become an ecclesiastic will become so against his will." The

[1] "Dicebant enim nunquam se audivisse Merovingum in regno sublimatum, voluntarium clericum fuisse. *Detestantibus ergo omnibus.*" — Vit. Columbani.

times had rapidly changed. From all parts of Western Christendom kings were coming, lowly penitents, to Rome, to lay aside the vain pomp of royalty, to assume the coarse attire, the total seclusion, and, as they hoped, the undisturbed and heaven-winning peace of the cloister. Ceolwulf is said to have been the eighth Anglo-Saxon prince who became a monk. Now, within a few years, from the thrones of France and of Lombardy, the kings descended of their own accord, laid their temporal government down before the head of Christendom, and entreated permission to devote the rest of their lives to the spiritual state.

Carloman, the elder son of Charles Martel, had commenced his reign with vigor, ability, and success. On a sudden he cast off at once the duties and the dignity of his station,[1] and surrendered to Pepin, his brother, the power and all the ambitious hopes of his family. Carloman left his country, appeared in Italy, humbly requested to be admitted into the monastic state, built a monastery on Mount Soracte, but finding that too near to Rome, retired to the more profound seclusion of Monte Casino. In that solitude the heir of Charles Martel hoped to pass the rest of his earthly days.[2]

Carloman. A.D. 747.

But Pope Zacharias beheld even a greater triumph of the faith. A Lombard king suddenly paused on

[1] Carloman had been preceded in this course by Hunald, Duke of Aquitaine, who having treacherously lured his brother Atto from the strong city of Poitiers, blinded him, and a few days after shut himself up in a monastery in the isle of Rhé. — H. Martin, Histoire de France, ii. p. 301. Hunald, however, on the death of his son, twenty-five years afterwards, scandalized Christendom by returning to the world, and resuming not only his dominions, but his wife also. — Muratori, ann. d' Italia, sub ann. 747.

[2] Vit. Zachariæ. Chronic. Moissiac. apud Pertz, i. 292.

the full tide of ambition and success, and from a deadly and formidable enemy of the Pope and of the Roman interest, became a peaceful monk.[1]

During the year of his last interview with Pope Zacharias had died Liutprand, the ablest and mightiest of the Lombard kings. Notwithstanding his pious deference for the Pope, his munificent ecclesiastical foundations in all parts of his dominions, the papal biographer attributes his death to the prayers of the Pope and the direct intervention of St. Peter.[2] The burden of ingratitude need not be laid on the Pope on account of the mature death of a sovereign who had reigned for thirty years. During a dangerous illness of Liutprand, nine years before, his nephew Hildebrand had been associated with him in the kingdom. After seven months of his sole dominion Hildebrand was deposed by the unanimous suffrage of the nation, and Rachis, Duke of Friuli, was raised to the throne. The first act of Rachis was to confirm the peace of twenty years with the Pope. The truce with the exarchate expired in the fifth year of his reign. But suddenly, incensed by some unknown cause of offence, or in a fit of ambition, Rachis appeared in arms, broke into the exarchate, and invested Perugia. The indefatigable Pope delayed not his interference. Again he was his own ambassador, and appeared in the camp of the Lombard king.[3] But he was not content with compelling King Rachis to

Death of Liutprand. A.D. 744

A.D. 713–743.

A.D. 749. Rachis.

1 Pauli i. Epist. ad Pepin. Regem; Muratori, R. I. Scrip. iii. 11. 116.

2 Anastasius in Zacharia.

3 Chronic. Salernit. i. 1; apud Muratori, i. 2. "Impensis eidem regi plurimis muneribus, atque . . . deprecans." See also account of conversion of King Rachis.

break up the siege; he pressed him so strongly with his saintly arguments, perhaps with the holy example of Carloman, that in a few days the king stood before the gates of Rome with his wife and daughter, having abdicated his throne, an humble suppliant for admission into the cloister. He too retired to Monte Casino, which thus boasted of two royal recluses. His wife and daughter entered the neighboring convent of Piombaruola. Carloman will appear again, somewhat unexpectedly, on the scene of political life.

Rachis a monk.

A.D. 749.

The last act in the eventful pontificate of Zacharias was the most pregnant with important results to Latin Christendom, the transference of the crown of France from the Merovingian line to the father of Charlemagne, with the sanction, it has been asserted, under the direct authority, of the Pope. To the Church and to Western Europe it is difficult to estimate all the consequences of the elevation of the Carlovingian dynasty.

A.D. 751.

Pepin, king of France.

The Pope has been accused of assuming an unwarranted power in virtually, as it were, by his sanction of Pepin's coronation, absolving the subjects of Chilperic from their allegiance; of want of stern principle in countenancing the violation of the great law of hereditary succession, and the rebellious ambition of the Mayor of the Palace, who thus degraded his lawful sovereign and usurped his throne. This is to confound the laws and usages of different ages. Hereditary succession among the Teutonic races had not yet attained that sanctity in which, in later times, it has been invested by supposed religious authority, and by the rational persuasion of its inestimable advantage. In theory it was admitted in the Roman empire; but the perpetual change of dynasty at Constantinople was not calculated to confirm the general reverence for its inviolability. Among the Lombards, as in most of the Gothic kingdoms, the nobles claimed and constantly exercised the privilege of throwing off the yoke of an unworthy prince, and advancing a more warlike or able chieftain, usually of the royal race, to the throne. The degradation of the successor to Liutprand, the accession of Rachis, were yet fresh in the memory of man. The Teutonic sovereign was still in theory the leader of an army; when he ceased to exercise his primary functions he had almost abdicated his state. It is difficult to conceive how such a shadow of a monarch had been so long permitted to rule over an enterprising and turbulent nation like the Franks. He was more like the Lama of an old, decrepit, Asiatic theocracy than the head of a young and conquering people. He sat on a throne with long hair and a flowing beard (these were the signs of royalty, worn indiscriminately whether he was young or old), he received ambassadors, and gave the answers put into his mouth: he had no domain but one small city, whose revenues hardly maintained his scanty retinue. In the spring alone, at the opening of the Champ de Mars, the idol was drawn forth from his sanctuary and offered to the sight of the people. He was slowly conveyed in a car drawn by oxen through the ranks of his wondering subjects, and was then consigned again to his secluded state.[1] For two or three

[1] "Crine profuso, barbâ submissâ . . . quocunque eundum erat, carpento ibat, bubulis rustico more agente trahebatur." Eginhard, c. 1. Compare Michelet, Hist. de France. Eginhard may perhaps have exaggerated the absolute and ostentatious insignificance of the dethroned Merovingian.

generations the effete Merovingian race had acquiesced in this despicable inactivity, and made no effort to break forth from the ignominious pomp in which they slumbered away their lives.

There are no details of this signal revolution.[1] Pe-
A.D 751. pin sent two ecclesiastics, Burchard, Bishop of Wurtzburg, and Fulrad his chaplain, to consult the Pope, but it appears not whether to relieve his conscience or as to a judge of recognized authority. A less decided pontiff than Zacharias might think the nation justified in its weariness of that hypocrisy which assigned to a secluded, imbecile pageant the name and ensigns of royalty, while its power was possessed by his Mayor of the Palace. It was time to put an end to this poor comedy of monarchy. Even if he took a higher view of his own power, there was full precedent in that which had long been the code of hierarchical privilege, the Old Testament, for the interference of the Priest, of God's representative on earth, in the deposition of unworthy kings, in the elevation of new dynasties.[2] It was indeed to usurp authority over a foreign kingdom, but what kingdom was foreign to the

[1] Eginhard, Ann. sub ann. 750, 751.

[2] "Et Zacharias Papa mandavit Pepino, ut melius esset illum regem vocari, qui potestatem haberet, quam illum, qui sine regali potestate manebat, ut non conturbaretur ordo." —Annal. Franc. apud Duchesne. Compare the Gesta Francorum, where it is more fully stated (Bouquet. p. 38). This passage is quoted in Lehuerou (Histoire des Institutions Carolingiens, p. 99): "Gens Merovingorum, de quâ Franci reges sibi creare soliti erant, usque in Hildericum regem, qui jussu Stephani, Romani Pontificis, depositus ac detonsus atque in monasterium trusus est, durâsse putatur. Quæ licet in illo finita possit videri, tamen jamdudum nullius vigoris erat, nec quicquam in se clarum præter inane regis vocabulum præferebat, nam et opes et potentia regni penes palatii præfectos, qui majores domus dicebantur et ad quos summa imperii pertinebat, tenebantur. . . . . Qui honor non aliis a *populo dari* consueverat, quam qui his et claritate generis et opum amplitudine cæteris eminebant." — Eginhard, Vit. Kar., iii. 1.

head of Christendom? The retirement of the deposed Chilperic into a monastery made but little change in his life; he was spared the fatigue and mockery of a public exhibition. The election of Pepin at Soissons was conducted according to the old usage of the Franks, the acclamation and clash of arms of the nobles and of the people, the elevation on the buckler; but it had now a new religious character, which marked the growing power of the clergy. The bishops stood around the throne, as of equal rank with the armed nobles. The Jewish ceremony of anointing was first introduced to sanctify a king perhaps of still somewhat doubtful title. The holy oil was poured on his head by the saintly archbishop of Mentz.[1] Two years after, on the visit of Pope Stephen, this ceremony was renewed by the august head of Christendom. King Chilperic was shaven and dismissed into a monastery, the retreat or the prison of all weary or troublesome princes.[2]

March, A.D. 752.

Little foresaw Pepin, little foresaw Zacharias, or his successor Stephen, the effects of the precedent which they were furnishing in the contemptuous dismissal of the poor foolish Chilperic from the throne of his ancestors, and the sanction of the Pope to this it might

[1] Clovis had also been *anointed* by St. Remi: "Elegi baptizari . . . et per ejusdem sacri chrismatis unctionem ordinato in regem . . . statuo." If he fails in his engagements "fiant dies ejus pauci, et principatum ejus accipiat alter." — Testament. S. Remig. ap. Flodoard. On the sacred character conferred by the holy unction, see Adlocutio duorum Episcoporum in eccles. S. Medard, A.D. 806. — Bouquet. According to the bishops, it gave the same right as that divinely bestowed on the kings of Israel. "Ainsi, par une réciprocité ordinaire dans les affaires humaines, le sacre, en donnant un titre, a imposé une sujétion; et de cette équivoque naîtra un jour le plus grand problème du moyen âge, la guerre du sacerdoce et de l'empire." — Lehuerou, p. 330.

[2] Eginhard, *loc. cit.*

seem almost insignificant act: that successors of Zacharias would assert that the kings of France, or rather the emperors, the successors of Charlemagne, held their crown only by the authority of the Pope; that the Pope might transfer that allegiance, to which the only title was the papal sanction, to a more loyal son of the Church.

In every respect, whether he contemplated the remote or the immediate interests of the Church or of Christianity, the Pope might hail with unmitigated satisfaction and hope the accession of Pepin. The whole race, since the alliance with Charles Martel, had been devoted to the Church and to the see of Rome. The prescient sagacity of Zacharias might discern in Astolph, the new king of the Lombards, that he inherited all the ambition without the strong religious feeling of his predecessors. Rome might speedily need a powerful Transalpine protector.

Nor could the Pope be blind to the pride, the ambition, the duty of establishing his own jurisdiction on a firmer basis beyond the Alps. In the German part of the Frankish kingdom, and in Germany itself, had now arisen a new clergy; if more devoted to the Pope, unquestionably of far higher Christian character than the degenerate hierarchy of France. They began as the humblest yet most enterprising missionaries, daily perilling their lives for the faith, and bringing gradually tribes of Barbarians within the pale of Christendom; they had become prelates of large sees, abbots of flourishing monasteries. But all this aggression on paganism, all these conquests of Christianity and civilization in the forests and morasses of Germany, had been made by men commissioned by Rome, and in strict subserviency to her discipline. Not even the jarring discrepancy between what Boniface and his followers saw and heard of the lives of Christian prelates in Rome, the venality of the public proceedings, and all which was strange to his lofty ideal of the faith, could in the least shake their conscientious devotion to the See of St. Peter.

To judge from the reports of these holy men, the monarchy itself was not more utterly effete and depraved than the old established clergy of France, which had boasted, in the century before, a hierarchy of saints. With due allowance for the rigidly monastic and celibate notions of Boniface and his disciples, which would induce them to condemn the marriage of the clergy as sternly as the loosest concubinage, there can be no doubt that the Frankish clergy were in general sunk low in character as in estimation.[1] Boniface, well informed, doubtless, of what he might expect to find, demands authority of the Pope to punish by summary degradation the incredible profligacy, especially of the lower ecclesiastics; as well as to interdict the unchristian occupations of the soldier-bishops, who indulged all the license of the camp — drunkenness, gambling, and quarrelling; and all the ferocity of the field of battle, even bloodshed, whether that of Pagans or Christians.[2]

1 Archbishop Boniface, it is said, Archbishop of Mentz, by papal authority (missus S. Petri), was set by Charles Martel over a synod, of which the object was to restore the law of God and the religion of the Church, which had gone to ruin under former kings, "quæ in diebus præteritorum principum corruit." — Epist. Boniface. Ellendorf, die Karolinger, i. p. 83. Carloman and his brother Pepin had followed the example of their father Charles Martel in supporting with all their power these better Christian ecclesiastics; they not only befriended them in their conversion of the Pagans, but in the correction of their own clergy.

2 Bonifac. Epist., with the permission to hold the Synod, and the reply

All the energy at least, the high principle, the pure morality, all the christianity of the time, might seem centred in these missionaries and in their followers; and this clergy at once so much more papal, and of so much higher character, was that of the new Carlovingian kingdom, a kingdom of Germany[1] rather than of Gaul. This clergy, the ancestors of Pepin, and Pepin himself, had always treated with the utmost respect and deference.[2] Boniface, in truth, as Papal Legate, or under the authority of Pepin, had early assumed the power of a primate of Gaul, consecrated three archbishops, of Rouen, and Sens, and Rheims. The last see was occupied by a soldier-prelate, named Milo, archbishop at once of Rheims and of Treves, who resisted for ten years all attempts to dispossess him; at the end of that time he was killed by a wild boar.

King Pepin was himself an Austrasian, the vast estates of his family lay on the Rhine. The accession of his house Teutonized more completely, till the division among the sons of Charlemagne, the whole Frankish monarchy.

Pope Zacharias did not live to behold the fulfilment of his great designs. He died in the same year on

of Pope Zacharias.—Labbe, Concil., p. 1495. He speaks of those who "in diaconatu concubinas quatuor vel quinque vel plures noctu in lectulo habentes," nevertheless dared to perform their sacred offices, and were promoted to the priesthood, evên to episcopacy. He proceeds: "Et inveniantur quidam inter eos episcopi, qui licet *dicant* se fornicarios vel adulterios non esse, sunt tamen ebriosi, et injuriosi, vel pugnatores; et qui pugnant in exercitu armati, et effundunt propriâ manu sanguinem hominum sive infidelium, sive Christianorum."

1 Compare Guizot, Essai iii.

2 Pope Zacharias writes to Boniface: "Quod (Carlomanus et Pepinus) tuæ prædicationis socii et adjutores esse niterentur ex divina inspiratura."—Epist. Bonifac. 144.

which Pepin became king of France. The election fell on a certain presbyter, named Stephen ; but the third day after, before his consecration, he was seized with a fit, and died the following day. He is not reckoned in the line of popes. Another Stephen, chosen immediately on his death, is usually called the second of that name. A.D. 752. March 14. March 26. Stephen II. or III.

The first act of Stephen's pontificate was to guard against the threatened aggressions of the Lombards. Already had Astolph, a prince as daring but less religious than Liutprand, entered the Exarchate, and seized Ravenna. The ambassadors of the Pope were received with courtesy, his gifts with avidity; a hollow truce for forty years was agreed on; but in four months (the terms of the treaty, and the pretext alleged by Astolph for its violation, are equally unknown) the Lombard was again in arms. In terms of contumely and menace he demanded the instant submission of Rome, and the payment of a heavy personal tribute, a poll-tax on each citizen. Astolph now treated the ambassadors of the Pope with scorn.[1] A representative of the empire, which still clung to its barren rights in Italy, John the Silentiary, appeared at Rome. He was sent to Ravenna, to protest against the Lombard invasion, and to demand the restoration of the Roman territory to the republic. Astolph dismissed him with a civil but evasive answer, that he would send an ambassador June October.

1 According to Anastasius, he was required to surrender to their rightful lord all that he had usurped by his *diabolic* ambition. This is a flower of ecclesiastical rhetoric, yet showing the papal abhorrence of the Lombards.

October. to the Emperor. Stephen wrote to Constantinople, that without an army to back the imperial demands, all was lost.

Astolph, exasperated, perhaps, at the demand of an army from the East, which might reach his ears, inflexibly pursued his advantages. He approached the Roman frontier; he approached Rome. Not all the litanies, not all the solemn processions to the most revered altars of the city, in which the Pope himself, with naked feet, bore the cross, and the whole people followed with ashes on their heads, and with a wild howl of agony implored the protection of God against the blaspheming Lombards, arrested for an instant his progress. The Pope appealed to heaven, by tying a copy of the treaty, violated by Astolph, to the holy cross.[1] Yet, during the siege of Rome, Astolph was digging up the bodies of saints, not for insult, but as the most precious trophies, and carried them off as tutelar deities to Lombardy.[2]

The only succor was beyond the Alps, from Pepin, the king, by papal sanction, of the Catholic Franks. Already the Pope had written to beseech the interference of the transalpine; and now, as the danger became more imminent, he determined to leave his beloved flock, though in a feeble state of health, to encounter the perils of a journey over the Alps, and so to visit the Barbarian monarch in person. He set forth among the tears and lamentations of the people. He was accompanied by some

Stephen leaves Rome.

1 "Alligans connectensque adorandæ cruci Dei nostri, pactum illud, quod nefandus Rex Longobardorum disrupit." — Anastas., in Vit. Steph. II.

2 "Ablata multa sanctorum corpora ex Romanis finibus, in Papiam . . . construxit eorum oracula." He founded a nunnery, in which he placed his own daughters. — Chronic. Salernit.

ecclesiastics, by the Frankish bishop Radigond, and the Duke Anscharis, already sent by Pepin to invite him to the court of France. Miracles, now the ordinary signs of a papal progress, were said to mark his course.[1] Instead of endeavoring to pass without observation through the Lombard dominions, he boldly presented himself at the gate of Pavia. He was disappointed if he expected Astolph to be overawed by his presence, as Liutprand and Rachis had been by that of his saintly predecessor; but he was safe under the protection of the ambassador of Pepin. Astolph received him not without courtesy, accepted his gifts, but paid no regard to his earnest tears and supplications; coldly rejected his exorbitant demands, — the immediate restoration of all the Lombard conquests — but respected his person, and tried only, by repeated persuasion, to divert him from his journey into France. Stephen, on leaving Pavia, anticipated any stronger measures to detain him by a rapid march to the foot of the Alps. In November he passed the French frontier, and reached the convent of St. Maurice. There he was met by another ecclesiastic, and another noble of the highest rank, with orders to conduct him to the court. At a distance of a hundred miles from the court appeared the Prince Charles, with some chosen nobles. Charles was thus to be early impressed with reverence

Oct. 14.

November.

Nov. 15.

Jan. 6, 754.

1 Compare, on the other hand, the curious story in Agnelli. Stephen wished to plunder on his way the treasures of the church of Ravenna. The Ravennese priests (among them Leo, afterwards archbishop) designed to murder him. He escaped, taking only part of the treasures. Those who had plotted the death of the Pope were sent to Rome, and remained till most of them died. Among them, says the writer, " avus patris mei fuit." —Apud Muratori.

for the Papal dignity. Three miles from the palace of Pontyon,[1] Pepin came forth with his wife, his family, and the rest of his feudatories. As the Pope approached, the king dismounted from his horse, and prostrated himself on the ground before him. He then walked by the side of the Pope's palfrey. The Pope and the ecclesiastics broke out at once into hymns of thanksgiving, and so chanting as they went, reached the royal residence. Stephen lost no time in adverting to the object of his visit. He implored the immediate interposition of Pepin to enforce the restoration of the domain of St. Peter. So relate the Italians. According to the French chroniclers, the Pope and his clergy, with ashes on their heads, and sackcloth on their bodies, prostrated themselves as suppliants at the feet of Pepin, and would not rise till he had promised his aid against the perfidious Lombard. Pepin swore at once to fulfil all the requests of the Pope; but as the winter rendered military operations impracticable, invited him to Paris, where he took up his residence in the abbey of St. Denys. Pepin and his two sons were again anointed by the Pope himself, their sovereignty thus more profoundly sanctified in the minds of their subjects. Stephen would secure the perpetuity of the dynasty under pain of interdict and excommunication. The nation was never to presume to choose a king in future ages, but of the race of Charles Martel.[2] From fatigue and the severity of the climate, Stephen became dangerously ill in the
July. monastery of St. Denys, but, after a hard

1 Pontyon on the Perche, near Vitry-le brulé.

2 "Tali omnes interdicto et excommunicationis lege constrinxit, ut nunquam de alterius lumbis regem in ævo præsumerent eligere." — Clausul. de Pippini Elect.

struggle, recovered his health. His restoration was esteemed a miracle, wrought through the prayers of St. Denys, St. Peter, and St. Paul.

Astolph, in the mean time, did not disdain the storm which was brooding beyond the Alps. He took an extraordinary measure to avert the danger. He persuaded Carloman, the brother of Pepin, who had abdicated his throne, and turned monk, to leave his monastery, to cross the Alps, and endeavor to break this close alliance between Pepin and the Pope. No wonder that the clergy should attribute the influence of Astolph over the mind of Carloman to diabolic arts, for Carloman appeared at least, whether seized by an access of reviving ambition, or incensed at Pepin's harsh treatment of his family, to enter with the utmost zeal into the cause of the Lombard. The humble slave of the Pope Zacharias presented himself in France as the resolute antagonist of Pope Stephen and of the Papal cause.[1] But the throne of Pepin was too firmly fixed; he turned a deaf and contemptuous ear to his brother's arguments. The Pope asserted his authority over the renegade monk, who had broken his vows; and Carloman was imprisoned for life in a cloister at Vienne; that life however, lasted but a few days.

Carloman in France.

Pope Stephen was anxious to avert the shedding of blood in the impending war.[2] Thrice before he col-

1 According to Anastasius, "vehementius decertabat, sanctæ Dei ecclesiæ causam subvertere." It is impossible to conceive how Astolph could persuade him to engage in this strange and perilous mission, and the arguments urged by Carloman on his brother are still more strange. Eginhard asserts that he came "jussu abbatis sui quia nec ille ablatis sui jussa contempnere, nec abbas ille præceptis Regis Longobardorum, qui ei et hoc imperavit, audebat resistere." Sub ann. 753.

2 "Obtestatur per omnia divina mysteria et futuri examinis diem ut

lected his forces, once on his march to Italy, Pepin sent ambassadors to the Lombard king, who were to exhort him to surrender peaceably the possessions of the Church and of the Roman Republic. Pope Stephen tried the persuasiveness of religious awe. Astolph rejected the menacing and more quiet overtures with scorn, and fell on an advanced post of the Franks, which occupied one of the passes of the Alps, about to be entered by the army. He was routed by those few troops, and took refuge in Pavia. The King of the Franks and Pope Stephen advanced to the walls of the city; and Astolph was glad to purchase an ignominious peace, by pledging himself, on oath, to restore the territory of Rome.[1]

Pepin in Italy.

Sept.—Oct.

Pepin had no sooner retired beyond the Alps with his hostages, than Astolph began to find causes to delay the covenanted surrender. After a certain time he marched with his whole forces upon Rome, to which Pope Stephen had then returned, wasted the surrounding country, encamped before the Salarian Gate, and demanded the surrender of the Pope.[2] The plunder, if the Papal historian is to be believed, which he chiefly coveted, was the dead bodies of the saints. These he dug up and carried away. He demanded that the Romans should give up the Pope into his hands, and on these terms only would he

November.

December. Siege of Rome.

pacifice sine ullâ sanguinis effusione propria sanctæ dei ecclesiæ et reipublicæ Romanorum reddat jura." — Vit. Steph.

1 The Pope attributed the easy victory of the Franks, not to their valor, but to St. Peter. "Per manum beati Petri Dominus omnipotens victoriam vobis largiri dignatus est." — Steph. Epist. ad Pepin. p. 1632.

2 Stephan. Epist. Gretser, 261. — "Aperite mihi portam Salariam ut ingrediar civitatem, et tradite mihi pontificem vestrum."

spare the city. Astolph declared he would not leave the Pope a foot of land.[1]

Stephen sent messengers in all haste by sea, for every way by land was closed to his faithful ally. His first letter reminded King Pepin how stern an exactor of promises was St. Peter; "that the king hazarded eternal condemnation if he did not complete the donation which he had vowed to St. Peter, and St. Peter had promised to him eternal life. If the king was not faithful to his word, the apostle had his handwriting to the grant, which he would produce against him in the day of judgment."

Pope Stephen's first letter.

A second letter followed, more pathetic, more persuasive. "Astolph was at the gates of Rome; he threatened, if they did not yield up the Pope, to put the whole city to the sword. He had burned all the villas and the suburbs;[2] he had not spared the churches; the very altars were plundered and defiled; nuns violated; infants torn from their mothers' breasts; the mothers polluted, — all the horrors of war were ready to break on the devoted city, which had endured a siege of fifty-five days. He conjured him, by God and his holy mother, by the angels of heaven, by the apostles St. Peter and St. Paul, and by the last day." This second letter was sent by the hands of the Abbot Warnerius, who had put on his breast-plate, and night and day kept watch for the city. (This is the first example of a warlike abbot.) With him were George, a bishop, and Count

Second letter.

Dec. 754–Feb. 755.

1 "Nec unius palmi terræ spatium B. Petro . . . . vel reipublicæ Romanorum reddere." — Steph. Epist. In the utmost distress, the very stones, the Pope says, might have wept at his grief and peril. — Epist. ad Pepin. Reg.

2 Epist. ii. ad Pepin. Reg.

Tomaric. Stephen summed up the certain reward which Pepin might expect if he hastened to the rescue — " Victory over all the Barbarian nations, and eternal life."

But the Franks were distant, or were tardy; the danger of the Pope and the Roman people more and more imminent. Stephen was wrought to an agony of fear, and in this state took the daring — to our calmer religious sentiment, impious step — of writing a letter, as from St. Peter himself, to hasten the lingering succor: — " I, Peter the Apostle, protest, admonish, and conjure you, the Most Christian Kings, Pepin, Charles, and Carloman, with all the hierarchy, bishops, abbots, priests, and all monks; all judges, dukes, counts, and the whole people of the Franks. The Mother of God likewise adjures you, and admonishes and commands you, she as well as the thrones and dominions, and all the host of heaven, to save the beloved city of Rome from the detested Lombards. If ye hasten, I, Peter the Apostle, promise you my protection in this life and in the next, will prepare for you the most glorious mansions in heaven, and will bestow on you the everlasting joys of paradise. Make common cause with my people of Rome, and I will grant whatever ye may pray for. I conjure you not to yield up this city to be lacerated and tormented by the Lombards, lest your own souls be lacerated and tormented in hell, with the devil and his pestilential angels. Of all nations under heaven, the Franks are highest in the esteem of St. Peter; to me you owe all your victories. Obey, and obey speedily, and, by my suffrage, our Lord Jesus Christ will give you in this life length of days, security, victory; in the life to come, will mul-

Third from St. Peter himself.

tiply his blessings upon you, among his saints and angels."[1]

A vain but natural curiosity would imagine the effect of this letter at the court of Pepin. Were there among his clergy or among his warrior nobles those who really thought they heard the voice of the apostle, and felt that their eternal doom depended on their instant obedience to this appeal? How far was Pepin himself governed by policy or by religious awe? How much was art, how much implicit faith wrought up to its highest pitch by terror, in the mind of the Pope, when the Pope ventured on this awful assumption of the person of the apostle? That he should hazard such a step, having had personal intercourse with Pepin, his clergy, and his nobles, shows the measure which he had taken of the power with which religion possessed their souls. He had fathomed the depths of their Christianity; and whether he himself partook in the same, to us extravagant, notions, or used them as lawful instruments to terrify the Barbarians into the protection of the holy see and the advancement of her dominion, he might consider all means justified for such high purposes. If it had been likely to startle men, by this overwrought demand on their credulity, into reasoning on such subjects, it would have hindered rather than promoted his great end.

1 Gretser, p. 17-23. Mansi, sub ann. A. D. 755. Fleury observes of this letter: "Au reste, elle est pleine d'équivoques, comme les précédentes. L'Eglise y signifie non l'assemblée des fidèles, mais les biens temporels consacrés à Dieu: le troupeau de Jésus Christ sont les corps et non pas les âmes: les promesses temporelles de l'ancienne loi sont mêlées avec les spirituelles de l'Evangile, et les motifs plus saints de la religion employés pour une affaire d'état."—Liv. xlvii. c. 17. After all, the ground of quarrel was for the excharchate, not for the estates of the Church. If the Pope had allowed the Lombards to occupy the exarchate, they would have been loyal allies of the Pope.

Not the least remarkable point of all is, that Christianity has now assumed the complete power, not only of the life to come, but of the present life, with all its temporal advantages. It now leagues itself with Barbarians, not to soften, to civilize, to imbue with devotion, to lead to Christian worship; but to give victory in all their ruthless wars, to confer the blessings of heaven on their schemes of ambition and conquest. The one title to eternal life is obedience to the Church — the Church no longer the community of pious and holy Christians, but the see, almost the city, of Rome. The supreme obligation of man is the protection and enlargement of her domain. By zeal in this cause, without any other moral or religious qualification, the most brutal and bloody soldier is a saint in heaven. St. Peter is become almost God, the giver of victory, the dispenser of eternal life. The time is approaching when war against infidels or enemies of the Pope will be among the most meritorious acts of a Christian.

Pepin in Italy. Lombards yield.

The Franks had alarmed the Pope by the tardiness of their succor; but their host once assembled and on its march, their rapid movements surprised Astolph. Scarcely could he return to Pavia, when he found himself besieged in his capital. The Lombard forces seem to have been altogether unequal to resist the Franks. Astolph yielded at once to the demands of Pepin, and actually abandoned the whole contested territory. Ambassadors from the East were present at the conclusion of the treaty, and demanded the restitution of Ravenna and its territory to the Byzantine Empire. Pepin declared that his sole object in the war was to show his veneration for St.

Peter; and he bestowed, as it seems, by the right of conquest, the whole upon the Pope.

The representatives of the Pope, who however always speak of the republic of Rome, passed through the land, receiving the homage of the authorities and the keys of the cities. The district comprehended Ravenna, Rimini, Pesaro, Fano, Cesena, Sinigaglia, Iesi, Forlimpopoli, Forli with the Castle Sussibio, Montefeltro, Acerra, Monte di Lucano, Serra, San Marino, Bobbio, Urbino, Cagli, Luciolo, Gubbio, Comachio, and Narni which was severed from the dukedom of Spoleto.[1]

Thus the successor, as he was declared, of the fisherman of the Galilean lake, the apostle of Him whose kingdom was not of this world, became a temporal sovereign. By the gift of a foreign potentate, this large part of Italy became the kingdom of the Bishop of Rome.

King Astolph did not long survive this humiliation: he was accidentally killed when hunting. A.D. 756. The adherents of the Pope beheld the hand of God in his death; they heap on him every appellation of scorn and hatred; the Pope has no doubt of his damnation.[2] The Lombards of Tuscany favored the pretensions of their Duke Des-

Desiderius King of Lombardy. A.D. 756.

[1] It is not quite clear how Stephen himself eluded the claims of the Greek Emperor — probably by the Emperor's heresy. In Stephen's letter of thanks for his deliverance to the King of the Franks, he desires to know what answer had been given to the Silentiary, commissioned to assert the rights of his master. He reminds Pepin that he must protect the Catholic Church against pestilent wickedness (malitia), (no doubt the iconoclastic opinions of the Emperor), and keep her *property* secure (omnia proprietatis suæ).

[2] "Divino ictu percussus est et in inferni voraginem demersus." — Epist. ad Pepin. vi.; Gretser, 60; Mansi, sub ann.

iderius to the throne. In the north of Italy, Rachis, the brother of Astolph, who had retired to a monastery, appeared at the head of a powerful faction, and reclaimed the throne. Desiderius endeavored to secure the influence of the pope. Stephen extorted, as the price of his interference, Faenza, Imola, with some other castles, and the whole duchy of Ferrara.[1] Stephen no doubt felt a holy horror of the return of a monk to worldly cares, even those of a crown. This would be rank apostasy with him who was thus secularizing the papacy itself.

During the later years of Stephen's pontificate, a strong faction had designated his brother Paul as successor to the see. Another party, opposed perhaps to this family transmission of the papacy, which was thus assimilating itself more and more to a temporal sovereignty, set up the claims of the Archdeacon Theophylact. On the vacancy the partisans of Paul prevailed. The brother of Stephen was raised to the throne of St. Peter. Paul has the fame of a mild and peace-loving prelate. He loved to wander at night among the hovels of the poor, and to visit the prisons, relieving misery and occasionally releasing the captives from their bondage. Yet is Paul not less involved in the ambitious designs of the advancing papacy. His first act is to announce his election to the King of the Franks, who had now the title, probably bestowed by Stephen, of Patrician of Rome. His letter does not allude to any further ratification of his election, made by the free choice of the clergy and people of Rome; there is no recognition whatever of supremacy.

A.D. 757. April 26.

Paul I. Pope.

[1] Perhaps also Osimo, Ancona, Humana, and he even demanded Bologna.

Desiderius, till he had secured his throne in Lombardy, remained on terms of amity with the Pope; but the old irreconcilable hostility broke out again soon after the accession of Paul.

Among the causes of the weakness of the Lombard kingdom, and the easy triumph of the Franks, was the disunion of the nation. The Dukes of Spoleto and Benevento renounced their allegiance to the King of Pavia, and declared their fealty to the King of the Franks. The chastisement of their revolt gave Desiderius a pretext for war. He marched, ravaging as he went with fire and sword, through the cities of the exarchate, surprised and imprisoned the Duke of Spoleto, forced the Duke of Benevento to take refuge in Otranto, and set up another duke in his place. He then proceeded to Naples, still occupied by the Greeks, and endeavored to negotiate a dangerous alliance with the Eastern emperor.[1] On his return he passed through Rome; and when the Pope demanded the surrender of the stipulated cities — Imola, Osimo, Ancona, and Bologna — Desiderius eluded the demand by requiring the previous restitution of the Lombard hostages carried by Pepin into France; but dreading perhaps a new Frankish invasion, Desiderius gradually submitted to the fulfilment of his treaty. Disputes arose concerning certain patrimony of the Church in some of the Lombard cities, but even these were amicably adjusted. The adulation of Paul to the King of the Franks passes bounds. He is another Moses; as Moses rescued Israel from the bondage of Egypt, so Pepin the Catholic Church; as Moses confounded idolatry, so Pepin heresy. The rapturous

1 Gretser, p. 81; Mansi, sub ann. 758.

expressions of the Psalms about the Messiah are scarcely too fervent to be applied to Pepin. All his acts are under divine inspiration.[1] The only apprehensions of Paul seemed to be on the side of the Greeks. On one occasion he writes that six Byzantine ships menaced a descent on Rome; on another he dreads an attack by sea on Ravenna. He entreats the King of the Franks to urge Desiderius to make common cause against the enemy; but he represents the hostility of the Greeks as arising not from their desire to recover their rights in Italy, but solely from the impious design of destroying the images, of subverting the Catholic faith and the traditions of the holy fathers. They are odious iconoclastic heretics, not the Imperial armies warring to regain their lost dominions in Italy. The Greeks have now succeeded to the appellation of the "most wicked," a term hitherto appropriated to the Lombards; but hereafter the epithet of all those who resisted the temporal or spiritual interest of the Papal See.[2]

The Greek empire

Such was the singular position of Rome and of the Roman territory. In theory they were still part of the Roman Empire, of which the Greek Emperor, had he been orthodox, would have been the acknowledged

[1] Gretser, Epist. xvi. "Novus quippe Moses, novusque David in omnibus operibus suis effectus est Christianissimus et a Deo protectus filius et spiritalis compater Dominus Pepinus." — Epist. xxii. Thou, after God, art our defender and aider; if all the hairs of our head were tongues, we could not give you thanks equal to your deserts. — Epist. xxxvi. Throughout it is St. Peter who has anointed Pepin king; St. Peter who is the giver of all Pepin's victories over the Barbarians; St. Peter whom he protects; St. Peter whose gratitude he has a right to command; and St. Peter is all powerful in heaven.

[2] Non ob aliud *nefandissimi* nos persequuntur Græci, nisi propter sanctam et orthodoxam fidem, et venerandorum patrum piam traditionem, quam cupiunt destruere et conculcare." — Epist. ad Pepin.

sovereign;[1] but his iconoclasm released the members of the true Church from their allegiance: he was virtually or actually under excommunication. In the mean time the right of conquest, and the indefinite title of Patrician, assigned by the Pope, acting in behalf and with the consent of the Roman republic, to Pepin — a title which might be merely honorary, or might justify any authority which he might have power to exercise — gave a kind of supremacy to the King of the Franks in Rome and her domain. The Pope, tacitly at least, admitted as the representative of the Roman people, awarded this title, which gave him a right to demand protection, while himself, by the donation of Pepin, possessed the actual property and the real power. In the Exarchate he ruled by the direct grant of Pepin, who had conquered this territory from the Lombards, they having previously dispossessed the Greeks. Popes of this time kept up the pious fiction that the donations even of sovereigns, though extending to cities and provinces, were given for holy uses, the keeping up the lights in the churches, and the maintenance of the poor.[2] But who was to demand account of the uses to which these revenues were applied? The Pope took possession as lord and master; he received the homage of the authorities and the keys of the cities. The local or municipal institutions remained; but the revenue, which had before been received by the Byzantine crown, became the

1 The Greeks still retained Naples and the South of Italy.

2 "Unde pro animæ vestræ salute indefessa luminarium concinnatio Dei ecclesiis permaneat, et esuries pauperum, egenorum, vel peregrinorum nihilominus relevetur, et ad veram saturitatem perveniant." — Steph. II. ad Pepin. Epist.

revenue of the Church: of that revenue the Pope was the guardian, distributor, possessor.

The pontificate of Paul, on the whole, was a period of peace. If Desiderius, after his first expedition against the rebel Duke of Spoleto, did not maintain strictly amicable relations with the Papal See, he abstained from hostility.

Papacy seized by Toto.

But, as heretofore, the loftier the papal dignity and the greater the wealth and power of the Pope, the more it became an object of unhallowed ambition. On the death of Paul, that which two centuries later reduced the Papacy to the lowest state of degradation, the violent nomination of the Pope by the petty barons and armed nobles of the neighboring districts was prematurely attempted. Toto, the Duke of Nepi, suddenly, before Paul had actually expired, entered the city with his three brothers and a strong armed force. As soon as Paul was dead, they seized a bishop and compelled him to ordain Constantine, one of the brothers, yet a layman. They then took possession of the Lateran palace, and after a hasty form of election, forced the same bishop, George of Palestrina, with two others, Eustratius of Alba and Citonatus of Porto, to consecrate Constantine as Pope.[1] The usurper retained possession of the see for more than a year, ordained and discharged all the offices of a pontiff, a period reckoned as a vacancy in the papal annals. At the end of that time two distinguished Romans, Christopher the Primicerius and Sergius his son, made their escape to the court of Pavia, to entreat the intervention of Desiderius. They obtained the aid of some Lombards, chiefly

Jan. 28, 767.

Constantine Pope. July 6, 767, to Aug. 1, 768.

[1] Vit. Stephan. III.

from the duchy of Spoleto, and appeared in arms in the city. Toto at first made a valiant de- July 29. fence, but was betrayed by his own followers and slain. Constantine, the false Pope, with his brother and a bishop named Theodorus, endeavored to conceal themselves, but were seized by their enemies.

During the tumult part of the successful insurgents hastily elected a certain Philip, and installed him in the Lateran palace. The stronger party assem- July 31. Philip. bled a more legitimate body of electors, the chief of the clergy, of the army, and of the people. The unanimous choice fell on Stephen III., who A.D. 768. Stephen III. Cruelties in Rome. had been employed in high offices by Paul.[1] The scenes which followed in the city of the head of Christendom must not be concealed.[2] The easy victory was terribly avenged on Constantine and his adherents. The Bishop Theodorus was the chief object of animosity. They put out his eyes, cut off his tongue, and shut him up in the dungeon of a monastery, where he was left to die of hunger and of thirst, vainly imploring a drop of water in his agony. They put out the eyes of Passianus, the brother of the usurping Pope, and shut him up in a monastery: they plundered and confiscated all their possessions. The usurper was led through the city riding on a horse with a woman's saddle, with heavy weights to his feet; then brought out, solemnly deposed (for he was yet Pope elect),[3] and thrust into the monastery of Centumcellæ. Even there he was not allowed to repent in peace of his ambition. A party of his ene-

1 He is called Vice Dominus.

2 Anastas. Vit. Stephan. III.

3 "Dum adhuc electus extitisset."—Vit. Steph. III.

mies first seized a tribune of his faction named Gracilis,
Aug. 6. put out his eyes, surprised the convent, treated the Pope in the same inhuman manner, and left him blind and bleeding in the street. These atrocities were not confined to the adherents of Constantine. A presbyter named Waldipert had taken a great part in the revolution, had accompanied Christopher, the leader of the deliverers, to Rome, but he had been guilty of the hasty election of Philip to the papacy. He was accused of a conspiracy to betray the city to the Duke of Spoleto. He fled to the church of the Virgin ad Martyres. Though he clung to and clasped the sacred image, he was dragged out, and plunged into one of the most noisome dungeons in the city. After a few days he was brought forth, his eyes put out, his tongue cut in so barbarous a manner that he died. Some of these might be the acts of a fierce, ungovernable, excited populace; but the clergy, in their collective and deliberative capacity, cannot be acquitted of as savage inhumanity.

The first act of Stephen was to communicate his election to the Patrician, the King of the Franks.
Aug. 1, 768. Pepin had expired before the arrival of the ambassadors. His son sent a deputation of twelve bishops to Rome. The Pope summoned the bishops of Tuscany, of Campania, and other parts of Italy, and with the Frankish bishops formed a regular Council in the Lateran. The usurper Constantine was brought in, blind and broken in spirit, to answer for
April 12, 769. his offences. He expressed the deepest contrition, he grovelled on the earth, he implored the mercy of the priestly tribunal. His sentence was deferred. On his next examination he was asked how,

being a layman, he had dared to venture on such an impious innovation as to be consecrated at once a bishop. It is dangerous at times to embarrass adversaries with a strong argument. He replied that it was no unprecedented innovation; he alleged the cases of the Archbishops of Ravenna and of Naples, as promoted at once from laymen to the episcopate. The indignant clergy rose up, fell upon him, beat him cruelly with their own hands, and turned him out of the church.

Punishment of Constantine.

All the instruments which related to the usurpation of Constantine were then burned; Stephen solemnly inaugurated; all who had received the communion from the hands of Constantine professed their profound penitence. A decree was passed interdicting, under the strongest anathema, all who should aspire to the episcopate without having passed through the inferior orders. All the ordinations of Constantine were declared null and void; the bishops were thrown back to their inferior orders, and could only attain the episcopate after a new election and consecration. The laymen who had dared to receive these irregular orders fared worse: they were to wear the religious habit for their lives, being incapable of religious functions. This Lateran Council closed its proceedings by an unanimous decree in favor of image-worship, anathematizing the godless Inconoclasts of the East.

April 14, 769.

These tragic scenes closed not with the extinction of the faction of Constantine: new victims suffered the dreadful punishment of blinding, some also seclusion in a monastery, the ordinary sentence of all whose lives were spared in civil conflict. But the causes of this new revolution and the conduct of the Pope are contested and obscure. All that is undoubted is that the King of the Lombards appears as the protector of the Pope; Carioman the Frank, the son of Pepin, threatens his dethronement.[1]

Desiderius, King of Lombardy, A.D. 757, in Rome, A.D. 769.

Desiderius, the Lombard King, presented himself before Rome with the avowed object of delivering the Pope from the tyranny of Christopher the primicerius, and his son Sergius. These men had been the leaders, with Lombard aid, in the overthrow of the usurper. Christopher and his son hastily gathered some troops, and closed the gates of the city. They were betrayed by Paul (named Afiarta), the Pope's chamberlain, seized, blinded: the elder, Christopher, died of the operation. Desiderius boasted of this service as equivalent to and annulling all the papal claims to certain rights in the cities of Lombardy. Carloman the Frank, on the other hand, espoused the cause of these oppressors, as they were called, of the Pope, who had menaced his life, in conjunction with Dodo, Carloman's ambassador. Carlo-

1 The great object of dispute, after the surrender of the exarchate, that which the popes constantly demanded, and the Lombard kings endeavored to elude, was the full restitution of the "justitiæ" claimed by the pope within the Lombard kingdom. — Vit. Stephan. III. This term, intelligible in the forensic language of the day, is now unmeaning. Muratori defines it, "Allodiale, rendite e diritte, che appartenevano alla chiesa Romana nel regno Longobardico." But what were these allodial rights, in a kingdom of which the full sovereignty was in the Lombards? Were they estates held by the Church, as landlords, like those in Sicily or elsewhere? or *dues* claimed at least of all *Roman* Christians in Italy? Sismondi's suggestion, that it means the royal cities, the property of the crown, which were administered in France by judges, seems quite inapplicable to the Lombard kingdom (Sismondi, Hist. des Français, ii. p. 281). Manzoni, in a note to his Adelchi, supposes that it was a vague term, intended to comprehend all the demands of the Church. Yet in the epistles of the several popes, the two Stephens, Paul, and Hadrian, it seems to mean something specific and definite. To me Muratori appears nearest to the truth.

man threatened to avenge their punishment by marching to Rome and dethroning the Pope. This strange statement is confirmed by a letter of Stephen himself, addressed to Bertha, the mother of the Frankish kings, and to Charlemagne.[1] The biographer of Pope Stephen gives an opposite version. The hostility of Desiderius to Christopher and Sergius arose from their zeal in enforcing the papal demands on the Lombard kings. He denounces the Lombards as still the enemies of the Pope, and accuses Paul, the Pope's chamberlain, their ally, of the basest treachery.

At all events this transitory connection between the pope and the Lombards soon gave way to the old implacable animosity. Whatever might be the claim of Desiderius on the gratitude of Stephen, the intelligence of a proposed intimate alliance between his faithful protectors the Franks, and his irreconcilable enemies the Lombards, struck the Pope with amazement and dismay.

1 "Unde (Christophorus et Sergius, cum Dodone Carlomanni regis misso) in basilicam domni Theodori papæ, ubi sedebamus, introierunt, sicque ipsi maligni homines insidiabantur nos interficere." Cenni, Monument. i. 267. Jaffe, p. 201. This letter is by some supposed to have been written under compulsion, when Desiderius was master of the Pope and of Rome. Muratori hardly answers this by showing that it was written after the execution of Christopher and Sergius.

CHAPTER XII.

CHARLEMAGNE ON THE THRONE.

Carloman and Charles.

The jealousies of Carloman and Charles, the sons of Pepin, who had divided his monarchy, were for a time appeased. Bertha, their mother, seized the opportunity of strengthening and uniting her divided house by intermarriages with the family of the Lombard sovereign. Desiderius was equally desirous of this connection with the powerful Transalpine kings. His unmarried son, Adelchis, was affianced to Gisela,[1] the sister of Charlemagne; his daughter Hermingard proposed as the wife of one of the royal brothers. Both Carloman and Charles were already married; Carloman was attached to his wife Gisberta, by whom he had children. The ambition of Charles was less scrupulous; he at once divorced his wife (an obscure person, whose name has not been preserved by history), and wedded the daughter of Desiderius. In this union the Pope saw the whole policy of his predecessors threatened with destruction: their mighty protector was become the ally, the brother of their deadly enemy. Already the splendid donation of Pepin seemed wrested from his unresisting hands. Who should now interpose to prevent the Lombards from becoming masters of the Exarchate, of Rome, of Italy? The Pope lost all self-

[1] Or Desiderata. Gisela became a nun. — Eginh. v. k. 1. xviii.

command; he gave vent to the full bitterness of Roman, of papal hatred to the Lombards and to the agony of his terror, in a remonstrance so unmeasured in its language, so unpapal, it might be said unchristian, in its spirit, as hardly to be equalled in the pontifical diplomacy.[1]

Letter of Pope Stephen.

"The devil alone could have suggested such a connection. That the noble, the generous race of the Franks, the most ancient in the world, should ally itself with the fetid brood of the Lombards, a brood hardly reckoned human, and who have introduced the leprosy into the land.[2] What could be worse than this abominable and detestable contagion? Light could not be more opposite to darkness, faith to infidelity." The Pope does not take his firm stand on the high moral and religious ground of the French princes' actual marriage. He reminds them of the consummate beauty of the women in their own land; that their father Pepin had been prevented by the remonstrances of the Pope from divorcing their mother; then briefly enjoins them not to dare to dismiss their present wives.[3] Again he urges the evil of contaminating their blood by any foreign admixture (they had already declined an alliance with the Greek emperor), and then insists on the absolute impossibility of their maintaining their fidelity to

1 Muratori faintly hints a doubt of its authenticity; a doubt which he is too honest to assert.

2 Manzoni has pointed out with great sagacity, that in the 170th law of Rotharis there is a clause prescribing the course to be pursued with lepers; thus showing that the nation was really subject to the disease. Stephen might thus be expressing a common notion, that from the Lombards, at least in Italy, "came the race of the lepers." Thus this expression, instead of throwing suspicion, as Muratori supposes, on the letter, confirms its authenticity. — Discorso Storico, subjoined to the tragedy "Adelchi," p. 199.

3 "Nec vestras quodammodo conjuges audeatis demittere." But it is the guilt of the alliance, not of the divorce, on which he dwells.

the papal see, "that fidelity so solemnly sworn by their father, so ratified on his death-bed, so confirmed by their own oaths," if they should thus marry into the perfidious house of Lombardy. "The enmity of the Lombards to the papal see is implacable. Wherefore St. Peter himself solemnly adjures them, he, the Pope, the whole clergy, and people of Rome adjure them by all which is awful and commanding, by the living and true God, by the tremendous day of judgment, by all the holy mysteries, and by the most sacred body of St. Peter, that neither of the brothers presume to wed the daughter of Desiderius, or to give the lovely Gisela in wedlock to his son. But if either (which he cannot imagine) should act contrary to this adjuration, by the authority of St. Peter he is under the most terrible anathema, an alien from the kingdom of God, and condemned with the devil and his most wicked ministers and with all impious men, to be burned in the eternal fire; but he who shall obey shall be rewarded with everlasting glory."

But Pope Stephen spoke to obdurate ears. Already Charlemagne began to show that, however highly he might prize the alliance of the hierarchy, he was not its humble minister. Lofty as were his notions of religion, he would rarely sacrifice objects of worldly policy. Sovereign as yet of but one half the dominions of his father Pepin, he had not now by the death of his brother and the dispossession of his brother's children consolidated the kingdom of the Franks into one great monarchy. It was to his advantage, in case of hostilities with his brother (already they had once broken out), to connect himself with the Lombard kingdom. He married the daughter of Desiderius; and his own irregular passions, not the dread of papal censure, dissolved, only a year after, the inhibited union.

The acts and the formal documents of the earlier Popes rarely betray traces of individual character. The pontificate of Stephen III. was short — about a year and a half. Yet in him there appears a peculiar passionate feebleness in his relation to the heads of the different Roman factions and to the King of the Lombards, no less than in his invective against the marriage of the French princes into the race of Desiderius.

His successors, Hadrian I. and Leo III., not only occupy the papal throne at one of the great epochs of its aggrandizement, but their pontificates were of much longer duration than usual. Hadrian entered on the 23d, Leo on the 21st year of his papacy, and Hadrian at least, a Roman by birth, appears admirably fitted to cope with the exigencies of the times; — times pregnant with great events, the total and final disruption of the last links which connected the Byzantine and Western empires, the extinction of the Lombard Kingdom, the creation of the Empire of the West.

A.D. 768-772. Feb. 1. Hadrian I.

If the progress of the younger son of Pepin, Charles the Great, to almost universal empire now occupied the attention of the West, it was watched by the Pope with the profoundest interest. If Stephen III. had trembled at the matrimonial alliance which he had vainly attempted to prevent, between the King of the Franks and the daughter of Desiderius, which threatened to strengthen the closer political relations of those once hostile powers, his fears were soon allayed by the sudden disruption of that short-lived connection. After one year of wedlock, Charles, apparently without alleging any cause, divorced Hermingard, threw back upon her father his repudiated daughter, and embittered the insult by an immediate marriage with Hildegard, a German lady of a noble Suabian house.[1] The careless indifference with which Charlemagne contracted and dissolved that solemn bond of matrimony, the sanctity if not the indissolubility of which the Church had at least begun to assert with the utmost rigor, shocked some of his more pious subjects. Adalhard, the Abbot of Corbey, could not disguise his religious indignation; so little was he versed in courtly ways, he would hold no intercourse with the unlawful wife.[2] Pope Hadrian maintained a prudent silence. He was not called upon officially to take cognizance of the case; and the divorce from the Lombard Princess, the severance of those unhallowed ties with the enemy of the Church against which his predecessor had so strongly protested, might reconcile him to a looser interpretation of the law. A marriage, not merely unblessed but anathematized by the Church, might be considered at least less binding than more hallowed nuptials.

Every step which the ambition of Charles made towards dominion and power, showed, it might be hoped, a more willing and reverent, as well as a more formidable defender of the Church. At his great national assemblies, as in those of his pious father, the bishops met on equal terms with the nobles, the peaceful prelates mingled with the armed counts and dukes in the councils of Charles the Great.

1 Eginhard. i. 18.

2 Paschas. Radbert., Vit. Adalhard Abbatis.—"Nullo negotio beatus senex persuaderi, dum adhuc esset *tiro palatii*, ut ei, quam vivente illâ, rex acceperat, aliquo communicaret servitutis obsequio."

Charlemagne's first Saxon war was a war of religion; it was undertaken to avenge the destruction of a church, the massacre of a saintly missionary and his Christian congregation.

Even his more questionable acts had the merit of estranging him more irrevocably from the enemies of the Pope. On the death of his brother Carloman, Charles seized the opportunity of reconsolidating the kingdom of his father Pepin. It is difficult to decide how far this usurpation offended against the justice or the usages of the age. The old Teutonic custom gave to the nobles the right of choosing their chieftain from the royal race.[1] A large party of the Austrasian feudatories, how induced or influenced we may conjecture rather than assert, deliberately preferred a mature and able sovereign to the precarious rule of helpless and inexperienced children. Some, however, of the nobles, more strongly attached to the right of hereditary succession, more jealous of the rising power of Charles, or out of generous compassion, adhered to the claims of Carloman's children, who, thus dispossessed, took refuge at the court of the Lombard Desiderius. The opportunity of revenge was too tempting for the rival king and the insulted father; he espoused their cause; but the alliance with Desiderius put the fatherless children at once out of the pale of the Papal sympathy. Desiderius thought he saw his advantage; he appealed to the justice, to the compassion, to the gratitude of the head

Charlemagne sole King. Dec. 771.

1 Eginhard may show that this was a right, claimed at least by the common sentiment of the day. Of the Merovingians he says, in the first sentence of his life of Charlemagne, "Gens . . . . . de qua Franci reges sibi creare soliti erant."

of Christendom; he urged him to befriend the orphans, A.D. 772. to anoint the heirs of the pious Carloman, and thus to recognize their royal title, as their papal predecessors had anointed Pepin, Carloman and Charles.

But Hadrian had too much sagacity not to discern the rising power of Charles, and would not be betrayed by any rashly generous emotions into measures hostile to his interests. Desiderius resented his steadfast refusal. He heard at the same time of the death of his faithful partisan in Rome, Paul Afiarta, whom the Pope had condemned to exile in Constantinople. Paul, accused of having blinded and killed the secondary Sergius, before the decease of Pope Stephen, had been put to death, not, it was declared, with the connivance of the Pope, before he could leave Italy.[1]

Desiderius supposed that Charles was fully occupied King Desiderius. in establishing his sovereignty over his brother's kingdom, and in the war against the Saxons. He collected his forces, fell on Sinigaglia, Montefeltro, Urbino, and Gubbio, and ravaged the whole country of Romagna with fire and sword. His troops besieged, stormed, and committed a frightful massacre in Blera, a town of Tuscany, and already threatened the Pope in his capital. Desiderius, at the A.D. 773. head of his army, and accompanied by all his family, advanced towards Rome to compel an interview declined resolutely by the Pontiff.

[1] The death of Paul Afiarta was attributed to the indiscreet zeal of Leo, Archbishop of Ravenna (Leo owed his archiepiscopate to Pope Stephen). It was disclaimed by Hadrian: "Animam ejus cupiens salvare, pœnitentiæ eum submitti decreveram . . . . huc Romam eum deferendum." — Vit. Hadrian. Paul Afiarta's crime was that he had pledged himself to bring the Pope, willing or unwilling, before Desiderius. — Ibid.

Hadrian relied not on the awe of his personal presence, by which Popes on former occasions had subdued the hostility of Lombard kings. He sent messengers in the utmost haste to solicit, to entreat immediate succor from Charles, but he himself neglected no means for the defence of Rome. Hadrian (a new office for a Pope) superintended the *military preparations; he gathered troops from* Tuscany, Campania, and every district within his power; strengthened the fortifications of Rome, transported the sacred treasures from the less defensible churches of St. Peter and St. Paul into the heart of the city; barricaded the gates of the Vatican, and having so done, reverted to his spiritual arms. He sent three Bishops, of Alba, Palestrina, Tibur, to meet the King, and to threaten him with excommunication if he dared to violate the territory of the Church. Desiderius had reached Viterbo; he was struck with awe, or with the intelligence of the preparations of Charles.

Hadrian sends to Charlemagne.

The ambassadors of the Frank arrived in Rome; on their return they passed through Pavia. Desiderius had returned to his capital: they urged him to reconciliation with the Pope. New ambassadors arrived, offering a large sum, ostensibly for his concessions to the demands of the Pope, but no doubt for the surrender of Carloman's children, whom Charles was anxious to get into his power.

Desiderius, who would not know the disproportion of his army to that of Charles, blindly resisted all accommodation. With his usual rapidity Charles, who had already assembled his forces, approached the passes of the Alps, one division that of Mont Cenis, the other that of the Mont St. Bernard.

Charlemagne's descent into Italy.

Treachery betrayed the passes,[1] in one of which, however, the hosts of Charlemagne suffered a signal defeat by the Lombards, under Adelchis, the king's son. This was no doubt the secret of the Lombard weakness. The whole of the Roman population of Lombardy looked to the Pope as their head and representative; to the Franks as their deliverers. The two races had not mingled; the Lombards were but an armed aristocracy, lording it over a hostile race. A sudden famine dispersed the victorious troops of Adelchis, who still guarded the descent from Mont Cenis. Adelchis shut himself up in Verona; and Charles, encountering no enemy on the open plain, laid siege to Pavia.[2] That city was, for those times, strongly fortified; it resisted for many months. During the siege in the Holy Week of the next year, the King of the Franks proceeded to Rome to perform his devotions at the shrine of St. Peter, and to knit more closely his league with the Pope. Charles was already the deliverer, it might be hoped he would be the faithful protector of the Church. Excepting the cities of Verona and Pavia, he was already master of all Northern Italy. With his father Pepin, he had been honored with the name of Patrician of Rome; by this vague adoption, which the lingering pride of Rome might still esteem an honor to a Barbarian, he was head of the Roman republic. He might become, in their hopes, the guardian, the champion of the old Roman society, while at the same time his remote

A.D. 774. April 2.

[1] "A suis quippe fideles callidè ei traditus fuit."—Chronic. Salernit. This chronicle shows the curious transition from the Latin inflection to the uninflected Italian, "et dum de fatus Karolus Sermo."

[2] A.D. 773, October. Muratori sub ann.

residence beyond the Alps diminished the danger which was always apprehended from neighboring barbarians. In Rome.

Accordingly the civil and ecclesiastical authorities vied in the honors which they paid to the Patrician of Rome and the dutiful son of the Church, who had so speedily obeyed the summons of his spiritual father, and had come to prostrate himself before the relics of the Apostles. At Novi, thirty miles distant, he was met by the Senate and the nobles of the city, with their banners spread. For a mile before the gates the way was lined by the military and the *schools*. At the gates all the crosses and the standards of the city, as was usual on the entrance of the Exarchs the representatives of the Emperor, went out to meet the Patrician. As soon as he beheld the cross, Charles dismounted from his horse, proceeded on foot with all his officers and nobles to the Vatican, where the Pope and the clergy, on the steps of St. Peter's, stood ready to receive him; as he slowly ascended he reverently kissed the steps; at the top he was affectionately embraced by the Pope. Charles attended with profound devotion during all the ceremonies of the Holy Season; at the close he ratified the donation of his father Pepin. The diploma which contained the solemn gift was placed upon the altar of St. Peter. Yet there is much obscurity as to the extent and the tenure of this most magnificent oblation ever made to the Church. The original record has long perished; its terms are but vaguely known. It is said to have comprehended the whole of Italy, the exarchate of Ravenna, from Istria to the frontiers of Naples, including the island of Corsica. The nature of the

Papal tenure and authority is still more difficult to define. Was it the absolute alienation of the whole temporal power to the Pope? In what consisted the sovereignty still claimed and exercised by Charlemagne over the whole of Italy, even over Rome itself?

Donation of Charlemagne.

Charlemagne made this donation as lord by conquest over the Lombard kingdom, and the territory of the Exarchate. For Pavia at length fell, and Desiderius took refuge in the usual asylum of dethroned kings, a monastery. His son, Adelchis, abandoned Verona, and fled to Constantinople. Thus expired the kingdom of the Lombards; and Charles added to his royal titles that of Lombardy. The Exarchate, by his grant, was vested, either as a kind of feud, or in absolute perpetuity, in the Pope.[1]

But, notwithstanding the grant of the conqueror, the Pope did not enter into undisputed possession of this territory. An ecclesiastic, Leo, the Archbishop of Ravenna, set up a rival claim. He withheld the cities
A.D. 775.
of Faenza, Forli, Forlimpopoli, Cesena, Bobbio, Comachio, Ferrara, Imola, the whole Pentapolis, Bologna, from their allegiance to the see of Rome, ejected the judges appointed by Rome, appointed others of his own authority in the whole region, and sent missives throughout the province to prevent their submission to the papal officers.[2] Hadrian became the

[1] See the passage quoted by Muratori from the anonymous Scriptor Salernitanus, sub anno 774. The Lombard dukedom of Benevento raised itself into a principality, and asserted its independence.

[2] Agnelli, Vit. Pontif. Ravennat. — "Troppo è credible, che questo sagace ed ambizioso prelato s' ingegnasse di far intendere a Carlo, chè avrebbe egualmente potuto servire a onor di Dio, e de' santi appostoli, la liberalità, chè fosse piaciuto al re di fare alla chiesa di Ravenna, come a quella di Roma; chè già non mancavano ai Romani pontifici ubertosi

scorn of his enemies, who inquired what advantage he had gained by the destruction of the Lombards. He wrote the most pressing letter to Charles, entreating him to prevent this humiliation of St. Peter and his successors. The Archbishop of Ravenna succeeded to the title which, in the language of the papal correspondence, belongs to all the adversaries of the Pope's temporal greatness, the "Most wicked of Men."[1] The Pope asserted his right to the judicial authority, not only over the cities of the Pentapolis, but in Ravenna itself.

But the rivalship of Ravenna did not long restrain the ambition of a pontiff, secure in the protection of Charlemagne.

Hadrian in possession of the Exarchate.

After some time, and some menaced interference from the East, Hadrian took possession of the Exarchate, seemingly with the power and privileges of a temporal prince. Throughout the Exarchate of Ravenna, he had "his men," who were judged by magistrates of his appointment, owed him fealty, and could not leave the land without his special permission. Nor are these only ecclesiastics subordinate to his spiritual power (that spiritual supremacy Hadrian indeed asserted to the utmost extent; Rome had a right of judicature over all churches.)[2]

patrimoni in più parte d' Italia è di Sicilia," &c. &c. This ingenious conjecture of Denina (Revoluz. d' Italia. vol. i. p. 352) is but conjecture.

[1] Nefandissimus. Compare Muratori, Annal. d' Italia, sub ann. 777. The epistle does not state on what the Archbishop of Ravenna rested his claim to this jurisdiction. This dispute shows still further the ambiguous and undefined supremacy supposed to be conferred, even in his own day, by the donation of Charlemagne. Did the Archbishop claim in any manner to be Patrician of the Exarchate? See following note.

[2] "Quanta enim auctoritas B. Petro Apostolorum principi, ejusque sacratissimæ sedi concessa est, cuiquam non ambigimus ignorari: utpote quæ de omnibus ecclesiis fas habeat judicandi, neque cuiquam liceat de ejus

His language to Charlemagne is that of a feudal suzerain also: "as your men are not allowed to come to Rome without your permission and special letter, so my men must not be allowed to appear at the court of France without the same credentials from me." The same allegiance which the subjects of Charlemagne owed to him, was to be required from the subjects of the See of Rome to the Pope. "Let him be thus admonished, we are to remain in the service, and under the dominion of the blessed apostle St. Peter, to the end of the world." The administration of justice was in the Pope's name; not only the ecclesiastical dues, and the rents of estates forming part of the patrimony of St. Peter, the civil revenue likewise came into his treasury. Hadrian bestows on Charlemagne, as a gift, the marbles and mosaics of the imperial palace in Ravenna, that palace apparently his own undisputed property.[1]

Such was the allegiance claimed over the Exarchate and the whole territory included in the donation of Pepin and of Charlemagne, with all which the ever watchful Pope was continually adding (parts of the old Sabine territory, of Campania and of Capua) to the immediate jurisdiction of the Papacy. Throughout these territories the old Roman institutions remained under the Pope as Patrician, the Patriciate seemed tantamount to imperial authority.[2] The city of Rome

judicare judicio. Quorumlibet sententias legati Pontificum, Sedes B. Petri Apostoli jus habet solvendi, per quos ad unam Petri sedem universalis ecclesiæ cura confluit, et nihil unquam a suo capite dissidet." — Epist. Hadrian. ad Carol. Magn. Cod. Carol. lxxxv., apud Bouquet, p. 579.

1 "Tam marmora, quamque mosivum, cæteraque exempla de eodem palatio vobis concedimus auferenda." — Epist. lxvii. apud Gretser.

2 The Frankish monarch, afterwards the Emperor, was the *Patrician* of Rome. On the vague yet extensive authority conveyed by this title of

alone maintained, with the form, somewhat of the independence of a republic. Hadrian, with the power, assumed the magnificence of a great potentate: his expenditure in Rome, more especially, as became his character, on the religious buildings, was profuse. Rome, with the increase of the papal revenues, began to resume more of her ancient splendor.

Charlemagne in Rome. A.D. 780, 781.

Twice during the pontificate of Hadrian, Charlemagne again visited Rome. The first time was an act of religious homage, connected with his future political plans. He came to celebrate the baptism of his younger son Pepin by the Pope, a son for whom he destined the kingdom of Italy. The second time he came as a protector, at the summons of the Pope, to deliver him from a new and formidable enemy at the gates of Rome. Arigiso the Lombard Duke of Benevento, who had married the daughter of Desiderius, had grown in power, and around him had rallied all the adversaries of the Papal and the Frankish interests. It was a Lombard league, embracing almost all Italy — Rotgadis Duke of Friuli, his father-in-law Stebelin Count of Treviso, the Duke of Spoleto. Arigiso had obtained the title of Patrician, with all its vague and indefinite pretensions,

Patrician, Muratori is the most full and satisfactory. Charlemagne, as his ancestors had been, was Patrician of Rome. Was this only an honorary title, while the civil supremacy over the city was vested in a republic (so Pagi supposes, but according to others this notion is purely imaginary), or did the office invest him in full imperial authority? That he had a theoretic supremacy, the surrender to the successive Frankish monarchs of the keys of the city and of the sepulchre of St. Peter clearly shows. As imperial representative, or substitute, there was a Patrician of Sicily. The Lombard Dukes of Benevento obtained a grant of the *Patriciate* from Constantinople. The Pope claimed to be *Patrician* of the Exarchate. (See above.)

from Constantinople; he was in close correspondence with Adelchis, the son of the fallen Desiderius. Hadrian accused this dangerous neighbor of hostile encroachments on the patrimony of St. Peter. He entreated the invincible Charlemagne to cross the Alps to his succor. Charlemagne obeyed. He passed the Christmas at Pavia. He appeared at Rome: the Lombard shrunk from the unequal contest, and purchased peace by an annual tribute of 7000 pieces of gold. He gave his two sons as hostages for the fulfilment of the treaty.[1] Hadrian, however, did not feel secure; he still suspected the designs and intrigues of the Lombard. The death of Arigiso, in the same year in which he swore allegiance to Charlemagne, did not allay the jealousies of Hadrian; for Charlemagne, in his generosity, placed the son of Arigiso, Grimoald, in the Dukedom of Benevento. Grimoald, during the lifetime of Charlemagne, repaid this generosity by a faithful adoption, not only of the interests, but even the usages of the Franks. He shaved his beard, and clothed himself after the Frank fashion. In later days he became a formidable rival of Pepin, the son of Charlemagne, for the ascendency in Italy.

Rebellion suppressed. A.D. 787.

A.D. 788.

While Charlemagne was yet at Rome, a more formidable rebellion began to lower. Adelchis, the son of Desiderius, was upon the seas with a considerable Greek force, supplied by order of the Byzantine Em-

[1] Eginhard, Vit. Karol., x.; Annal. sub ann. 786. Compare the very strange account in the Chronic. Salernit. 9, 10, 11, of the interference of the bishops at Benevento to save Arigiso from the wrath of Charlemagne; and the conspiracy of Paulus Diaconus, the historian, to murder Charlemagne. "How," says the Emperor, when urged to punish him, "can I cut off one who writes so elegantly?"

peror, Constantine. The Huns broke into Bavaria and Friuli. Tassilo, Duke of Bavaria, whose wife Liutberga was the sister of Adelchis, meditated revolt. Charlemagne, with his wonted rapidity, appeared in Germany. Tassilo was summoned before a diet at Ingelheim. He dared not refuse to appear; was condemned to capital punishment; in mercy shut up, with his son, in a monastery. His Lombard wife suffered the same fate. The Huns were driven back; the Greek army deserted Adelchis; the son of Desiderius fled; John, the Byzantine general, was strangled in prison.

This great pontiff Hadrian, who, during above twenty-four years, had reposed, not undisturbed, but safe under the mighty protection of Charlemagne, died before the close of the eighth century. The coronation of Charlemagne, as Emperor of the West, was reserved for his successor. At that coronation our history will pause to take a survey of Latin Christendom, now a separate Western Empire, under one temporal, and under one spiritual sovereign. Charlemagne showed profound sorrow for the death of Hadrian. He wept for him, according to his biographer,[1] as if he had been a brother or a dear son. An epitaph declared to the world the respect and attachment of the Sovereign of the West for his spiritual father.

A.D. 795. Death of Hadrian.

On the death of Hadrian,[2] an election of unexampled rapidity, and, as it seemed, of perfect unanimity among the clergy, the nobles, and the people, raised

1 Eginhard, c. xix.

2 Hadrian died on Christmas day. The election was on the following day, that of St. Stephen, A.D. 795.

Leo III. Leo III. to the pontifical throne.[1] The first act of Leo was to recognize the supremacy of Charles, by sending the keys, not only of the city, with the standard of Rome, but those also of the sepulchre of St. Peter, to the Patrician. This unusual act of deference seems as if Leo anticipated the necessity of foreign protection; even the precipitancy of the election may lead to the suspicion that the unanimity was but outward. Secret causes of dissatisfaction were brooding in the minds of some of the leading men in Rome. The strong hand of Hadrian had kept down the factions which had disturbed the reign of his predecessor Stephen; now it is among the court, the family of Hadrian, even those whom he had raised to the highest offices, that there is at first sullen submission, erelong furious strife. Dark rumors spread abroad of serious charges against the Pope himself. Leo III. ruled, however, in seeming peace for three years and two months, at the close of which a frightful scene betrayed the deep and rooted animosity.

Hadrian had invested his two nephews, Paschalis and Campulus, in two great ecclesiastical offices, the Primicerius and Sacellarius. This first example of nepotism was a dismal omen of the fatal partiality of future Popes for their kindred. These two men, or one of them, may have aspired to the Pontificate, or they hoped to place a pontiff, more under their own influence, on the throne: their dark crime implies dark motives. The Pope was to ride in solemn pomp, on St. April 25, 799. George's day, to the church of St. Lawrence, called in Lucinâ. These ecclesiastics formed part of the procession. One of them excused himself for some in-

[1] Ann. Til. sub ann. 796; Eginhard, Annal.

formality in his dress.[1] On a sudden, a band of armed men sprang from their ambush. The Pope was thrown from his horse, and an awkward attempt was made to practice the Oriental punishment of mutilation, as yet rare in the West, to put out his eyes, and to cut out his tongue. Paschalis and Campulus, instead of defending the Pope, dragged him into a neighboring church, and there, before the high altar, attempted to complete the imperfect mutilation, beat him cruelly, and left him weltering in his blood. From thence they took him away by night (no one seems to have interposed in his behalf), carried him to the convent of St. Erasmus, and there threw him into prison. Leo recovered his sight and his speech; and this restoration, of course, in process of time became a miracle.[2] His enemies had failed in their object, the disqualifying him by mutilation for the Papacy. A faithful servant rescued him, and carried him to the church of St. Peter. There, no doubt, he found temporary protectors, until the Duke of Spoleto (Winegis), a Frank, marched into Rome to his deliverance, and removed him from the guilty city to Spoleto.

Assault on Pope Leo.

Urgent letters entreated the immediate presence of the Patrician, of Charles the protector of the Papacy,

[1] He was sine planetâ.

[2] "Carnifices geminas traxerunt fronte fenestras,
Et celerem abscindunt lacerato corpore linguam.
* * * * * * *
Sed manus alma Patris oculis medicamina ademptis
Obtulit atque novo reparavit lumine vultum;
* * * * * * *
Explicat et celerem truncataque lingua loquelam."
— See the poem of Angilbert, the poet of Charlemagne's court, Pertz, ii. p. 400. The papal biographer is modest as to the miracle.

in Rome. But Charles was at a distance, about to engage in quelling an insurrection of the Saxons.[1] The Pope condescended, or rather was compelled by his necessities, to accept the summons to appear in person before the Transalpine monarch. Charles was holding his court and camp at Paderborn, one of the newly-erected German bishoprics. The reception of Leo was courteous and friendly, magnificent as far as circumstances might permit. The poet describes the imperial banquet; nor does he fear to shock his more austere readers by describing the Pope and the Emperor as quaffing their rich wines with convivial glee.[2]

But at the same time arrived accusations of some unknown and mysterious nature against the Pope; accusations, according to the annalists, made in the name of the Roman people.[3] Charles did not decline, but postponed till his arrival in Rome the judicial investigation of these charges; but he continued to treat the Pope with undiminished respect and familiarity.

The return of Leo to Rome is said to have been one long triumph. Throughout Italy he was received with the honors of the apostle. The clergy and people of Rome thronged forth to meet him, as well as the military, among whom were bands (scholars) of Franks, of Frisians, and of Saxons, either at Rome for purposes of devotion, or as a foreign body-guard of the Pope.

Charlemagne sets out for Rome.

The journey of Charles to Rome was slow. He went to Rouen, and to Tours, to pay his adorations at the shrine of St. Martin. There

[1] Eginhard, Ann. 799.

[2] Angilbert, apud Pertz, ii. 401, describes, as an eye-witness, the meeting of the Pope and the Emperor.

[3] "Quæ a populo Romano ei objiciebantur."

his wife, Liutgarda, died, and her funeral caused further delay. He then held a great diet at Mentz; and towards the close of the following year crossed the Alps, and halted at Ravenna. At Nomentana he was met by the Pope with high honors. After Nov. 23, 800. he had entered Rome he was received on the Nov. 24. steps of St. Peter's by the Pope, the bishops, and the clergy; he passed into the church, the whole assembly joining in the solemn chant of thanksgiving.

But Charles did not appear at Rome as the avowed protector and avenger of the injured Pope Dec. 1. against those who had so barbarously violated his sacred person. He assumed the office of judge.[1] At a synod held some days after, a long and difficult investigation of the charges made against Leo by his enemies proceeded, without protest from the Pope.[2] Paschalis and Campulus were summoned to prove their charges. On their failure, they were condemned to death; a sentence commuted, by the merciful interposition of the Pope, to imprisonment in France. Their other noble partisans were condemned to decapitation. Yet this exculpation of Leo hardly satisfied the public mind. It was thought necessary that the Pope should openly, in the face of the people, in the sight of God, and holding the holy Gospels in his hands, avouch his own innocence. There was no complaint of Dec. 23. the majesty of heaven insulted in his person, no reproof for the indignity offered to St. Peter in his suc-

1 The clergy, according to the biographer, refused to judge the Pope, declaring their incompetency.

2 "In quibus vel maximum vel difficillimum erat." — Eginhard, Ann. Eginhard expressly says, "Hujus factionis fuere principes Paschalis nomenclator et Campulus Sacellarius et multi alii Romanæ urbis habitatores nobiles." — Ibid.

cessor; it was a kind of recognition of the tribunal of public opinion. The humiliation had something of the majesty of conscious blamelessness, — "I, Leo, Pontiff of the Holy Roman Church, being subject to no judgment, under no compulsion, of my own free will, in your presence, before God who reads the conscience, and his angels, and the blessed Apostle Peter in whose sight we stand, declare myself not guilty of the charges made against me. I have never perpetrated, nor commanded to be perpetrated,[1] the wicked deeds of which I have been accused. This I call God to witness, whose judgment we must all undergo; and this I do, bound by no law, nor wishing to impose this custom on my successors, or on my brother bishops, but that I may altogether relieve you from any unjust suspicions against myself."[2]

This solemn judgment had hardly passed when Christmas day arrived: the Christmas of the last year in the eighth century of Christ. Charles and all his sumptuous court, the nobles and people of Rome, the whole clergy of Rome, were present at the high services of the Nativity. The Pope himself chanted the mass, the full assembly were wrapt in profound devotion. At the close the Pope arose, advanced towards Charles, with a splendid crown in his hands, placed it upon his brow, and proclaimed him Cæsar Augustus. "God grant life and victory to the great and pacific Emperor." His words were lost in the acclamations

[1] These words positively negative the notion that the crime of which Leo was accused was adultery or unchastity, which some expressions in Alcuin's letters seem to intimate. I cannot help suspecting that the charge was some simoniacal proceeding (spiritual adultery) by which he had thwarted the ambitious views of Hadrian's relatives.

[2] Baronius gives this form as "ex sacris ritibus Romanæ Ecclesiæ."

of the soldiery, the people, and the clergy. Charles, with his son Pepin, humbly submitted to the ratification of this important act, and was anointed by the hands of the Pope.

Was this a sudden and unconcerted act of gratitude, a magnificent adulation of the Pope to the unconscious and hardly consenting Emperor? Had Leo deliberately contemplated the possible results of this assumption of authority — of this creation of a successor to the Cæsars over Latin Christendom? In what character did the Pope perform this act — as vicegerent of God on earth, as the successor of St. Peter, or as the representative of the Roman people? What rights did it convey? In what, according to the estimation of the times, consisted the Imperial supremacy? To these questions history returns but vague and doubtful answers. Charlemagne — writes Eginhard the secretary of the Emperor, the one contemporary authority — declared that holy as was the day (the Lord's nativity), if he had known the intention of the Pope he would not have entered the church.[1] To treat this speech as mere hypocrisy agrees neither with the character nor the position of Charles; yet the Pope would hardly, even in the lavish excess of his gratitude, have ventured on such a step, if he had not reason, from his long conferences with the Emperor at Paderborn and his intercourse in Rome, to suppose that it was in accordance at least with the unavowed and latent ambition of Charles. In its own day it was perhaps a more daring and violent measure than it appears in

[1] Eginhard, in Vit. xx.; but Eginhard adds, "Insidiam tamen suscepti nominis Romanis Imperatoribus super hoc indignantibus, *magnâ tulit patientiâ*, vicitque eorum contumaciam magnanimitate." — Vit. Kar., xxviii.

ours. A Barbarian monarch, a Teuton, was declared the successor of the Cæsars. He became the usurper of the rights of the Byzantine emperors, which, though fallen into desuetude, had never been abandoned on their part, or abrogated by any competent authority.[1] The Eastern Cæsars had not been without jealousy of the progress of the Frankish dominion. The later Greek emperors sent repeated but vain remonstrances. It was alleged that the Greek Empire having fallen to a woman, Irene, and that woman detestable as the murderess of her son, in her the Byzantine Empire had come to an end. But the enmity of the Byzantine court to Charlemagne had betrayed itself by acts of hostility. Adelchis, the heir of the Lombard kingdom, that kingdom of which Charlemagne had assumed the title, still held the dignity of Roman Patrician in Constantinople.[2]

The significance of this act, the coronation, the subsequent anointing, the recognition by the Roman peo-

[1] "Imperatores etiam Constantinopolitani, Nicephorus, Michael et Leo, ultro amicitiam et societatem ejus expetentes, complures ad eum misere legatos; cum quibus tamen propter susceptum a se Imperatoris nomen et ob hoc quasi qui Imperium eis præripere vellet, valde suspectum, fœdus firmissimum statuit, ut nulla inter partes cujuslibet scandali remaneret occasio. Erat enim semper Romanis et Græcis suspecta Francorum potentia, quia ipsam Romam matrem Imperii tenebat, ubi semper Cæsares et Imperatores soliti erant sedere." — Chron. Moissiac. In the other copy of this Chronicle (apud Bouquet, p. 79), we read, "Delati quidem sunt ad eum dicentes, quod apud Græcos nomen Imperii cessasset, et femina apud eos nomen Imperii teneret, Hirena nomine, quæ filium suum Imperatorem fraude captum oculos eruit, et nomen sibi imperii usurpavit." Compare, for a curious passage, Annal. Lauresheimenses, sub eodem anno. The chronicle of Salerno says: "Imperator quippe omnimodis non dici possit, nisi qui regnum Romanum præest, hoc est Constantinopolitanum. Reges Galliarum nunc usurparunt sibi talem nomen, nam antiquitus omnimodis sic non vocitati sunt." — c. ii.

[2] "In Constantinopoli itaque in patriciatus ordine atque honore consenuit." — Eginhard, 774.

ple, was not merely an accession of vague and indefinite grandeur (which it undoubtedly was), but added to the substantive power of Charlemagne. It was the consolidation of all Western Christendom under one monarchy. By establishing this sovereignty on the basis of the *old Roman* empire, it could not but gain something of the stability of ancient right.[1] It was the voluntary submission of the Barbarians to the title at least of Roman dominion. In Rome Charlemagne affected to be a Roman: he condescended to put off his native Frankish dress, and appeared in the long tunic and chlamys, and with Roman sandals. While the Barbarians were flattered by this their complete incorporation with the old disdainful Roman society, the Latins, conscious that in the Franks resided the real power, still aimed at maintaining their traditionary superiority in intellectual matters — a superiority which Charlemagne might hope to emulate, not to surpass. The Pope (for Charlemagne swore at the same time to maintain all the power and privileges of the Roman Pontiff) obtained the recognition of a spiritual dominion commensurate with the secular empire of Charlemagne. The Emperor and the Pope were bound in indissoluble alliance; and notwithstanding the occasional outbursts of independence, or even superiority, asserted by Charlemagne himself, he still professed and usually showed the most profound veneration for the Roman spiritual supremacy; and left to his successors

1 Eginhard, c. 23. But compare Lehuerou, p. 362, who attributes Charlemagne's reluctance to assume the empire, and his apparent depreciation of the importance of the title of Cæsar, to the dominant Teutonism of his character. Lehuerou espouses the theory that the emperor was only the advocate of the Church of Rome. But this was a purely German theory utterly unknown to Pope Hadrian or Pope Leo, and to the Roman Italians.

and to their subjects an awful sense of subjugation, from which they were not emancipated for ages.

The imperial title was understood, no doubt, by the senate and people of Rome, to be conferred by themselves, as representing the republic, not by the Pope, of his sole religious authority. Without their assenting acclamations, in their estimation it would not have been valid. The Pope, as one of the people, as his subject therefore, paid adoration to the Emperor.[1]

But it is even more difficult to ascertain the rights which the imperial title conveyed in Rome itself, especially in one important particular. Rome became, it is clear, one of the subject cities of Charlemagne's empire. Even if the Pope had ever possessed any actual or asserted magisterial power, the events of the last year had shown that he did not govern Rome. He had no force, even for his personal security, against conspiracy or popular tumult. But the Emperor of Rome was bound to protect the Bishop of Rome: he was the conservator of the peace in this as in all the other cities of his empire, though here, as elsewhere, there was no abolition of the old Roman municipal institutions. The Senate still subsisted, the people called itself the Roman people; the shadow of a republic which had been suffered to survive throughout the Empire, and had occasionally seemed to acquire form, if not substance, still lurked beneath the Teutonic, as in later times beneath the Papal, sovereignty. The great undefined, undefinable point was the conflicting right of the Emperor,

[1] "Et summus eundem
Præsul adoravit, sicut mos debitus olim
Principibus fuit antiquis, ac nomine dempto
Patricii, quo dictus erat prius, inde vocari
Augustus meruit pius, Imperii quoque princeps."
Poeta Saxo, sub ann. 801.

the clergy, and the people, in the election and ratification of the election to the Popedom; as well as that which was hereafter to be the source of such long and internecine strife, the boundary of the two sovereignties, the temporal and the spiritual. This was the fatal feud which for centuries distracted Latin Christendom.

It was perhaps in its vagueness that chiefly dwelt its majesty and power, both as regards the Pope who bestowed and the Frank who received the Empire. In some unknown, undefined manner, the Empire of the West flowed from the Pope; the successor of St. Peter named, or sanctioned the naming of, the successor of Augustus and of Nero. The enormous power of Charlemagne, as contrasted with that of the Pope, disguised or ennobled the bold fiction, quelled at least all present inquiry, silenced any insolent doubt. If Charlemagne acknowledged the right of the Pope to bestow the Empire by accepting it at his hands, who should presume to question the right of the Pope to define the limits of the Imperial authority thus bestowed and thus received? And Charlemagne's elevation to the Empire invested his protection of the Pope in the more sacred character of a duty belonging to his office, ratified all his grants, which were now those not only of a conqueror[1] but of a successor to all the rights of the Cæsars. On one side the Teuton became a Roman, the King of the Franks was merged in the Western Emperor; on the other, Rome created the sovereign of the West, the sovereign of Latin Christendom.

[1] All writers, even ecclesiastics, call Charlemagne's descent into Italy a conquest. — See epitaph on his Queen Hildegard at Metz.

"Cumque vir armipotens sceptris junxisset avitis
Cycniferumque Padum, Romuleumque Tibrim."
Pauli Gesta Episc. Met. Pertz, i. 266.

BOOK V.

CONTEMPORARY CHRONOLOGY.

POPES. A.D.		A.D.
795	Leo III.	816
816	Stephen III.	817
817	Paschal I.	824
824	Eugenius II.	827
827	Valentinus	
827	Gregory IV.	844
844	Sergius II.	847
847	Leo. IV.	855
855	Benedict III.	858
855	(Anastasius, antipope)	
858	Nicolas I.	867
867	Hadrian II.	872
872	John VIII.	882
882	Marinus I.	884
884	Hadrian III.	885
885	Stephen V.	891
891	Formosus	896
896	Boniface II.	
896	Stephen VI.	897
897	Romanus	
897	Theodore II.	

PATRIARCHS OF CONSTANTINOPLE. A.D.		A.D.
784	Tarasius	806
806	Nicephorus, deposed	815
815	Theodotus Cassiteras	821
821	Antonius	832
832	John VII., expelled	842
842	Methodius	846
846	Ignatius, deposed	857
857	Photius, deposed	867
867	Ignatius, restored	877
877	Photius, restored Again deposed	886
886	Stephen	893
893	Antonius II.	895
895	Nicolas, deposed	906

EMPERORS OF THE WEST. A.D.		A.D.
800	Charlemagne	814
814	Louis the Pious	840
817	Lothair I.	855
850	Louis II.	875
875	Charles the Bald	876
884	Charles the Fat	887
888	Arnulf, emperor in Germany	

KINGS OF GERMANY. A.D.		A.D.
840	Louis the German	875
876	Louis II.	
880	Charles the Simple	
	In Italy, Guido. Berengar	
896	Lambert	

KINGS OF FRANCE. A.D.		A.D.
840	Charles the Bald	
876	Louis the Stammerer	879
879	Louis III. and Carloman	884
888	Eudes	

EMPERORS OF THE EAST. A.D.		A.D.
797	Irene, deposed	802
802	Nicephorus	811
811	Staurasius, deposed	811
811	Michael Rhangabes	813
813	Leo the Armenian, murdered	820
820	Michael the Stammerer	829
829	Theophilus	842
842	Michael the Drunkard	867
867	Basil the Macedonian	886
886	Leo the Philosopher	911

		GERMAN EMPERORS.	KINGS OF ITALY.		
898 John IX. 900				898 Charles the Simple 923	
900 Benedict IV. 903		900 Louis III. 912	899 Louis 904		
903 Leo V. 903					
903 Christopher 904					
904 Sergius IV. 911			904 Berengar, restored 923		
	906 Euthymius I., deposed 911				
911 Anastasius III. 913	911 Nicolas, restored 925				911 Alexander
		912 Conrad 920			912 Constantine Porphyrogenitus 919
913 Lando 914					
914 John X. 928		920 Henry the Fowler 920	923 Rodolph of Burgundy 926	923 Rodolf 936	
					919 Romanus
	925 Stephen II. 928		926 Hugh of Arles 947		
928 Leo VI. 929	928 Tryphon, deposed 931				
929 Stephen VII. 931					
931 John XI. 936	931 Vacant 933				
936 Leo VII. 939	936 Theophylact 956	936 Otho I., the Great 973		936 Louis d'Outre-Mer 954	
					951 Constantine IX. 959
939 Stephen VIII. 942					
942 Marinus II. 946					
946 Agapetus II. 955			947 Lothair 950		
			950 Berengar II. 964	954 Lothair 986	
955 John XII. 963					
	956 Polyeuc s 970				
963 Leo VIII. 965					959 Romanus II. 963
964 Benedict V., antipope (?)			964 Otho		963 Nicephorus Phocas 969
965 John XIII. 972					969 John Zimisces 975
	970 Basil I., deposed 974				
972 Benedict VI. 974					
		973 Otho II. 983			
974 Benedict VII. 983	974 Antonius III. Studites 983				
					975 Basil II. and Constantine X. 1025
983 John XIV. 984	983 Nicolas II. 996	983 Otho III. 1002			
984 Boniface VII., antipope (?) 985					
985 John XV. 996				986 Louis le Faineant 987	
				987 Hugh Capet 996	
996 Gregory V. 999	996 Sisinnius II. 999			996 Robert I.	
999 Silvester II. 1003	999 Sergius II. 1019				
		1002 Henry the Lame 1024			
1003 John XVII. 1003					
1003 John XVIII. 1009					
1009 Sergius IV. 1012					
1012 Benedict VIII. 1024					
	1019 Eustathius 1025				
1024 John XIX. 1033		1024 Conrad the Salic 1039			
	1025 Alexius 1043				
1033 Benedict IX. 1048				1031 Henry I. 1060	
		1039 Henry III. 1056			
1044 Silvester III., antipope 1046	1043 Michael Cerularius 1059				
1046 Gregory VI. 1046					

BOOK V.

CHAPTER I.

CHARLEMAGNE.

Empire of Charlemagne.

The empire of Charlemagne was almost commensurate with Latin Christendom;[1] England was the only large territory which acknowledged the ecclesiastical supremacy of Rome, not in subjection to the Empire. Two powers held sway in Latin Christendom, the Emperor and the Pope: of these incomparably the greatest at this time was the Emperor. Charlemagne, with the appellation, assumed the full sovereignty of the Cæsars, united with the commanding vigor of a great Teutonic conqueror. Beyond the Alps he was a German sovereign, assembling in his Diet the whole nobility of the Romanized Teutonic nations, and bringing the still barbarous races by force under his yoke. In Italy he was a Northern Conqueror, though the ally of the Pope and of Rome. But he was likewise an Emperor attempting to organize his vast dominions with the comprehensive policy of Roman administration, though not without respect for Teutonic freedom. He was the sole legislator in ecclesiastical as well as civil affairs; the Carolinian institutions em-

[1] Compare limits of the empire of Charles — Eginhard, Vit. Car. xv. He includes within it the whole of Italy, from Aosta to Lower Calabria.

brace the Church as well as the State; his Council at Frankfort dictates to the West, in despite of Papal remonstrances, on the great subject of image-worship. For centuries no monarch had stood so high, so alone, so unapproachable as Charlemagne. He ruled — ruled absolutely — by that strongest absolutism, the overawed or spontaneously consentient, cordially obedient, coöperative will of all other powers. He ruled from the Baltic to the Ebro, from the British Channel to the duchy of Benevento, even to the Straits of Messina. In personal dignity, who, it must not be said rivalled, approximated in the least degree, to Charlemagne? He had added, by his personal prowess in war, and this in a warlike age, by his unwearied activity, and by what success would glorify as military skill, almost all Germany, Spain to the Ebro, the kingdom of the Lombards, to the realm of the Franks, to Christendom. Huns, Avars, Slavians, tribes of unknown name and descent, had been repelled or subdued. His one defeat, that of Roncesvalles, is only great in recent poetry.[1] Every rebel, the independent German princes, like Tassillo of Bavaria, had been crushed; the obstinate Saxon, pursued to the court of the Danish King, at last became a subject and a Christian. On the Byzantine throne had sat an iconoclastic heretic, a boy, and a woman a murderess. Hadrian, during his long pontificate, had worn the Papal tiara with majesty. His successor, maimed and maltreated, had fallen to implore protection before the throne of Charlemagne; he

[1] See in H. Martin, Histoire de France, ii. p. 373, the very curious and spirited song (from a French historic periodical), called the Chant d'Altabiçar, said to have been preserved from the ninth or tenth century among the Pyrenean mountaineers.

had been obliged to clear himself of enormous crimes, to purge himself by oath before, what seemed to all, the superior tribunal of the Emperor. The gift of the Imperial crown had been the flattering homage of a grateful subject, somewhat loftily and disdainfully received; the donations of Charlemagne to the Pope were the prodigal but spontaneous alms of a religious King to the Church which he condescended to protect — free grants, or the recognition of grants from his pious ancestors.

Nor was it on signal occasions only that Charlemagne interfered in the affairs of the Church. His all comprehending, all pervading, all compelling administration was equally and constantly felt by his ecclesiastical as by his civil subjects. The royal commissioners inspected the conduct, reported on the lives, fixed and defined the duties, settled the tenure of property and its obligations, determined and apportioned the revenues of the religious as well as the temporal hierarchy. The formularies of the Empire are the legal and authorized rules to bishops and abbots as to nobles and knights. The ecclesiastical unity is but a subordinate branch of the temporal unity. The State, the Empire, not the Church, is during the reign of Charlemagne a supreme unresisted autocracy. Later romance has fallen below, rather than heightened, the full reality of his power and authority.

His power personal.

But it was only during his long indeed but transitory reign. For the power of Charlemagne was altogether personal, and therefore unenduring: it belonged to the man, to the conqueror, to the legislator, to the patron of letters and arts, to Charles the Great. At his death the Empire inevitably fell to pieces, only to be reunited occasionally and partially by some one great successor like Otho I., or some great house like that of Swabia. It was the first and last successful attempt to consolidate, under one vast empire, the Teutonic and Roman races, the nations of pure German origin and those whose languages showed the predominance of the Roman descent. It had its inherent elements of anarchy and of weakness in the first principles of the Teutonic character, the independence of the separate races, the vague notions of succession, which fluctuated between elective and hereditary sovereignty with the evils of both; the empire transmitted into feeble hands by inheritance, or elections contested by one half of the Empire; above all, in the ages immediately following Charlemagne, the separation of the Empire into independent kingdoms, which became the appanages of several sons, in general the most deadly enemies to each other. It was no longer, it could not be, a single realm united by one wide-embracing administration, but a system of hostile and conflicting states, of which the boundaries, the powers, the wealth, the resources, were in incessant change and vicissitude.

The Papacy must await its time, a time almost certain to arrive. The Papacy, too, had its own source of weakness, the want of a settled and authoritative elective body. It had its periods of anarchy, of menaced — it might seem, at the close of the tenth century, inevitable — dissolution. But it depended not on the sudden and accidental rise of great men to its throne. It knew no minorities, no divisions or subdivisions of its power between heirs of coequal and therefore conflicting rights. It was a

The Papacy.

succession of mature men; and the interests of the higher ranks of its subjects, of the hierarchy, even of the great ecclesiastical potentates throughout the West, were so bound up with his own, that the Pope had not to strive against sovereigns as powerful as himself. Till the times of the antipopes the papal power, though often obscured, especially in Rome itself, appeared to the world as one and indivisible. Its action was almost uniform; at least it had all the steadiness and inflexibility of a despotism — a despotism, if not of force, of influence, or of sympathy, and of cordial concurrence among all its multifarious agencies throughout the world to its aggrandizement.

But the empire of Charlemagne, as being the great epoch in the annals of Latin Christendom, demands more full consideration. Out of his universal Empire in the West and out of his Institutes rose, to a great degree, the universal empire of the Church and the whole mediæval polity; feudalism itself. Western Europe became, as it were, one through his conquests, which gathered within its frontiers all the races of Teutonic origin (except the formidable Northmen, or Normans, who, after endangering its existence, or at least menacing the rebarbarizing of many of its kingdoms, were to be the founders of kingdoms within its pale), and those conquests even encroached on some tribes of Slavian descent. It became a world within the world; on more than one side bordered by Mohammedanism, on one by the hardly less foreign Byzantine Empire. The history, therefore, of Latin Christianity must survey the character of the founder of this Empire, the extent of his dominions, his civil as well as his ecclesiastical institutes. As yet we have only traced him in his Italian conquests, as the ally and protector of the Popes. He must be seen as the sovereign and lawgiver of Transalpine as well as of Cisalpine Europe.[1]

The character of Charlemagne.

Karl, according to his German appellation, was the model of a Teutonic chieftain, in his gigantic stature, enormous strength, and indefatigable activity; temperate in diet, and superior to the barbarous vice of drunkenness. Hunting and war were his chief occupations; and his wars were carried on with all the ferocity of encountering savage tribes. But he was likewise a Roman Emperor, not only in his vast and organizing policy, he had that one vice of the old Roman civilization which the Merovingian kings had indulged, though not perhaps with more unbounded lawlessness. The religious Emperor, in one respect, troubled not himself with the restraints of religion. The humble or grateful Church beheld meekly, and almost without remonstrance, the irregularity of domestic life, which not merely indulged in free license, but treated the sacred rite of marriage as a covenant dissoluble at his pleasure. Once we have heard, and but once, the Church raise its authoritative, its comminatory voice, and that not to forbid the King of the Franks from wedding a second wife while his first was alive, but from marrying a Lombard princess. One pious ecclesiastic alone in his dominions, he a relative, ventured to protest aloud. Charles repudiated his first wife to marry the daughter of Desiderius; and after a year repudiated her to marry Hildegard, a Swabian lady. By Hildegard he had six children. On her death he married Fastrada, who bore him two; a nameless concubine another. On

[1] Eginhard. Vit. Car. sub fine.

Fastrada's death he married Liutgardis, a German, who died without issue. On her decease he was content with four concubines.[1] A darker suspicion, arising out of the loose character of his daughters, none of whom he allowed to marry, but carried them about with him to the camp as well as the court, has been insinuated, but without the least warrant from history. Under the same double character of the Teutonic and the Roman Emperor, Charlemagne introduced Roman arts and civilization into the remoter parts of his dominions. Aix-la-Chapelle, his capital, became, in buildings and in the marble and mosaic decorations of his palace, a Roman city, in which Karl sat in the midst of his Teutonic Diet. The patron of Latin letters, the friend of Alcuin, encouraged the compilation of a grammar in the language of his Teutonic subjects. The hero of the Saxon poet's Latin hexameter panegyric collected the old bardic lays of Germany. Even Charlemagne's fierce wars bore Christianity and civilization in their train.

Saxon wars.

The Saxon wars of Charlemagne, which added almost the whole of Germany to his dominions, were avowedly religious wars. If Boniface was the Christian, Charlemagne was the Mohammedan, Apostle of the Gospel. The declared object of his invasions, according to his biographer, was the extinction of heathenism;[2] subjection to the Christian faith or

[1] The reading is doubtful. Bouquet has *quatuor*. Pertz has followed a MS. which gives three.

[2] Some of the heathen Frisian temples appear to have contained much wealth. St. Luidger was sent out to destroy some. His followers brought back a considerable treasure, which they found in the temples. Charlemagne took two thirds, and gave one to the Church. — Vit. S. Luidg. apud Pertz. ii. p. 408.

extermination.[1] Baptism was the sign of subjugation and fealty: the Saxons accepted or threw it off according as they were in a state of submission or of revolt. These wars were inevitable, they were but the continuance of the great strife waged for centuries, from the barbarous North and East, against the civilized South and West; only that the Roman and Christian population, now invigorated by the large infusion of Teutonic blood, instead of awaiting aggression, had become the aggressor. The tide of conquest was rolling back; the subjects of the Western kingdoms, of the Western Empire, instead of waiting to see their homes overrun by hordes of fierce invaders, now boldly marched into the heart of their enemies' country, penetrated the forests, crossed the morasses, and planted their feudal courts of justice, their churches, and their monasteries in the most remote and savage regions, up to the Elbe and the shores of the Baltic.

The Saxon race now occupied the whole North of Germany, from the Baltic along the whole Eastern frontier of the Frankish kingdom. The interior of the land was yet an unknown world, both as to extent and population. Vast forests, in which it was said that squirrels might range for leagues without dropping to the ground,[2] broken only by wide heaths, sandy moors, and swamps, were peopled by swarms which still were thought inexhaustible. These countless hosts, which seemed but the first wave of a yet undiminished flood, might still precipitate themselves or be precipitated by the impulse of nations from the further

The Saxons.

1 "Eo usque perseveravit, dum aut victi Christianæ religioni subjicerentur aut omnino tollerentur." — Eginhard, sub ann. 775.

2 Vit. S. Lebuini.

North or East, on the old Roman empire and the advanced settlements beyond the Rhine. The Saxons were divided into three leading tribes, the Ostphalians, the Westphalians, and the Angarians; but each clan or village maintained its independence, waged war, or made peace. Each clan, according to old Teutonic usage, consisted of nobles, freemen, and slaves; but at times the whole nation met in a great armed convention. A deadly hatred had grown up between the Franks and Saxons, inevitable between two warlike and restless races separated by a doubtful and unmarked border, on vast level plains, with no natural boundary, neither dense forests, nor a chain of mountains, nor any large river or lake.[1] The Saxons were not likely, when an opportunity of plunder or even of daring adventure might offer itself, to respect the frontier of their more civilized neighbors; or the Franks to abstain from advancing their own limits wherever the land offered any advantage for a military, commercial, or even religious outpost. But it was not merely this casual hostility of two adventurous and unquiet people, encountering on a long and doubtful border — the Saxons scorned and detested the Romanized Franks, the Franks held the Saxons to be barbarians and heathens. The Saxons no doubt saw in the earlier and peaceful Christian missionaries the agents of Frankish as well as of Christian conquest. Even where their own religion hung so loosely on their minds, they could not but be suspicious of foreigners who began by undermining their

[1] "Suberant et causæ, quæ quotidie pacem conturbare poterant, termini videlicet nostri et illorum pæne ubique in plano contigui, præter pauca loca in quibus, vel silvæ majores, vel montium juga interjecta utrorumque agros certo limite disterminant, et rapinæ et incendia vicissim fieri non cessabant." — Eginhard, Vit. Carol. cvii.

national faith, and might end in endangering the national independence. They beheld with impatience and jealousy the churches and monasteries, which gradually rose near to, upon, and within their frontier; though probably the connection of the missionaries with the Romanized Franks, rather than the religion itself, which otherwise they might have admitted with the usual indifference of barbarians, principally excited their animosity.

First Saxon invasion. A.D. 772.

The first expedition of Charlemagne against the Saxons before his Lombard conquest arose out of religion. Among the English missionaries who, no doubt from speaking a kindred language, were so successful among the Teutonic tribes, was St. Lebuin, a man of the most intrepid zeal. Though the oratory which he had built on the Saxon bank of the Ysell had been burned by the Saxons, he determined to confront the whole assembled nation in their great diet on the Weser. Charles was holding at the same time his Field of May at Worms: this Saxon diet might be a great national council to watch or obtain intelligence of his proceedings.[1] The Saxons were in the act of solemn worship and sacrifice, when Lebuin stood up in the midst, proclaimed himself the messenger of the one true God, the Creator of heaven and earth, and denounced the folly and impiety of their idolatries.[2] He urged them to repentance, to belief, to baptism, and promised as their reward temporal and eternal peace. So far the Saxons seemed to have listened with decent or awe-struck reverence; but when

[1] May, however, was probably the usual month for the German national assemblies.

[2] Vit. S. Lebuini, apud Pertz.

Lebuin ceased to speak in this more peaceful tone, and declared that, if they refused to obey, God would send against them a mighty and unconquerable King who would punish their contumacy, lay waste their land with fire and sword, and make slaves of their wives and children, the proud barbarians broke out into the utmost fury; they threatened the dauntless missionary with stakes and stones: his life was saved only by the intervention of an aged chieftain. The old man insisted on the sanctity which belonged to all ambassadors, above all the ambassadors of a great God.

The acts and language of Charles showed that he warred at once against the religion and the freedom of ancient Germany. Assembling his army at Worms, he crossed the Rhine, and marched upon the Eresburg, a strong fortress near the Drimel.[1] Having taken this, he advanced to a kind of religious capital, either of the whole Saxon nation or at least of the more considerable tribes. It was situated near the source of the Lippe,[2] and contained the celebrated idol, the Irmin-Saule.[3]

The Irminsul.

This may have been simply the great pillar, the trunk of a gigantic tree, consecrated by immemorial reverence, or the name may imply the war-god, or the parental-god, or demigod of the race. This no-

1 Supposed Stadbergen, in the bishopric of Paderborn.

2 Eckhart (Pertz, p. 151) says distinctly that it was some way beyond the Eresburg.

3 Grimm, Deutsche Mythologie, 81 *et seq.*, 208 *et seq.*, "Irmânsaul, colossus, altissima columna." He quotes Rudolf of Fulda: "Truncum quoque ligni non parvæ magnitudinis in altum erectum sub divo colebant, patriâ eum linguâ Irminsul appellantes, quod Latine dicitur universalis columna, quasi sustinens omnia." Yet Irmin seems to have been the name of a national god or demigod.

tion suits better with the simpler description of the idol in the older writers. This rude and perhaps, therefore, not less imposing idol, has been exalted into a great symbolic image, either of the national deity or of the nation, arrayed in fanciful attributes, which seem to belong to a later mythology;[1] and German patriotism has delighted to recognize in this image consecrated by the Teutonic worship, that of the great Teutonic hero, Herman, the conqueror of Varus. Throughout the neighborhood the names and places are said to bear frequent and manifest allusion to this great victory over Rome, — the field of victory, the stream of blood, the stream of the bones. Not far off is the field of Rome, the mountain of Arminius, the forest of Varus.[2]

But whether rude and shapeless trunk, or symbolic image of the Saxon god, or the statue of the Teutonic hero, the Irmin-Saule fell by the remorseless hands of the Christian Frank.[3]

The war of the Franks and the Saxons lasted for thirty-three years;[4] it had all the horrors of an internecine strife between two hordes of barbarians. The

[1] He was clothed in armor; his feet rested on a field of flowers; in his right hand he held a banner with a rose in the centre, in his left a balance; on his buckler was a lion commanding other animals. — Spelman, in Irminsul.

[2] The neighborhood of Dethmold abounds with these sacred reminiscences. At the foot of the Teutberg is Wintfield, the field of victory; the Rodenbach, the stream of blood; and the Knochenbach, where the bones of the followers of Varus were found. Feldrom, the field of the Romans, is at no great distance. Rather farther off, near Pyrmont, Hermansberg, the mountain of Arminius; and on the banks of the Weser, Varenholz, the wood of Varus. — Stapfer., art. Arminius, in Biograph. Universelle.

[3] Luden is indignant at the destruction of this monument of German freedom by the renegade Charlemagne. — Geschichte, iv. p. 234.

[4] From 772 to 805.

armies of Charles were almost always masters of the field; but no sooner were they withdrawn than the indefatigable Saxons rose again, burst through the encroaching limits of the Empire, and often reached its more peaceful settlements. Hardly more than two years after the capture of Eresburg, and of their more sacred place, the site of the Irmin-Saule, they revenged the destruction of their great idol by burning, or attempting to burn, the church in Fritzlar, founded by St. Boniface. It was said to have been saved by the miraculous appearance of two angels in white garments; possibly two of the younger ecclesiastics.[1] In their inroads they respected neither age, nor sex, nor order, nor sacred edifice; all was wrapped in one blaze of fire, in one deluge of blood. But their especial fury was directed against the monasteries and churches. Widekind, the hero of these earlier exploits, was no less deadly an enemy of Christianity than of the Franks. He began his career by destroying all the Christian settlements in Friesland, and restoring the whole land to heathenism.[2]

Aug. 1, 775.

The historians of Charlemagne denounce the perfidy of the Saxons to the most solemn engagements; but in fact there was no supreme government which

1 Ann. Franc. A.D. 774. Bouquet, p. 19.

2 The Saxon Campaigns, according to Boehmer, Regesta: 1. Taking of Eresberg, A.D. 772. 2. Charlemagne crosses the Weser, Aug. 776. 3. To the Lippe, 776. 4. Diet of Paderborn, 777. 5. Revolt of Saxons, who waste as far as the Moselle, 778. 6. Advance to the Weser, 779. 7. To the Elbe, 780. 8. Diet at Lippe Brunnen. 9. Capitulation of the Saxons, 782. 10. Great victory at Thietmar, 783. 11. Readvance to the Elbe. 12. Further campaign, 784. 13. Widekind surrenders, and is baptized, 785. There were, however, later insurrections, and later progresses of Charlemagne through the subjugated land.

had the power or could be answerable for the fulfilment of treaties. Each village had its chieftain and its freemen, independent of the rest; the tribes whose land Charles occupied, or whose forests he menaced, submitted to the yoke, but those beyond them held themselves in no way bound by such treaties.[1]

After a few years, at a great Diet at Paderborn, the whole nation seemed to obey the summons of Charles to acknowledge him as their liege lord. Multitudes were baptized; and all the more considerable tribes gave hostages for their peaceful conduct. Yet but two years after, on the news of Charlemagne's defeat at Roncesvalles, they appeared again in arms, with the indefatigable Widekind at their head; he alone had kept aloof from the Diet at Paderborn, having taken refuge, it was said, with the King of Denmark, no doubt beyond the Elbe. Notwithstanding their baptism and the hostages, they reached the Rhine, ravaging as they went, threatened Cologne from Deutz, and were only prevented from invading France by the difficulty of crossing the river; along its right bank they burned and slaughtered from Cologne to Coblentz. This sudden outburst was followed by the most formidable revolt, put down by Charles's victories at Dethmold and near the river Hase. Throughout the war Charlemagne endeavored to subdue the tribes as he went on by the terror of his arms; and terrible indeed were those arms! On one occasion, at Verdun-on-

Diet at Paderborn, A.D. 777.

A.D. 778.

A.D. 779.

1 "Quæ nec rege fuit saltem sociata sub uno
Ut se militiæ pariter defenderet usu,
Sed variis divisa modis plebs omnis habebat
Quot pagos tot pæne duces."
Poeta Saxo. ad ann. 772, v. 24.

the-Allier, he massacred 4000 brave warriors who had surrendered, in cold blood. Nor did he trust to the humanizing influence of Christianity alone, but to the diffusion of Roman manners, and what might appear Roman luxury. The more submissive chieftains he tried to attach to his person by honors and by presents. The poor Saxons first became acquainted with the produce of wealthy Gaul. To some he gave farms, whence they were tempted and enabled to purchase splendid dresses, learned the use of money, the pleasures of wine.[1]

His frontier gradually advanced. In his first expedition he had crossed the Drimel and the Lippe, and reached the Weser; but twelve years of alternate victory and revolt had passed before he arrived at the Elbe. In four years more, during which Widekind himself submitted to baptism, although the unquiet people still renewed their revolt, he reached the sea, the limit of the Saxon territory.[2]

The policy of Charlemagne in the establishment of Christianity in the remote parts of Germany was perhaps wisely incongruous. Though wars of religion, they were waged entirely by the secular arm. He encouraged no martial prelate to appear at the head of his vassals, or to join in the work of bloodshed. On no point are his edicts more strong, more frequent, or more precise, than in prohibiting the clergy from bearing arms, or joining any military ex-

Establishment of Christianity.

[1] "Prædia præstiterat cum rex compluribus illis
Ex quibus acciperent pretiosæ tegmina vestis
Argenti cumulos, dulcisque fluenta Lyæi."
Poeta Saxo. iv. 130.

[2] "Usque ad oceanum trans omnes paludes et invia loca transitum est." — Ann. Tiliac. sub ann.

pedition.[1] They followed in the wake of war, but did not mingle in it. A few priests only remained with the camp to perform divine service, and to offer ministrations to the soldiers. The religion, though forced upon the conquered, though baptism was the only security (a precarious security, as it often proved) which the conqueror would accept for the submission of the vanquished, yet this was part of the treaty of peace, and as a pledge of peace was fitly performed by the ministers of peace. The conquest was complete, the carnage over, before the priests were summoned to their office to baptize the multitudes, who submitted to it as the chance of war, as they would to the surrender of property or of personal freedom. For this baptism no preparation was deemed necessary; the barbarians assented by thousands to the creed, and were immediately immersed or sprinkled with the regenerating waters. The clergy on the other hand were exposed to the fury of the insurgent people on every revolt; to hew down the crosses was the first sign that the Saxons renounced allegiance, and baptism was, according to their notion, cancelled by the renunciation of allegiance.

Foundations of bishoprics and monasteries.

The subjugation of the land appeared complete before Charlemagne founded successively his great religious colonies, the eight bishoprics of Minden, Seligenstadt, Verden, Bremen,[2]

1 "Hortatu omnium fidelium nostrorum et maxime episcoporum et reliquorum sacerdotum consultu, servis Dei per omnia omnibus armaturam portare vel pugnare, aut in exercitum et in hostem pergere, omnino prohibemus, nisi illi tantummodo qui propter divinum ministerium." — Caroli M. Capit. General. A.D. 769. Carloman, A.D. 742, Pepin, 744, had made similar enactments; but it appears that the restraint was unwelcome to some of the more warlike of the order. Charlemagne was supposed to detract from their dignity by prohibiting them from bearing arms.

2 Bremen, founded July 14, 787.

Munster, Hildesheim, Osnaburg, and Paderborn. These, with many richly-endowed monasteries, like Hersfeld, became the separate centres from which Christianity and civilization spread in expanding circles. But though these were military as well as religious settlements, the ecclesiastics were the only foreigners. The more faithful and trustworthy Saxon chieftains, who gave the security of seemingly sincere conversion to Christianity, were raised into Counts; thus the profession of Christianity was the sole test of fealty. The Saxon remained a conquered, but in some respects an independent, nation; it was ruled by a feudal nobility and a feudal hierarchy. The Saxons paid no tribute to the Empire; Charlemagne was content with their payment of tithes to the clergy,— a part of his ecclesiastical system, which was extended throughout his Transalpine dominions. Yet even after this period another great general insurrection broke out while Charles was engaged in a war with the Avars; the churches were destroyed, dreadful ravages committed. The revolt arose partly from the severe avarice with which the clergy exacted their tithes, and the impatience of the rude Germans at this unusual taxation. It was not till ten thousand men had been transplanted from the banks of the Elbe into France that the contest came to an end. The gratitude of the Saxon poet, who wrote under the Emperor Arnulf, for the conversion of his ancestors to Christianity, dwells but slightly on the sanguinary means used for their conversion, and their obstinate resistance to his persuasive sword.[1] On

[1] "Tum Carolum gaudens Saxonum turba sequatur,
Illi perpetuæ gloria lætitiæ;
O utinam vel cunctorum sequar ultimus horum." — v. 685.

the day of judgment, when the Apostles render an account of the nations which they have converted, when Charlemagne is followed into heaven by the hosts of his Saxon proselytes, the poet expresses his humble hope that he may be admitted in the train.

Charlemagne's legislation.

Charlemagne, in Christian history, commands a more important station even than for his subjugation of Germany to the Gospel, on account of his complete organization, if not foundation, of the high feudal hierarchy in great part of Europe. Throughout the Western Empire was, it may be said, constitutionally established this double aristocracy, ecclesiastical and civil. Everywhere the higher clergy and the nobles, and so downwards through the different gradations of society, were of the same rank, liable to many of the same duties, of equal, in some cases of coördinate, authority. Each district had its Bishop and its Count; the dioceses and counties were mostly of the same extent. They held for some purposes common courts, for others had separate jurisdiction, but of coequal power.

At the summit of each social pyramid, which rose by the same steps from the common base, the vast servile class, which each ruled with the right of master and possessor, or that of serfs attached to the soil, which were gradually succeeding to the baser and more wretched slavery of the Roman Empire,[1] stood the Sovrans, the Emperor, and the Pope. So at least it was in later times. At present Charlemagne stood alone on his unapproachable height. As monarch of

1 On the slow and gradual transition from slavery to serfdom and villeinage, see Mr. Hallam's supplemental note 79, and the remarkable quotation from M. Guerard.

the Franks, as King of Italy, still more as Emperor of the West, he was supreme, the Pope his humble, grateful subject. Charlemagne, with the title, assumed the imperial power of a Theodosius or a Justinian. His legislation embraces ecclesiastical as well as civil affairs. In the general assembly, of which, with the nobles, they were constituent parts, the assent of the bishops may be expressed or implied; but the laws which fix the obligations, the revenues, even the duties of the clergy, are issued in the name of the Emperor: they are monarchical and imperial, not papal or synodical canons. Already, indeed, the principles on which the loftier pretensions of the Church were hereafter to be grounded, had crept imperceptibly in under the specious form of religious ceremonies. The very title to the Frankish monarchy, the Empire itself, had to the popular view something of a papal gift. The anointing of the Kings of France had become almost necessary for the full popular recognition of the royal title.[1] The part taken by the pope in the offer of the Empire to Charlemagne, his coronation by the hands of the Pope in the same manner, gave a vague notion, a notion to be matured by time, that it was a Papal grant. He who could bestow could withhold; and, as it was afterwards maintained, he who could elevate could degrade; he who could crown could discrown the Emperor.

Authority of Charlemagne.

But over the Transalpine clergy, Charlemagne had not only the general authority of a Teutonic monarch and a Roman Emperor, he had like-

1 The Old Testament, which had suggested and sanctioned this ceremony, had become of equal authority with the New. The head of the Church was not merely the successor of the chief apostle. He was the high priest of the old Law, Samuel or Joas as well as St. Peter.

wise the same feudal sovereignty, founded on the same principles, which he had over the secular nobility. Their estates were held on the same tenure; they had been invested in them, especially in Germany, according to the old Teutonic law of conquest. Every conquered territory, or a portion of it, became the possession of the conquerors; it was a vast farm, granted out in lots, on certain conditions; the king reserved certain portions as the royal domain, others were granted to the warriors (the leudes), under the title first of allodes, which gradually became benefices.[1] But bishoprics and abbacies were originally, or became, in the strictest sense, benefices. The great ecclesiastics took the same oath with other vassals on a change of sovereign. They were bound, bishops, abbots and abbesses, to appear at the Herr-bann of the sovereign. Charlemagne submits them without distinction to the visitation of his officers, who are to make inquest as to their due performance of their duties as beneficiaries, the maintenance not merely of the secular buildings, but also of the churches, and the due solemnization of the divine offices.[2] The men of the church were

Transalpine hierarchy.

1 French learning, especially that of M. Guizot, of M. Lehuerou, and of the authors of the prefaces to the valuable volumes of the "Documents Inédits," has exhausted every subject relating to the national and social institutions of the prefeudal and feudal times; the ranks and orders of men: the growth of the cities; their guilds and privileges; the particular tenure and obligations of land. Mr. Hallam has diligently watched, and in his supplemental notes summed up with his characteristic strong English sense and fairness, the results of all these vast and voluminous inquiries; not only those of France, but those of Belgium, England, Italy, Germany.

2 "Volumus atque jubemus ut missi nostri per singulos pagos prævidere studeant omnia beneficia quæ nostri et aliorum homines habere videntur, quomodo restaurata sint post annuntiationem nostram sive destructa. Primum de ecclesiis, quomodo structæ aut destructæ sint in tectis, in maceriis, sive parietibus, sive in pavimentis, necnon in picturâ, etiam in

bound to obey the summons to military service, as duly as any other liegemen, only that they marched under a lay captain. The same number were allowed to stay at home to cultivate the land. The great prelates, even in the days of Charlemagne, resisted the laws which prohibited their appearing in war at the head of their own troops, as lowering their dignity, and depriving the Church of some of its honors.[1] Bishops and abbots, in return for the oath of protection from the sovereign, took an oath of fealty as counsellors and as aids to the sovereign; but the great proof of this ecclesiastical vassalage is that they were amenable to the law of treason, were deposed as guilty of violating their allegiance.[2]

Estates of the Church.

Charlemagne himself was no less prodigal than weaker kings of immunities and grants of property to churches and monasteries. With his queen Hildegard he endows the church of St. Martin, in Tours, with lands in Italy. His grants to St. Denys, to Lorch, to Fulda, to Prum, more particularly to Hersfeld, and many Italian abbeys, appear among the acts of his reign.[3]

luminariis, sive officiis. Similiter et alia beneficia, casas cum omnibus appendiciis eorum." — K. Magn. Cap. Aquense, A.D. 807; Lehuerou, p. 517.

1 "Quia instigante antiquo hoste audivimus quosdam nos suspectos habere propterea quod concessimus episcopis et sacerdotibus ac reliquis Dei servis ut in hostes . . . non irent . . . nec agitatores sanguinum fierent . . . quod honores sacerdotum et res ecclesiarum auferre vel minuere voluissemus." — Cap. Incert. Ann.; Lehuerou, 520.

2 "Promitto et perdono vobis . . . defensionem, quantum potero, adjuvante Domino, exhibebo . . . ut vos mihi secundum Deum et secundum sæculum sic fideles adjutores et consilio et auxilio sitis sicut vestri antecessores boni meis melioribus prædecessoribus extiterunt." — Promiss. Dom. Karlomanni regis, A.D. 882; Lehuerou, p. 519. Ebbo, Archbishop of Rheims, was deposed as traitor to Louis the Debonnaire; Tertoldus, Bishop of Bayeux, was accused of treason against Charles the Bald. — Bouquet.

3 See the Regesta in Boehmer, passim. Leuhuerou (p. 539) gives an

Nor were these estates always obtained from the pious generosity of the king or the nobles. The stewards of the poor were sometimes the spoilers of the poor. Even under Charlemagne there are complaints against the usurpation of property by bishops and abbots, as against counts and laymen. They compelled the poor free man to sell his property, or forced him to serve in the army, and that on permanent or continual duty, and so to leave his land either without owner, with all the chances that he might not return, or to commit it to the custody of those who remained at home in quiet and seized every opportunity of entering into possession.[1] No Naboth's vineyard escaped their watchful avarice.

In their fiefs the bishop or abbot exercised all the rights of a feudal chieftain. At first, like all seignorial privileges, their administration was limited, and with appeal to a higher court, or in the last resort, to the king. Gradually, sometimes by silent usurpation, sometimes by actual grant, they acquired power over all causes and all persons. The right of appeal, if it

instance of the enormous possessions of some of the monasteries: they were larger in the north than in the south of France (compare Thierry, Temps Mérovingiens). The abbey of S. Wandrille, or Fontenelle, according to its chartulary, owned, less than 150 years after its foundation (A.D. 650–788) 3974 manses (the manse contained 12 jugera, acres), besides mills and other property. Compare the lands heaped on churches and monasteries by the Merovingians, p. 221.

[1] "Quod pauperes se reclamant expoliatos esse de eorum proprietate; et hoc æqualiter supra episcopos et abbates et eorum advocatos et supra comites et eorum centenarios. . . . Dicunt etiam quod quicunque proprium suum episcopo, abbati, comiti aut judici . . . dare noluerit, occasiones quærunt super illum pauperem, quomodo eum condemnare possint, et illum semper in hostem faciant ire, usque dum pauper factus, volens nolens suum proprium aut tradat aut vendat; alii vero qui traditum habent, absque ullius inquietudine domi resideant."—Kar. M. Capit. de Exped. Exercit. A.D. 811. Compare Capit. Longobard. ap. Pertz, iii. p. 192, and Lehuerou, p. 311.

existed, was difficult to exercise, was curtailed, or fell into desuetude.[1]

Thus the hierarchy, now a feudal institution, parallel to and coördinate with the temporal feudal aristocracy, aspired to enjoy, and actually before long did enjoy, the dignity, the wealth, the power of suzerain lords. Bishops and abbots had the independence and privileges of inalienable fiefs; and at the same time began either sullenly to contest, or haughtily to refuse, those payments or acknowledgments of vassalage, which sometimes weighed heavily on other lands. During the reign of Charlemagne this theory of spiritual immunity slumbered, or rather had not quickened into life. It was boldly (so rapid was its growth) announced in the strife with his son, Louis the Pious. It was then asserted by the hierarchy (become king-makers and king-deposers) that all property given to the Church, to the poor, and to the servants of God, or rather to the saints, to God himself (such were the specious phrases) was given absolutely, irrevocably, with no reserve. The king might have power over knight's fees, over those of the Church he had none whatever. Such claims were impious, sacrilegious, and implied forfeiture of eternal life. The clergy and their estates belonged to another realm, to another commonwealth; they were entirely, absolutely independent of the civil power. The clergy belonged to the Herr-bann of Christ, and of Christ alone.[2]

[1] Compare the luminous discussion of Lehuerou, p. 243, *et seq.* The right of basse justice was inseparable from property. The bishop or abbot was head of the family; all were in his mundium. He afterwards acquired moyenne, finally haute justice. In the cities he became chief magistrate by another process.

[2] "Quod semel legitime consecratum est Deo, in suis militibus, et pauperi-

These estates, however, thus sooner or later held by feudal tenure, and liable to feudal service, were the aristocratic possessions of the ecclesiastical aristocracy; on the whole body of the clergy Charlemagne bestowed their even more vast dowry — the legal claim to tithes.[1] Already, under the Merovingians, the clergy had given significant hints that the law of Leviticus was the perpetual and unrepealed law of God.[2] Pepin had commanded the payment of tithe for the celebration of peculiar litanies during a period of famine.[3] Charlemagne made it a law of the Empire: he enacted it in its most strict and comprehensive form, as investing the clergy in a right to the tenth of the substance and of the labor alike of freeman and of serf.[4] The collection of tithe was regulated by compulsory statutes; the clergy took note of all who paid or refused to pay;[5] four, or eight, or more jurymen were summoned from each parish, as witnesses for the claims disputed;[6] the contumacious were three times summoned; if still obstinate, excluded from the church;

bus ad usus militiæ suæ libere concedatur. Habeat igitur Rex rempublicam libere in usibus militiæ suæ ad dispensandum; habeat et Christus res ecclesiarum quasi alteram rempublicam, omnium indigentium et sibi servientium usibus. . . . Sin alias ut apostolus ait, qui aliena diripiunt, regnum non possidebunt eternum. Quanto magis qui ea quæ Dei sunt et ecclesiarum defraudantur, in quibus sacrilegia copulantur." — Vit. Walæ, apud Pertz. Wala's doctrines were not unopposed. Compare Lehuerou, p. 538.

1 On Tithes, see Planck, ii. pp. 402 and 411.

2 Sirmond, Concil. Eccles. Gall. i. p. 543; Council of Macon, A.D. 585.

3 Peppini Regis Capitul. A.D. 764.

4 "Similiter secundum Dei mandatum præcipimus ut omnes decimam partem suis ecclesiis et sacerdotibus donent, tam nobiles quam ingenui, similiter et liti." — Capit. Paderborn. A.D. 785. See also Cap. A.D. 779. It was confirmed by the Council of Frankfort, Capitul. Frankfurtense, A.D. 794.

5 Capit. Aquisgran. A.D. 801.

6 Capitul. Longobard. A.D. 803.

if they still refused to pay, they were fined over and above the whole tithe, six solidi; if further contumacious, the recusant's house was shut up; if he attempted to enter it, he was cast into prison, to await the judgment of the next plea of the crown.[1] The tithe was due on all produce, even on animals.[2] The tithe was usually divided into three portions — one for the maintenance of the Church, the second for the Poor, the third for the Clergy. The bishop sometimes claimed a fourth. The bishop was the arbiter of the distribution: he assigned the necessary portion for the Church, and apportioned that of the clergy.[3] This tithe was by no means a spontaneous votive offering of the whole Christian people — it was a tax imposed by Imperial authority, enforced by Imperial power. It had caused one, if not more than one, sanguinary insurrection among the Saxons. It was submitted to in other parts of the Empire, not without strong reluctance.[4]

1 Capitul. Longobard. A.D. 803, et Capitul. Hlotharii, i. 825, et Hludovici, ii. 875.

2 Capitul. Aquisgran. 801.

3 The tithe belonged to the parish church; that in which alone baptisms were performed. But there was a constant struggle to alienate them to churches founded by the great land-owners on their own domain, of which churches they retained the patronage. Charlemagne himself set a bad example in this respect, alienating the tithes to the succursal churches on his own domain. — Capitul. de Villis. Compare Lehuerou, p. 489.

4 Even Alcuin ventures to suggest, that if the Apostles of Christ had demanded tithes they would not have been so successful in the propagation of the Gospel: — "An Apostoli quoque ab ipso Christo edocti, et ad prædicandum mundo missi, exactiones decimarum exegissent . . . considerandum est. Scimus quia decimatio substantiæ nostræ valde bona est; sed melius est illam amittere quam fidem perdere. Nos vero in fide catholicâ nati, nutriti, edocti, vix consentimus substantiam nostram pleniter decimare. Quanto magis tenera fides et infantilis animus, et avara mens." — Alcuin, Epist. apud Bouquet, I. v. Compare a note of Weissenberg (Die grossen Kirchen Versammlungen, vol. i. p. 178), on some curious consequences of enforcing the law of tithes.

Ecclesiastical laws of Charlemagne.

But in return for this magnificent donation, Charlemagne assumed the power of legislating for the clergy with as full despotism as for the laity: in both cases there was the constitutional control of the concurrence of the nobles and of the higher ecclesiastics, strong against a feeble monarch, feeble against a sovereign of Charlemagne's overruling character. His Institutes are in the language of command to both branches of that great ecclesiastical militia, which he treated as his vassals, the secular and the monastic clergy.[1] He seemed to have a sagacious foresight of the dangers of his feudal hierarchical system; the tendency still further to secularize the secular clergy; the inclination to independence in the regulars, which afterwards led to the rivalry and hostility between the two orders. The great church fiefs would naturally be coveted by men of worldly views, seeking only their wealth and power, without discharging their high and sacred offices; they would become hereditary in certain families, or at least within a limited class of powerful claimants. Each separate benefice would be exposed to perpetual dilapidation by its successive holders; there was no efficient security against the illegal alienation of its estates to the family, kindred, or friends of the incumbent;[2] it might be squandered in war by a martial, in magnificence by a princely, in rude voluptuousness by a dissolute prelate.[3] Charle-

[1] See, on the kind of spiritual jurisdiction exercised by former kings of France, Ellendorf, i. 231.

[2] "Si sacerdotes plures uxores habuerint:" that probably means married more than once. — Caput. lib. i.

[3] There are many sumptuary provisions. Bishops, abbots, abbesses, are not to keep hounds, falcons, hawks, or jugglers. Drunkenness is forbidden, as well as certain oaths.

magne endeavored to bring the great monastic rule of mutual control to hallow the lives and secure the property of the clergy. The scheme of St. Augustine, that the clergy should live in common, under canonical rule, and under the immediate control and superintendence of the Bishop, had never been entirely obsolete. Charlemagne endeavored to marshal the whole secular clergy under this severe discipline; he would have all either under canonical or monastic discipline.[1] But the legislator passed his statutes in vain; rich chapters were founded, into which the secular spirit entered in other forms. The great mass of the clergy continued to lead their separate lives, under no other control than the more or less vigilant rule of the Bishop.

The monasteries.

Charlemagne endeavored with equal want of success to prevent the monastic establishments from growing up into separate and independent republics, bound only by their own rules, and without the pale of the episcopal or even metropolitan jurisdiction. The abbots and the monks were commanded to obey in all humility the mandates of their Bishops.[2] The abbot received his power within the walls of his convent from the hands of the Bishop; the doors of

1 "Qui ad clericatum accedunt, quod nos nominamus canonicam vitam volumus ut episcopus eorum regat vitam. Clerici — ut vel veri monachi sint vel veri canonici." — Capit. A.D. 789, 71 et 75. "Canonici . . . in domo episcopali vel etiam in monasterio . . . secundum canonicam vitam erudiantur." A.D. 802. *Ut omnes clerici unum de duobus eligant, aut pleniter secundum canonicam*, aut secundum regularem institutionem vivere debeant." A.D. 805.

2 "Abbates et monachos omnismodis volumus et præcipimus, ut episcopis suis omni humilitate et hobhedientiâ sint subjecti, sicut canonica constitutione mandati." — Capit. Gen. A.D. 769; Hludovic. i.; Imp. Capit. Aquisgran. 825.

the monastery were to fly open to the Bishop; an appeal lay from the Bishop to the Metropolitan, from the Metropolitan to the Emperor.[1] The Bishops themselves too often granted full or partial immunities, which gradually grew into absolute exemption from episcopal authority.[2] In later times many of the more religious communities, to escape the tyranny and rapacity of a secular bishop, placed themselves under the protection of the King, or some powerful lord, whose tyranny in a certain time became more grinding and exacting than that of the Bishop.[3]

The extent of Charlemagne's Empire may be estimated by the list of his Metropolitan Sees: they were Rome, Ravenna, Milan, Friuli (Aquileia), Grado, Cologne, Mentz, Saltzburg, Treves, Sens, Besançon, Lyons, Rouen, Rheims, Arles, Vienne, Moutiers in the Tarantaise, Ivredun, Bordeaux, Tours, Bourges.[4] To these Metropolitans lay the appeal in the first instance from the arbitrary power of the Bishop. This power it was the policy of Charlemagne to elevate to the utmost.[5] The Capitularies enact the

Extent of empire.

1 "Statutum est a domino rege et sancto synodo, ut episcopi justitias faciant in suas parrochias. Si non obedierit aliqua persona episcopo suo de *abbatibus*, presbyteris . . . *monachis* et cæteris clericis, veniant ad metropolitanum suum, et ille dijudicet causam cum suffraganeis suis . . . Et si aliquid est quod episcopus metropolitanus non possit corrigere vel pacificare, tunc tandem veniant accusatores cum accusatu, cum literis metropolitani, ut sciamus veritatem rei." — Capitul. Frankfurt. 705.

2 Lehuerou, p. 493.

3 Baluzius, Formula 38.

4 Eginhard, c. xxxiii. The omission of Narbonne and one or two others perplexes ecclesiastical antiquarians. To these 21 archbishoprics of his realm Charlemagne in his last will bequeathed a certain legacy, two thirds of his personal property.

5 Ellendorf (Die Karolinger) asserts that the capitularies nowhere recognize appeals to the Pope. The metropolitans and metropolitan synods were the courts of last resort, except, it should seem, the emperors'.

regular visitation of all the parishes within their diocese by the Bishops, even those within peculiar jurisdiction.[1] Their special mission, besides preaching and confirmation and the suppression of heathen ceremonies, was to make inquisition into all incests, parricides, fratricides, adulteries, heresies, and all other offences against God. The Bishop on this visitation was received at the expense of the clergy and the people (he was forbidden to oppress the people by exacting more than was warranted by custom.)[2] The monasteries were subject to the same jurisdiction. The clergy made certain fixed payments, either in kind or money, as vassals to their superiors of the hierarchy;[3] the Bishops, notwithstanding the prohibition of the canons, persisted in demanding fees for the ordination of clerks. Both these are, as it were, tokens of ecclesiastical vassalage, strikingly resembling the commuted services and the payments for investiture.

The clergy were under the absolute dominion of the Bishop; they could be deposed, expelled from communion, even punished by stripes. No priest could officiate in a diocese, or leave the diocese, without permission of the Bishop.[4]

Election of bishops.

The primitive form of the election of the Bishop remained, but only the form; the popular election had, in all higher offices, faded into

[1] "Similiter nostras in beneficio datas, quam et aliorum ubi reliquiæ præesse videntur." — Capitular. A.D. 813.

[2] Capitular. A.D. 769 and 813.

[3] "Ut unum modium frumenti, et unum modium ordei, atque unum modium vini . . . . episcopi a presbyteris accipiant, et frischingam (a lamb) sex valentem denarios. Et si hæc non accipiant, si volunt, pro his omnibus duos solidos in denariis." — Karol. ii. Syn. apud Tolosam, A.D. 844.

[4] Capitular. vi. 163. "Clerici, quos increpatio non emendaverit, verberibus coerceantur." — vii. 302.

a shadow. That of the clergy retained for a long time more substantive reality. It was this growing feudality of the Church, which, if it gave not to the sovereign the absolute right of nomination, invested him with a coördinate power, and made it his interest if not his royal duty to assert that power. The Metropolitan, the Bishop, the Abbot, had now a double character; he was a supreme functionary in the Church, a beneficiary in the realm. The Sovereign would not and could not abandon to popular or to ecclesiastical election the nomination to these important fiefs; Charlemagne held them in his own hands, and disposed of them according to his absolute will.

Charlemagne himself usually promoted men worthy of ecclesiastical dignity; but his successors, like the older Merovingian kings, were not superior to the ordinary motives of favor, force, passion, or interest; they were constantly environed by greedy and rapacious candidates for Church preferments; helmeted warriors on a sudden became mitred prelates, needy adventurers wealthy abbots. Still was the Church degraded, enslaved, disqualified for her own office, by her power and wealth. The successors of Boniface, and his missionary clergy on the shores of the Rhine, became gradually, as they grew rich and secure, like the Merovingian hierarchy who had offended the austere virtue of Boniface. The pious and death-defying men whom Charlemagne planted in his new bishoprics and abbeys in the heart of Germany, with the opulence assumed the splendor, princely pride, secular habits, of their rival nobles. Even his son witnessed and suffered by the rapid, inevitable, melancholy change.

The parochial clergy were still appointed by the

Parochial clergy.

election of the clergy of the district, with the assent of the people; the Bishop nominated only in case a fit person was not found by those with whom lay the ordinary election.[1] Nor could he be removed unless legally convicted of some offence. Yet even in France there was probably not as yet a regular, and by no means an universal division of parishes; certainly not in the newly-conquered dominions. They were either chapels endowed, and appointed to by some wealthy prince or noble (the chaplain dwelt within the castle-walls, and officiated to the immediate retainers or surrounding vassals): or the churches were served from some cathedral or conventual establishment, where the clergy either lived together according to canonical rule, or were members of the conventual body. The Bishop alone had in general the title to the distribution of the tithes, one third, usually, to himself and his clergy (of his clergy's necessities and his own he was the sole, not always impartial or liberal judge); one to the Fabric, the whole buildings of the See; one to the Poor. Each, however, in his narrower sphere, and according to his personal influence, the devotion or respect of his people, had his sources of wealth; the gifts and oblations, the fees, which were often prohibited but always prohibited in vain. The free gratuity became an usage, usage custom, custom right. Where spiritual life and death depended on priestly ministration, that which love and reverence might not be

[1] "Et primum quidem ipsius loci presbyteri, vel cæteri clerici, idoneum sibi rectorem eligant; deinde populi qui ad eamdem plebem aspicit, sequatur assensus. Si autem in ipsâ plebe talis inveniri non poterit, qui illud opus competenter peragere possit, tunc episcopus de suis quem idoneum judicaverit, inibi constituat." — Hludowici, ii. Imp. Convent. Ticin. A.D. 855.

strong enough to lure forth would be wrung from fear. Where the holy image might be veiled, the relic withdrawn from worship, the miracle unperformed, to say nothing of the actual ritual services, the priest might exact the oblation. Whether from the higher or lower, the purer or more sordid motive, neither the land nor the tithes of the Church were the measure of the popular tribute. While, on the other hand, the alms of the clergy themselves out of their own revenues, those bestowed at their instance by the wealthy, by the princely or the vulgar robber as an atonement or commutation for his sins, the bequests made on the deathbed of the most wicked as well as the most holy, redistributed a vast amount of that fund of riches — if not wisely, at least without stint, without cessation.

Yet, no doubt, by the deference which Charlemagne paid to the clergy, by his own somewhat ostentatious religion, by his munificent grants and donations, above all by his elevation of their character through his wise legislation, however imperfect or unenduring the success of his laws, Charlemagne raised the hierarchical power far more than he depressed it by submitting it to his equal autocracy. There was no humiliation in being, with the rest of Western Christendom, subject to Charlemagne. Even if the Church did feel some temporary obscuration of her authority, some slight limitation of her independence, conscious of her own strength, she might be her own silent prophet of her future emancipation and more than emancipation.

Council of Frankfort.

The Council of Frankfort displays most fully the power assumed by Charlemagne over the hierarchy as well as the lay nobility of the realm, the mingled character, the all-embracing comprehen-

siveness of his legislation. The assembly at Frankfort was at once a Diet or Parliament of the Realm and an ecclesiastical Council. It took cognizance alternately of matters purely ecclesiastical and of matters as clearly secular. Charlemagne was present and presided in the Council of Frankfort.[1] The canons as well as the other statutes were issued chiefly in his name. The Council was attended by a great number of bishops from every part of the Western Empire, from Italy, Germany,
A.D. 794. Gaul, Aquitaine, some (of whom Alcuin was the most distinguished, though Alcuin was now chiefly resident at the court of Charlemagne) from Britain. Two bishops, named Theophylact and Stephen, appeared as legates from Pope Hadrian. The powerful Hadrian was still on the throne, in the last year of his pontificate, when Charlemagne summoned and presided over this Diet-Council.

The first object of this Council was the suppression of a new heresy, and the condemnation of its authors, certain Spanish bishops. Nestorianism, which had been a purely Oriental heresy, now appeared in a new form in the West. Two Spanish prelates, Elipand, Archbishop of Toledo, and Felix, Bishop of Urgel (whether to conciliate their Mohammedan masters,[2] or trained to more than usual subtlety by communication with

[1] "Præcipiente et *præsidente* piissimo et gloriosissimo domino nostro Carolo rege." — Synod. ad Episc. Gall. et German. Labbe, 1032. Charles himself writes: "Congregationi sacerdotum auditor et *arbiter* adsedi." — Car. Magn. Epist. ad Episc. Hisp.

[2] Charlemagne expresses his sympathy with the oppression of Elipand under the Gentiles: "Vestram quam patimini inter gentes lacrymabili gemitu condoleamus oppressionem." But his language almost implies that he considers them as subjects of his Empire, as well as subjects of the Church. Urgel, near the Pyrenees, was in the dominions of Charlemagne.

Arabian writers),[1] had framed a new scheme, according to which, while they firmly maintained the coequality of the Son as to his divine nature, they asserted that, as to his humanity, Christ was but the adopted Son of the Father. Hence the name of the new sect, the Adoptians. It was singular that, while the Greeks exhausted the schools of rhetoric for distinctive terms applicable to the Godhead, the Western form of the heresy chose its phraseology from the Roman law. This strange theory had been embraced by a great number of proselytes.[2] Felix of Urgel, a subject of Charlemagne, had already been summoned before a synod at Ratisbon, at which presided Charles himself. Felix recanted his heresy, and swore never to teach it more. He was sent to Rome, imprisoned by order of Pope Hadrian, and condemned to sign and twice most solemnly to swear to his abandonment of his opinions. He resumed his bishopric, and returned to his errors; he was again prosecuted, and took refuge among the Saracens.

A.D. 752.

The doctrines of Elipand and Felix were condemned as wicked and impious with the utmost unanimity. Already Pope Hadrian, in a letter to the Bishops of Spain and Gallicia, had condemned these opinions; but the Emperor, not content with communicating the unanimous decision of the Pope and the Bishops of Italy, of those of Gaul and Germany, with certain

[1] According to Alcuin, the scheme had originated in certain writers at Cordova. — Alcuin, Epist. v. 11, 5.

[2] St. Leidrad is said to have converted 20,000 bishops, priests, monks, laymen, men and women. — Paullin. Epist. ad Episc. Arno. edited by Mabillon. Compare Walch, p. 743. Leo III. Epist.; Alcuin, v. 11, 7; other authorities in Walch, ix. p. 752. Walch wrote a history of the Adoptionists.

wise and holy doctors whom he had summoned from Britain, thinks it necessary to address the condemned bishops in his own name. He enters into the theology of the question; and it must be said that both the divinity and the mild and even affectionate tone of the royal letter are much superior to that of Pope Hadrian and of the Italian bishops.[1]

But the more important act of the Council of Frankfort was the rejection of the Second Council of Nicea, or, as it was inaccurately called, the Council of Constantinople. To this Council the East had given its assent. It had been sanctioned by Pope Hadrian, it spoke the opinions of successive pontiffs, it might be considered as the established law of Christendom. This law Charlemagne and his assembly of feudal prelates scrupled not to annul and abrogate. Image-worship in the East had gained the victory, and was endeared to the Byzantine Greeks as distinguishing them more decidedly from the iconoclastic Mohammedans (the Image-worshippers branded Iconoclasm as Mohammedanism). It had a strong hold on all the population of Southern Europe, as the land of the yet unextinguished arts, as the birthplace of the new polytheistic Christianity, but it was far less congenial to the Teutonic mind. The Franks were at war with the Saxon idolaters; and though there was no great similitude between the rude and shapeless deities of the

[1] According to the report of the Italian bishops, a letter arrived from Elipand of Toledo while Charlemagne was seated in his palace in the midst of his clergy. It was read aloud. At its close the imperial theologian immediately rose from his throne, and from its steps addressed the meeting in a long speech, refuting all the doctrines of Elipand. When he had ended, he inquired, "What think ye of this?"—Epist. Episcop. Ital. apud Labbe, p. 1022.

Teutonic forests and the carved or painted saints and angels of the existing Christian worship, yet, though with the passion of most savage nations for ornament and splendor the Franks delighted in the brilliant decorations of their churches (Charlemagne laid Italy under contribution to adorn his palace); still their more profound spirituality of conception, their inclination to the vague, the mystic, the indefinite, or their unhabituated deadness to the influence of art, made them revolt from that ardent devotion to images which prevailed throughout the South. Such at least was the disposition of Charlemagne himself, and the author of the Carolinian Books.

Constantine Copronymus, the Iconoclast, had endeavored to make an alliance with Pepin the A.D. 767.
Frank. Pepin held a council on image-worship at Gentilly, at which the ambassadors of Copronymus appeared, it is not known for what ostensible purpose, perhaps to negotiate a matrimonial union between the courts, but no doubt with the view to detach Pepin from the support of the Italian rebels to the Eastern Empire. Of these the real head was the Pope, whose refusal of allegiance to the Emperor, and alliance with the Franks, were defended on the plea that the Emperor was an iconoclast and a heretic. Pepin probably took no great pains to understand the religious question; in that he was content to acquiesce in the judgment of the Pope; nor were the offers of Constantine sufficiently tempting to incline him to break up his Italian policy. Image-worship remained an undecided question with the Franks.

But Charlemagne and the Council of Frankfort proclaimed their deliberate judgment on a question already, it might seem, decided by a Council which aspired to be thought Œcumenic, and by the notorious sanction of more than one Pope. The canon of the Council of Frankfort overstates the decrees of Nicea. It arraigns that synod as commanding, under the pain of anathema, the same service and adoration to be paid to the images as to the Divine Trinity. This adoration they reject with contempt, and condemn with one voice. But the brief decree of Frankfort must be considered in connection with the deliberate and declared opinions of Charlemagne, as contained in the famous Carolinian Books. These books speak in the name of the Emperor; Charlemagne himself boldly descends into the arena of controversy. The real authorship of these books can never be known; it is difficult not to attribute them to Alcuin, the only known writer equal to the task. It is probable indeed that the Emperor may have called more than one counsellor to his assistance in this deliberate examination of an important question, but to Christendom the books spoke in the name and with the authority of the Emperor.

Throughout the discussion, Charlemagne treads his middle path with firmness and dignity. He rejects, with uncompromising disdain, all worship of images; he will not tamper, perhaps he feels or writes as if he felt the danger of tampering, in the less pliant Latin, with those subtile distinctions of meaning which the Western Church was obliged to borrow, and without clear understanding, from the finer and more copious Greek. He rejects alike adoration, worship, reverence, veneration.[1] He will not admit the kneeling before

[1] Lib. ii. 21, 23; iii. 18; ii. 27; ii. 30.

them; the burning of lights or the offering of incense;[1] or the kissing of a lifeless image, though it represent the Virgin and the Child. Images are not even to be reverenced, as the saints, as living men, as relics, as the Bible, as the Holy Sacrament, as the Cross, as the sacred vessels of the Church, as the Church itself.[2] But, on the other hand, Charlemagne is no Iconoclast: he admits images and pictures into churches as ornaments, and, according to the definition of Gregory the Great, as keeping alive the memory of pious men and of pious deeds.[3] The representatives of the Pope ventured no remonstrance either against the accuracy or the conclusion of the Council. The Carolinian Books were sent to the Pope at Rome. Hadrian still ruled: he was too prudent not to dissemble the indignation which he must have felt at this usurpation of spiritual authority by the temporal power, at least by this assertion of independence in a Transalpine Council, a Council chiefly of barbarian prelates; or to betray his wounded pride at this quiet contempt of his theological arguments, which could hardly be unknown as forming part of the proceedings in the Nicene Council, yet were not even noticed by the Imperial controversialist. There is no peremptory declaration of his own infallibility, no anathema against the contumacious prelates, no protest against the Imperial interference. A feeble answer, still extant, testi-

A.D. 795. Hadrian died Dec. 26, 796.

1 "Quod ante imagines luminaria concinnentur, et thymiamata adoleantur." — iv. 3; iv. 23.

2 Lib. ii. 21, 24; iii. 25; ii. 30, 27; i. 28, 29; iii. 27; iv. 3, 12. Walch, vol. xi. pp. 57, 59.

3 See the very curious description of Charlemagne's own splendid palace at Ingelheim. — Ermondus Nigellus, iv. The whole Scripture history was painted on the walls. There were sculptures representing all the great events in profane history. "Regia namque domus late *persculpta* nitescit."

fies at once the authenticity of the Carolinian Books, the embarrassment of the Pope within the grasp of a more powerful reasoner and more learned theologian, his awe of a superior power. Nor did this controversy lead to any breach of outward amity, or seem to deaden the inward feelings of mutual respect. Hadrian writes this, his last letter, with profound deference. Charlemagne shed tears at the death of the Pontiff; and, as has been said, showed the strongest respect for his memory.

These theological questions settled before the Council of Frankfort, a singular spectacle was exhibited, as though to make an ostentatious display of the power and dubious clemency of Charlemagne. Tassilo, the Duke of Bavaria, cousin to the Emperor, who had been subdued, deposed, despoiled of his territory, was introduced, humbly to acknowledge his offences against the Frankish sovereign, to entreat his forgiveness, to throw himself and all his family on the mercy of Charlemagne. The Emperor condescended to be merciful, but he kept possession of the territory. The unfortunate Tassilo and all his family ended their days in a monastery. The Council added to its canons, condemnatory of the Spanish heresy and of image-worship, a third, ratifying this degradation, spoliation, and life-long imprisonment of the Duke of Bavaria.

Of the two following canons, one regulated the sale of corn, and fixed a price beyond which it was unlawful to sell it. The other related to the circulation of the coin, and enacted that whoever should refuse the royal money, when of real silver and of full weight, if a freeman, should pay a fine of fifteen shillings to the

Crown; if a slave, forfeit what he offered for sale, and be publicly flogged on his naked person.

The ninth canon decreed that Peter, a Bishop, should appear, with the two or three bishops who had assisted at his consecration, or at least his Archbishop, as his compurgators, and should swear before God and the angels that he had not taken counsel concerning the death of the King, or against his kingdom, or been guilty of any act of disloyalty.[1] But as the Bishop could not bring his compurgators into court, he proposed that *his man* should undergo the ordeal, the judgment of God; that himself should swear, without touching either the holy relics or the Gospel, to his own innocence; and that God would deal with *his man* according to the truth or falsehood of his oath. What the ordeal was does not appear, but *the man* passed through it unhurt; and the Bishop, by the clemency of the King, was restored to his honors.

Other canons, of a more strictly ecclesiastical character, were passed:—I. To enforce discipline in monasteries.[2] II. On the residence of the clergy. III. On Ordinations, which were fixed for presbyters to the age of thirty. Virgins were not to take the vows before twenty-two. No one was to receive the slave of another; no bishop to ordain a slave without permission of his master. IV. The payment of tithe. V. For the maintenance of churches by those who held the benefices.[3] VI. Against the worship of new saints

[1] This conspiracy is alluded to in Eginhard, sub ann. 792. See the note of Sirmond in Labbe, p. 1066.

[2] No abbot was to blind or mutilate one of his monks for any crime whatever. "Nisi regulari disciplinæ subjaceant."

[3] If any one was found "by true men" to have purloined timber, stone, or tiles, from the churches, for his own house, he was compelled to restore them.—xxvi.

without authority. VII. For the destruction of trees and groves sacred to pagan deities. VIII. Against the belief that God can be adored only in three languages; "there is no tongue in which prayer may not be offered." The Teutonic spirit is here again manifesting itself. The last statute of the Council, at the suggestion of the Emperor, admitted the Briton Alcuin, on account of his ecclesiastical erudition, to all the honors, and to be named in the prayers of the Council.[1]

Such was the Council of Frankfort, the first example of that Teutonic independence in which the clergy appear as feudal beneficiaries around the throne of their temporal liege lord, with but remote acknowledgment of their spiritual sovereign, passing acts not merely without his direct assent, but in contravention of his declared opinions. Charlemagne, not yet Emperor, is manifestly lord over the whole mind of the West. Except that he condescends to take counsel with the prelates instead of the military nobles, he asserts the same unlimited authority over ecclesiastical and civil affairs. He is too powerful for the Pope not to be his humble and loyal subject. The Pope might take refuge in the thought that the assembly at Frankfort was but a local synod, and aspired not to the dignity of an Ecumenic Council; and to local or national synods much power had always been allowed to regulate the discipline of their Churches, provided they issued no canons which infringed on the Catholic doctrines: yet these were statutes for the whole realm of Charlemagne, almost commensurate with the Western Patriarchate the actual spiritual dominion of the Roman Pontiff, with Latin Christendom. Yet, on the other hand, the

[1] Canon lii.

hierarchy of the Church is advancing far beyond the ancient boundaries of its power; it is imperceptibly, almost unconsciously, trenching on temporal ground. The Frankfort assembly is a diet as well as a synod. The prelates appear as the King's counsellors, not only in religious matters, or on matters on the doubtful borders between religion and policy, but likewise on the affairs of the Empire — affairs belonging to the internal government of the State.

And though Charlemagne, as liege lord of the Teutonic race, as conqueror of kingdoms beyond the Teutonic borders, as sovereign of almost the whole Transalpine West, and afterwards as Emperor, stood so absolutely alone above all other powers; though the Pope must be content to lurk among his vassals; yet doubtless, by his confederacy with the Pope, Charlemagne fixed, even on more solid foundations, the papal power. The Pope as well as the hierarchy was manifestly aggrandized by his policy. The Frankish alliance, the dissolution of the degrading connection with the East, the magnificent donation, the acceptance of the Imperial crown from the Pope's hand, the visits to Rome, whether to protect the Pope from his unruly subjects or for devotion; everything tended to throw a deepening mysterious majesty around the Pope, the more imposing according to the greater distance from which it was contemplated, the more sublime from its indefinite and boundless pretensions. The Papacy had yet indeed to encounter many fierce contentions from without, and still more dangerous foes around, before it soared to the plenitude of its power and influence in the period from Gregory VII. to Innocent III. It was to sink to its lowest point of degradation in the tenth century, before it emerged again to contest the dominion of the world with the Empire, with the successors of Charlemagne, to commit the spiritual and temporal powers in a long and obstinate strife, in which for a time it was to gain the victory.

Arts and letters under Charlemagne.

The brief epoch of renascent letters, arts, education, during the reign of Charlemagne, was as premature, as insulated, as transitory, as the unity of his Empire. Alcuin, whom one great writer[1] calls the intellectual prime minister of Charlemagne, with all his fame, his well-merited fame, and those whom another great writer[2] calls the Paladins of his literary court, Clement, Angilbert,[3] all but Eginhard, were no more than the conservators and propagators of the old traditionary learning, the Augustinian theology, the Boethian science, the grammar, the dry logic and meagre rhetoric, the Church music, the astronomy, mostly confined to the calculation of Easter, of the trivium and quadrivium. The Life of Charlemagne by Eginhard is unquestionably the best historic work which had appeared in the Latin language for centuries; but Eginhard, during his later years, in his monastery in the Odenwald, stooped to be a writer of legend.[4] Perhaps the Carolinian books are the most

[1] M. Guizot.

[2] Mr. Hallam.

[3] Agobard, Archbishop of Lyons, of a much higher cast of mind, was bred under Charlemagne.

[4] The history of the Translation of the relics of St. Marcellinus and St. Peter Martyr,* and their miracles, is one of the most extraordinary works of this extraordinary age, written, as it was, by a statesman and counsellor of two emperors. Two clerks, servants of Abbot Eginhard and the abbot of St. Médard in Soissons, are sent to Rome to *steal* relics. They

* An exorcist martyred at Rome. The martyrdom is related in a curious trochaic poem, not without spirit and vigor, ascribed also to Eginhard. — Eginhardi Opera, by M. Teulet. Soc. Hist. de France.

remarkable writings of the time. It might seem as if Latin literature, as it had almost expired in its originality among the great lawyers, so it revived in jurisprudence. Even the schools which Charlemagne established, if he did not absolutely found, on a wide and general scale,[1] had hardly a famous teacher, and must await some time before they could have their Erigena, still later their Anselm, their Abelard, with his antagonists and followers. What that Teutonic poetry was which Charlemagne cherished with German reverence, it is vain to inquire: whether tribal Frankish songs, or the groundwork of those national poems which, having passed through the Latin verse of the monks,[2] came forth at length as the Nibelungen and the Heldenbuch.

make a burglarious entry by night into a tomb (such sacrilege was a capital crime), carry off the two saints, with difficulty convey the holy plunder out of Rome and through Italy (some of the party pilfering a limb or two on the way). Eginhard is not merely the shameless receiver of these stolen treasures; there is no bound to his pious and public exultation. The saints are fully consentient, rejoice in their seduction from their inglorious repose; their restless activity reveals itself in perpetual visions, till they are settled to their mind in their chosen shrines. A hundred and fifty pages of miracles follow; wrought in all quarters, even in the imperial palace. It might almost seem surprising that there should be a blind, lame, paralytic, or demoniac person left in the land.

1 See the schools in Hallam, ii. p. 478.

2 See the poem De Expeditione Attilæ

CHAPTER II.

LOUIS THE PIOUS.

The unity of the Empire, so favorable to the unity of Christendom, ceased not at the death of Charlemagne, it lasted during some years of the reign of his successor. But the unity of the Church, as it depended not on the personal character of the sovereign, remained undissevered. In the contests among Charlemagne's descendants the Pope mingles with his full unbroken authority; while the strife among the military feudatories of the Empire only weakens, or exposes the weakness of the imperial power. The influence of the great Transalpine prelates, so often on different sides in the strife, aggrandizes that of the Pope, whom each party was eager, at any sacrifice, to obtain as an ally. Already the Papal Legates, before the pontificate of Nicolas I., begin to appear, and to conduct themselves with arrogance which implies conscious power. The awful menace of excommunication is employed to restrain sovereign princes. The Emperor for a time still holds his supremacy. Rome is, in a certain sense, an imperial city. The Pope is not considered duly elected without the Emperor's approbation; the successor of Leo III. throws the blame of his hasty consecration on the clergy and people. But, first the separation of the

Jan. 28, A.D. 814.

Italian kingdom from the Empire, and afterwards the feebleness, or the distance, or the preoccupation of the Emperor, allows this usage to fall into desuetude.

Yet, during the whole of this period, and indeed much later, in the highest days of the Papacy, the limited and contested power of the Pope in Rome strongly contrasts with his boundless pretensions and vast authority in remoter regions. The Pope and the Bishop of Rome might appear distinct persons. Already that turbulence of the Roman people, which afterwards, either in obedience to, or in fierce strife with, the lawless petty sovereigns of Romagna, degraded the Papacy to its lowest state, had broken out, and was constantly breaking out, unless repressed by some strong friendly arm, or overawed by a pontiff of extraordinary vigor or sanctity. The life of the Pope, in these tumults, was not secure. While mighty monarchs in the remotest parts of Europe were trembling at his word, he was himself at the mercy of a lawless rabble. The Romans still aspired to maintain their nationality. It was rare at that time for any one but a born Roman to attain the Papacy;[1] and no doubt at each promotion there would be bitter disappointment among rival prelates and conflicting interests. It was at once the strength and weakness of the Pope; it arrayed sometimes a powerful party on his side, sometimes condensed a powerful host against him. Though the Romans had been overawed by the magnificence and grandeur of Charlemagne, and had joined, it might seem, cordially in their acclamations at his as-

1 Of nearly fifty Popes, from Hadrian to Gregory V. (a German created by Otho the Great), there appears one Tuscan (Martin or Marinus), and three or four of doubtful origin: every one of the rest is described as "patriâ Romanus."

sumption of the Empire, (which still implied dominion over Rome,) yet the Franks, the Transalpines, were foreigners and barbarians. The Pope was constantly compelled by Roman turbulence to recur to his imperial protector (among whose titles and offices was Defender of the Church of Rome) ; yet the presence of the Emperor, while it flattered, wounded the pride of the Romans: if it gratified one faction, imbittered the hatred of the others.

Leo III. must have been among the most munificent and splendid of the Roman Pontiffs. Charlemagne had made sumptuous and imperial offerings on the altar of St. Peter. His donation seems to have endowed the Pope with enormous wealth. Long pages in Leo's Life are filled with his gifts to every church in Rome — to many in the Papal territories. Buildings were lined with marble and mosaic: there were images of gold and silver of great weight and costly workmanship (a silent but significant protest against the Council of Frankfort), priestly robes of silk and embroidery, and set with precious stones; censers and vessels of gold, columns of silver. The magnificence of the Roman churches must have rivalled or surpassed the most splendid days of the later republic, and the most ostentatious of the Cæsars.[1]

Leo, like other prodigal sovereigns, may have exacted the large revenues, which he spent with such profusion, with hardness, which might be branded as avarice; and hence the Pope, who was thus gorgeously

[1] Anastasius in Vit. Leo expended 1320 pounds of gold (pounds weight?) and 24,000 of silver on the churches in Rome. Thirty-five pages of this faithful chronicler of the wealth and expenditure of the Roman See are devoted to the details. — Compare Ellendorf, Die Karolinger und die Hierarchie ihrer Zeit, ii. p. 65.

adorning the city and all his dominions with noble buildings, and decorating the churches with unexampled splendor, was still in perpetual danger from popular insurrection. Even during the reign of Charlemagne, Leo was hardly safe in Rome. Immediately on the death of the Emperor, the embers of the old hostility broke out again into a flame; and the Pope held his throne only through the awe of the imperial power, at the will of Charlemagne's successor, Louis the Pious.

Death of Charlemagne.

There was a manifest conflict, during his later years, in the court, in the councils, in the mind of Charlemagne, between the King of the Franks and the Emperor of the West; between the dissociating independent Teutonic principle, and the Roman principle of one code, one dominion, one sovereign. The Church, though Teutonic in descent, was Roman in the sentiment of unity. The great churchmen were mostly against the division of the Empire. The Empire was still one and supreme. The vigorous impulse given to the monarchical authority by its founder maintained for a few years the majesty of his son's throne. That unity had been threatened by the proclaimed division of the realm between the sons of Charlemagne. The old Teutonic usage of equal distribution seemed doomed to prevail over the august unity of the Roman Empire. What may appear more extraordinary, the kingdom of Italy was the inferior appanage: it carried not with it the Empire, which was still to retain a certain supremacy; that was reserved for the Teutonic sovereign. It might seem as if this were but the continuation of the Lombard kingdom, which Charlemagne still held by the right of

A.D. 806.

conquest. It was bestowed on Pepin; after his death intrusted to Bernhard, Pepin's illegitimate but only son. Wiser counsels prevailed. The two elder sons of Charlemagne died without issue; Louis the third son was summoned from his kingdom of Aquitaine, April, 813. and solemnly crowned at Aix-la-Chapelle, as successor to the whole Empire.

Louis,[1] — his name of Pious bespeaks the man, — thus the heir of Charlemagne, had inherited the religion of his father. But in his gentler and less resolute character that religion wrought with an abasing and enfeebling rather than ennobling influence. As King of Aquitaine Louis had been distinguished for some valor, activity, and conduct in war against the Saracens of Spain;[2] but far more for his munificence to the churches and convents of his kingdom. The more rigid clergy had looked forward with eager hope to the sole dominion of the pious king; the statesmen among them had concurred in the preservation of the line of the Empire; yet Louis would himself have chosen as his example his ancestor Carloman, who retired from the world into the monastery of Monte Casino, rather than that of his father, the lord and conqueror of so many realms. It required the author-

[1] Ermoldus gives the German derivation of the name Louis (Hludwig): "Nempe sonat Hluto præclarum, Wigch quoque Mars est." — Apud Pertz, ii. p. 468.

[2] The panegyrist of Louis, the poet Ermondus Nigellus, asserts his vigorous administration of Aquitaine. He describes at full length the siege of Barcelona, giving probably a much larger share of glory than his due to Louis. For his general character see Thegan. c. xix. Louis understood Greek; spoke Latin as his vernacular tongue. On the youth of Louis see the excellent work of Funck, "Ludwig der Fromme." Sir F. Palgrave highly colors the character and accomplishments of Louis. Louis the Pious renounced the Pagan (Teutonic?) poetry which he was accustomed to repeat in his youth. — Thegan. p. 19.

ity of Charlemagne, not unsupported even by the most austere of the clergy, the admirers of his piety, to prevent him from turning monk.[1]

Yet, on his accession, the religion of Louis might seem to display itself in its strength rather than in its weakness. The license of his father's court shrank away from the sight of the holy sovereign. The concubines of the late Emperor, even his daughters and their paramours, disappeared from the sacred precincts of the palace. Louis stood forward the reformer, not the slave of the clergy. To outward appearance, like Charlemagne, he was the Pope, or rather the Caliph of his realm. He condescended to sit in council with his bishops, but he was the ostensible head of the council; his commissioners were still bearers of unresisted commands to ecclesiastical as to temporal princes. Yet the discerning eye might detect the coming change. The ascendency is passing from the Emperor to the bishops. It is singular, too, that the nobles almost disappear; in each transaction, temporal as well as ecclesiastical, the bishops advance into more distinct prominence, the nobles recede into obscurity. The great ecclesiastics, too, are now almost all of Teutonic race. The effete and dissolute Roman hierarchy has died away. German ambition seizes the high places in the church; German force animates their counsels. The great prelates, Ebbo of Rheims, Agobard of Lyons, Theodolf of Orleans, are manifestly of Teutonic descent. Benedict of Aniane is the assumed name of Witiza, son of the Gothic Count of Mage-

[1] Louis was a serious man. When at the banquet the jonglers and mimes made the whole board burst out into laughter, Louis was never seen to smile.

lone; Benedict, the most rigorous of ascetics, who stooped to the name, but thought the rule of the elder Benedict of Nursia far below monastic perfection. The bastard descendants of Charles Martel appear, two of them even now, not as kings or nobles, but as abbots or monks; compelled, perhaps, to shroud themselves from the jealousy of the legitimate race by this disqualification for temporal rule, only to exercise a more powerful influence through their sacred character.[1] Adalhard, Wala, Bernarius, were the sons of Bernhard, an illegitimate son of Charles Martel. Adalhard, Abbot of Corvey, and Bernarius, were already monks: the Count Wala was amongst the most honored counsellors of Charlemagne. The nomination of Louis to the sole empire had not been unopposed. Count Wala, some of the higher prelates, Theodolf of Orleans, no doubt Wala's own brothers Adalhard and Bernarius, would have preferred, and were known or suspected to have pressed upon the Emperor the young Bernhard, the son, whom Charlemagne had legitimated, or might have legitimated, of the elder Pepin, rather than the monk-King of Aquitaine. Wala indeed had hastened, after the death of Charlemagne, to pay his earliest homage at Orleans to Louis. He thought it more safe, however, to shave his imperilled head, and become a monk. The whole family was proscribed. Adalhard was banished to the island of Noirmoutiers; Bernarius to Lerins; Theodrada and Gundrada the sisters, Gundrada, who alone
Aug. 1. had preserved her chastity in the licentious

[1] Funck, p. 42. He observes further: "Die lustigen Gesellen an Karls Hof, die Buhlen seiner Töchter, denen Ludwig mit seiner Heiligkeit, lächerlich war, konnten naturlich den Bibelleser und Psalmsinger nicht an die Stelle Karls wünschen." Politics make strange coalitions!

court of Charlemagne, were ignominiously dismissed from the court.[1]

A diet at Aix-la-Chapelle was among the earliest acts of Louis the Pious. From this council commissioners were despatched throughout the empire to receive complaints and to redress all acts of oppression.[2] Multitudes were found who had been unrighteously despoiled of their property or liberty by the counts or other powerful nobles. The higher clergy were not exempted from this inquest, nor the monasteries. In how many stern and vindictive hearts did this inquest sow the baleful seed of dissatisfaction!

The Emperor is not only the supreme justiciary in his Gallic and German realm; it is his unquestioned right, it is his duty, to decide between the Pope and his rebellious subjects — on the claims of Popes to their throne. Leo III. had apparently bestowed the imperial crown on Charlemagne, had recreated the Western Empire; but he had been obliged to submit to the judicial award of Charlemagne. He is again a suppliant to Louis for aid against the Romans and must submit to his haughty justice. Whether, as suggested, the prodigality of Leo had led to intolerable exactions — whether he had tyrannically exercised his power, or the turbulent Romans would bear no control — (these animosities must have had a deeper root than the disappointed ambition of Pope Hadrian's nephews) — a conspiracy was formed to depose Pope

[1] "Quæ inter venereos palatii ardores et juvenum venustates, etiam inter deliciarum mulcentia, et inter omnis libidinis blandimenta, *sola* meruit (ut credimus) reportare pudicitiæ palmam." — Vit. Adalh. apud Pertz, ii. p. 527. Theodrada had been married; as a widow, could only claim the secondary praise of unblemished virtue.

[2] See the Constitutio, Bouquet, vi. p. 410.

Leo, and to put him to death. Leo attempted to suppress the tumults with unwonted rigor: he seized and publicly executed the heads of the adverse faction.[1] The city burst out in rebellion. Rome became a scene of plunder, carnage, and conflagration. Intelligence was rapidly conveyed to the court of Louis. King Bernhard, who had been among the first to render his allegiance to his uncle at Aix-la-Chapelle, had been confirmed in the government of Italy. He was commanded to interpose, as the delegate of the Emperor. Bernhard fell ill at Rome, but sent a report by the imperial officer, the Count Gerhard, to the sovereign. With him went a humble mission from the Pope, to deprecate the displeasure of that sovereign, expressed at the haste and cruelty of his executions, and to answer the charge made against him by the adverse faction. No sooner had King Bernhard withdrawn from Rome than, on the illness of Leo, a new insurrection broke out. The Romans sallied forth, plundered and burned the farms on the Pope's estates in the neighborhood. They were only compelled to peace by the armed interference of the Duke of Spoleto.

The death of Leo, and, it should seem, the unpopular election of his successor, Stephen IV., exasperated rather than allayed the tumults. Stephen's first acts were to make the Romans swear fealty to the Emperor Louis;[2] to despatch a mission, excusing, on account of the popular tumults, his consecration without the approbation of the Emperor, or the presence of his legates.[3] In the third

June 12, 816.

June 22.

1 A.D. 815, Eginhard, sub ann.

2 Thegan., Vit. Hludovici, ii. 594.

3 "Missis interim duobus legatis, qui quasi pro suâ consecratione imperatori suggererent." — Eginhard. ann. 816.

month of his pontificate Stephen was compelled to take refuge, or seek protection, at the feet of the Emperor, against his intractable subjects.[1] He was received in Rheims with splendid courtesy, and with his own hand crowned the emperor. Thus the fugitive from his own city aspires to ratify the will of Charlemagne, the choice of the whole empire, the hereditary right of Louis to the throne of the Western world. In Rome the awe of Louis commanded at least some temporary cessation of the conflict, and a general amnesty. Stephen returned to Rome, accompanied by those who had been the most daring and obstinate rebels against his predecessor Leo and the Church.[2] Stephen died soon after his return to Rome.

On his death Paschal I. was chosen by the impatient clergy and people, and compelled to assume the Pontificate without the Imperial sanction. But Paschal was too prudent to make com- Jan. 24, 817. Pope Paschal I.

1 The poet disguises the flight of Stephen; he comes to Rheims at the invitation of Louis: —

"Tum jubet acciri Romana ab sede patronum."

The interview is described in his most florid style. He makes the Pope draw a comparison between his visit and that of the Queen of Sheba to Solomon: —

"Rex tamen ante sagax flexato poplite adorat
Terque quaterque, Dei sive in honore Petri,
Suscipit hunc supplex Stephanus, manibusque sacratis
Sublevat e terrâ, basiat ora libens,
Nunc oculos, nunc ora, caput, nunc pectora, colla,
Basiat alterutri Rexque sacerque pius." — ii 221.

All accounts agree in the festivities. The poet says —

"Pocula densa volant, tangitque volentia Bacchus Corda." — ii. 227.

The pious king was not averse to wine. Funck erroneously ascribes Stephen's journey in the first instance to the Pope's desire of crowning the Emperor.

2 "Qui illic captivitate tenebantur, propter scelera et iniquitates suas, quas in sanctam Ecclesiam Romanam et erga dominum Leonem Papam gesserant." — Anastas. in Vit.

mon cause with the Romans in this premature assertion of their independence; he sent a deprecatory embassy across the Alps, throwing the blame on the disloyal precipitancy of the people. The Romans received a grave admonition not again to offend against the majesty of the Empire.

Louis the Pious held his plenary Court a second time at Aix-la-Chapelle. The four great acts of this Council were among the boldest and most comprehensive ever submitted to a great national assembly. The Emperor was still in theory the sole legislator; not only were the secret suggestions, but the initiatory motions in the Council, from the supreme power. It might seem, that in the three acts which regarded the hierarchy, the Emperor legislated for the Church; but it was in truth the Church legislating for herself through the Emperor. It was Teutonized Latin Christianity organizing the whole transalpine Church with no regard to the Western Pontiff. The vast reforms comprehended at once the whole clergy and the monasteries. It was the completion, ratification, extension of Charlemagne's scheme, a scheme by its want of success or universality still waiting its consummation. Chrodogang, Bishop of Metz, another Teuton, had, under the last Merovingians and Pepin, aspired to bring the clergy to live together under the canonical discipline. Charlemagne had given the sanction of his authority to this plan. Now the Archbishops and Bishops are invested in autocratic power to extend, if not absolutely to enforce this rigorous mode of life on all the Priesthood.[1] The sumptu-

Died at Aix-la Chapelle. July, A.D. 817.

Church laws.

[1] Wala, the exiled counsellor of Charlemagne, hereafter to succeed to the influence of Benedict of Aniane, held the same ecclesiastical notions as

ary laws were universal, minute; the prohibition to bear arms; the proscription of their worldly pomp, of their belts studded with gold and precious stones; their brilliant and fine apparel; their gilded spurs. But if stripped of their pomp, it is only to increase immeasurably their power. If the sacerdotal army is to be arrayed under more rigid order and under more absolute command, it is only that it may be more efficient. Church property is strictly inviolable. II. The monasteries (which it might have seemed the sole object of Louis, since his accession, to endow with ampler wealth)[1] are submitted to the iron rule of Benedict of Aniane. III. This hierarchy, so reformed, so reinvigorated, aspires to sever itself entirely from the state. A special Capitular asserted their full and independent rights. The election of Bishops was to be in the clergy and the commonalty; that of the abbots in the brotherhood of monks. The Crown, the nobles, surrendered or were excluded from all interposition. The right of patronage, even in nobles who built churches on their own domain, was limited to the nomination; once instituted, only the Bishop could depose or expel the priests. The whole property of the Church was under their indefeasible, irresponsible administration. The Teutonic aristocracy of the Church maintained its lofty tone. No unfree man could be admitted to holy orders; if he stole into orders, might be degraded and

to the rigorous subordination of monks and clergy to rule. He denounces even the court chaplains: "Quorum itaque vita neque sub regulâ est monachorum, neque sub episcopo militat canonicè, præsertim cum nulla alia tirocinia sint ecclesiarum, quam sub his duobus ordinibus," *et seq.* — Vita Walæ, Pertz, ii. 560.

1 In the Regesta, during the first years of Louis, it is difficult to find out the public acts, among the long succession of grants to churches and monasteries. — Boehmer, Regesta, Frankfort, 1833.

restored to his lord. If the Bishop would ordain a slave, he must be first emancipated before the whole Church and the people. Yet were there provisions to limit abuses as well as to increase power. The threefold division of the church revenues is enacted, two-thirds to the poor, one to the monks and clergy. The clergy are prohibited from receiving donations or bequests to the wrong of near relations. None were to be received into monasteries in order to obtain their property. Church treasures might on one account only be pawned — the redemption of captives. Youths of either sex were not to be persuaded to receive the tonsure or take the veil without consent of their parents. All these laws are enacted by the Emperor in council for the whole empire, almost tantamount to Latin Christendom; of approbation, ratification, confirmation by the Pope, not one word!

The Council Diet of Aix-la-Chapelle, having thus legislated for the Church, contemplated the dangers of the State. The accidental fall of a gallery had endangered the life of the Emperor; he was seriously hurt. What, the wiser men bethought them, or had long before thought, were the Emperor thus suddenly cut off, had been the fate of the Empire? They clearly foresaw the danger of the old Teutonic principle, which had been threatened even under Charlemagne — equal division among the three sons of Louis. The mother of these three sons, as well as their closer adherents, might look with profound solicitude at the rivalry of Bernhard, son of Pepin, whom some of the most powerful had in their hearts, probably in their counsels, designated as the successor of Charlemagne. The Council must not separate without regu

Succession to the empire.

lating the succession of the Empire. His counsellors urged this upon Louis. "I love my sons with equal affection; but I must not sacrifice the unity of the Empire to my love." He laid this question before the Council, — "Is it right to delay a measure on which depends the welfare of the state?" "That," was the universal acclamation, "which is necessary or profitable brooks no delay." But such determination must be made with due solemnity. A fast of three days, prayer for divine grace, is ordered by the pious Emperor. After these three days the decree was promulgated. It proclaimed the great principle of primogeniture. The whole empire fell in its undivided sovereignty, at the death of Louis, to his eldest son, Lothair. Two royal appanages were assigned, with the title of King, to Pepin II., Aquitaine, the Basque Provinces, the March of Toulouse, four Countships in Septimania and Burgundy: to Louis, the third son, Bavaria, Bohemia, Carinthia, the Slavian and Avarian provinces subject to the Franks. But the younger sons were every year to pay homage and offer gifts to the Emperor. Without his consent they could not make war or peace, send envoys to foreign lands, or contract marriage. If either died without heirs, his appanage fell back to the Empire. If he should leave more sons than one, the people were to choose one for their king, the Emperor to confirm the election. If one of the younger brothers should take arms against the Emperor, he was to be admonished; if contumacious, deposed.

This decree was fatal to Bernhard, the son, by a concubine, of Pepin,[1] who still held, by the unrevoked

[1] Funck observes that illegitimate is an unknown word; the term is usually ex ancillâ.

Bernhard king in Italy.

grant of Charlemagne, the kingdom of Italy. He alone was not summoned, had no place, in the great council of Aix-la-Chapelle. In the decree there was a total, inauspicious, significant silence as to his name. And this was the return for the early and ready allegiance which he had sworn to Louis, his fidelity in the affairs of Rome. Bernhard had nothing left but the energy of despair. Italy, weary and indignant, seemed ready to cast off the transalpine yoke. The Lombards may have aspired to restore their ruined kingdom. Two great Bishops, Anselm of Milan, Wulfhold of Cremona, and many of the nobles, tendered him their allegiance, as their independent sovereign. The cities and people as far as the Po were ready or were compelled to take the oath of fealty. Pope Paschal was believed at least not unfriendly to the ambitious views of Bernhard. He was not without powerful partisans beyond the Alps. Theodulf, Bishop of Orleans, was still faithful to his cause. Wala and his brothers were at least suspected of the same treasonable inclinations; the three were placed, each in his convent, under more rigid care.

Defeat and death of Bernhard.

But Louis raised an overpowering force; the Lombards were not united. The Count of Brescia, the Bishop Rathald of Verona, retired across the Alps to the Emperor. The powerful dukes of Friuli and Spoleto adhered to the Imperial cause. Bernhard had nothing left but submission. He passed the Alps, and threw himself at his uncle's feet at Châlons on the Saone.[1] The mild Louis interposed to

[1] Funck asserts that the Empress Hermingard decoyed him over the Alps, with promise of full pardon. I do not think that his authorities bear him out. — p. 65, and note.

mitigate the capital sentence pronounced against the rebel and the leaders of his party at Aix-la-Chapelle. His sterner counsellors, it is said the implacable Hermingard, insisted that Bernhard should be incapacitated for future acts of ambition by the loss of his eyes. The punishment was so cruelly or unskilfully executed, that he died of exhaustion or a broken heart. April 15, 518. Some of the rebellious leaders suffered the same penalty: one died like Bernhard. The traitor Bishops, Orleans, Milan, Cremona, were shut up in monasteries. Now, too, were the three natural sons of Charlemagne, Drogo, Hugh, and Thierry, compelled to submit to the tonsure. Louis had sworn to be their guardian; the pious Emperor forced them to perpetual holy imprisonment.

Lothair, the eldest son of Louis, now crowned, by the sole authority of Louis, King of Italy, assumed the dominion of the Peninsula. But the turbulent state of the whole country compelled him to return to Germany, and to demand succor in men and arms from his father. Rome was not behind the rest, as will speedily appear, in acts of violence and insubordination.

Lothair king of Italy.

So far the son of Charlemagne had reigned in splendor, in justice, in firmness, in wisdom. He had been the legislator of the Empire, both as to its religious and temporal affairs. He had, it might seem, secured the succession in his house; he had suppressed all rebellion with a strong hand, had only yielded to mercilessness, which could not injure him in the estimation of his Teutonic subjects. On the death of his wife Hermingard his mind was shaken, if not partially disturbed; his old religious feelings

Death of the Empress Hermingard.

came back in all their rigour; it was feared that the pious Emperor would abdicate the throne, and retire into a monastery. His counsellors, to bind him to the world, persuaded him to take a second wife. His choice was made with a singular union of the indifference of a monk and the arbitrary caprice of an Eastern sultan.[1] The fairest daughters of the nobles were assembled for his inspection.[2] The monarch was at once captivated by the surpassing beauty of Judith, daughter of the Bavarian Count Wippo.[3] Judith was not only the most beautiful, according to the flattering testimony of bishops and abbots, she was the most highly educated woman of the time. She played on the organ; she danced with perfect grace; she was eloquent as well as learned. The uxorious monarch yielded himself up to his blind passion.

Marriage of Louis. Feb. 819.

From this time a strange feebleness comes over the character of Louis. The third year after his marriage the great diet of the Empire is summoned to Attigny-on-the-Aisne, not to take counsel for the defence, extension, or consolidation of the Empire; not to pass ecclesiastical or civil laws, but to witness the humiliating public penance of the Emperor. His sensitive conscience had long been preying upon him; it reproached him with the barbarous blinding and death of his nephew Bernhard; the chastisement of the insurgent Bishops; the presumptuous restraint which he had imposed on the holy monks Adalhard,

Diet of Attigny. Aug. 822.

[1] "Timebatur a multis, ne regium vellet relinquere gubernaculum. Tandemque eorum voluntati satisfaciens, et undique adductas procerum filias inspiciens, Judith, filiam Wipponis." — Astronomus, c. 32.

[2] "Inspectis plerisque nobilium filiabus." — Eginhard, p. 332.

[3] "The marriage was but four months after the death of Hermingard." — Agobard, Oper. ii. p. 65.

Wala, Bernarius; the enforced tonsure of his father's three sons.

Penance of Louis.

Even in his own time, this act of Louis was compared by admiring Churchmen with the memorable penance of Theodosius the Great. How great the difference between the crimes and character of the men! Theodosius, in a transport of passion, had ordered the promiscuous massacre of all the inhabitants of a flourishing city. Bernhard and his partisans had forfeited their lives according to the laws of the Franks: the Emperor had interposed, though vainly and weakly, only to mitigate the penalty. His offence against Adalhard and Wala was banishment from the court, confinement to monasteries of men who had aimed at excluding him from the Empire, whose abilities and influence he might still dread.[1] And for these delinquencies the trembling son of Charlemagne, the lord of his Empire, stood weeping and imploring the intercession of the clergy, and endeavored to appease the wrath of Heaven by prodigal almsgiving and the most abject acts of penitence.[2] He supplicated the forgiveness of Adalhard and Wala, whom he had already recalled to his court, Wala, now that Benedict of Aniane was dead, speedily to assume absolute power over the mind of Louis.[3] Against them it would be difficult to show how he had grievously sinned. He deplored his having compelled the sons of

1 "Timebatur enim quam maximè Wala, summi apud Karolum Imperatorem habitus loci, ne forte aliquid sinistrum contra imperatorem moliretur." — Astronomus, ii. p. 618. Pertz, ii.

2 "Eleemosynarum etiam largitione plurimarum, sed et servorum Christi orationum instantiâ, necnon et propria satisfactione, adeo divinitatem sibi placare curabat, quasi hæc quæ super unumquemque legaliter decucurrerant, sua gesta fuerant crudelitate." — p. 626.

3 "Venerabatur passim secundus a Cæsare." — Vit. Walæ, p. 535.

Charlemagne to the tonsure. If we respect the conscientious scruples which induced Louis publicly to own his offences, to seek reconciliation with his enemies, some compassion and more contempt mingle with that respect when we see him thus prostrating the imperial dignity at the feet of the hierarchy. The penance of Theodosius was the triumph of religion over the pride and cruelty of man — a noble remorse; in Louis it was the slavery of superstition: he had lost all moral discrimination as to the nature and extent of his own guilt. The slightest act of authority against monk or priest is become a crime, reconciliation with Heaven only to be obtained by propitiating their favor.

The hierarchy failed not to discover the hour of the monarch's weakness. At the autumnal Diet four great ecclesiastical councils were summoned to meet at Pentecost in the following year, to treat of affairs of religion and the abuses of the civil power. Among the crimes which it was determined to suppress was the granting of monasteries to laymen; the grants of Church property at pleasure to the vassals of the Crown, without consent of the bishops. Thus the bishops aspired to be co-legislators in the diets, sole legislators in the councils of which themselves determined the powers.

Yet even in his prostrate humiliation before the transalpine clergy, Louis, through his son Lothair, is exercising full sovereignty over Rome. Lothair, accompanied by Wala, now at once the confidential adviser of Louis in the highest matters, had descended into Italy to command disquieted Rome into peace. He had received the crown from the obsequious Pope. Hardly, however, had Lothair recrossed the Alps when he was overtaken by hasty messengers with intelligence of new tumults.

Two men of the highest rank (Theodorus, the Primicerius of the Church, and Leo, the Nomenclator, who had held high functions at the coronation of Lothair) had been seized, dragged to the Lateran palace, blinded, and afterwards beheaded. The Pope was openly accused of this inhuman act.[1] Two imperial commissioners, Adelung, Abbot of St. Vedast, and Hunfrid, Count of Coire, were despatched with full powers to investigate the affair. At the same time came envoys from the Pope to the court of Louis.[2] The imperial commissioners were baffled in their inquiry. Paschal refused to produce the murderers; he asserted that they were guilty of no crime in putting to death men themselves guilty of treason; he secured them by throwing around them a half-sacred character as servants of the Church of St. Peter.[3] Himself he exculpated by a solemn expurgatorial oath, before thirty bishops, from all participation in the deed. The Emperor received with respect the exculpation May, 824. of the Pope. But Paschal was summoned before a higher judgment: he died immediately after the arrival of the Emperor's messengers. The Romans, though Paschal had vied with his predecessor, Leo III., in his magnificent donations to the churches of Rome,

1 Both Leo and Theodorus had been sent as ambassadors by Paschal, one to the Emperor, the other to Lothair.—Eginhard. "Erant et qui dicerent, vel jussu vel consilio Paschalis Pontificis rem fuisse perpetratam."—Eginhard, Annal. sub ann. 823. "Qua in re fama Pontificis quoque ludebatur, dum ejus consensui totum ascriberetur."—Astronom. p. 302.

2 John, Bishop of Silva Candida; the librarian Sergius; Quirinus subdeacon, Leo, master of the military.

3 Thegan., Vit. Hludovic. apud Pertz, c. 30. Eginhard sub ann.

would not permit his burial in the accustomed place, nor with the usual pomp.[1]

The contest for the vacant see arrayed against each other the two factions in Rome under their undisguised colors. It was a strife between a transalpine and a cisalpine, a Teutonic and a Roman interest. June, 824. The patricians, the nobles of Rome, many of Lombard blood, were in the Imperialist party; the plebeians, the commons, asserted their independence, and scorned the subservience of the Popes. They were more papal than the Popes themselves. Wala, now ruling the Emperor's counsels, had remained at Rome. By his dexterous management Eugenius prevailed over his rival, Zinzinnus. Yet the presence of Lothair was demanded to overawe the city, and to maintain the Imperialist Pope.[2] Lothair again in Rome. Lothair issued his mandates in a high tone. He strongly remonstrated with the Pope against the violence and insults suffered by all who were faithful to the Emperor and friendly to the Franks. Oct., Nov. Some had been put to death, others made the laughing-stock of their enemies. There was a general clamor against the Roman pontiffs and against the administrators of justice. By the ignorance or indolence of the popes, by the insatiable avarice of the judges, the property of many Romans had been unjustly confiscated. Lothair had determined to redress these abuses. By his supreme authority many judgments were reversed; the confiscated estates restored to their rightful owners. In other words, the Imperialist nobles obtained redress of all grievances, real or imaginary. The heads of the

[1] Thegan.

[2] "Eugenius, vincente nobilium parte, ordinatus est." —Eginhard.

popular party were surrendered and sent to France. A constitution was publicly affixed on the Vatican, regulating the election of the Pope, for which no one had a suffrage but a Roman of an approved title: it thus vested the election in the nobles.[1] Annual reports were to be made, both to the Pope and to the Emperor, on the administration of justice. Each of the senate or people was to declare whether he would live according to the Roman, the Lombard, or the Frankish law. On the Emperor's arrival at Rome, all the great civil authorities were to pay him feudal service. There were other provisions for the maintenance of the Papal estates, and prohibiting plunder on the vacancy of the see. As a still more peremptory assertion of the Imperial supremacy, the unrepealed statute was confirmed, that no Pope should be consecrated till his election had been ratified by the Emperor. The Emperor declared his intention of sending commissioners from time to time to watch over the administration of the laws, to receive appeals, and to remedy acts of wrong or injustice.[2]

Constitution.

But while the Empire thus asserted its supremacy in Rome, beyond the Alps it was gradually sinking into decay. The vast dominions of Charlemagne, notwithstanding the decree of Aix-la-Chapelle, were severing into independent, soon to become hostile, kingdoms. The imperial power,

Growing weakness and division of the empire.

[1] The Constitution in Sigonius, Hist. Italica; and in Holstenius; Labbe cum Notis Binii, p. 1541, sub ann. Bouquet.

[2] "Statutum est quoque juxta antiquorum morem, ut ex *latere* imperatoris mitterentur, qui judiciariam potestatem exercentes justitiam omni populo facerent, et tempore quo visum foret imperatori, æqua lance penderent." — Apud Bouquet, vi. 410. The Emperor Henry II. afterwards appealed to this constitution. — Ellendorf, p. 31.

out of which grew the unity of the whole, was losing its awful reverence. The Emperor was but one of many sovereigns, with the title, but less and less of the substance, of preëminent power. The royal authority itself was becoming more precarious by the rise of the great feudal aristocracy; and in the midst of, above great part of that aristocracy, the feudal clergy of France and Germany were more and more rapidly advancing in strength, wealth, and influence.

In the miserable civil wars which distracted the latter part of the reign of Louis the Pious, in the rebellions of his sons, in the degradation of the imperial authority, the bishops and abbots not merely take a prominent part, but appear as the great arbiters, as the awarders of empire, the deposers of kings.

The jealousies of the sons of Louis by his Queen Hermingard, which broke out into open insurrection, into civil wars with the father, began with the birth of his son by the Empress Judith;[1] and became more violent and irreconcilable as that son, afterwards Charles the Bald, advanced towards adolescence. These jealousies arose out of the apprehension, that in the partition of the Empire, according to Frankish usage confirmed by Charlemagne, on the death or demise of Louis, some share, and that more than a just share, should be extorted by the dominant influence of the beautiful stepmother from the uxorious Emperor. Louis was thought to be completely ruled by his wife and her favorite, Bernhard, Duke of Septimania. Rumors, of which it is impossible to know the truth, accused Duke Bernhard not only of swaying the counsels, but of dishonoring the

Bernhard of Septimania.

[1] Charles, born June 13, 823, at Frankfort.

bed, of his master.[1] The sons of Louis propagated these degrading reports, and indignantly complained that the bastard offspring of Duke Bernhard should aspire to part of their inheritance. But to Duke Bernhard the unsuspecting Louis, besides the cares of empire, intrusted the education of his son Charles. He had dismissed all his old counsellors: Abbot Elisachar, the chancellor; the chief chaplain, Hilduin; Jesse, Bishop of Amiens; and other lay officers and ministers of the court. Ebbo, Archbishop of Rheims, must withdraw to his diocese.[2] The whole time of Louis seemed to be indolently whiled away between field-sports, hunting and fishing in the forest of Ardennes, and the most rigid and punctilious religious practices.

These melancholy scenes concern Christian history no further than as displaying the growing power of the clergy, the religion of Louis gradually quailing into abject superstition, the strange fusion and incorporation of civil and ecclesiastical affairs. But in this consists the peculiar and distinctive character of these times. The Church gives refuge to, or punishes and incapacitates, by its disqualifying vows, the victims of political animosity. The dethroned Empress is forced into a convent. Civil incapacity is not complete, at least is not absolutely binding, without ecclesiastical censure. The Pope himself appears in person: prin-

1 "Thorum occupavit." — Vit. Walæ. Paschasius Radbert, the friend, partisan, and biographer of Wala, is the fierce accuser of the queen, the fury, the adulteress; and of Bernhard, the most factious monster, the defiler of matrons, the cruel beast. — Vit. Walæ. "Fit palatium prostibulum, ubi mœchia dominatur, adulter regnat." Bernhard is even accused of a design to murder Louis and his sons. Thegan declares that these charges were all lies (p. 36): "Mentientes omnia."

2 Compare Funck, p. 102.

cipally by his influence, Louis is abandoned by his army, and left at the mercy of his rebellious sons. The degraded monarch, recalled to his throne, will not resume his power without the removal of the ecclesiastical censure.

The first overt act of rebellion by the elder sons of Louis, chiefly Pepin (for Louis held a doubtful course, and Lothair was yet in Italy), was the refusal of the feudal army to engage in the perilous and unprofitable war in Bretagne.[1] Already the fond and uxorious father had awakened jealousy by assigning to the son of Judith the title of King of Alemania.[2] Pepin, King of Aquitaine, placed himself at the head of the mutinous forces. The Emperor, with a few loyal followers (who, though like the rest they refused to engage in the Breton war, yet would not abandon their sovereign), lay at Compiègne, while his sons, with the mass of the army, were encamped three leagues off at Verberie. Around Pepin had assembled the discarded ecclesiastical ministers, Elisachar, Wala, Hilduin, Jesse; with Godfrey and Richard, and the Counts Warin, Lantbert, Matfrid, Hugo. The demands of the insurgents were stern and peremptory: the dismissal and punishment of Duke Bernhard, the degradation of the guilty Judith. Bernhard made his escape to the south, and took refuge in Barcelona; Judith, by the Emperor's advice, retired into the convent of St. Mary of Laon. There she was seized by the adherents of her step-sons, and compelled to promise that she would use all her influence, if she had opportunity, to urge the Emperor to retire to a cloister.[3]

1 The herrban was summoned to Rennes, April 14, 830.

2 Aug. 829, at Worms.

3 "Quam usque adeo intentatam per diversi generis pœnas invite adegere,

Before herself was set the dreary alternative of death or of taking the veil. She pronounced the fatal vows; and, as a nun, edified by her repentance and piety the sisters of St. Radegonde at Poitiers. To the people she was held up as a wicked enchantress, who by her potions and by her unlawful bewitchments alone could have so swayed the soul of the pious Emperor. Lothair, the King of Italy, now joined his brothers, and approved of all their acts. Deliberations were held, in which the higher ecclesiastics Jesse, Bishop of Amiens; Hilduin, Abbot of St. Denys; Wala (by the death of his brother Adalhard now Abbot of Corbey) urged the stronger measure, the degradation of the Emperor. The sons, either from fear or respect, hesitated at this extreme course. Some of the Imperial ministers were punished; two brothers of the Empress forced to submit to the tonsure; and Heribert, brother of Duke Bernhard, blinded. In a general Diet of the Empire at Compiègne, Lothair was associated with his father in the Empire.

April, 830.

But the unpopularity of Louis with the Roman Gauls and with the Franks of Gaul was not shared by the German subjects of the Empire. Throughout this contest, the opposition between the Teutonic and the Gaulish Franks (the French, who now began to form a different society and a different language, with a stronger Roman character in their institutions) foreshowed the inevitable disunion which awaited the Empire of Charlemagne. In the Diet of Nimeguen the cause of the Emperor predominated so completely

ut promitteret, se, si copia daretur cum imperatore colloquendi persuasuram quatenus Imperator abjectis armis, comisque recisis monasterio sese conferret." — Astron. Vit. Ludov. A.D. 829.

that Lothair would not listen to the advice of his more desperate followers to renew the war.[1] He yielded to the gentle influence of his father, and abandoned, with but little scruple, his own adherents and those of his brothers. The Emperor and his son appeared in public as entirely reconciled. Sentence of capital condemnation was passed on all who had taken part in the proceedings at Compiègne. Jesse, Hilduin, Wala, Matfrid and the rest were in custody; and it was the clemency of the Emperor rather than the interposition of Lothair in favor of his partisans which prorogued their punishment till the meeting of another Diet at Aix-la-Chapelle, summoned for the 2d of February. Louis returned in triumph to pass the winter in that capital. His first act was to release his wife from her monastic prison. She returned from Aquitaine, but the scrupulous Emperor hesitated to restore her to her conjugal rights while the impeachment remained upon her honor, perhaps likewise on account of the vows which she had been compelled to take. On the solemn day of the purification of the Virgin, Judith appeared (no one answering the citation to accuse the Empress of adultery or witchery) to assert her own purity. The loyal assembly at once declared that no accuser appeared against her; an oath was tendered, and without further inquiry her own word was held sufficient to establish her spotless virtue. The gentle Louis seized the opportunity of mercy to commute the capital punishment of all the conspirators against his authority.[2]

1 Funck, I think, does not make out his case of the craft of Louis: he seems to have followed rather than guided events.

2 Hilduin had appeared with a great armed retinue of the vassals of the abbeys of St. Denys, St. Germain de Prés, and St. Médard. — Funck, p. 111. Jesse of Amiens was deposed by a council of bishops, headed by

His monkish biographer rebukes his too great lenity.[1] The sons of Louis, humiliated, constrained to assent to the condemnation of their partisans, withdrew, each to his separate kingdom — Pepin to Aquitaine, Louis to Bavaria, Lothair to Italy. Duke Bern- A.D. 831. hard presented himself at the court at Thionville in the course of the autumn; he averred his innocence; according to the custom, defied his accusers to come forward and prove their charge in arms. The wager of battle was not accepted, and Duke Bernhard was admitted to purge himself by oath.

Hardly more than a year elapsed, and the three sons were again in arms against their father. Louis seems now to have alienated the able Duke Bernhard, and to have surrendered himself to the undisputed rule of Gombard, a monk of St. Médard in Soissons.

The whole Empire is now divided into two hostile parties: on each side are dukes and counts, bishops and abbots. The Northern Germans espouse the cause of the Emperor; the Gaulish Franks and some of the Southern Germans obey the Kings of Aquitaine and Bavaria. Among the clergy, another element of jealousy and disunion was growing to a great height. Even under the Merovingian kings, it has been seen, the nobles had endeavored to engross the great ecclesiastical dignities. Under the Carlovingians, men of the highest rank, of the noblest descent, even the younger

Ebbo of Rheims; Hilduin imprisoned at Corbey; Wala in a castle on the lake of Geneva.

1 Astronomus, in Vit. xlv. According to Boehmer (Regesta), Lothair and Louis were present at this diet. At this diet too appeared envoys from the Danes to implore the continuance of peace; from the Slavians, and the Caliph of Bagdad, with splendid presents. The Empire appeared still in its strength at a distance.

or illegitimate branches of the royal family, had become Churchmen; but the higher these dignitaries became, and more and more on a level with the military feudatories, the more the Nobles began to consider the ecclesiastical benefices their aristocratical inheritance and patrimony. They were indignant when men of lower or of servile birth presumed to aspire to these high places, which raised them at once to a level with the most high-born and powerful. They almost aimed at making a separate caste, to whom should belong, of right, all the larger ecclesiastical as well as temporal fiefs. But abilities, piety, learning, in some instances no doubt less lofty qualifications, would at times force their way to the highest dignities. Louis, whether from policy or from a more wise and Christian appreciation of the clerical function in the Church, was considered to favor this humbler class of ecclesiastics. One of his biographers, Thegan, himself an ecclesiastical dignitary of noble birth, thus contemptuously describes the low-born clergy:—"It was the great weakness of Louis that he did not prevent that worst of usages by which the basest slaves obtained the highest dignities of the Church. He followed the fatal example of Jeroboam, 'who made of the lowest of the people priests of the high places. . . . . And this thing became sin unto the house of Jeroboam, even to cut it off and to destroy it from the face of the earth.' No sooner have such men attained elevation than they throw off their meekness and humility, give loose to their passions, become quarrelsome, evil-speaking, ruling men's minds by alternate menaces and flatteries. Their first object is to raise their families from their servile condition: to some they give a good education,

Low-born clergy.

others they contrive to marry into noble families. No one can lead a quiet life who resents their demands and intrigues. Their relatives, thus advanced, treat the older nobles with disdain, and behave with the utmost pride and insolence. The apostolic canon is obsolete, that, if a bishop has poor relations, they should receive alms like the rest of the poor, and nothing more." Thegan devoutly wishes that God would put an end to this execrable usage.[1] In all this there may have been truth, but truth spoken in bitterness by the wounded pride of caste. These ecclesiastics were probably the best and the worst of the clergy. There were those who rose by the virtues of saints, by that austere and gentle piety, by that winning evangelic charity, united with distinguished abilities, which is sure of sympathy and admiration in the darkest times: and those who rose by the vices of slaves, selfishness, cunning, adulation, intrigue, by the worldly abilities which in such times so easily assume the mask of religion. Now, however, all the higher clergy, of gentle or low birth, seem to have joined the confederates against the Emperor. Ebbo of Rheims, Agobard of Lyons, Barnard of Vienne, Heribald of Auxerre, Hilduin of Beauvais, are united with Jesse of Amiens and the indefatigable Wala. Afterwards appear also, with Lothair at Compiègne, Bartholomew of Narbonne, Otgar of Mentz, Elias of Troyes, Joseph of Evreux.

At length — after many vicissitudes, hostilities, negotiations, in which Louis, under the absolute control of the ambitious Judith, seemed determined to depress

1 "Jamdudum illa pessima consuetudo erat, ut ex vilissimis servis fiant summi Pontifices . . . et ideo omnipotens Deus cum regibus et principibus hanc pessimam consuetudinem amodo et deinceps eradicare et suffocare dignetur, ut amplius non fiat in populo Christiano. Amen!"

his elder sons to advance the young Charles (he had now named him King of Aquitaine) — the armies of the Emperor and of his rebellious sons (all three sons were now in arms) stood in array against each other on the plains of Rothfeld in Alsace, at no great distance from Strasburg. The Pope was announced as in the camp of the King of Italy. This Pope was Gregory IV., by birth a Roman. Eugenius had been succeeded by Valentinus, who died five weeks after his accession. Gregory IV. had then ascended the papal throne, with the sanction of the King of Italy, Lothair.[1] The Pope may have placed himself in this unseemly position, supporting rebellious sons against the authority of their father, either from the desire of courting the favor of Lothair, who was all-powerful in Italy; or, it may be hoped, with the more becoming purpose of interposing his mediation, and putting an end to this unnatural conflict.

Civil war. June 20, 833.

Pope Gregory IV.

But the Emperor Louis and the clergy of his party beheld in Gregory an avowed enemy. He addressed a strong letter to the Frankish hierarchy assembled at Worms. Gregory's answer was in the haughty tone of later times: it was suggested by Wala,[2] now again in the camp of the foes of Louis.

Field of Lies.

1 "Non prius ordinatus est, quam legatus Imperatoris Romani venit et electionem populi qualis esset examinavit." — Eginhard, p. 390.

2 "Unde ei dedimus (Wala, &c.) nonnulla SS. Patrum auctoritate formata prædecessorumque suorum conscripta, quibus nullus contradicere possit, quod ejus esset potestas, imo Dei et B. Petri apostoli, suaque auctoritas ire, mittere ad omnes gentes pro fide Christi, et pace ecclesiarum, pro prædicatione evangelii et assertione veritatis, et in eo esset omnis auctoritas B. Petri excellens et potestas viva, a quo oporteret universos judicari ita ut ipse a nemine judicandus esset." — Vit. Walæ, xvi. It is curious to find the Pope, no humble Pope, needing this prompting from a Frankish monk, a higher High Churchman than the Pope. Yet I see nothing here of the false Decretals.

But the enmity of the Pope was not so dangerous as what he called his friendly mediation. He appeared suddenly in the camp of Louis. The clergy, Fulco the chief chaplain, and the bishops, had the boldness to declare that, if he came to threaten them and their Imperial master with excommunication, they would in their turn excommunicate him, and send him back to Italy.[1] There were even threats that they would depose him. Even the meek Emperor received the Pope with cold courtesy, and without the usual honors. He had summoned him indeed, but rather as a vassal than as a mediator. The Pope passed several days in the Imperial camp. Other influences were likewise at work. Unaccountably, imperceptibly, the army of Louis melted away like a heap of snow. The June 29.
nobles, the ecclesiastics, the troops, gradually fell off and joined his sons. Louis found himself encircled only by a few faithful followers.[2] "Go ye also to my sons," said the gentle Louis; "no one shall lose life or limb in my behalf."[3] Weeping they left him. Ever after this ignominious place was named Lügenfeld, the field of falsehood.[4]

The Emperor, Judith his Queen, and their young son Charles, were now the prisoners of Lothair. The Emperor was at first treated with some marks of respect. Judith was sent into Italy, and imprisoned in

[1] "Sed si excommunicans advenerit, excommunicatus abiret, cum aliter se habeat antiquorum auctoritas canonum." — Thegan.

[2] Of these were four bishops, his brother Drogo of Metz, Modoin of Autun, Wilerich of Bremen, Aldric of Mons.

[3] "Ite ad filios meos, nolo ut ullus propter me vitam aut membra dimittat. Illi infusi lacrymis recedebant ab eo." — Thegan, c. xlii.

[4] "Qui ab eo quod ibi gestum est perpetuâ est ignominiâ notatus ut vocetur campus mentitus." — Astronom. Vit. Thegan calls it "campus mendacii."

the fortress of Tortona. The boy was conveyed to the abbey of Prüm: probably on account of his youth he escaped the tonsure. The sons divided the Empire; the Pope, it is said, in great sorrow returned to Rome.[1]

Lothair was a man of cruelty, but he either feared or scrupled to take the life of his father. Yet he and his noble and episcopal partisans could not but dread another reaction in favor of the gentle Emperor. A Diet was held at Compiègne. They determined to incapacitate him by civil and ecclesiastical degradation for the resumption of his royal office. They compelled him to perform public penance in the church of St. Médard, at Soissons. There the Emperor, the father of three kings, before the shrine which contained the relics of St. Médard, and of St. Sebastian the Martyr, laid down upon the altar his armor and his imperial attire, put on a dark mourning robe, and read the long enforced confession of his crimes. Eight weary articles were repeated by his own lips. I. He confessed himself guilty of sacrilege and homicide, as having broken the solemn oath made on a former occasion before the clergy and the people; guilty of the blood of his kinsmen, especially of Prince Bernhard (whose punishment, extorted by the nobles, had been mitigated by Louis). II. He confessed himself guilty of perjury, not only by the violation of his own oaths, but by compelling others to forswear themselves through his frequent changes in the partition of the Empire. III. He confessed himself guilty of a sin against God, by having made a military expedition during Lent, and having held a Diet on a high festival. IV. He confessed himself guilty of

Oct 833.

Penance of Louis.

1 "Cum maximo mœrore." — Astronom. Vit.

severe judgments against the partisans of his sons — whose lives he had spared by his merciful intervention! V. He confessed himself again guilty of encouraging perjury, by permitting especially the Empress Judith to clear herself by an oath. VI. He confessed himself guilty of all the slaughter, pillage, and sacrilege committed during the civil wars. VII. He confessed himself guilty of having excited those wars by his arbitrary partitions of the Empire. VIII. And lastly, of having, by his general incapacity, brought the Empire, of which he was the guardian, to a state of total ruin. Having rehearsed this humiliating lesson, the Emperor laid the parchment on the altar, was stripped of his military belt, which was likewise placed there; and having put off his worldly dress, and assumed the garb of a penitent, was esteemed from that time incapacitated from all civil acts.

The clergy.

The most memorable part of this memorable transaction is, that it was arranged, conducted, accomplished in the presence and under the authority of the clergy. The permission of Lothair is slightly intimated; but the act was avowedly intended to display the strength of the ecclesiastical power, the punishment justly incurred by those who are disobedient to sacerdotal admonition.[1] Thus the hierarchy assumed cognizance not over the religious delinquencies alone, but over the civil misconduct of the sovereign. They imposed an ecclesiastical penance, not solely for his asserted violation of his oaths before the altar, but for the ruin of the Empire. It is strange to see the pious sov-

1 "Manifestare juxta injunctum nobis ministerium curavimus, qualis sit vigor et potestas sive ministerium sacerdotale, et quali mereatur damnari sententiâ, qui monitis sacerdotalibus obedire noluerit." — Acta Exautorationis Ludov. Pii, apud Bouquet, v. p. 243.

ereign, the one devout and saintly of his race, thus degraded by these haughty Churchmen, now, both high-born and low-born, concurring against him. The Pope had ostensibly, perhaps sincerely, hoped to reconcile the conflicting parties. His mission may have been designed as one of peace, but the inevitable consequence of his appearance in the rebellious camp could not but be to the disadvantage of Louis. He seemed at least to befriend the son in his unnatural warfare against his father. Agobard, Bishop of Lyons, issued a fierce apology for the rebellious sons of Louis, filled with accusations of incontinence against the Empress Judith.[1] Her beauty and the graces of her manner had even seduced the admiration of holy priests and bishops towards this Delilah, who had dared to resume her royal dignity and conjugal rights after having taken the veil: to her he attributes all the weaknesses of the too easy monarch. In the words of the aristocratic Thegan, all the bishops were the enemies of Louis, especially those whom he had raised from a servile condition, or who were sprung from barbarous races. But there was one on whom Thegan pours out all his indignation. One was chosen, an impure and most inhuman man, to execute their cruel decrees, a man of servile origin, Ebbo, the Archbishop of Rheims. "Unheard-of words! Unheard-of deeds! They took the sword from his thigh; by the judgment of his servants he was clad in sackcloth; the prophecy of Jeremiah was fulfilled—'Slaves have ruled over us.'[2] Oh, what a return for his goodness! He made thee free, noble he

[1] "Domina Palatii . . . ludat pueriliter, spectantibus etiam aliquibus de ordine sacerdotali et plerisque conludentibus, qui secundum formam quam apostolus scribat de eligendis episcopis . . ."

[2] Lamentat. v. 8.

could not, for that an enfranchised slave cannot be. He clothed thee in purple and in pall, thou clothedst him in sackcloth; he raised thee to the highest bishopric, thou by unjust judgment hast expelled him from the throne of his ancestors. . . . . . . O Lord Jesus! where was thy destroying angel when these things were done?" Thegan goes on to quote Virgil, and says that the poet would want the combined powers of Homer, Virgil, and Ovid to describe the guilt of these deeds. The miseries of Louis were greater than those of Job himself. The comforters of Job were kings, those of Louis slaves.[1]

It is astonishing to find that this was the same Ebbo, Archbishop of Rheims, who undertook a perilous mission to the heathen Northmen, brought the Danish King to the court of Louis to receive baptism, and is celebrated by the monkish poet of the day in the most glowing strains for his saintly virtues.[2]

This strange and sudden revolution, which had left the Emperor at the mercy of his son, was followed by another no less sudden and strange. No doubt the pride of many warlike nobles was insulted by this display of ecclesiastical presumption. The degradation of the Emperor was the degradation of the Empire. The character of Louis, however, could not but command the fond attachment of many. The people felt the profoundest sympathy in his fate; and even among the clergy there were those who could not but think these

1 "Qui beato Job insultabant Reges fuisse leguntur in libro beati Thobiæ; qui illum vero affligebant, legales ejus servi erant, et patrum suorum." — Thegan. Vit. Ludov. xliv.

2 Ermoldi Nigelli, Carm. iv. Ermoldus makes Louis deliver a charge to Ebbo, when setting out to convert the Normans. Munter, Geschichte der Einführung des Christenthüms in Dänemark und Norwegen, has collected the passages about Ebbo's mission. — Page 238 *et seq.*

insults an ungracious and unchristian return for his piety to God, his tenderness to man, his respect for the ecclesiastical order.[1] A revulsion took place in the whole nation. The other sons of the Emperor, Pepin and Louis, had taken no part in this humiliation of their father, and expressed their strong commiseration of his sufferings, their reprobation of the cruelty and insult heaped upon him. The murmurs of the people were too loud to be mistaken. Leaving his father at St. Denys, Lothair fled to Burgundy. No sooner had he retired than the whole Empire seemed to assemble, in loyal emulation, around the injured Louis.

But Louis would not resume his power, and his arms, the symbol of his power, but with the consent of the Bishops. His subjects' reviving loyalty could not remove the ecclesiastical incapacitation. But bishops were not wanting among those who thronged to renew their allegiance.[2] Louis was solemnly regirt with his arms by the hands of some of these prelates, and, amid the universal joy of the people, the Pious resumed the Empire. So great was the burst of feeling, that, in the language of his biographer, the very elements seemed to sympathize in the deliverance of the Emperor from his unnatural son. The weather, which had been wet and tempestuous, became clear and serene. Once more the Empress Judith returned to court;[3] and Louis might again enjoy his quiet hunting

A.D. 834. March 1.

1 "Nithard says, "Plebs autem non modica, quæ præsens erat, etiamque Lothario pro patre vim inferre volebat." — Apud Bouquet, p. 13. The Astronomer says on one occasion, "Miseratio tamen hujusce rei et talis rerum permutationis, exceptis authoribus, omnes habebat." — c. 39.

2 Among these, Otgar of Mentz, who had been present at his penance in Soissons.

3 The empress was brought from Tortona by officious nobles, eager to merit the gratitude of the restored emperor.

and fishing, and his ascetic usages, in the forest of Ardennes. Yet it was not a bloodless revolution. The armies of Louis and Lothair encountered Aug. 834. near Châlons. That unfortunate town was burned by the victorious Lothair, whose savage ferocity did not spare even females. Not content with the massacre of a son of Duke Bernhard in cold blood, his sister was dragged from her convent, shut up in a wine-cask, and thrown into the Saone.[1]

But the year after a pestilence made such ravages in the army of Lothair, that he was obliged to A.D. 836. return into Italy. Before long he had to deplore the death of almost all his great Transalpine partisans, Wala, Count Hugo, Matfrid, Jesse of Amiens. During this time a Diet at Thionville had annulled the proceedings of that at Compiègne. In a sol- Feb. 28. emn assembly at Metz, eight archbishops[2] and thirty-five bishops condemned the acts of themselves and their rebellious brethren at that assembly. In the cathedral of Metz, seven archbishops chanted the seven prayers of reconciliation, and the Emperor was then held to be absolutely reinvested in his civil and religious supremacy. At a later Diet at Cremieux, near Lyons, Ebbo of Rheims (the chief chaplain, Fulco, the faithful adherent of Louis, who had defied the June, 835. Pope in his cause, aspired to the metropolitan see) submitted to deposition.[3] He was imprisoned in the abbey of Fulda. Yet Rome must be consulted before the degradation is complete, at all events before the succes-

1 "More maleficorum," says Nithard. No doubt the punishment of a witch.—Apud Bouquet, p. 13.

2 Mentz, Treves, Rouen, Tours, Sens, Bourges, Arles, even Ebbo of Rheims.

3 Funck, p. 153, with authorities.

sor is consecrated. Agobard of Lyons was condemned. The Archbishop of Vienne appeared not; he incurred sentence of deposition for his contumacy. The Archbishop of Narbonne, and other bishops, were deposed. A new division of the Empire took place at a later diet at Worms, in which Lothair received only Italy: the Transalpine dominions were divided between the three other sons, Pepin, Louis, and Charles; the Empress Judith secured the first step to equality in favor of her son.[1]

The few remaining years of the life of Louis were still distracted by the unallayed feuds in his family. A visit of devotion to Rome was prevented by a descent of the Normans, who had long ravaged the coasts of France. A new partition was made at Nimeguen; Charles was solemnly crowned. The Empress Judith contrived to bring about a reconciliation between Lothair and his father, to the advantage of her own son Charles,[2] and a division of interests between Lothair and his brothers, Louis of Bavaria and Pepin of Aquitaine. Pepin, King of Aquitaine, died, and the claims of his children to the succession were disregarded. Judith knit still closer the alliance of the Emperor and the elder son. Yet one more partition. With the exception of Bavaria, with which Louis was obliged to be content, the Empire was divided between Lothair and the son of Judith.

May, A.D. 837.

June, 838. Sept. 838.

Dec. 13, 838. May 30, 839.

The death of Louis was in harmony with his life. In a state of great weakness (an eclipse of the sun had thrown him into serious alarm, and from that day he

1 Carta Divisionis, Bouquet, vi. 411; compare Funck, 158, 9.
2 Astronomus, l. ii. Nithard, p. 14, lib. i.

began to fail[1]), he persisted in strictly observing the forty days of Lent; the Eucharist was his only food. Almost his last words were expressive of forgiveness to his son Louis, who was in arms against him,[2] and "bringing down his gray hairs in sorrow to the grave." He continued, while he had strength, to hold the crucifix, which contained a splinter of the true cross, to his breast; when his strength failed, he left that office to Drogo, Bishop of Metz, his natural brother, who, with the Archbishops of Treves and Mentz, attended his dying hours. His last words were the German, *aus*, *aus*. His attendants supposed that he was bidding an evil spirit, of whose presence he was conscious, avaunt. He then lifted up his eyes to heaven, and, with serenity approaching to a smile, expired.[3]

May 5, A.D. 839.

June 20, A.D. 840.

Christian history has dwelt at some length on the life of this monarch. His appellation, the Pious, shows what the religion was which was held in especial honor in his day, its strength and its weakness, its virtue, and what in a monarch can hardly escape the name of vice. It displays the firmer establishment of a powerful and aristocratic clergy, not merely in that part of Europe which became the French monarchy, but also in great part of trans-Rhenane Germany; the manner in which they attained and began to exercise that power; the foundation, in short, of great national Churches, in acknowledged subordination, if not always in rigid

1 Annales Francorum, Fuldenses, Bertiniani, sub ann.

2 Louis of Bavaria had not rushed into war without provocation. The Emperor had at least sanctioned the last partition, which left him a narrow kingdom, while Lothair and his younger brother shared the realm of Charlemagne.

3 Louis died on an island of the Rhine, opposite to Ingelheim.

obedience, to the See of Rome, but also mingling, at times with overruling weight, in all the temporal affairs of each kingdom.

But throughout the reign of Louis the Pious, not only did the Empire assert this supremacy in ecclesiastical as in temporal affairs; Teutonic independence maintained its ground, more perhaps than its ground, on the great question of image-worship. The Council of Paris enforced the solemn decree of the Council of Frankfort. The Iconoclastic Byzantine Emperor, Michael the Stammerer, entered into negotiations with the Western Emperor, of which the manifest object was to compel the Pope at least to amity, and to recede from the decrees of the second Council of Nicea asserted by his predecessors. The ambassadors of Constantinople appeared in Rome, accompanied by ambassadors from Louis. The Pope Eugenius, who owed his Popedom to the Franks, who sat on his throne only through their support, was in great embarrassment; he was obliged to elude what he dared not oppose. At no other time could a bishop like Claudius of Turin have acted the fearless Iconoclast in an Italian city, removed all images and pictures, condemned even the cross, and lived and died, if not unassailed by angry controversialists, yet unrebuked by any commanding authority, undegraded, and in the full honors of a Bishop. Claudius was a Spaniard who acquired fame as a commentator on the scriptures in the court of Louis at Aquitaine. Among the first acts of Louis as Emperor was the promotion of Claudius to the bishopric of Turin. The stern reformer at once began to wage war on what he deemed the superstitions of the people. Claudius went

Image-worship in the West.

A.D 824.

Claudius of Turin.